Miami

& the Keys

Kim Grant

LONELY PLANET PUBLICATIONS
Melbourne • Oakland • London • Paris

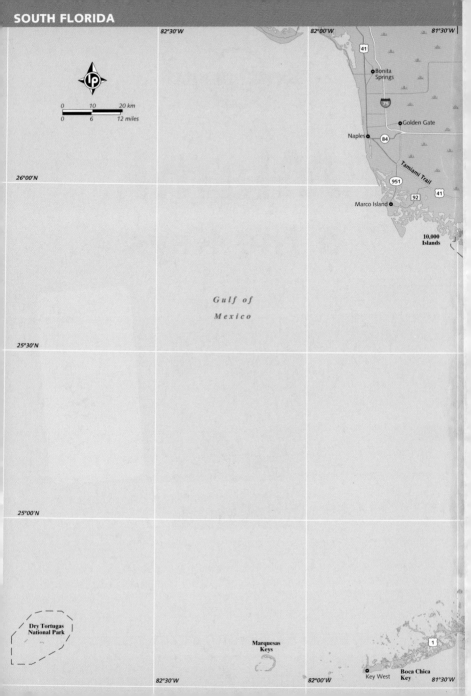

82°30'W

82°00'W

81°30'W

41

Bonita
Springs

75

Golden Gate

Naples

84

Tamiami Trail

951

92

41

Marco Island

10,000
Islands

26°00'N

Gulf of

Mexico

25°30'N

0   10   20 km

0   6   12 miles

25°00'N

Dry Tortugas
National Park

Marquesas
Keys

1

Key West

Boca Chica
Key

82°30'W

82°00'W

81°30'W

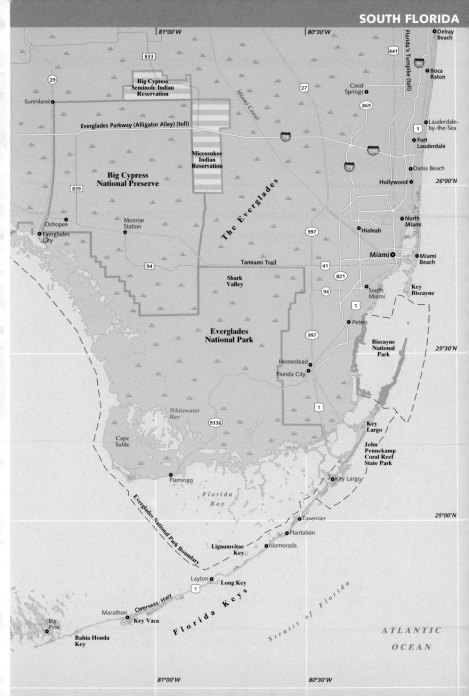

Miami & the Keys
3rd edition – September 2002
First published – October 1996

Published by
Lonely Planet Publications Pty Ltd ABN 36 005 607 983
90 Maribyrnong St, Footscray, Victoria 3011, Australia

Lonely Planet Offices
Australia Locked Bag 1, Footscray, Victoria 3011
USA 150 Linden St, Oakland, CA 94607
UK 10a Spring Place, London NW5 3BH
France 1 rue du Dahomey, 75011 Paris

Photographs
Many of the images in this guide are available for licensing from
Lonely Planet Images.
W www.lonelyplanetimages.com

Front cover photograph
Classic car and palm trees, Miami Beach (Jon Davison)
Map section photograph
West Indian flamingos, Miami (Tom Boyden)

ISBN 1 74059 183 6

text & maps © Lonely Planet Publications Pty Ltd 2002
photos © photographers as indicated 2002

Printed by The Bookmaker International Ltd
Printed in China

Contents

2 Contents

The Author

Kim Grant

Kim's family drove from New England to Florida every winter for 15 years of family vacations – from Key West to Amelia Island. Shortly thereafter, she hitchhiked from Montreal to Gainesville and Pensacola. After that, she started flying. She grew up in the Boston area and graduated from Mt Holyoke College in western Massachusetts in 1984. After two years of traveling around Europe on $10 a day, she was determined to make a living traveling, writing and taking pictures. Almost 20 years later, she finds herself the author or co-author of Lonely Planet's *Boston, New England, Miami & the Keys, Florida* and *USA*, as well as books by other publishers, including *Cape Cod, Martha's Vineyard & Nantucket: An Explorer's Guide, Best Places to Stay in Hawaii* (someone's gotta do it) and *Best Places to Stay in New England*. Represented by Lonely Planet Images, Kim's photography is also published under the Bindu Press imprint. Kim lives with her partner in a circa-1900 Victorian in Dorchester, Boston's largest, oldest and most diverse neighborhood.

FROM THE AUTHOR

Heartfelt compassion goes out to the really fine Oaktown production crew, for whom this is the last title. LP authors will miss you. Thank you.

Great thanks go to the ever-respectful, meticulous, hands-on editor Rebecca Northen, who should be moving to Boston to work with me, but isn't. I'm sorry not to have the chance to work with her again. Thanks to soft-spoken but extremely effective senior editor David Zingarelli, and Suki Gear for her smart briefing. And to the vision of senior carto Sean Brandt and the microcosmic day-to-day, dot-to-dot work of Sherry Veverka and Kat Smith. And to Mariah Bear for pitching me the job. Nice throw.

Special thanks go to the knowledgeable and professional Michelle Revuelta, media relations manager at the Greater Miami Convention & Visitors Bureau; to ever-engaging Andrea Chassen, a volunteer guide for the Miami Design Preservation League; and to Dr Paul George, a renowned historian and tour guide. Wish waiters Nicole Schargel and Robert Elliott are thanked for brainstorming creatively about their favorite insider haunts – without spilling a drop of wine or missing a beat between courses.

And finally, thanks – as always – to the infinitely supportive Lisa Otero, for walking the walk with me, enlivening my forays into Miami's heat, and for searching out next year's orange.

This Book

This is the 3rd edition of *Miami & the Keys*. The last edition was written by Nick and Corinna Selby. This edition expanded on coverage of the Florida Keys, Key West, the Everglades and Fort Lauderdale. Material was drawn from the 2nd edition of Lonely Planet's *Florida* guide, which was also written by the Selbys.

FROM THE PUBLISHER

This guide was one of the swan songs of Lonely Planet's Oakland production team. Thanks to the wonderful work of the thoroughly enjoyable Kim Grant, it was joyfully edited by Rebecca Northen. Rebecca also had the pleasure of working with senior editor David Zingarelli, who oversaw the project, and Wendy Smith, who helped with the editing and proofread most of the book. Other co-conspirators included associate senior editors Suki Gear, who wrote the brief, and Wade Fox, who lent a hand with proofing, and senior editor Michele Posner. The ever-reliable Ken DellaPenta indexed the book.

Lead cartographers Sherry Veverka and Kat Smith drew and perfected the maps, with assistance from cartographic data specialist John Spelman and cartographers Herman So, Anneka Imkamp, Justin Colgan and Laurie 'CGE' Mikkelsen. Senior cartographer Sean Brandt oversaw the mapping until baby Ellis Townsend Brandt came onto the scene, at which point Annette Olson took over. All cartographic work was headed up by Alex 'King of all Mapworld' Guilbert.

The ever-creative Lora Santiago designed the 'Art Deco Architecture' special section and the supplemental color pages. She also laid out the book, with the guidance of senior designers Tracey Croom and Ruth Askevold. Justin Marler designed the cover and drew most of the book's illustrations; those he didn't draw were done by Hugh D'Andrade and Hannah Reineck.

Thanks again to Kim for being the author of our dreams.

Foreword

ABOUT LONELY PLANET GUIDEBOOKS

The story begins with a classic travel adventure: Tony and Maureen Wheeler's 1972 journey across Europe and Asia to Australia. There was no useful information about the overland trail then, so Tony and Maureen published the first Lonely Planet guidebook to meet a growing need.

From a kitchen table, Lonely Planet has grown to become the largest independent travel publisher in the world, with offices in Melbourne (Australia), Oakland (USA), London (UK) and Paris (France).

Today Lonely Planet guidebooks cover the globe. There is an ever-growing list of books and information in a variety of media. Some things haven't changed. The main aim is still to make it possible for adventurous travelers to get out there – to explore and better understand the world.

At Lonely Planet we believe travelers can make a positive contribution to the countries they visit – if they respect their host communities and spend their money wisely. Since 1986 a percentage of the income from each book has been donated to aid projects and human rights campaigns, and, more recently, to wildlife conservation.

Although inclusion in a guidebook usually implies a recommendation, we cannot list every good place. Exclusion does not necessarily imply criticism. In fact, there are a number of reasons why we might exclude a place – sometimes it is simply inappropriate to encourage an influx of travelers.

UPDATES & READER FEEDBACK

Things change – prices go up, schedules change, good places go bad and bad places go bankrupt. Nothing stays the same. So, if you find things better or worse, recently opened or long-since closed, please tell us and help make the next edition even more accurate and useful.

Lonely Planet thoroughly updates each guidebook as often as possible – usually every two years, although for some destinations the gap can be longer. Between editions, up-to-date information is available in our free, quarterly *Planet Talk* newsletter and monthly email bulletin *Comet*. The *Upgrades* section of our website (**W** www.lonelyplanet.com) is also regularly updated by Lonely Planet authors, and the site's *Scoop* section covers news and current affairs relevant to travelers. Lastly, the *Thorn Tree* bulletin board and *Postcards* section carry unverified, but fascinating, reports from travelers.

Tell us about it! We genuinely value your feedback. A well-traveled team at Lonely Planet reads and acknowledges every email and letter we receive and ensures that every morsel of information finds its way to the relevant authors, editors and cartographers.

Everyone who writes to us will find their name listed in the next edition of the appropriate guidebook and will receive the latest issue of *Comet* or *Planet Talk*. The very best contributions will be rewarded with a free guidebook.

We may edit, reproduce and incorporate your comments in Lonely Planet products such as guidebooks, websites and digital products, so let us know if you don't want your comments reproduced or your name acknowledged.

How to contact Lonely Planet:
Online: **e** talk2us@lonelyplanet.com.au, **W** www.lonelyplanet.com
Australia: Locked Bag 1, Footscray, Victoria 3011
UK: 10a Spring Place, London NW5 3BH
USA: 150 Linden St, Oakland, CA 94607

Introduction

RICHARD CUMMINS

There's more to Miami than sex in South Beach. Certainly, this city is sultry. It attracts a wildly diverse cauldron of pleasure-seekers – happy hedonists who'd rather gyrate the night away (not to mention the dawn!) at discos and doze on the beach during the day than go to a museum. And there are plenty of justifiably trendy and wonderfully shallow reasons why exotic models, celebrities and *you* are drawn to SoBe's circuit of chichi nightclubs, mod martini bars, sophisticated restaurants and renovated art deco hotels. When we say it's the hottest and steamiest city in America, we're not just talking weather.

And yet, if you limit yourself to sensuous pastimes and don't venture beyond the physical and psychological parameters of South Beach, you'll miss making a wealth of richer memories. (Unless, of course, you met your sugar daddy the night before. In that case, stay in bed and order in.) From outrageously opulent Coconut Grove villas to the industrial chic of the seedy Miami

River area; from artfully lit downtown skyscrapers to diverse contemporary art collections; from the haunting Holocaust memorial to Little Havana's religious botánicas; from the chic Design District to funky monkeys and performing parrots; and from bountiful botanical gardens to wacky coral castles – greater Miami has it all, and a lot more.

The environmental diversity of South Florida is downright astonishing – coastal hardwood hammocks, brilliant coral in the Keys, prairies in the Everglades and unimpeded stretches of prime beachfront all over. And it all begs active pursuits. Miamians love to play outdoors – with all that endless ocean and fair weather, only the agoraphobic would shun bicycling, windsurfing, kayaking and snorkeling. Besides, for a city whose number one objective is having fun, a healthy glow and a high degree of fitness is essential.

In the quirky Keys – remote islands connected like a strand of pearls – you've got to get out on the water to truly appreciate the region's serenity and fragility. To deeply understand the mysterious Everglades, you'll need to walk or paddle your way around (or take a cruise of some sort). To appreciate Fort Lauderdale, hit the beach or explore the tranquil Intracoastal Waterway. And in Key West, heavy lifting means philosophizing over margaritas about the effects of isolationism, or who makes the best Key lime pie and conch chowder.

The land of pink flamingos and palms, Miami and South Florida are a veritable menu of kitsch, the rich, political posturing and multiculturalism, all wrapped together like a messy Cuban sandwich. This, after all, is the town that embraced Elian Gonzales and anti-Castro fervor as easily as Madonna and gay adoption. It's a town where 'minorities' – Cubans, Haitians, African Americans, Bahamians – make up the majority.

It's not that all is perfect in the land of South Florida. Quite the contrary. Open the *Miami Herald* with your morning shot of espresso and you'll be confronted with corruption, crime and cultural oddities and eccentricities. Miami-Dade County is one of the 10 poorest in the country, and yet it encompasses leafy Mediterranean-style Coral Gables.

Perhaps Miami's indescribable allure has something to do with the future. After all, it's a young city, always seeming to be on the verge of breaking out, full of hope. Just like all the immigrants who settle here. Just like the land developers waiting to strike it rich. Just like the drug traffickers looking to expand their territory like any good salesperson would. This is the end of the USA, and the air is thick with potential. No worries here. Like the cruise ships setting off into the sunset, let yourself drift beyond the limitless horizons. Let these South Florida trade winds carry you; it'll be a far lighter trip. And isn't that why we choose sultry holidays?

Facts about Miami

HISTORY

Miami Beach and Miami are very new cities, even by American standards. They were developed mainly during the 20th century.

Tequesta Indians

Miami's earliest known inhabitants, the Tequesta (or Tekesta) Indians, are something of a mystery. Their culture, including their language and customs, did not withstand European settlement long enough to be sufficiently recorded. The apparently non-agrarian tribal group occupied much of South Florida beginning about 10,000 BC. The remains of a permanent settlement were recently discovered at the mouth of the Miami River.

The 2.3-acre site includes the carved-stone foundation of a large circular building that archaeologists believe was used as a meeting place or temple. There is evidence that the layout was designed to correspond with astronomical bodies and events, like many Aztec and Mayan structures. Artifacts made of bone, shark teeth and basalt – a nonnative stone for which the closest sources are the Appalachian Mountains of North America and the Guatemalan highlands – have been recovered. Charcoal found at the site has been dated at 1800 to 2000 years old.

Shortly after the Spanish made contact with the Tequesta, the combination of disease and violence decimated their population. The Miami River site was probably abandoned shortly after Spanish Conquest. Although no Tequesta tribal members are currently recognized by the US government, it is likely that survivors joined forces with the Mikosukee or Seminole tribes.

European Settlement

A full 50 years before the Pilgrims washed ashore on Plymouth Rock, and 40 before the establishment of Jamestown, Virginia, Florida was settled by Spanish explorer Don Pedro Menéndez de Avilés. The area would become to North America what Poland is to Europe: the flattest piece of land between battling superpowers. Before Florida was officially ceded to the US by Spain in 1821, the entire northeast section of the state was sacked, looted, burned and occupied by Spanish, English and US forces.

Although the Spanish had claimed Florida after its European discovery in 1513 by Juan Ponce de León, the French sailed in (as they tended to) and established Fort Caroline, on the St Johns River, in 1564. In 1565, Menéndez arrived at Cape Canaveral with about 1500 soldiers and settlers, who made their way north and established St Augustine.

Menéndez headed farther north and was whupped by the French. The Spaniards retreated south to St Augustine, and soon after, the French, in an effort to fight *fuego* with *feu,* launched a fleet to head south and take on the pesky Spaniards. But the French fell victim to one of Florida's famous coastal storms, and their fleet was destroyed. Menéndez, no shirk when it came to opportunism, immediately forged north to the then relatively unpopulated French fort and destroyed it.

The Spanish retained control of the region despite repeated British attacks in 1586, 1668 and 1702.

The Brits

Beaten finally by fighting elsewhere in the French and Indian War, the Spanish ceded Florida in 1763 to Great Britain in a swap for Havana, Cuba. The British would hold the territory throughout the American Revolution, though as part of the Treaty of Paris ending that war, the fort was ceded back to Spain in 1783.

And the Spanish Again

With two rather significant interruptions, the Spanish ran the show from 1783 until

1817, when the US moved in to hold the territory 'in trust' for Spain – in rather the same way shakedown artists 'protect' the merchandise of shopkeepers from potential 'damage' by 'bad guys.'

In 1812, a group of rebels financed and backed by the US took over Amelia Island, in far northeast Florida. The next day, they turned over control to the US, but after the Spaniards expressed their rather understandable and considerable dismay, the US conceded that they really had no right to keep the place. The island's strategic location – that is, off the mainland – became key. In 1807, US President Jefferson established his Embargo Act forbidding trade with any European powers during the Napoleonic Wars and, in 1808, a prohibition on slavery importation. Amelia Island became black market central: Pirates, cutthroats and smugglers traded slaves and rum, and prostitutes did brisk business.

In 1817, Sir Gregor MacGregor, a Scottish mercenary with revolutionary experience in Venezuela and the financial support of businesspeople in Savannah, Georgia, and Charleston, South Carolina, hired a force that again took over the island from the Spanish on June 29, 1817. When the money ran out, so did MacGregor, who left two lieutenants in command. But wait…there's more!

The US Moves In

The two left holding the bag, Lieutenants Ruggles Hubbard and Jared Irwin, formed a joint venture with a Mexico-based French pirate named Louis Aury (who was permitted to fly the Mexican flag anywhere he wanted, so long as he kicked back a percentage of his plunders to the Mexican government). These three managed to turn the place into an even *more* scandalous town – it's said that there were more bars than street corners, and even more brothels.

Perhaps using moral outrage as an excuse to nab some nifty real estate, US troops moved in and took over that December. In a face-saving compromise, Spain officially turned Florida over to the US in 1821 in exchange for US promises to pay

the land claims of Spanish subjects (none of which, by the way, were ever paid).

In 1825, the US Army built the Cape Florida Lighthouse, the first permanent structure in South Florida, then mostly marshy wetlands. A mere 10 years later, the Cape Florida Lighthouse was destroyed during the Seminole Wars. These would last seven years, resulting in the massive displacement of the majority of Seminoles to a reservation in Oklahoma. (An interesting note is that the Seminoles are still technically at war with the USA – they say they never signed a valid peace treaty.)

In 1843, William F English settled in Miami, bringing investments, settlers and slaves. By 1850, a post office had been established, and a few dozen handfuls of people had moved into the area; by 1870, William B Brickell had established an Indian trading post at Miami.

In 1881, Henry B Lum bought up and cleared most of Miami Beach (for between 35¢ and $1.25 an acre) in an ill-conceived attempt to grow coconuts on the island. The plants either failed in poor soil or were lost to rabbits and deer, and by 1890 he admitted defeat. But the Lum family held on to much of the land.

Tuttle & Flagler

The first real shot at developing Miami Beach came with John S Collins. He bought the 5-mile strip between the Atlantic and Biscayne Bay (what is now 14th to 67th Sts) and began selling parcels of beachfront property in 1896. But the two most significant arrivals were Julia Tuttle in 1875, and Henry Morrison Flagler in 1895.

Tuttle had stayed in the area earlier with her husband, who had tuberculosis, and after his death she returned to land she had inherited. Over the next 20 years, she bought up quite a bit more property in the area.

Flagler, a developer and the business partner of John D Rockefeller in Standard Oil, had been developing the Florida coast at the northern end of the state, building resorts in St Augustine and Palm Beach. He also built the Florida East Coast Railroad, which extended down as far as Palm Beach. Tuttle contacted Flagler with a proposition: If he would extend his railroad to Miami, Tuttle would split her property with him. Flagler wasn't interested.

Then, in 1895, a record freeze enveloped most of the state of Florida, wiping out citrus crops and sending vacationers scurrying. Legend has it that Tuttle – who is said to have been rather quick both on the uptake and with an 'I told you so' – went into her garden at Fort Dallas on the Miami River, snipped off some orange blossoms and sent them to Flagler, who hightailed it down to Miami to see for himself.

What he found was a tropical paradise that was very warm indeed. Flagler and Tuttle came to terms, after which Flagler announced the extension of the railroad. Soon after, thousands of people whose livelihoods had been wiped out by the big freeze, including citrus growers and workers, and service industry professionals such as doctors and merchants, headed down to Miami in anticipation of the boom that was to come.

Passenger train service to Miami began April 22, 1896, the year the city of Miami became incorporated.

Spanish-American War

The USA showed the world it was a power to be reckoned with during the 10-week-long Spanish-American War in 1898. As Cuba struggled for independence from Spanish rule, reports drifted back of Cuban farmers being gathered into prison camps. Newspapers such as William Randolph Hearst's New York *Journal* began a campaign of 'yellow journalism' that riled the American public. The stories ostensibly supported the 'humanitarian annexation' of Cuba, that perhaps not coincidentally would have been a culmination of the USA's manifest destiny and a darned happy windfall to US businesspeople.

President William McKinley resisted intervention, but when the battleship *Maine* was destroyed in Havana's harbor, McKinley declared war on Spain. Congress ratified the declaration on April 25. Debate

continues today about the *Maine*'s destruction. On one hand, it is suspicious that almost all the ship's officers were ashore at the time of the detonation. On the other, new evidence that the explosion was an accident has also surfaced.

The main fighting took place in two theaters, the North Pacific and Cuba. After handy victories in Manila and Guam, US army and volunteer regiments landed in Cuba in late June, including the Rough Riders (who actually had to leave all their horses in Florida), led by Leonard Wood and Theodore Roosevelt. The Spanish surrendered on July 17.

Early Boom

Flagler extended his railway into farming-rich areas in Homestead and Cutler, and in 1905 the Overseas Highway (a railroad causeway connecting the Keys to the mainland) was begun. It fueled yet another, bigger wave of settlement. Development of Miami and Miami Beach kicked off, and in 1914 Chicago industrialist James Deering began building the eye-popping Vizcaya mansion (see the Coconut Grove section of the Things to See & Do chapter).

The wave peaked during WWI, when the US military established an aviation training facility here. Many of the thousands who came to work and train here also settled in the area.

After the war, the first full-fledged Miami boom (1923–25) was fueled not just by the area's idyllic beachfront location and perfect weather, but also by gambling and a lax implementation of prohibition. Though it was illegal, liquor flowed freely throughout the entire Prohibition period.

But the boom was cut short by a devastating hurricane, which was immediately followed by a statewide recession and national depression. After the boom, though, Miami remained a favorite haunt of gangsters. Al Capone's Palm Island mansion was a pleasure palace, and he wasn't alone.

Great Depression & WWII

The Great Depression hit Miami quite badly, and the city and state were major supporters of Franklin Delano Roosevelt and his socialist New Deal. When elected, Roosevelt made his way to Miami to thank South Florida for its support. During that visit an attempt was made on his life by Guiseppe Zangora, a deranged young man. Although FDR escaped unharmed, Chicago mayor Anton Cermas was shot and later died of his injuries.

In the mid-1930s, a mini-boom resulted in the creation and development of Miami Beach's famous art deco buildings. This reasonably prosperous period continued until 1942, when a German U-boat sank a US tanker off Florida's coast. The ensuing reaction created a full-scale conversion of South Florida into a massive military base, training facility and staging area. The Army's central Anti–U-boat Warfare School was based in Miami. Miami Beach's hotels were full of soldiers, who marched up and down the beach in full combat gear.

After the war, many of Miami's trainee soldiers returned and settled here; the city was maintaining its pre-war prosperity. In 1947, the Everglades, a sensitive marsh and swamp area that is home to thousands of indigenous wildlife species, was granted national park status by President Truman.

1950s Boom

In the 1950s, Miami Beach had another boom, as the area became known as the 'Cuba of America.' Gamblers and gangsters, enticed by Miami's gaming, as well as its proximity to the fun, sun and fast times of Batista-run Cuba, moved in en masse. Even a hurricane didn't discourage people *that* much. In 1954, Leroy Collins became the first Southern governor to publicly declare racial segregation 'morally wrong.' Oranges and cotton were becoming huge business in northern Florida, and as the aerospace industry moved to Florida near the end of the decade, an entire 'Space Coast' was created around Cape Canaveral to support the development of the National Aeronautics & Space Administration (NASA)'s Mercury, Gemini and, later, Apollo space programs.

Cuba & the Bay of Pigs

After the 1959 Cuban Revolution, Miami was flooded with anti-Castro immigrants who, in gathering to organize a counter-revolutionary force, managed to establish a permanent Cuban community. A group of exiles formed the 2506th Brigade, sanctioned by the US government, which provided weapons and CIA training for the purpose of launching an attack on Cuba.

In April, 1961, the counterrevolutionaries (CRs) launched an attack against the beaches at Playa Girón, a debacle remembered in the US as the Bay of Pigs. But the US state department had already leaked a warning to the Cubans. A *New York Times* correspondent says he heard about the attack weeks before it happened. The resulting pathetic, half-baked, poorly planned and badly executed attack was little more than an ambush.

To add insult to injury, when the magnitude of the botch-up became clear, President Kennedy refused to send air cover or naval support in the name of 'plausible deniability.' The first wave of CRs, left on the beach without reinforcements or supplies, were all captured or killed (though all prisoners were released by Cuba about three months later).

Kennedy vs Krushchev

Kennedy and the CIA both looked rather silly after the Bay of Pigs fiasco, which is probably why Kennedy stood his ground so firmly during the event that brought the world to the brink of nuclear war: the Cuban Missile Crisis.

Smelling blood after the Bay of Pigs, the USSR's general secretary Nikita Krushchev began secretly installing missile bases in Cuba. By some stroke of luck or by accident, the CIA managed to take photographs of the unarmed warheads. They were shown to Kennedy on October 16, 1962. The Kennedy administration debated what to do about it, and for almost a week after Kennedy was shown the photos, the Soviet embassy denied the existence of the bases.

The Cuban Revolutions

While most people mark the influx of Cubans to the rise of Castro in 1959, Cubans have been flocking to Miami – and Florida – for more than a century. The first large immigration wave began in 1868, when socialist-minded cigar workers fleeing the Ten Years War made Key West sort of an 'enlightened-masses–tobacco combine.'

Those enlightened masses, educated about the struggle in Cuba, began demanding more money and benefits at a time when the economy was in a downturn. Cigar maker Vicente Martínez Ybor practically single-handedly squashed Key West's cigar industry by moving his factory to Tampa and shipping in Cuban laborers from Havana.

The relocation to Miami began during the Spanish-American War (1898), but took off after Cuban independence (the turn of the century) and really soared after regular aviation between Miami and Havana was established in the late 1920s.

Despite intrigue and the murderous Batista regime, the Roaring Twenties to Castro's Revolution were the swinging days of the Cuban-American relationship. Gamblers and hot shots poured into Cuba on hourly flights from Miami, and wealthy Cubans poured right back into Miami to purchase clothes and American products.

What ended these heady days has continued to play a key role in US attitudes toward Cuba and Cubans to this very day.

Most people agree that Fulgencio Batista, whose regime controlled Cuba for almost 20 years before the rise of Fidel Castro, was a horrible gangster who terrorized a nation. At the time, it seemed the best hope of displacing him was to back his adversaries, a coalition headed by Fidel Castro that had been trying for years to oust Batista.

In late 1958, US President Eisenhower announced an arms embargo against the Batista government, which was interpreted by many to be tacit US support for Fidel Castro and his revolutionary coalition. Castro had made a formal promise to the coalition to hold free elections as soon as they took power.

Batista abdicated on January 1, 1959. Although there is some dispute as to just how forthcoming Castro was about his intentions, over the next year and a half, Castro broke his promise of free elections, consolidated his power, and in a move that would set the tone of the next three decades, nationalized business – including major US-owned businesses – and property without compensation.

The US responded by canceling its Cuban sugar quota. Castro, pressed for cash, turned to the great Soviet market. The Soviet Union offered to buy Cuba's entire cash crop, bailing out the struggling new government. Thumbing its nose at the USA, which was reaching the height of its Cold War with the Soviet Union, Castro allied himself with Moscow.

On October 22, Kennedy went on national television and announced that the USSR was installing missiles on Cuba and that installing missiles in such close proximity to Florida was a direct threat to the safety and security of the country. He then announced a naval 'quarantine' of Cuba (a nice euphemism for a naval blockade, which would have been an act of war) and further, that any attack on the USA from Cuba would be regarded as an attack by the USSR.

As tensions mounted, a flurry of letters passed between Washington and Moscow, beginning with: Well, okay, we *do* have missiles, but they're there as a deterrent not as an offensive threat. The exchange culminated in two offers from the Soviets for ending the stalemate. The first, dated October 26, agreed to remove the missiles in exchange for a promise by the USA not to attack Cuba. The second, on the 27th, tied the removal to the USA's elimination of similar sites it had in Turkey.

Publicly, Kennedy responded to the first offer. When it was announced that the USA would not invade Cuba, the Soviets began removing their missiles. Several months later, and with markedly less fanfare, the US removed its missiles from Turkey.

Miami's population swelled as Cubans immigrated there in record numbers. A special immigration center was established in Miami's Freedom Tower to handle the overflow. It became known as the Ellis Island of the South.

Racial Tensions

Miami's record of harmonious race relations is not altogether impressive. The Ku Klux Klan has been active in Florida since the 1920s, and bombings of black-owned housing were not unknown. Blacks were segregated to an area north of downtown known as Colored Town, later called Overtown. And in the 1950s, as the city grew, many were displaced to the federal housing projects at Liberty City, a misnomer if ever there was one. (See the Things to See & Do chapter for more information.)

During 1965, the two 'freedom flights' that ran daily between Miami and Havana disgorged more than 100,000 Cuban refugees. Sensing the tension that was building between blacks and Cubans, Dr Martin Luther King Jr pleaded with the two sides not to let animosity lead to bloodshed.

Riots and skirmishes broke out nonetheless, and acts of gang-style violence occurred. But not all were caused by simmering Cuban/black tensions: Whites got into the fray as well. In 1968, a riot broke out after it was discovered that two white police officers had arrested a 17-year-old black male, stripped him naked and hung him by his ankles from a bridge.

In 1970, the 'rotten meat' riot began when blacks picketed a white-owned shop they had accused of selling spoiled meat. After three days of picketing, white officers attempted to disperse the crowds and fired

on them with tear gas. During the 1970s, there were 13 other race-related violent confrontations.

The Mariel Boatlift

As Florida's economy began recovering in the late 1970s after the oil crisis and recession, Fidel pulled a fast one. He opened the floodgates, allowing anyone who wanted to leave Cuba access to the docks at Mariel. Before the ink was dry on the proclamation, the largest flotilla ever launched for nonmilitary purposes set sail (or paddle) from Florida in practically anything that would float the 90 miles between Cuba and the USA.

The Mariel Boatlift, as the largest of these would be called, brought 150,000 Cubans to Florida. This included an estimated 25,000 prisoners and mental patients that Fidel had cleverly decided to foist off on the Cuban-American population. The resulting strain on the economy, logistics and infrastructure of South Florida only added to still-simmering racial tensions.

Liberty City Riots

Miami's racial tensions would explode on May 17, 1980, when four white police officers, being tried on charges that they beat a black suspect to death while he was in custody, were acquitted by an all-white jury. When the verdict was announced, severe race riots broke out all over Miami and lasted for three days. The riots resulted in 18 deaths, $80 million in property damage and 1100 arrests.

Drugs, Money & Vice

In the indulgent 1980s, the area gained prominence as the major East Coast entry port for drug dealers, their products and the unbelievable sums of money that went along with them. As if to keep up, many savings and loans (S&Ls) opened here in newly built headquarters. While *Newsweek* magazine called Miami 'America's Casablanca,' locals dubbed it the 'City with the S&L Skyline.'

CenTrust, a particularly heinous S&L, used a helicopter to load a marble staircase into its IM Pei–designed downtown headquarters, installed gold-plated faucets in the bathrooms and hung several million dollars worth of art on the walls. This was all before the company went down in flames. Today the building is the Bank of America Tower (see the Things to See & Do chapter).

A plethora of businesses – legitimate concerns as well as drug-financed fronts – and buildings sprung up all over Miami. The downtown was completely remodeled. But it was still being reborn while in the grip of drug smugglers. Shoot-outs were common, as were gangland slayings by cocaine cowboys.

The police, Coast Guard, Drug Enforcement Agency (DEA), Border Patrol and FBI were in a tizzy trying to keep track of it all. Roadblocks were set up along the Overseas Highway to Key West. Police on I-95, the main East Coast north-south highway, were given extraordinary powers to stop vehicles that matched a 'drug runner profile.' According to one public defender who believed in civil rights, this amounted to the power to stop anyone. (Rather sounds like today's terrorist profiling.)

Then it happened: *Miami Vice*.

The show starred Don Johnson and Philip Michael Thomas as two outrageously expensive (and yet pastel-) clad narcotics detectives driving around in a Ferrari Testarossa and million-dollar cigarette boats. It was single-handedly responsible for Miami Beach rising to international attention in the mid-1980s. The show's unique look, slick soundtrack and music video–style montages glamorized the rich South Florida lifestyle. Before long, people were coming down to check it out for themselves.

Photographer Bruce Weber began using South Beach as a grittily fashionable backdrop for modeling shoots in the early 1980s, leading to imitators and eventually to the situation that exists today: model-jam.

By the late 1980s, Miami Beach had risen to international Fabulousness. Celebrities were wintering in Miami, international photographers were shooting here, and the Art Deco District, having been granted federal protection, was going through a renovation and renaissance. A city filled with drug addicts was fast becoming a showpiece of fashion and trendiness.

The Roaring '90s & Beyond

The city rode the peak of a boom during most of the 1990s. The city hosted the Summit of the Americas in 1994 (everyone attended but Castro), celebrated its centennial in 1996 and jumped for joy as the US military moved its Central and South American command center to Miami. But it wasn't all smooth sailing. Miami weathered the storms with grit, a mighty public relations machine, good intentions, decent follow-through and a smattering of luck.

Hurricane Andrew On August 24, 1992, Hurricane Andrew, with sustained 145mph winds and gusts of up to 170mph, slammed Homestead. By the time it passed, the costliest weather disaster to ever hit the USA had damages pegged at $30 billion. It could have been worse, but a) people had had time to prepare and evacuate; and b) the category 4 storm was obliging enough to keep moving and not sit on the area. Had the storm been 20 miles farther north when it hit land (as was expected), the surge surely would have destroyed Miami Beach. (See the Dangers & Annoyances section of the Facts for the Visitor chapter for complete hurricane information.) Fortunately, Andrew barely affected the tourist industry, the city's economic backbone.

Crime Tries for a Comeback Policing had never been a strong suit for Miami. After the gangsters and mobsters of the '20s and '50s, and the 1980s *Miami Vice* era, came the serious carjackings and other crimes against tourists in 1993 (see the Dangers & Annoyances section of the Facts for the Visitor chapter). Miami didn't shake its dangerous reputation until the economic engine of tourism threatened to chug to a complete standstill. Tourist-oriented community policing and other visible programs reversed the curse. Miami went from being the US city with the most violent crime to one with average crime statistics for a city

Elian Gonzales

Is there a soul in the world who doesn't know the story of the little boy whose mother died at sea while trying to flee Cuba for a better life in America? Of a little boy who was rescued from an inner tube 2 miles off the coast of Fort Lauderdale on Thanksgiving Day 1999, then protectively mothered by his cousin Marisleysis while he rode around with an impish grin on bicycles in the front yard of his great-uncle Lazaro Gonzalez, whom he'd not met before his arrival? And who was later seized at gunpoint from his closet in an early-morning raid by US Border Patrol agents and then reunited with his Cuban father and his second family, who remained in the US for another two months while all the political wrangling played itself out? Is there anyone?

It quickly became a struggle between the exiles and Fidel. Is it better for a boy to grow up under communism or capitalism? Is capitalism stronger than blood? Underlying this was an uglier polarization of the local community. Other immigrant groups had long resented the inordinate influence Cubans had and preference they were shown. On a national level, the debate raged between taking a hard-line approach or appeasing Castro. Democratic attorney general Janet Reno, a former federal prosecutor and current Miami-Dade resident, took a lot of flack for the decision and it may haunt her as she tries to secure the governorship in 2002.

its size. From 1992 to 1998, tourist-related crimes decreased a whopping 80%. It remains the third-most-popular US city for international visitors, after Los Angeles and New York.

Drug smuggling also became fashionable again in the 1990s. Smaller traffickers, who make runs between the Florida coast and 'mother' ships and air-drops in the Bahamas, reclaimed their voices. During the opening ceremonies for the Brickell Ave Bridge, news cameras panned away from the speaking dignitaries to photograph a speedboat chase right beneath them on the Miami River, a route that one bridge tender said is like a hospital gown – wide open at the back.

As the very fabulous South Beach scene sprouted, so did a drug-dependent club culture. Ecstasy, ketamine and GHB were as popular as topless models. It finally got so bad in the late 1990s that the police couldn't avoid it any longer and started cracking down. While politicians knew the value of clubs to the local economy, they didn't want to be seen as condoning drug use. Very popular clubs were closed. These days, if Miami Beach won't issue 24-hour liquor licenses, the city of Miami will. New clubs are springing up downtown, but there have been problems with policing. The saga continues. One-ton drug busts regularly feed nightly news reports.

Cuban Run-Ins & Embargos In the early 1990s, the US stopped instantly accepting Cuban refugees in an effort to keep the hotheads with Fidel rather than on Miami streets. The US started its Communism deathwatch as anti-Castro demonstrators stepped up pressure, and as Cuba sank deeper into debt and became more desperate for hard currency. Pundits predicting Castro's imminent fall were generally disappointed by a dictator who kept fighting back.

In early 1995, Castro may have made things far more difficult, though, by shooting down two American planes flown by Brothers to the Rescue (BTTR). A Miami-based group that patrols the Caribbean looking for refugee rafters, these rabid anti-Castro, Miami-based Cubans characterize their work as 'humanitarian aid.' BTTR claims to have rescued thousands of rafters and boat people, who, it also claims, are shot at by Cuban patrol boats and helicopters. After BTTR planes skirted Cuban airspace as part of a flotilla-and-airborne demonstration, they were downed by the Cuban Air Force. The US government's outrage over the attack raised one of the biggest flaps between the countries since the Bay of Pigs.

Most foreign governments permit their citizens to travel and do business with Cuba; the USA, however, does not. Americans, though, can still surreptitiously visit Cuba via Cancún, Jamaica and the Bahamas. Families with close kin, journalists and academics can officially visit (although families can only visit once yearly). In 1998 sweeping trade embargoes were lightly loosened for the first time since commercial transactions ceased in 1963. Medical supplies were first allowed, then came agricultural products, as long as Cuba paid in cash. Although Cuba was struck hard by a hurricane, Fidel's pronouncement in 2000 that he'd not take 'one grain of rice' from the USA was tempered by his cash acquisition in 2002 of $17 million worth of US grain.

While the US house of representatives has twice voted to resume travel to Cuba, the US senate has quashed it the same number. President Bush, mindful of his brother's bid for reelection as governor of Florida in 2002, and his own close call in Florida in 2000 (and bid in 2004), has ordered a top-to-bottom review of the government's policies toward Cuba. The expatriate population always watches with great interest.

Versace & the Gap The highly publicized murder of fashion designer Gianni Versace in 1997 stunned the celebrity world and once again brought negative media coverage to the area (see the Things to See & Do chapter for more information). Yet again, the boom continued. Creeping gentrification has made inroads, and South Beach has long since left the growing stages of a funky, hip destination and become a multinational hot spot. Small family-run shops and restaurants are out, the Gap and Starbucks are in.

What Now? How long the boom will last is subject to conjecture, but not really to heated debate. The crazy eight ball is neither clear nor cloudy, but we might 'try again later.' To be sure, South Beach simultaneously excels at reinventing itself and maintaining a central core. Gay travelers are very loyal; the sun still shines and the

beach is still golden; hotels get groovier by the minute; kitchens churn out celebrity chefs faster than one-minute eggs; and the club scene stays hot to the Touch, distinct like Rain and Liquid, morphing faster than you can BED Lola (see the Entertainment chapter for more on these clubs).

On the one hand, more people than ever are coming. Miami remains the hottest American city and Americans always relish a good night on the town. On the other hand, though, there are murmurs among Europeans and the supermodel crowd that South Beach is imploding and getting – gasp – passé.

Locals are not worried. After the film, TV and European fashion shoots are over; after the Stallones and Schwarzeneggers, Rosies and Madonnas, and the thousands who swarm the neon-emblazoned cafés and boutiques of SoBe depart, South Beach will still be here. And it will be better than ever.

CLIMATE
South Florida's warm weather was the only reason anyone dreamed of inhabiting the area in the first place.

Ideal conditions in Miami Beach exist between December and May, when temperatures average between 60°F and 85°F

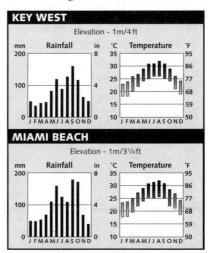

(16°C and 30°C), and average rainfall is a scant 2.14 inches per month.

Summer is very hot and humid with thunderstorms rolling in at 3pm or 4pm. June is the rainiest month (with an average of 7.14 inches), when temperatures are usually between 75°F and 88°F (24°C and 32°C). August is the hottest month, with average temperatures between 78°F and 87°F (26°C and 31°C), but you have to take the heat index – a combination of heat and humidity – into account. It feels a *lot* hotter than 89°F when there's 90% humidity! See the climate chart.

You can call ☎ 305-229-4522 for a weather report.

GOVERNMENT & POLITICS

Miami-Dade County, which includes the city of Miami and environs, has a two-tiered governmental system including a large unincorporated area and 27 separate municipalities. Miami-Dade provides services such

Politics as Usual

State senators from Miami-Dade are re-elected despite being under indictment. Mayor Xavier Suarez, the first Cuban-born mayor of Miami, elected in 1985, was thrown out of office when it was discovered that a few too many corpses cast ballots for him. Here's another fairly run-of-the-mill influence-peddling scenario: In 2002 it was discovered that politicians lobbied for and received hefty contributions from the very consultants whose salaries are paid by the local government and who then seek rehiring from those same politicians. This was all in connection with the $5.4 billion airport renovation and new Transit Center, by the way. To this, mayor Alex Penelas (who received funds from the consultants) responded: 'I think it all stinks. I wish I didn't have to call for any contributions. But that's the way the system works.' Right. If it's not your money, it's almost funny. If it is, well, you get used to it or you move.

as the police and fire departments, and trash collection to the unincorporated areas, which make up about 60% of the county. In some cases, such as police and fire coverage, Miami-Dade may overlap with an incorporated municipality. Buses and other public transportation within the entire county fall under the domain of Miami-Dade. Each municipality within Miami-Dade has its own city government, police force, fire department etc. The Miami-Dade board of county commissioners consists of 13 commissioners elected by districts.

While that summarizes the structure of Miami government, it doesn't address Miami's far more interesting and often absurd political shenanigans and chicanery. The city's insular political culture spawns borderline racist nicknames like 'Banana Republic.' Corruption usually stems from issues of power or money, both of which are essential components of the drug trade, which in turn is inextricably tied to laundering, development and crime in Miami. Sounds like the makings of a good novel, eh? Perhaps it's no coincidence that so many *Miami Herald* writers win awards for their writings about South Florida perversions. Issues are always messy where population growth and limited natural resources butt heads.

Cubans hold the reins as the overriding political force, but it wasn't always that way. When the first waves began arriving in the late 1950s, they were more concerned with regaining their economic independence. (Most were middle-class merchants and social elitists who had their property and money confiscated when they left Cuba.) They intended to go back to Cuba, after all. But after the Mariel Boatlift, when negative media coverage got really bad, Cubans started taking a more active role in their futures. These days a nephew of Castro and the daughter of a Bay of Pigs leader represent Miami-Dade as Republicans in the US house of representatives. With the 1997 death of Jorge Mas Canosa, leader of the Cuban American National Foundation, which lobbies for Cuban democracy, and with the coming of age of second-generation Cubans born in this country, the Cubans have become a tad less hard-line.

An attorney by trade, and never having held public office, mayor Manny Diaz took over in November 2001. Critics, who have labeled him a 'phantom mayor,' carp that since taking office he's been to lots of ceremonial events but has not put forward any substantial policy initiatives. Supporters claim that he's working behind the scenes building relationships, bringing sorely needed stability to the office. Elected with great support from Cubans, but practically none from blacks, Diaz has his work cut out for him.

ECONOMY

Miami's economy relies heavily on tourism, but its position as gateway to Latin America has given it powerhouse status as an international business city. More than 150 multinational companies have operations in Miami, and at least 100 have their Latin American headquarters here. Among the top 20 are Johnson & Johnson, the Gap, American Airlines, Sony, IBM, Cisco Systems, Canon, Oracle, UPS, FedEx, ExxonMobil and ChevronTexaco.

Miami customs processes 50% of all US exports to Central America and the Caribbean and 30% of all US exports to South America. The city is also establishing itself as an international banking center – almost 45 international banks call it home. To be sure, brokerage houses, banking, imports, exports and commodities drive the local economy. But, more than a few people admit in hushed tones that 'Miami is the city that drugs built.' If there is a kilo of truth to that, it's worth noting that there is more high-rise construction here than in any major metropolitan center I've visited in the last few years. To paraphrase a James Carville adage: 'It's the drugs, stupid.'

The Beacon Council (☎ 305-579-1300, W www.beaconcouncil.com) is a nonprofit organization that provides business introductions, research studies and many business services at no charge.

POPULATION & PEOPLE

Miami Beach has 95,000 residents. Population figures for the city of Miami are misleading; while there are about 650,000 people living within the city limits, 2.25 million live in Miami-Dade County. There are slightly more Latinos than whites. And of those Latinos, 60% are Cuban. It's also interesting to note that in the early 1980s the median age in Miami Beach was 65; these days it's the early 40s.

ARTS

Over the past decade, Miami's gentrification and redevelopment have resulted in an explosion of artistic and cultural activity, and it's coming from all demographic sectors. Many artists based in other areas of the country, notably the Northeast, headed south to take advantage of lower real estate prices and more quirky and affluent visitors. With artists came the collectors and galleries who invigorated the scene.

The influx of foreigners has also resulted in a boom in Caribbean and South American art. If your tastes tend toward conventional Western art and culture, you may be slightly disappointed. There are some very good works, but it's not the overwhelming theme.

The name of the game is diversity.

Literature

Every mid- to late November, you can visit the Miami Bookfair International, among the finest in the USA (see the Special Events section of the Facts for the Visitor chapter). Books & Books runs a delightful series of events throughout the year; check their Web site (W www.booksandbooks.com) for a calendar of events.

Fiction While inroads are being made in poetry and experimental fiction, the Miami literature scene remains primarily a hotbed of mystery, scandal and detective novels. You're not surprised, are you?

Miami's most notable poets include Richard Blanco (*City of a Hundred Fires*), Campbell McGrath (*American Noise*), Michael Hettich (*Small Boat*), John

Looking for Love in All the Right Places

Looking for love? Come to Miami, where girls – and boys – just wanna have fun, at least according to Forbes.com's guide to the best places to be single. In a list of 40 metropolitan areas, Miami came in at number two, right behind…Washington, DC?

To come up with the rankings, Forbes.com took statistical data on everything from census figures to job growth to the number of nightspots and singles. The cost of living was factored in, too. Along with the cost of renting an apartment, they calculated the cost of a pizza, movie tickets and a six-pack of beer. Not exactly Miami fare – Miamians prefer to think of themselves as a mango-salsa–mahimahi and martini set – but what the heck.

The guide made special note of Miami's physical attractions (gorgeous bodies covered by little clothing), its international flavor (English is almost a second language) and its intense nightlife.

Incidentally, Orlando came in at number 20 and Tampa at number 23, making the Sunshine State one of the best places to find love.

Balaban (*Blue Mountain* and *Words for My Daughter*) and Ricardo Pau-Llosa (*Cuba*).

The region has spawned more than a dozen major suspense/thriller writers, and more are writing themselves into publication daily. If you're short on time, pick up *Naked Came the Manatee,* a series by 13 of Miami's best-known writers.

Some Miami heavy-hitters include Carl Hiaasen, whose books *Stormy Weather, Native Tongue* and *Striptease* offer snarling satire of South Florida, especially its tourists and developers. Hiaasen's *Team Rodent: How Disney Devours the World* is an eminently readable rant against Mauschwitz.

Other bright stars include Pulitzer prize–winning *Miami Herald* columnist Edna Buchanan (*Miami, It's Murder);* Pulitzer prize–winning columnist Liz Balmaseda; and Les Standiford, author of the ecothriller *Spill,* and several other novels that star building contractor John Deal, *Deal to Die for, Done Deal* and *Book Deal.*

Not to be forgotten, of course, is Elmore Leonard, the author of dozens of books including *Get Shorty, Gold Coast, Stick* and *Maximum Bob.* Charles Willeford, the quintessential grizzled Miami author, is best known for *Miami Blues.*

Peter Matthiessen's novel *Killing Mister Watson* details the settlement of the Everglades. Papa Hemingway's *To Have and Have Not* is his only book set in his beloved Key West. Pick up Zora Neale Hurston's *Their Eyes Were Watching God.* John Sayles, film director extraordinaire, has penned his take on Cubans in Miami (*Los Gusanos*).

James W Hall writes Florida Keys–based mysteries, including *Mean Hightide, Beginning Algebra, Buzz Cut* and *Hard Aground.* Keep one eye on Lynn Barrett, whose collection of short stories is entitled *The Land of Go,* and the other eye on Cuban-born mystery writer Carolina Garcia-Aguilera, whose first book, *Bloody Waters,* has been very successful.

Nonfiction Reality is more colorful than fiction in Miami. Look for Edna Buchanan's *The Corpse Had a Familiar Face;* Buchanan's *Herald* beat was grisly crime and this is her story of covering those stories. The irrepressible Joan Didion's *Miami* expresses her take on the Cuban community (fiction or nonfiction?).

Rolf Shields' *Bought and Sold* tells the history of Miami like it was. In the same vein, John Rothchild's *Up for Grabs* exposes the state's wacky commercial transactions. Stuart McIver's *Dreamer, Schemers & Scallawags: The Florida Chronicles* gives the lowdown on the state's colorful underground characters.

Art deco savior Babara Beer Capitman's *Deco Delights* is mostly a photo essay on South Beach architecture. Marjory Stoneman Douglas' *The Everglades: River of Grass* is a must-read for anyone remotely interested in the complex ecological issues of that area. Michael Gannon's *The New History of Florida* tells the state's story by way of historical themes.

Arva Moore Parks' *Miami, the Magic City* chronicles local lore with a good dose of historic photos. David Leon Chandler's *Henry Flagler* chronicles the story of Miami's 'Robber Baron' who laid out the city.

Those scant on time, or who can't read on the beach, might pick up *The Florida Reader,* edited by Maurice O'Sullivan and Jack Lane, a great collection of writings about the state from 1530 to the present.

Film

At the turn of the century, before Hollywood, California, became filmmaking central, places like Jacksonville and even Hollywood, Florida, were cranking out films. These days, filmmakers are flocking back to the area with a vengeance. In the last few years, the Beach has starred in staggeringly successful films, including *There's Something about Mary, The Bodyguard, Donnie Brasco, Ace Ventura: Pet Detective, True Lies, Get Shorty* and *The Birdcage.*

But Miami and Miami Beach have been featured in a string of stinkers, too, including Eddy Murphy's *Holy Man;* the unspeakably embarrassing *The Specialist,* starring Sly Stallone, Sharon Stone and James Woods; *Striptease,* proof that a wonderful novel (by Carl Hiaasen) can make the worst movie of the year; and the unfathomable *Fair Game,* featuring the most obvious thespian in the world, Cindy Crawford, as a tough-talkin', no-nonsense attorney.

Luckily, Miami has provided a backdrop for some of America's most beloved classics, such as *The Cocoanuts* (the Marx Brothers' first feature); *Where the Sidewalk Ends,* filmed entirely at Miami Studios; *Citizen Kane,* which used the South Florida coastline as the setting for Xanadu, the largest pleasure palace in the world; *Key Largo,* with Bogie and Bacall; Elvis Presley's *Clambake; The Bellboy,* with funnyman Jerry Lewis doing his shtick at the gaudy Fontainebleau Hotel; *The Barefoot Mailman; Scarface,* starring Al Pacino exploring the glitzy and glamorous world of cocaine dealing and organized crime; and three Bond films, *Dr No, Live and Let Die* and *Goldfinger.*

By the time Alec Baldwin played a sicko in *Miami Blues,* based on Charles Willeford's book, everyone in the world knew about Miami thanks to a television phenomenon: *Miami Vice.* If you watch the show today (it's available in many larger video-rental shops) you'll see the Beach at its turning point from scuzzball alley to fashion central. Although the series was filmed primarily in Miami Beach, it's funny to watch the action jump to elsewhere in the city. Now that the place is so universally recognizable, no film could possibly get away with that.

It's not surprising that annual film festivals (see the Special Events section in the Facts for the Visitor chapter and the Cinemas section in the Entertainment chapter) showcase the area's rising talents. Independent filmmaking is making inroads, and foreign productions are streaming into the area so quickly that the local film commission started saying things like 'pay or play,' and knowing what they meant.

Music

The big story in Miami, of course, is Latin and Caribbean music. Think salsa, reggae, merengue, mambo, rumba, cha-cha-cha and calypso. The big stars have been Gloria Estefan, Celia Cruz, Ricky Martin and the androgynous Albita, but what's *really* exciting is that you're very likely to encounter the *next* Gloria Estefan or Celia Cruz. Ah, you knew them when…. See the Entertainment chapter for venues.

The best time to see ensemble Cuban bands – often with up to 20 musicians and singers – is during special celebrations, such as the annual Calle Ocho Festival (see the Special Events section in the Facts for the Visitor chapter). But there are also intimate places on Calle Ocho where you can catch concerts almost nightly. See the Entertainment chapter for venues.

And then there's classical. Established in 1987, the New World Symphony is a 'learning and performing experience for gifted graduates of the most prestigious music schools.' Darn tootin' it is. The country's best and brightest young (usually in their 20s) musicians spend about three years of post-graduate time performing in NWS concerts around the country and the world.

Members live in tiny rooms in a renovated South Beach deco hotel, and spend most of their waking hours immersed in all aspects of music. The energy level in the dorms is enough to guarantee a good concert, so by the time these people get into the Lincoln Theatre for a concert – whoa, Nelly, hold onto your hat. See the Entertainment chapter for more information.

Architecture

Miami architecture suffers from boom-bust cycles of drought and downpour when it comes to building. The early settlement's improbable obstacles – mangroves, mosquitoes, swamps and sand – didn't do much to encourage a long-term vision. That also accounts for the infrastructure problems of buildings that were not designed with so many people in mind. Most construction has reflected popular whims that blow in as fast as a tropical storm.

Although Miami is a young city with relatively little architectural heritage, in contrast to Miami Beach, Miami-Dade County hasn't done much to preserve it. You should seek out the few remaining early structures: the 1891 Barnacle State Historic Site, the 1897 Flagler cottage and the 1917 Plymouth Congregational Church (all are covered in the Things to See & Do chapter).

So while Miami's boom-era construction made a few concessions to various styles

here and there, it's famous for three distinct architectural styles – Mediterranean revival, towering skyscrapers and art deco. For a complete immersion in Mediterranean style, head down S Bayshore Dr, to the extravagant Vizcaya Museum & Gardens or almost anywhere in Coral Gables. (Also see the boxed text 'Master Planner' about George Merrick, in the Things to See & Do chapter.) After a while Merrick's 'City Beautiful' will seem, perhaps, a bit too beautiful: Coral Gables city ordinances require houses to be painted within a very narrow palette and that lawns be kept trim and tidy.

Downtown soars with skyscrapers, including the tallest one south of the Mason-Dixon line (it was under construction at press time). Look for the private Atlantis Condominium, at 2025 Brickell Ave, which you might recognize from the opening of *Miami Vice.* It's the building with the architecturally arresting hole containing a circular staircase and a palm tree on the 12th floor. It was designed by a big-time Miami architecture firm, Arquitectonica, which has its own headquarters on Brickell Ave. They also designed the mod American Airlines Arena and Sawgrass Mills.

Miami Beach is best known, of course, for its art deco buildings. The term was a contraction of the 1925 Parisian *Exposition Internationale des Arts Décoratifs et Industriels Modernes,* in which a strong emphasis was placed upon *Arts Décoratifs,* or decorative arts. The Exposition wasn't the starting point, but rather the dawn of a style that combined many existing forms. These mostly included turn-of-the-century and pre-WWI European movements like art nouveau, Arts and Crafts, the Vienna secession and Italian futurism, and the more geometric modernism. For a complete discussion of art deco in Miami Beach, see the 'Art Deco Architecture' special section.

Theater

Partly because of the University of Miami-Coral Gable campus' acting program (Sylvester Stallone's and Ray Liotta's alma mater), and partly because of the model/

actors migrating to Miami looking for that big break, there are plenty of places to catch a show. The best bets for new and independent theater productions are those smaller venues like the Gable Stage, New Theatre and Coconut Grove Playhouse. Most of the ethnic theater companies are itinerant, so you'll want to keep an eye peeled for them.

When civic leaders were making their mark on Miami in the early 20th century, they wanted to impress their northern brethren. They sure did. There are many gorgeous performance venues, such as the Colony Theatre, the Lincoln Theatre and the Gusman Center for the Performing Arts. Don't pass up an opportunity to see something there.

Also because of that continuing Northeast and New York City connection, many touring Broadway road shows stop in Miami. There are several area Spanish-language theaters; don't forget to check what's going on at the Tower Theater (see the Entertainment chapter for details). The oft-overlooked Lyric Theatre (see the Things to See & Do chapter) might be hosting something when you're in town, too.

Dance

Miami nourishes start-ups. There are dozens of nonprofit dance organizations, and hundreds of dance-related businesses like studios, schools and production companies. And the mix of American, African, Cuban, Haitian, European and Latin American cultures is obvious in the productions you'll see here. The big player is the Miami City Ballet, one of the top 10 funded companies in the country; see the Entertainment chapter for more information.

Perhaps more unique to Miami, though, would be taking salsa or flamenco lessons from the hot shots at the Performing Arts Network. Then you could really put the moves on your friends back home.

Painting & Sculpture

Perhaps surprisingly, as recently as the early 1980s, Miami's art scene was virtually nonexistent. But in the mid-1980s, artists discovered that they could get more space and live more cheaply in South Beach than in other art centers like New York and Los Angeles. About the same time the South Beach boom began, which in turn supplied the cash to fuel an explosion in local art. Even today, though, while the lack of many major galleries or a truly world-class museum is still an issue, the arts market is still only one notch above fledgling.

Unfortunately, as the gentrification of Miami Beach becomes more complete, the very artists who made the scene fledgling have had to move on to find new, cheaper digs. South Beach rents skyrocketed, and the art scene became exclusive without ever really experiencing a heyday. It went from bust to boom too quickly to establish a real culture of its own. But that's not to say that there isn't art everywhere you look.

Real estate developers encouraged the arts by incorporating local artists' projects in the designs of private and public spaces. The Margulies sculpture garden, which includes works by Richard Serra, Isamu Noguchi, Mark di Suivero and Jonathan Borofsky, is on long-term loan to the campus of Florida International University (FIU). The outstanding, artist-run ArtCenter/South Florida bought and leased buildings to provide affordable studios and exhibition space in the mid-'80s, which helped to significantly revitalize South Beach's Lincoln Road. You'll definitely want to pop in. The Museum of Contemporary Art, designed by Charles Gwathmey, fused urban and cultural planning by placing a civic and cultural center within a residential and commercial area. It's a schlep to visit, but worth it. The Rubell family, formerly of New York City and now South Beach hotel developers, houses their modern art collection in a former DEA-confiscated drug warehouse.

As you can imagine, Cuban and Latin American artists have a major impact on Miami's growing art community. Watch for group shows and check out the monthly exhibits at the Latin American Art Museum in Little Havana. The Miami Art Museum also specializes in post-WWII art of the Western Hemisphere.

For more Eurocentric art, the Bass Museum of Art and the Lowe Art Museum will satisfy your cravings. You'll find more information on most of these sights in the Things to See & Do chapter.

Galleries along Lincoln Road are the area's most accessible, although tonier ones can be found in Coral Gables and hipper ones in Miami's Design District (which also has lots of cool design shops). Of all the contemporary venues, perhaps the most interesting and diverse is the Wallflower Gallery. See the Shopping chapter for information on these places.

RELIGION
Christianity & Judaism

The area's residents are predominantly Christian, but there are significant numbers of Jewish people here as well. Many are transplants from the northeastern USA, but there is also a healthy number of Jewish immigrants from Russia and Cuba. More are Reform Jews, who do not adhere as strictly to the religious and social teachings of the Torah, as opposed to Conservative Jews, who are more religious and ceremonial, and the extremely religious Orthodox community. Miami Beach is home the country's second-largest Hassidic community.

Miami is also the home of the Florida branch of the Chabad Lubavitchers, a faction of Orthodox Jews who proselytize within the Jewish faith. If a long-haired, bearded man dressed in a black suit and white shirt and wearing a black hat or *yarmulke* asks you a) if you're Jewish and b) to step inside a recreational vehicle, you've just met a Lubavitcher.

Afro-Caribbean Religions

Santería, a syncretism of the west African Yoruba religion with Catholicism, is one of the area's commonly practiced Afro-Caribbean religions. It was brought to Cuba by slaves who settled there, and is primarily practiced in Cuba. Vodou is Yoruba as practiced by Haitians. Both of these religions practice animal sacrifice as a token of fidelity to the gods and spirits, and it's not uncommon to come upon animal remains at various

The Voodoo Squad

Each weekday morning, members of the janitorial staff at the Miami-Dade Courthouse, at 1351 NW 12th St, patrol the grounds outside the building as part of the Voodoo Squad. According to the *Miami Herald*, they're on the lookout for the remains of voodoo rituals performed by family members of those in custody in an effort to sway the outcome of trials. The squad regularly encounters dead goats, roosters, chickens and lizards with their mouths tied closed (though sometimes a cow tongue tied with twine is substituted), ceremonial powder, corn kernels, cakes and eggs.

places around the city, such as along the Miami River, in parks and, strangely, near the Bass Museum of Art.

Afro-Brazilian Cults

Afro-Brazilian cults do not follow the ideas of major European or Asian religions; neither do they use doctrines to define good and evil. One of the most shocking things to Europeans in their first contact with various subSaharan African images and rituals was the cult of Exú. This entity was generally represented by a combined human/animal image, complete with a horn and an erect penis. Seeking parallels between their own beliefs and African religions, European Catholics and Puritans identified Exú as the devil. For practitioners of this African religion, however, Exú represents the transition between the material and the spiritual worlds.

Candomblé, an African word denoting a dance in honor of the gods, is the most orthodox of the cults brought to Brazil from

Africa by the Nago, Yoruba and Jeje peoples. In the ritual of Candomblé, Exú acts as a messenger between the gods and human beings. For example, everything related to money, love and protection against thieves comes under the watchful eye of Exú. Ultimately, Exú's responsibility is the temporal world.

LANGUAGE

'One of the nicest things about Miami,' goes an old joke, 'is how close it is to the USA.' Indeed, while English is the predominant language in the USA, Miami has an above-average number of non-English–speaking residents. In fact, more Miamians speak Spanish than English. How could it be otherwise with Miami's proximity to countries that have generated mass refugee migrations. It's a somewhat unique situation in the USA. While pockets of foreigners have formed in other large cities like New York, Chicago and Los Angeles, there seems to be a higher degree of linguistic assimilation there than in Miami.

Visitors can certainly get away with English only, but to do so is to essentially write off experiencing a huge chunk of Miami culture and life. Spanish is the main language in almost every shop, café, coin laundry and restaurant in Little Havana, as well as in a surprising number of businesses elsewhere in the city.

See the Language chapter at the end of the book for a brief glossary of both Spanish and Creole. If you plan to spend a lot of time in Spanish-speaking neighborhoods, take along Lonely Planet's comprehensive and compact *Latin American Spanish phrasebook*. If you're planning on romancing some Latin types, the finest resources are *Hot Spanish for Guys and Girls* and *Hot Spanish for Guys and Guys*, both of which contain an amazing number of useful phrases.

Facts for the Visitor

WHEN TO GO

The boundaries of 'the season' have been blurred by the stampede of models, photo and film shoots, and the huge number of people moving here from both other parts of the US and abroad. Nonetheless, the most popular time to visit is still December to April. See the Climate section in the Facts about Miami chapter for specifics on temperature and rainfall.

The advantage of coming early in summer or fall, despite the higher temperatures and increased rainfall, is that you get more of the place to yourself. Although oppressive humidity takes a couple of days to get accustomed to, ocean breezes do help temper it.

Hurricane season, from June to November, can be a perfectly pleasant time to visit. But remember, one little hurricane can ruin your holiday. See the Dangers & Annoyances section, later in this chapter, for more information.

ORIENTATION

The city of Miami covers an enormous, sprawling area that's subdivided into neighborhoods, and is adjacent to several cities. City lines are so indistinct that you may not even realize you've left Miami and entered, say, Coral Gables or Hialeah. Neighborhoods and cities are detailed below.

Miami is on the mainland, while the city of Miami Beach occupies a thin barrier island about 4 miles east across Biscayne Bay. Locals call it the Billion-Dollar Sandbar.

On the mainland, the street numbering system is based on north-south and east-west dividers. With the exception of Coral Gables and Hialeah (whose founders should be arrested for making their street systems so stupid) getting around the area is a snap, despite how intimidating it looks on a map.

The north-south divider is Flagler St and the east-west divider is Miami Ave; prefixes

are given to streets – N, S, E, W, NW, NE, SW, SE – based on that street's position relative to the intersection of Flagler St and Miami Ave.

Most avenues and streets are numbered: Avenues begin at 1st and count upward the farther east and west they are from Miami Ave, so E 1st Ave would be one block east of Miami Ave, while W 42nd Ave would be 42 blocks west of Miami Ave. Streets are numbered similarly, increasing in number progressively the farther north or south of Flagler St they are, so N 1st St would be one block north of Flagler etc.

With the exception of Coral Gables and Hialeah, most streets, terraces, lanes and drives run east-west, and most avenues, places, courts and roads run north-south.

Addresses

Most of Miami operates on the 'hundred-block' system, so the first digits of an address are the product of its lower-number cross-street. So, a specific address is based on the streets it's between: 7012 NW X St is on X St between 70th and 71st Sts, northwest of the intersection of Flagler St and Miami Ave.

South Beach (Maps 3 & 4)

The southern part of the city of Miami Beach encompasses the widest section of the island. As for its footprint, streets run east-west, avenues run north-south. Unlike the city of Miami, major arteries (Washington, Collins, Alton and Ocean) are named rather than numbered. There are no directional sectors such as NW or SE.

Washington Ave is the bustling main drag and Collins Ave is the famous deco-hotel–lined thoroughfare. The chic outdoor cafés and restaurants along Ocean Drive overlook the wide Atlantic beach shorefront.

Alton Rd is the utilitarian main drag on the west side, gaining in popularity as the sexier eastern end becomes more and more crowded.

Lincoln Road is pedestrian-only between Washington Ave and Alton Rd.

South Pointe is below 5th St at the southern tip of Miami Beach, directly across Government Cut from Fisher Island.

Northern Miami Beach (Map 5)

Northern Miami Beach (which for our mapping purposes is separated by narrow Indian Creek north of 25th St) should not be confused with an entirely different city on the mainland called North Miami Beach, which borders the city of North Miami. Indian Creek separates Collins Ave, almost exclusively lined with high-rise condominiums and luxury hotels, from the residential districts at the west. Alton Rd winds through this exclusive neighborhood and connects with Collins Ave at 63rd St.

The official northern border of Miami Beach is 96th St. But for our purposes we've mapped a large stretch of the beach – including the neighborhoods of Surfside, Bal Harbour, Sunny Isles and some of Golden Beach.

Note that there are major differences between the northern and southern sections of Miami Beach, and these can be far more than the stodginess of the former and the trendiness of the latter.

Downtown Miami (Map 6)

Downtown Miami is a fairly straightforward grid, with Flagler Ave as much the main drag as any. The downtown area is divided by the lazy Miami River, which is crossed by the Brickell Ave Bridge. Biscayne Blvd runs north from the river and Brickell Ave runs south of it; both are on the eastern side of the district.

From South Beach, the MacArthur Causeway dumps you right into downtown.

Key Biscayne (Map 7)

The Rickenbacker Causeway ($1 toll), with exits off US Hwy 1 and I-95 and most directly accessible from Biscayne Blvd, leads over to Key Biscayne. It turns into Crandon Blvd, the key's only real main road, which runs all the way to the southernmost tip and the Cape Florida Lighthouse.

Little Havana (Map 8)

Calle Ocho, or SW 8th St, doesn't just cut *through* the heart of the neighborhood, it *is* the heart of the neighborhood. For the purposes of our exploration, the neighborhood extends roughly from W Flagler St to SW 13th St and from SW 3rd Ave to SW 37th Ave. The Miami River separates Little Havana from downtown on the northeast border.

Coconut Grove (Map 9)

The Grove unfolds along S Bayshore Dr (south of the Rickenbacker Causeway), which hugs the shoreline. S Bayshore Dr turns into the central village where it becomes Main Hwy and eventually leads to Douglas Rd (SW 37th Ave), Ingraham Hwy, Old Cutler Rd and attractions in South Dade. US Hwy 1 acts as the northern boundary for the Grove.

Coral Gables (Map 10)

The lovely Mediterranean-style city of Coral Gables is essentially bordered by Calle Ocho to the north, Sunset Dr (SW 72nd St/Hwy 986) to the south, Le Jeune Rd (SW 42nd Ave/Hwy 953) to the east and Red Rd (SW 57th Ave/Hwy 959) to the west. US Hwy 1 slashes through at a 45-degree angle from northeast to southwest. The main campus of the University of Miami is located just south of the enormous Coral Gables Biltmore Golf Course, north of US Hwy 1.

Now, here's the fun part: The address system in Coral Gables is bass-ackwards when compared to Miami; avenues here run east-west, while streets run north-south.

MAPS

All rental car companies are required by law to hand out decent city and area maps when they rent a car. Rand McNally, AAA and Dolph Map Company all make maps of the Miami area. Lonely Planet produces a laminated foldout map of the Miami area that includes Key West and Fort Lauderdale. The best free map is from the Greater Miami & the Beaches Convention & Visitor's Bureau (see next section).

TOURIST OFFICES

There are several tourist offices in the Greater Miami area, all of which give advice of varying usefulness and hand out visitor's guides, pamphlets and, especially, flyers and discount tickets to many area attractions.

South Beach

Run by the Miami Design Preservation League (MDPL), the Art Deco Welcome Center (☎ 305-672-2014, W www.mdpl.org; Map 4), 1001 Ocean Dr, has tons of Deco District information. It's open 10am to 10pm daily. The MDPL also organizes walking tours of the District (see the South Beach section of the Things to See & Do chapter).

The informative Miami Beach Chamber of Commerce (☎ 305-672-1270, W www .miamibeachchamber.com; Map 3), 1920 Meridian Ave, is open 9am to 5pm Monday to Friday.

Downtown & Elsewhere

The Greater Miami & the Beaches Convention & Visitor's Bureau (☎ 305-539-3000, 800-933-8448, W www.miamiandbeaches .com; Map 6) has luxurious headquarters on the 27th floor of 701 Brickell Ave, a five-minute walk south of the Miami River. It's open 8:30am to 5pm Monday to Friday.

The Coconut Grove Chamber of Commerce (☎ 305-444-7270, W www.coconut grove.com; Map 9), 2820 McFarlane Rd, is open 9am to 5pm Monday to Friday.

Coral Gables Chamber of Commerce (☎ 305-446-1657, W www.gableschamber .org; Map 10), inside the Omni-Colonnade Hotel, at 2333 Ponce de León Blvd, Suite 650, is open 9am to 5pm Monday to Friday.

The Black Archives History & Research Center of South Florida (☎ 305-636-2390; Map 2), at 5400 NW 22nd Ave, Suite 101, in Liberty City, has information about black culture and can arrange tours of Liberty City and other areas of Miami.

DOCUMENTS

With the exception of Canadians, who only need proper proof of Canadian citizenship, all foreign visitors to the USA must have a valid passport and may also require a US visa.

If you could, on the best of days, be mistaken as being under 30, carry a photo ID card with your age on it or a national ID card. Anyone who appears to be under 30 is asked for identification at bars and nightclubs.

If you qualify, you can sometimes use an International Student Identity Card (ISIC) for discounts to museums, tourist attractions and on some airfares.

Visas

A reciprocal visa-waiver program applies to citizens of certain countries who may enter the USA for stays of 90 days or less without having to obtain a visa. Under this program you must have a roundtrip ticket on an airline that participates in the visa-waiver program; have proof of financial solvency; sign a form waiving the right to a hearing of deportation; and will not be allowed to extend your stay beyond 90 days. Consult with your travel agent or contact the airlines directly for more information.

Other travelers (except Canadians) will need to obtain a visa from a US consulate or embassy. In most countries you can do this by mail; for others, you'll need show up at the nearest US consulate or embassy.

Your passport should be valid for at least six months longer than your intended stay in the USA and you'll need to submit a recent photo with the application. Documents of financial stability and/or guarantees from a US resident are sometimes required, particularly for visitors from developing countries.

Visa applicants may be required to 'demonstrate binding obligations' that will ensure their return back home. Because of this requirement, those planning to travel through other countries before arriving in the USA are generally better off applying for their US visa while they are still in their home country, rather than after they have hit the road.

The validity period for US visitor visas depends on what country you're from. The

HIV & Entering the USA

Anyone entering the USA who is not a US citizen is subject to the authority of the Immigration & Naturalization Service (INS), which has the power to keep someone from entering or staying in the USA. Being HIV positive is not grounds for deportation, but it is a grounds for exclusion, and the INS can refuse to admit HIV-positive visitors.

Although the INS does not test people for HIV when they try to enter the USA, the form for the non-immigrant visa asks: 'Have you ever been afflicted with a communicable disease of public health significance?' The INS will try to exclude anyone who answers 'yes' to this question.

If you have HIV but can prove to consular officials that you are the spouse, parent or child of a US citizen or legal resident (green-card holder), you are exempt from the exclusionary rule.

For legal immigration information and referrals to immigration advocates, visitors may contact the National Immigration Project of the National Lawyers Guild (☎ 617-227-9727), 14 Beacon St, Suite 602, Boston, MA 02108.

length of time you'll be allowed to stay in the USA is ultimately determined by US immigration authorities at the port of entry.

Visa Extensions Tourists are usually granted a six-month stay on arrival. If you try to extend at that time, the first assumption will be that you are working illegally, so come prepared with concrete evidence that you've been traveling extensively and will continue to be a model tourist.

Extensions are manhandled by the US Government Justice Department's Immigration & Naturalization Service (INS; ☎ 800-375-5283, ⓦ www.ins.usdoj.gov; Map 2), at 7880 Biscayne Blvd. Get there early, bring along a good, long book and pack a lunch.

Other Documents

Bring your driver's license if you intend to rent a car; visitors from some countries may find it wise to back up their national license with an International Driving Permit, available from many local auto clubs. A comprehensive travel or health insurance policy is very important for overseas visitors, and foreign tourists should bring documentation of membership. See the Health section, later in this chapter, for more on health insurance.

Copies

All important documents (passport data page and visa page, credit cards, travel insurance policy, air/bus/train tickets, driver's license etc) should be photocopied before you leave home. Leave one copy with someone at home and keep another with you, separate from the originals.

EMBASSIES & CONSULATES

As a tourist, it's important to realize what your own embassy – the embassy of the country of which you are a citizen – can and can't do to help you if you get into trouble. Generally speaking, it won't be much help in emergencies if the trouble you're in is remotely your own fault. Remember that you are bound by the laws of the country you are in. Your embassy will not be sympathetic if you end up in jail after committing a crime locally, even if such actions are legal in your own country.

In genuine emergencies you might get some assistance, but only if other channels have been exhausted. For example, if you need to get home urgently, a free ticket home is exceedingly unlikely – the embassy would expect you to have insurance. If your money and documents are stolen, it might assist you with getting a new passport, but a loan for onward travel is out of the question.

Some embassies used to keep letters for travelers or have a small reading room with home newspapers, but these days most of the mail-holding and other such services have been stopped.

US Embassies & Consulates

To find US embassies in countries other than those listed below, visit W www.usembassy.state.gov.

US diplomatic offices abroad include the following:

Australia
(☎ 2-6214-5600) 21 Moonah Place, Yarralumla ACT 2600
(☎ 2-9373-9200) Level 59 MLC Center, 19-29 Martin Place, Sydney NSW 2000
(☎ 3-9526-5900) 553 St Kilda Rd, Melbourne, Victoria 3004

Austria
(☎ 1-313-39) Boltzmanngasse 16, A-1091, Vienna

Belgium
(☎ 2-508-21-11) Blvd du Regent 27, B-1000, Brussels

Canada
(☎ 613-238-5335) 490 Sussex Dr, Ottawa, Ontario, K1N 1G8
(☎ 604-685-4311) 1095 W Pender St, Vancouver, BC, V6E 2M6
(☎ 514-398-9695) 1155 Rue St-Alexandre, Montréal, Québec, H2Z 1Z2

Denmark
(☎ 45-3555-3144) Dag Hammarskjolds Allé 24, Copenhagen

Finland
(☎ 9-171-931) Itainen Puistotie 14A, Helsinki

France
(☎ 1-4312-2222) 2 Av Gabriel, 75382 Paris

Germany
(☎ 30-238-5174) Neustaedtische Kirchstrasse 4-5, 10017 Berlin

Greece
(☎ 1-721-2951) 91 Vasilissis Sophias Blvd, 10160 Athens

India
(☎ 11-419-8000) Shanti Path, Chanakyapuri 110021, New Delhi

Ireland
(☎ 1-668-8777) 42 Elgin Rd, Ballsbridge, Dublin

Israel
(☎ 3-519-7575) 71 Hayarkon St, Tel Aviv

Italy
(☎ 6-46-741) Via Vittorio Veneto 119A-121, 00187 Rome

Japan
(☎ 3-224-5000) 1-10-5 Akasaka, Minato-ku, Tokyo

Kenya
(☎ 2-537-800) Mombasa Rd, Unit 64100, Nairobi (E)

Korea
(☎ 2-397-4114) 82 Sejong-Ro, Chongro-ku, Seoul

Malaysia
(☎ 3-2168-5000) 376 Jalan Tun Razak, 50400 Kuala Lumpur

Mexico
(☎ 5-209-9100) Paseo de la Reforma 305, Cuauhtémoc, 06500 Mexico City

Netherlands
(☎ 70-310-9209) Lange Voorhout 102, 2514 EJ The Hague
(☎ 20-5755-309) Museumplein 19, 1071 DJ Amsterdam

New Zealand
(☎ 4-472-2068) 29 Fitzherbert Terrace, Thorndon, Wellington

Norway
(☎ 22-44-85-50) Drammensvein 18, Oslo

Russia
(☎ 95-728-5000) Bolshoy Devyatinckiy Pereulok No 8, 121099 Moscow

Singapore
(☎ 476-9100) 27 Napier Rd, Singapore 258508

South Africa
(☎ 12-342-1048) 877 Pretorius St, Box 9536, Pretoria 0001

Spain
(☎ 1-91587-2200) Calle Serrano 75, 28006 Madrid

Sweden
(☎ 8-783-5300) Dag Hammarskjolds Vag 31, S-115 89 Stockholm

Switzerland
(☎ 31-357-70 11) Jubilaumsstrasse 93, 3005 Berne

Thailand
(☎ 2-255-4365) 120 Wireless Rd, Bangkok

United Kingdom
(☎ 020-7499-9000) 24/31 Grosvenor Square, London W1A 1AE
(☎ 131-556-8315) 3 Regent Terrace, Edinburgh EH7 5BW
(☎ 2890-328-239) Queens House, 14 Queens St, Belfast BT1 6EQ

Foreign Consulates in Miami

Check under Consulates in the white pages of the telephone book for diplomatic representation in Miami. Be patient:

Miami is considered a cushy post by the always-hardworking diplomatic set, and some consular offices have ridiculously limited hours and act as if you're really interfering with their day if you ask for things.

Most consulates are in Miami, but a few are in Coral Gables. Citizens of Australia and New Zealand may contact the British or Canadian consulates for emergency assistance, as neither country maintains consular offices in Miami.

Antigua & Barbuda
(☎ 305-381-6762) 25 SE 2nd Ave, Suite 300

Argentina
(☎ 305-373-7794) 800 Brickell Ave

Austria
(☎ 305-325-1561) 1454 NW 17th Ave, Suite 200

Bahamas
(☎ 305-373-6295) 25 SE 2nd Ave, Suite 818

Belgium
(☎ 305-932-4263) 4100 N Miami Ave

Bolivia
(☎ 305-670-0709) 9100 S Dadeland Blvd, Suite 406

Brazil
(☎ 305-285-6200) 2601 S Bayshore Dr, Suite 800, Coconut Grove

Canada
(☎ 305-579-1600) 200 S Biscayne Blvd, Suite 1600

Chile
(☎ 305-373-8623) 800 Brickell Ave, Suite 1230

Colombia
(☎ 305-448-5558) 280 Aragon Ave, Coral Gables

Costa Rica
(☎ 305-871-7485) 1600 NW Le Jeune Rd, Suite 102

Denmark
(☎ 305-446-4284) 2655 Le Jeune Rd, Coral Gables

Dominican Republic
(☎ 305-358-3220) 1038 Brickell Ave

Ecuador
(☎ 305-539-8214) 1101 Brickell Ave, Suite 102

El Salvador
(☎ 305-371-8850) 300 Biscayne Blvd Way, Suite 1020

France
(☎ 305-372-9798) 2S Biscayne Blvd, Suite 1710

Germany
(☎ 305-358-0290) 100 Biscayne Blvd

Guatemala
(☎ 305-443-4828) 300 Sevilla Ave, Suite 210, Coral Gables

Haiti
(☎ 305-859-2003) 259 SW 13th St

Honduras
(☎ 305-447-8927) 300 Sevilla Ave, Coral Gables

Israel
(☎ 305-925-9400) 100 N Biscayne Blvd, Suite 1800

Italy
(☎ 305-374-6322) 1200 Brickell Ave, 7th floor

Jamaica
(☎ 305-374-8431) 25 SE 2nd Ave, Suite 842

Mexico
(☎ 305-716-4977) 1200 NW 78th Ave, Suite 200

Netherlands
(☎ 305-789-6646) 801 Brickell Ave, 9th floor

Nicaragua
(☎ 305-220-6900) 8532 SW 8th St, Suite 201

Norway
(☎ 305-358-4386) 1007 N American Way

Panama
(☎ 305-371-7031) 2800 Ponce de León Blvd, Suite 1050

Paraguay
(☎ 305-374-9090) 300 Biscayne Blvd Way, Suite 907

Peru
(☎ 305-374-1305) 444 Brickell Ave, Suite 135

Portugal
(☎ 305-444-6311) 1901 Ponce de León Blvd, Coral Gables

Spain
(☎ 305-446-5511) 2655 Le Jeune Rd, Suite 203, Coral Gables

Switzerland
(☎ 305-377-6700) 825 Brickell Bay Dr, Suite 1450

Trinidad & Tobago
(☎ 305-374-2199) 1000 Brickell Ave, Suite 800

United Kingdom
(☎ 305-374-1522) 1001 Brickell Bay Dr, Suite 2880

Uruguay
(☎ 305-443-9764) 1077 Ponce de León Blvd, Suite B, Coral Gables

Venezuela
(☎ 305-577-3834) 1101 Brickell Ave, Suite 901

CUSTOMS

You'll pass first through immigration, where US officials will check your passport and visa. Then they'll pass you through to clear customs.

US customs allows each person over the age of 21 to bring one liter of liquor and 200 cigarettes duty-free into the country. US citizens are allowed to import, duty-free, $400 worth of gifts from abroad, while non-US citizens are allowed to bring in $100 worth. US law permits you to bring in, or take out, as much as US$10,000 in American or foreign currency, traveler's checks or letters of credit without formality. Larger amounts of any or all of the above – there are no limits – must be declared to customs.

It's forbidden to bring in to the USA chocolate liqueurs, pornography, lottery tickets, items with fake brand names and goods made in Cuba or Iraq. Any fruit, vegetables, or other food or plant material must be declared or left in the bins in the arrival area. Most food items are prohibited to prevent the introduction of pests or diseases.

The USA, like 140 other countries, is a signatory to CITES, the Convention on International Trade in Endangered Species. As such, it prohibits the import and export of products made from species that may be endangered in any part of the world, including ivory, tortoise shell, coral, and many fur, skin and feather products. If you want to bring a snakeskin belt with you, you may have to show a certificate that it was not made from an endangered species. The easiest option is not to bring anything even remotely suspect. CITES restrictions apply to what you take home, too. Alligator-skin boots might be a great souvenir, but be ready to convince customs authorities that they're not made from endangered gators.

Due to Miami's infamous popularity as a drug-smuggling gateway, customs officers in Miami are known to be...let's call them *thorough* in their examination of backpackers and other travelers who may fit a profile they have of a 'mule,' or someone ferrying narcotics. They may not be very polite – but you should be, and you should dress neatly

and carry lots of traveler's checks and credit cards, or show other signs of prosperity lest they think you're here to work illegally.

Both customs and immigration officers have the right to drag you into a room for questioning, or worse. If you are taken back there, make certain that a representative of your airline (who can call your relatives and get you information) knows you're there and who you want told of your predicament.

MONEY
Currency

The US dollar (US$ or just $) is divided into 100 cents (100¢) with coins of one cent (penny), five cents (nickel), 10 cents (dime), 25 cents (quarter) and relatively rare 50 cents (half dollar). There are even a few $1 coins in circulation; they're gold-colored and feature a design by American artist Glenda Goodacre.

Bank notes are called bills. Be sure to check the corners for amounts, as they're all the same size and color. Circulated bills come in denominations of $1, $2 (rare), $5, $10, $20, $50 and $100. The US has two designs of bills in circulation, but you'd have to study them closely to notice. On the newer bills the central portrait is bigger and off-center.

There are three straightforward ways to handle payments: cash, US dollar traveler's checks and credit or debit cards. The ubiquitous ATMs (automated teller machines, see that section, later) facilitate the process of acquiring cash.

Exchange Rates

These are particularly volatile, but at press time exchange rates were as follows:

country	unit		US dollars
Australia	A$1	=	$0.54
Canada	C$1	=	$0.64
EU	€1	=	$0.91
Hong Kong	HK$10	=	$1.28
Japan	¥100	=	$0.78
New Zealand	NZ$1	=	$0.45
Singapore	S$1	=	$0.56
UK	£1	=	$1.47

LEE FOSTER

One of the reasons people flock to South Beach

NEIL SETCHFIELD

SoBe art deco lifeguard…hut

WILLIAM HARRIGAN

Blocks and blocks of Miami Beach high rises greet the ocean.

NEIL SETCHFIELD

Hit 'the Drive.' South Beach

RICHARD CUMMINS

Neon signs light up Ocean Drive.

ALFREDO MAIQUEZ

South Beach: Vintage cars, mobsters, stakeouts – and that's just last week.

Exchanging Money

Cash The best advice for people who need to exchange a foreign currency for US$ is to do so at home, before you arrive. Exchange rates are generally worse in the US than in other countries. If you must change money in the States, head to a real bank, rather than an exchange office. Bank of America (☎ 305-350-6350) offers foreign-exchange services in all its branches, and has branches throughout the city and state.

Private exchange offices generally offer the least competitive rates and charge the highest commissions. There are private exchange offices around town, in places such as drugstores and record shops.

Some good exchange offices include the following:

American Express (☎ 305-358-7350; Map 6) 100 N Biscayne Blvd

Thomas Cook (☎ 305-285-2348, 800-287-7362; Map 6) 80 N Biscayne Blvd

SunTrust Bank (☎ 305-591-6000) 777 Brickell Ave, and (☎ 305-591-6743; Map 3) 1111 Lincoln Road

Traveler's Checks Denominated in US dollars, traveler's checks are virtually as good as cash in the USA; most establishments (not just banks) will accept them just like cash. The major advantage of traveler's checks over cash is that they can be replaced if lost or stolen. But changing traveler's checks denominated in a foreign currency is rarely convenient, economical or practical. Get larger denomination US$100 checks, as you may be charged service fees per check when cashing them at banks.

ATMs You can usually withdraw money straight from your bank account at home at these ubiquitous machines. Most ATMs (automated teller machines) in the Miami area accept bank cards from the Plus and Cirrus systems, the two largest ATM networks in the USA, as well as Visa and MasterCard credit cards.

Keep in mind that you will be charged a fee from the bank that is dispensing the money as well as your bank at home. These can add up if you are withdrawing money daily. As for credit card cash advances, remember that you are charged interest on the withdrawal, often at a higher rate than for a standard purchase, beginning immediately and until you pay it back.

Credit & Debit Cards Major credit cards are accepted at hotels, most restaurants, gas stations, shops and car rental agencies throughout the USA. In fact, you'll find it hard to perform certain transactions, such as renting a car or purchasing tickets to performances, without one. Visa and MasterCard are the most widely accepted.

Even if you loathe credit cards and prefer to rely on traveler's checks and ATMs, carry one for emergencies. Banks in Australia, New Zealand and the UK are now selling Visa Travel Money, a pre-paid Visa card similar to a telephone card: Your credit limit is the amount you buy the card with, and while it's not rechargeable, it's accepted like a regular Visa card. It charges a fee that is usually around 2% of the card's purchase price, so it's more expensive than traveler's checks, but is also more accessible.

Places that accept Visa and MasterCard are also likely to accept debit cards. Unlike a credit card, a debit card deducts payment directly from the user's checking account. Instead of an interest rate, users are charged a minimal fee for the transaction. Be sure to check with your bank to confirm that your debit card will be accepted in other states or countries. Debit cards from large commercial banks can often be used worldwide.

Carry copies of your credit card numbers separately from the cards. If they are lost or stolen, contact the company immediately. Following are toll-free numbers for the main credit card companies. Contact your bank if you lose your ATM card.

American Express	☎ 800-528-4800
Diners Club	☎ 800-234-6377
Discover	☎ 800-347-2683
MasterCard	☎ 800-826-2181
Visa	☎ 800-336-8472

Costs

Luxury or penury, both are accommodated in Miami. Cheap hotels and digs with all the fixin's abound; there are good choices for everyone from backpackers to business travelers.

Getting to Miami is often very cheap, especially from the UK, where package deals are readily available. It's also cheap from within the USA, especially if you take a bus or drive here. See the Getting There & Away chapter for more information.

Rental cars in Florida tend to be cheaper than elsewhere. Rates start at around $25 a day or $125 a week, but you really have to seek those out; an average rate can be figured at $35/175 a day/week.

If you're staying in South Beach most of the time, a car will be expensive to park at $6 to $8 a day with no in-and-out privileges (see the Getting Around chapter). You're better off on foot or bicycle (rentals run around $15 to $20 a day or $45 to $70 a week; see the Activities section of the Things to See & Do chapter for some options). If you are staying in South Beach but plan on doing some exploring beyond the Beach (which we presume you are, after reading this guidebook), consider renting a car for a few days.

Tipping

Tipping is a US institution that can, initially, be a little confusing for foreign visitors. Waitstaff at restaurants, bartenders, taxi drivers, bellhops, hotel cleaning staff and others are paid a mere stipend. Customers are expected to compensate these people directly: Tips are actually part of their salary.

So tipping is not really an option; the service has to be absolutely *appalling* before you should consider not tipping. In a bar or restaurant a tip is customarily 15% (for a standard tip, double the tax and add a smidge) of the bill; a tip for outstanding service in a restaurant is 20%. You needn't tip at fast-food restaurants or self-serve cafeterias. Hotel cleaning staff should be tipped about $2 a day, unless they don't deserve it. Tip daily, as they rotate shifts. Add about 10% to taxi fares even if you

Say 'No! No!' to Tipping Twice

There's an insidious plot afoot in many Miami-area restaurants: A 15% tip may already be included in the bill. Of course, the staff may not go to heroic lengths to point this out. If you forget to look, and leave a cash tip as well, staff gets tipped twice. Unless you're feeling inordinately philanthropic, or were really happy with the service, make absolutely certain that you're not tipping twice. Examine the bill carefully before you pay.

think your driver should be institutionalized. Hotel porters who carry bags a long way expect $3 to $5, or add it up at $1 per bag. Valet parking is worth about $2, to be given when your car is returned to you.

Taxes & Refunds

You must add tax to rates listed in this book. In Miami, the tax on goods and services is 6.5% (6% state and .5% local). The tax on hotel accommodations varies with each community, but ranges from 9.5% to 12.5%. In Miami Beach it is 11.5%. If you eat and drink in a hotel the tax is also 11.5%. Rental cars are subjected to the 6.5% sales tax and, frankly, a myriad of other surcharges, which add up quickly.

POST & COMMUNICATIONS
Postal Rates

Currently, rates for 1st-class mail within the US are 34¢ for letters up to 1 ounce (28g) and 20¢ for postcards. International airmail rates differ from country to country, but in general run about 80¢ for a half-ounce letter (60¢ to Mexico and Canada). International postcard rates are 70¢ (50¢ to Mexico and Canada). Aerogrammes are 70¢.

Parcels airmailed anywhere within the USA are $3.45 (slower parcel post) or $3.95 (faster 1st class) for 2lb or less, increasing by about $1 per pound up to $6 for 5lb. Private companies such as Federal Express and UPS offer similar rates. For heavier items, rates differ according to the distance mailed. Books, periodicals and computer disks can be sent by a cheaper 4th-class rate.

Sending Mail

Mail within Florida takes from one to two days to reach its destination; it generally takes two to three days to destinations within the USA. To Europe, allow at least a week, and two weeks at peak times of the year like Christmas. If you have the correct postage, you can drop your mail into any blue official mailbox, found on many street corners. Look inside the lid of the mailbox for the mail pickup times.

Receiving Mail

You can have mail sent to you care of General Delivery at any post office that has its own zip (postal) code. In South Beach, send it to: USPS, General Delivery, 1300 Washington Ave, Miami Beach, FL 33139 (Map 3). If you're staying elsewhere in Miami, send it to: USPS, General Delivery, Miami FL 33101. Pick this mail up at the Flagler Station, 500 NW 2nd Ave (Map 6). It's best to have your intended date of arrival clearly marked on the envelope. Mail is usually held for 30 days before it's returned to the sender. Alternatively, have mail sent to the local representative of American Express or Thomas Cook, both of which provide mail service for their members. Call ☎ 800-275-8777 for postal zip codes and post offices nearest you.

Telephone

Area Codes The ☎ 305 and ☎ 786 area codes cover the Metropolitan Miami area and the Florida Keys. Fort Lauderdale's area code is ☎ 954. The eastern Everglades have ☎ 305 and ☎ 786, the western Everglades have ☎ 941.

Dialing All phone numbers within the USA consist of a three-digit area code followed by a seven-digit local number. If you are calling locally in Miami, you must dial the area code + the seven-digit number. Leave off the preceding 1 before local

Local Calls

To make up for the huge numbers of cell phone and fax numbers crowding the ☎ 305 area code, the local telephone company powers-that-be initiated a new system of dialing. Even if you are calling the restaurant next door in Miami, you must dial ☎ 305 + the seven-digit number, or in the case of the new numbers being doled out, ☎ 786 + the seven-digit number. Leave off the preceding '1' before local calls – just start with ☎ 305 or ☎ 786.

calls – just start with ☎ 305 or ☎ 786. If you are calling locally in the Keys or Key West, you only have to dial the seven-digit number.

If you are calling long distance, dial 1 + the three-digit area code + the seven-digit number.

If you're calling from abroad, the international country code for the USA is '1.'

The ☎ 800, ☎ 888, ☎ 877 and ☎ 866 area codes are toll-free numbers within the USA and sometimes from Canada as well.

The ☎ 900 area codes have a reputation for catering to sleazy operations – a smorgasbord of phone sex at $2.99 a minute, perhaps. Regardless of the nature of the business, you will be charged a fee when calling ☎ 900 numbers.

Directory assistance is reached locally by dialing ☎ 411. This is free from most pay phones, but costs as much as $1.25 from a private phone. For directory assistance outside your area code, dial ☎ 1 + the three-digit area code + 555-1212.

Cell Phones Anyone who's anyone in Miami has a cell phone, and you can rent one almost as easily as you can buy soda from a machine. You can often rent cell phones in larger hotels and at rental car agencies. Make certain you only have to pay for air time (not equipment rental), and find out if there's a daily minimum – it's usually about three minutes. Air time on rental phones is much more expensive than on normal cellular phones. Count on spending about $1 a minute on outgoing and incoming calls.

Unicom (☎ 305-538-9494, ⓦ www.unicom .com), 742 Alton Rd in South Beach, rents phones and they're open 9am to 6pm Monday to Friday, 11am to 4pm Saturday. To give you an idea of the prices we're talking, count on rental charges of $3 daily, plus air time. You can buy a $25 card that will get you either 71 local minutes or 38 national minutes. That works out to be 35¢ a minute for local calls, 65¢ a minute for national calls. You can make local calls with a national card, but not national calls with a local card.

Pay Phones Local calls cost 35¢ at pay phones, and they don't give change. Almost all hotels add a service charge of 50¢ to $1 for each local – and sometimes toll-free – call made from a room phone. They also add hefty surcharges for long-distance calls, 50% or even 100% on top of their carrier's rates. Public pay phones, which can be found in many lobbies, are always cheaper.

Long-distance rates vary depending on the destination and which telephone company you use. There are literally hundreds of long-distance companies in the US, and rates vary by several hundred percent – call the operator (☎ 0, ☎ 3050 or ☎ 00) for rate information. Don't ask the operator to put your call through, however, because operator-assisted calls are much more expensive than calls dialed directly. Generally, nights (11pm to 8am) and all day Saturday and Sunday are the cheapest times to call. Discounts also apply in the evening from 5pm to 11pm daily.

Many area pay phones accept incoming calls; the number will be posted on the phone.

Phone Debit Cards Phone debit cards in denominations of $5, $10, $20 and $50 allow purchasers to pay in advance, with access through a toll-free number. Look for these ubiquitous cards in small convenience stores and large drugstores. You shouldn't have to pay more than 25¢ per minute on domestic long-distance calls, but some are as high as 45¢ per minute. Wal-Mart and

other discount retailers sell them for as little as 6¢ a minute. If a card merely says that you'll 'save up to 60%,' move on. When using phone debit or calling cards, be cautious of people watching you dial in the numbers – thieves will memorize numbers and use your card to make calls to all corners of the earth.

International Calls To place an international call direct, dial ☎ 011 + country code + area code (dropping the leading 0) + number. From a pay phone, dial all those numbers before inserting coins; a voice will come on telling you how much to put in the phone after you dial the number. For international operator assistance and rates dial ☎ 00. Canada is treated like a domestic call.

In general, it's cheaper to make international calls at night, but this varies with the country you're calling and the long-distance company. Calls from a private phone to Australia or Europe, from a non-discounted long-distance carrier, should be about $1 for the first minute and 50¢ for each subsequent minute. Calls to other continents usually cost about twice that. From private phones with a discount plan for long-distance service, the cost could be as low as 20¢ a minute to Europe, 50¢ a minute to Australia – check before you dial!

eKno Communication Service Lonely Planet's eKno global communication service provides low-cost international calls – for local calls, you're usually better off with a local phone card. eKno also offers free messaging services, email, travel information and an online travel vault, where you can securely store all your important documents. You can join online at ⓦ www.ekno.lonelyplanet.com, where you will find the local-access numbers for the 24-hour customer-service center. Once you have joined, check the eKno Web site for the latest access numbers for each country and for updates on new features.

Collect & Country Direct You can call collect (reverse charges) from any phone. There is an increasing number of providers, but beware that there really is a difference in price, so check before you dial. The main players at the time of writing were AT&T (☎ 800-225-5288) and MCI (☎ 800-265-5328). You can also just dial ☎ 0 + the area code and number, eg, 0+212+555-4567, but this is generally the most expensive option of all.

Country-direct service connects you, toll-free, with an operator from another country and allows you to make collect calls via that country's phone system, which may be cheaper than doing it from the USA. With country direct, you may also use your telephone company charge card from home.

The following are some country-direct numbers:

Australia	☎ 800-682-2878
Austria	☎ 800-624-0043
Belgium	☎ 800-472-0032
Denmark	☎ 800-762-0045
France	☎ 800-537-2623
Germany	☎ 800-292-0049
Ireland	☎ 800-562-6262
Italy	☎ 800-543-7662
Japan	☎ 800-543-0051
Netherlands	☎ 800-432-0031
New Zealand	☎ 800-248-0064
Norway	☎ 800-292-0047
Portugal	☎ 800-822-2776
Spain	☎ 800-247-7246
Sweden	☎ 800-345-0046

Copy Shops

Mail Boxes Etc (☎ 305-538-5076; Map 3), 1521 Alton Rd, has self-service and color photocopiers, as well as standard shipping, mailing and mailbox services. Kinko's (☎ 305-373-4910, 600 Brickell Ave; Map 6) has a copy supercenter.

Fax

Fax machines are easy to find in the USA; they're at shipping outlets such as Mail Boxes Etc, as well as most hotel business service centers and photocopy shops like Kinko's. Be prepared to pay high prices

(more than $1 a page to the US, $4 or more to Europe and elsewhere). Prices for incoming faxes are usually half the outgoing domestic rate.

Email & Internet Access

Email is probably the preferred method of communication for travelers. However, unless you have a laptop and modem that can be plugged into a telephone socket, it's sometimes difficult to get online. See the Digital Resources section, following, for some suggestions on how to stay connected.

Before heading off, consider signing up for a free email account with any of the larger search engines. Companies such as Yahoo! (W www.yahoo.com), Microsoft (W www.hotmail.com), Pobox (W www.pobox.com) and Excite (W www.excite.com) will give you a free email address (for example, e janedoe@excite.com). You can then access your email account from any Web browser, such as those at Internet cafés or libraries. Don't forget your user name and password, and remember to log off before you leave to avoid misuse of your account.

Most hostels have computers with Internet connections for a minimal fee. Otherwise, the appropriately cluttered Kafka Kafé (☎ 305-673-9669; Map 3), 1464 Washington Ave, the Beach's biggest Internet café, has about 20 PCs with reasonably fast connections. It charges $7 an hour for access.

The austere Cybr Caffe (☎ 305-534-0057; Map 3), 1574 Washington Ave, has about 20 terminals and also charges $7 an hour. It's all about the Internet here – there are very few distractions.

For standard online services, the access numbers in Miami are:

America Online
  ☎ 800-827-6364, 305-621-8500 local access
CompuServe
  ☎ 800-848-8990, 305-262-9325 local access
Earthlink
  ☎ 800-719-4664, 786-380-4492 local access

DIGITAL RESOURCES

The World Wide Web is a rich resource for travelers. You can research your trip, hunt down bargain airfares, book hotels, check on weather conditions and chat with locals and other travelers about the best places to visit (or avoid!).

There's no better place to start your Web exploration than the Lonely Planet Web site (**w** www.lonelyplanet.com). Here you'll find succinct summaries on traveling to most places on earth, postcards from other travelers and the Thorn Tree bulletin board, where you can ask questions before you go or dispense advice when you get back. You can also find travel news and updates for many of our most popular guidebooks, and the subWWWay section links you to the most useful travel resources elsewhere on the Web.

Lonely Planet produces a guide to Miami as part of its *CitySync* series of digital city guides for handheld computers. *CitySync* lets travelers and locals use their Palm OS handheld to search and sort hundreds of detailed listings. For more information, go to **w** www.citysync.com.

BOOKS

Most books are published in different editions by different publishers in different countries. As a result, a book might be a hardcover rarity in one country but readily available in paperback in another. Fortunately, bookstores and libraries can search by title or author, so your local bookstore or library is best placed to advise you on the availability of the following recommendations.

Most of the books listed here are available locally, some nationally and internationally. For literature set in the area, check the Arts section of the Facts about Miami chapter. If you'll be traveling around the state, a key resource is Lonely Planet's *Florida*. Other good books on the area include Nixon Smiley's *Yesterday's Miami*, a fascinating photo history book (probably only available in the library), and Donald C Gaby's *The Miami River*. TD Allman's *Miami: City of the Future* is a solid general-interest read, though also somewhat dated.

What Sucks about South Florida – Strategies for Survival is a very fresh look at the area by Scott Marcus, giving commentary that could only come from a white boy living in South Florida.

If you're coming with kids, Lonely Planet's *Travel with Children,* by Cathy Lanigan, is a must-read for strategy, and don't miss the excellent *Places to Go with Children in Miami & South Florida* by Cheryl Lani Juárez and Deborah Ann Johnson, which is indispensable for keeping the little darlings calm and entertained.

If you plan on heading to the Keys for some diving or snorkeling, pick up a copy of Lonely Planet's Pisces book *Diving & Snorkeling Florida Keys* by William Harrigan. It covers all the top dive sites along the Overseas Highway, and is full of colorful underwater photos.

Marjory Stoneman Douglas' classic *The Everglades: River of Grass* should be required reading for those heading into the 'Glades. Also check out Susan D Jewell's excellent *Exploring Wild South Florida,* Allen de Hart's *Adventuring in Florida* and Frank Zoretich's *Cheap Thrills Florida – The Bottom Half,* written by an admittedly very stingy man who has found lots of really cheap things to do around here.

For a thorough exploration of Miami Beach deco in words and pictures, pick up *Tropical Deco: The Architecture and Design of Old Miami Beach* by Laura Cerwinske and David Kaminsky; and *Deco Delights: Preserving the Beauty and Joy of Miami Beach Architecture* by Barbara Baer Capitman and Steven Brooke.

NEWSPAPERS & MAGAZINES

The *Miami Herald* is the city's only major daily. While local coverage tends to draw fire from all sides, it's a good source of international and national news.

The weekly alternative *New Times* has, hands down, the best coverage of local issues, along with superb listings of restaurants, clubs, pubs, bars, theaters and cinema, as well as a special-events calendar and music and film reviews. It's available free around town.

Wire, a gay freebie, is more focused on partying at the beach.

On Fridays, the *Herald* features a pullout *Weekend* section with movie and music reviews and listings, gallery information for Miami and the surrounding area, and a whole lot of other stuff. Not to be outdone, they also publish a very good free weekly, *The Street*.

Other locally available newspapers include the Florida editions of the *New York Times* and *Wall Street Journal,* sold at vending boxes around town. For excellent, unbiased and thoughtful international news, pick up the *Christian Science Monitor.*

The *Miami Herald* publishes *El Nuevo Herald,* an excellent Spanish daily (in fact, if you speak Spanish, you should look here first for coverage of Latin America). Most major Western European newspapers are available at good newsstands.

RADIO

Miami radio is colorful, with lots of Spanish and Creole-language programming, and salsa and oldies. You can't avoid the standard American offerings of vulgar talk shows featuring convicted felons and the predictable smattering of musical styles. For balanced coverage and an international take on the news, National Public Radio (NPR)'s *Morning Edition* airs from 7am to 9am, and *All Things Considered* airs from 5pm to 7pm, on WLRN, 91.3 FM.

Some other stations include the following:

frequency	station	type of music
940 AM	WINZ	news, sports, traffic
1320 AM	WLQY	French & Creole-language news and information
88.9 FM	WDNA	Latin jazz and world music
90.5 FM	WVUM	progressive rock from a college station
94.9 FM	WZTA	classic rock
96 FM	WPOW	hip-hop
99.9 FM	WKIS	country
103.5 FM	Mega 103	classic disco

TV

Gore springs eternal in Miami, where the local news motto is 'If it bleeds, it leads.' Most of the local news stuff is as sensationalistic as a British daily newspaper. Look for WLTV (Univision, Spanish) and WSCV (Telemundo, Spanish). Tune into the local public-access cable TV station channel 3 for off-beat, low-budget programming. On AT&T Cable Miami, CNN is on channel 42, HBO on channel 16, MTV on channel 48, and Nickelodeon on channel 52.

The local stations are as follows:

network	station	channel
ABC	WPLG	10
CBS	WFOR	4
NBC	WTVJ	6
Fox	WSVN	7
PBS	WPBT	2

PHOTOGRAPHY & VIDEO
Film & Equipment

Color print film, widely available at supermarkets and discount drugstores, has greater latitude than color slide film. This means that print film can handle a wider range of light and shadow than slide film, and that the printer can fix your mistakes. However, slide film, particularly the slower speeds (under 100 ASA), has better resolution than print film. B&W film is most likely found at camera shops. Both B&W film and slide film are rarely sold outside of major cities and when available, they're more expensive. With the abundance of reflective surfaces in Miami, consider using a polarizing filter.

Drugstores process film cheaply. If you drop it off by noon, you can usually pick it up the next day. Processing a roll of 100 ASA 35mm color film with 24 exposures costs about $6 to $8. One-hour processing services are listed in the yellow pages under 'Photo Processing.' Expect to pay double the drugstore price.

Film can be damaged by excessive heat, so don't leave your camera and film in the sun (next to you on the beach towel) or car on hot days (read: most of the year). It's worth carrying a spare battery for your camera in case it dies in the middle of nowhere. If you're buying a new camera for your trip, practice using it before taking it on the trip.

For equipment, Wolf Camera & Video (☎ 305-931-5839) at the Aventura Mall (Map 5; see Northern Miami Beach in the Where to Shop section of the Shopping chapter) has honest salespeople and decent prices. On South Beach, head to Tropicolor Photo (☎ 305-672-3720; Map 3), at 1442 Alton Rd, or LIB Color Labs (☎ 305-538-5600; Map 4), at 851 Washington Ave, for film and processing.

Pros patronize Apeture Pro Supply (☎ 305-673-4327; Map 3), at 1330 18th St. If you're a stickler for fresh film, picky about processing film quickly (film wilting in the humidity), need another camera body or some studio space to rent, contact these folks.

Video

The USA uses the National Television System Committee (NTSC) color TV standard, which is not compatible with other standards (Phase Alternative Line, or PAL; Systeme Electronique Couleur avec Memoire, or SECAM) used in Africa, Europe, Asia and Australia unless converted.

Properly used, a video camera can yield a fascinating record of your holiday. Often the most interesting things occur when you're actually intent on filming something else.

Beginners should try to film in long takes; don't move the camera around too much. If your camera has a stabilizer, you can obtain decent footage while traveling on various means of transportation. But, really, don't let the video take over your life and turn your trip into a Cecil B DeMille production. It's better to be an active participant in your holiday than film it through a lens and watch it on a screen later.

Finally, remember to follow the same rules regarding people's sensitivities as for still photography – having a video camera shoved in their face is probably even more annoying and offensive for locals than a still camera. Always ask permission first.

Airport Security

It's tighter than ever. X-ray machines scan all carry-on baggage; more bags than ever are hand-searched. Sharp objects like nail files, forks and Swiss Army knives will be confiscated from your carry-on baggage; pack everything sharp in your checked baggage. Today's technology doesn't jeopardize computers, lower-speed film or cameras, so don't worry about these things going through the machine. If you are carrying high-speed film (1600 ASA and above), take the film out of the canisters and pack them in a clear plastic bag or container. Ask the X-ray inspector to visually check your film. Never *ever* pack film in your checked luggage; it is subjected to much more potent X-ray machines.

TIME

For the accurate time call ☎ 305-754-8463, or ☎ 305-279-4672 for Spanish. Miami is in the US Eastern standard time zone, three hours ahead of San Francisco and Los Angeles, and five hours behind GMT/UTC. Daylight saving time takes place from the first Sunday in April through the last Sunday in October. The clocks 'spring forward' one hour in April and 'fall back' one hour in October. Clocks are reset at 1am.

When it's noon in Miami it's:

city	time
Auckland	4am in winter, 6am in summer
London	5pm
Munich	6pm
Sydney	4am in summer, 2am in winter

ELECTRICITY

Electric current in the USA is 110V to 115V, 60Hz. Outlets may be suited for flat two- or three-prong plugs. If your appliance is made for another electrical system, you will need a transformer or adapter; if you didn't bring one along, check Radio Shack or another consumer electronics store.

WEIGHTS & MEASURES

The US continues to resist the imposition of the metric system. Distances are in feet, yards and miles; weights are in ounces, pounds and tons. Gasoline is measured in US gallons, about 20% smaller than the Imperial gallon and equivalent to 3.79L. Temperatures are given in degrees Fahrenheit. See the conversion chart on the inside back cover for more information.

LAUNDRY

Coin laundries are scattered throughout the area. Generally the cost is $1.50 to wash and either a flat rate (like $1.50) to dry or 25¢ for five to 10 minutes in a timed dryer. On the Beach, head to Wash Time (☎ 305-672-7110; Map 3), 14th Court at Alton Rd. It's open 7am to 11pm daily.

Mark's Quality Cleaners (☎ 305-538-6275; Map 3), at 1201 20th St, has same-day service if you drop off your clothes by 10am. They also pick up and deliver.

For a good time *and* clean clothes, head to the Laundry Bar (Map 3; see the Bars section of the Entertainment chapter).

TOILETS

There are public toilets at several spots on South Beach (like South Pointe Park and the Art Deco Welcome Center), but generally speaking, the area doesn't offer much in the way of public facilities. Usually restaurants will allow you to use their toilets if you're reasonably presentable and ask politely. In fact, even the ones with signs boldly proclaiming that their rest rooms are for customers only will often let you in if you ask very nicely. Bars are also a good bet; in crowded ones, just walk to the back and to the right or left, as if you're a customer.

HEALTH

Miami is a typical first-world destination when it comes to health. For most foreign visitors no immunizations are required for entry, though cholera and yellow fever vaccinations may be required of travelers from areas with a history of those diseases. There are no unexpected health dangers and excellent medical attention is readily available. The only real health concern is that, as elsewhere in the USA, a collision with the

> ### The Porcelain God
>
>
>
> For a country with a world-wide reputation for its outspoken, sometimes coarse and even foul-mouthed citizenry, few of them can utter the word that denotes the porcelain appliance into which they empty their bowels and bladders. For ladies and gentlemen to refer to anything vaguely personal was to open themselves to scorn and embarrassment – even today, American television commercials hawk 'bathroom tissue,' not toilet paper.
>
> So, Americans don't have toilets. They have (and these are just a few of the euphemisms you will come across in your travels): rest rooms, facilities, comfort stations, commodes, johns, latrines, powder rooms, little girl's/boy's rooms, bathrooms, way stations and potties.

medical system can cause severe injuries to your financial state.

Health Insurance

No sensible visitor will arrive in the USA without a good traveler's health insurance policy. When looking for a policy, what you're really after is coverage against a true catastrophe. Your travel agent will have suggestions about travel insurance; many policies offer higher levels of coverage for the USA. Check the fine print, as some policies may exclude coverage for 'dangerous' activities like scuba diving, motorcycling, surfing and the like. Policies issued through student-travel–oriented organizations like STA Travel, Travel Cuts and Campus Travel are usually good values.

If you do require medical attention, save all receipts and documentation and make an insurance claim as soon as possible.

Medical Attention

For physician referrals 24 hours daily, contact the Mount Sinai Medical Center Visitor's Medical Line (☎ 305-674-2222).

The Miami Beach Community Health Center (☎ 305-538-8835; Map 4), 710 Alton Rd, charges fees based on your income. Get there early (it's open 7am to 3:30pm Monday to Friday) since walk-in clinic lines are usually very long. Bring ID. If you're foreign born, bring your passport and I-94 card; US citizens should bring proof of residence and income.

If you need dental attention, check the white pages under Dentists or try ☎ 800-DENTIST (☎ 800-336-8478), a free referral service. Or, head to the 2nd-floor Beach Dental Center (☎ 305-532-3300; Map 3), 1370 Washington Ave.

In a serious emergency, call ☎ 911 for an ambulance to take you to the nearest hospital's emergency room. Mount Sinai Medical Center (☎ 305-674-2121; Map 5), 4300 Alton Rd, is the area's best. But ER fees are also stellar: Mount Sinai charges a *minimum* ER fee of $290. Then there are additional charges for X rays, casting, medicines, analysis...*everything,* so the cost of a visit can easily top $1000. The moral: Don't get sick or hurt in the USA without insurance!

Pharmacies

Some shops in the statewide Eckerd (☎ 305-538-1571) chain are open 24 hours daily; call for the nearest location.

Walgreens (☎ 305-261-2213), a national pharmacy, also sells liquor, so if you should ever require a shot of whiskey and a bandage.... Call for the nearest location.

Glasses & Contact Lens Supplies

Saline solution and other contact lens supplies are readily available at pharmacies like Eckerd and Walgreens. Express optometrist offices are located in every shopping mall; Pearle Vision Center is probably the largest (call ☎ 305-665-8660 for the location closest to you). In northern Miami Beach they're located at 1400 NE 163rd St (☎ 305-948-6017).

WOMEN TRAVELERS

Women travelers, especially solo women travelers, should develop the habit of traveling with a little extra awareness of their surroundings.

Men may interpret a woman drinking alone in a bar as a bid for male company, whether you intend it that way or not. If you don't want the company, most men will respect a firm but polite 'no thank you.'

Women must recognize the extra threat of rape, which is a problem in both urban and rural areas. The best way to deal with the threat of rape is to avoid putting yourself in vulnerable situations. Conducting yourself in a common-sense manner will help you avoid most problems. Shouting 'Fire!' may draw assistance more effectively than yelling 'Help!'

If you are assaulted, call the police. In an emergency, calling ☎ 911 will connect you with the emergency operator for police, fire and ambulance services. The Miami Rape Crisis Hotline (☎ 305-585-RAPE or 7273), open daily around the clock, provides resources for women who have been raped or assaulted. The free service offers comprehensive medical and psychological treatment. Using the service does *not* necessarily mean filing a police report (except in cases involving children). The center is at the University of Miami/Jackson Memorial Hospital, at 1611 NW 12th Ave. Call for directions.

Planned Parenthood (W www.planned parenthood.org), 2900 Bridgeport Ave, Coconut Grove, provides reproductive and complimentary health-care services, as well as emergency contraception that can prevent pregnancy after unprotected intercourse.

GAY & LESBIAN TRAVELERS

In the 1970s, Miami was one of the first municipalities in the USA to pass legislation barring discrimination of homosexuals in the workplace and housing. Before long came the backlash. Miami then became the highly publicized target of a campaign by conservative witch Anita Bryant in 1977 and the law was repealed. The biggest news in the Miami gay and lesbian scene was the

1998 reenactment of the law after a close vote.

Gay and lesbian visitors account for nearly $100 million in annual revenues to the Miami area. And with financial clout comes respect. Ah, capitalism; it runs deeply in Miami. Partying also runs deeply. South Beach hosts two flamboyant circuit parties; see the boxed text 'Circuit Parties' in the Entertainment chapter. Since the club scene is constantly changing, for absolutely up-to-date information during your trip, grab the indispensable free weeklies.

Organizations & Resources

The best source for unbiased information is the bookstore Lambda Passage (☎ 305-754-6900; Map 2), 7545 Biscayne Blvd, a fixture in Miami since the mid-1980s. Look for the rainbow flag at their store, park behind the building and enter through the back door. It's open 11am to 9pm Monday to Saturday, noon to 6pm Sunday.

A few well-known national gay publications with sections on South Florida are worth checking out. Try Damron's *Women's Traveller,* with listings for lesbians; *Men's Travel Guide* for men; and *Damron Accommodations,* listing gay-owned and gay-friendly hotels, B&Bs and guest houses nationwide. All three are published by Damron Company (☎ 415-255-0404, 800-462-6654, W www.damron.com). *Ferrari's Places for Women* is also useful. Out & About (☎ 212-645-6922, 800-929-2268, W www.outandabout.com) publishes books and a newsletter.

Another good resource, the Gay & Lesbian Yellow Pages (☎ 212-674-0120, W www.glyp.com) has national and regional editions. You can also contact the National Gay and Lesbian Task Force (☎ 202-332-6483, W www.ngltf.org) or the Lambda Legal Defense Fund (☎ 212-995-8585 in New York City, ☎ 213-937-2728 in Los Angeles).

A local weekly newspaper focusing on gay and lesbian community issues is *twn* ('the weekly news'). The weekly *Hotspots,* packed with ads for dance clubs to straightforward classifieds, concentrates more on Fort Lauderdale than Miami. *She Times,* a lesbian-oriented monthly, has a hodgepodge of self-help, poetry, useful listings and personals (from a mix of men, women, drag queens and others).

Contact the gay and lesbian Dade Human Rights Foundation (☎ 305-572-1841, W www.dhrf.com) for a calendar of events they participate in and sponsor.

DISABLED TRAVELERS

Miami is mainly wheelchair friendly, though many Deco District doorways may be too tight. Many buses, all Tri-Rail trains and stations, and Metromovers are wheelchair accessible. Special-needs travelers can contact the Metro-Dade Transit Agency Special Transportation Service (STS; ☎ 305-263-5406), which provides door-to-door transportation for disabled people; contact them a few weeks before your visit since the application process takes a bit of time.

The Deaf Services Bureau (☎ 305-668-4407, 800-955-8770), at 1320 S Dixie Hwy, Suite 760, has interpreters and an information and referral service. It's open 9am to 5pm Monday to Thursday, 9am to noon Friday. The Florida Relay Service (☎ 305-579-8644, 800-955-8771 TDD, 800-955-8770 voice, 800-955-8013 customer service) connects TDD (Telecommunication Device for the Deaf) users to people without TDDs, 24 hours a day.

For information for the blind, contact the Lighthouse for the Blind (☎ 305-856-2288), at 601 SW 8th Ave.

Organizations & Resources

A number of organizations and tour operators specialize in serving disabled travelers.

Access-Able Travel Source (☎ 303-232-2979, W www.access-able.com), PO Box 1796, Wheat Ridge, CO 80034 – an excellent Web site with many links

Mobility International USA (☎ 541-343-1284, fax 541-343-6812, W www.miusa.org), PO Box 10767, Eugene, OR 97440 – advises disabled travelers on mobility issues and runs an educational exchange program

MossRehab ResourceNet (☎ 215-456-9600, 215-456-9602 TTY, **W** www.mossresourcenet.org/travel.htm), 1200 W Tabor Rd, Philadelphia, PA 19141 – a concise list of useful contacts

Society for Accessible Travel & Hospitality (SATH; ☎ 212-447-7284, **W** www.sath.org), 347 Fifth Ave, No 610, New York, NY 10016 – lobbies for better facilities and publishes *Open World* magazine

Travelin' Talk Network (☎ 615-552-6670, **W** www.travelintalk.net), PO Box 3534, Clarksville, TN 37047 – offers a global network of people providing services to disabled people

Twin Peaks Press (☎ 360-694-2462, **W** home .pacifier.com/~twinpeak), PO Box 129, Vancouver, WA 98666 – publishes a quarterly newsletter, plus directories and access guides

SENIOR TRAVELERS

Travelers age 55 years and up can expect to receive discounts and benefits, though the applicable age varies. It's worth asking about a senior discount rate at hotels, museums and restaurants. Contact the following national advocacy groups to help plan your travels.

AARP (formerly known as the American Association of Retired Persons; ☎ 800-424-3410, **W** www.aarp.org), 601 E St NW, Washington, DC 20049 – an advocacy group for Americans 50 years and older, and a good resource for travel bargains. A one-year membership costs $10.

Elderhostel (☎ 877-426-8056, **W** www.elderhostel.org), 11 Ave de Lafayette, Boston, MA 02111 – a nonprofit organization that offers people 55 years and older the opportunity to attend academic college courses and study tours throughout the USA and Canada

MIAMI FOR CHILDREN

With all that beachfront, Miami is very kid-friendly. Watch out for the topless spots if that sort of thing bothers you and you'll have a great time. Warm-weather Miami is very outdoor-oriented and kids love the action of in-line skating, cycling, windsurfing and kayaking (see the Activities section of the Things to See & Do chapter). Equipment can be rented in many parks and on beachfronts. Ocean Drive certainly has a couple of playgrounds, with public toilets and water fountains, but you'll also want to head to Haulover Beach Park and Oleta River State Recreation Area (both Map 5); the Marjory Stoneman Douglas Biscayne Nature Center, Crandon Park and Bill Baggs Cape Florida State Recreation Area (all Map 7); or Matheson Hammock Park (Map 2). Crandon Park, especially, has some great hands-on programs for kids. The Venetian Pool (Map 10), one of the most distinctive pools in the county, is a must-visit (see the entry in the Things to See & Do chapter for age and height restrictions for toddlers).

On a rainy day (or even a sunny one, for that matter) the following places will educate and entertain the kids: the Historical Museum of Southern Florida (Map 6), Miami Museum of Science & Space Transit Planetarium (Map 9), American Police Hall of Fame & Museum (Map 2). Kids will also like riding the Metromover around downtown, especially at dusk with all the pretty lights. You could also consider taking them to little Elian Gonzales' house, Unidos en Casa Elian (Map 8), and using it as a starting point for discussing some thought-provoking issues.

Miami has a number of attractions, with varying degrees of seriousness, to introduce kids to the natural world: the Miami Seaquarium (Map 7), Miami Metrozoo and Monkey Jungle (both Map 1) and Parrot Jungle & Gardens (Map 2). As an alternative diversion, Miami boasts a big-screen IMAX theater, and Steven Spielberg's Gameworks (☎ 305-667-4263, **W** www.gameworks.com, Map 7), 5701 Sunset Dr. With virtual-reality games and old-fashioned arcade games, this multilevel entertainment emporium is fun for the whole family. Tickets cost $1 to $5, and it's open 11am to midnight Sunday to Thursday, 11am to 2am Friday and Saturday.

When it's time to head out for some adult entertainment, ask for baby-sitter recommendations at your hotel. For more information, advice and anecdotes, check out

Lonely Planet's *Travel with Children* by Cathy Lanigan.

LIBRARIES

With almost four million books and a surprisingly helpful staff, the Miami-Dade Public Library (☎ 305-375-2665/5184, w www.mdpls.org; Map 6), 101 W Flagler St, is an excellent resource for locals and visitors alike. It has an enormous Florida room containing thousands of books on all aspects of Florida life, history and travel, as well as a large video- and audio-tape library. The library is open 9am to 6pm Monday to Wednesday and Friday and Saturday, 9am to 9pm Thursday, and 1pm to 5pm Sunday.

A good branch of the library is on Miami Beach (☎ 305-535-4219; Map 3), at 2100 Collins Ave. It's open 10am to 8pm Monday and Wednesday, 10am to 5:30pm Tuesday and Thursday to Saturday, closed Sunday.

UNIVERSITIES

The state-run liberal arts Florida International University (FIU; Map 2) has an enrollment of more than 26,000 students. Its University Park campus is located on US Hwy 41 (west of Calle Ocho) between SW 107th Ave and Florida's Turnpike. The North Campus is located off US Hwy 1 at NE 151st St.

The University of Miami's Coral Gables campus (made up of two colleges and 10 schools) occupies 260 acres within the city of Coral Gables. Founded in 1925, UM has a total enrollment of about 13,000 full- and part-time students.

DANGERS & ANNOYANCES
Unsafe Areas

There are a few areas considered by locals to be dangerous, and racism – overt or implied – may be responsible for some such classifications, such as Liberty City, a predominantly black neighborhood in northwest Miami, and Little Haiti. Obviously, in these and other reputedly 'bad' areas, you should avoid walking around alone late at night, use common sense and travel in groups.

Deserted areas below 5th St in South Beach are more dangerous at night. In downtown Miami, use particular caution near the Greyhound station and around causeways, bridges and overpasses where homeless people and some refugees have set up shantytowns.

If you're considering sex on the beach or in Miami's public toilets, it's not a very original idea: Both the police and muggers patrol, albeit for different reasons.

Use caution when changing money, as muggers sometimes hang around exchange offices looking for victims.

Highway Robbery & Carjackings

In the early 1990s, several highly publicized attacks on tourists in Miami made international headlines. As a result, tourism revenue dropped off considerably. Because money talks, action was taken, and since then, the number of attacks has been halved. You'd still do well to use caution. Official police cars have flashing blue *and* red lights; if any other vehicle attempts to pull you over, keep driving until you get to a well-lighted area, such as a gas station, and call the police. That's also what you should do if someone rams your car from behind. Forget about stopping to exchange insurance information; just get to someplace safe and call the police. Consider the situation carefully if you are inclined to stop for a stranded motorist.

When a someone approaches you at a stoplight, points a gun at you, orders you out of the vehicle and drives off with your car, it's called a carjacking. It's a federal offense. Police say that resisting a gun-wielding person is not wise; just follow instructions and hope for the best.

Panhandlers & the Homeless

Miami has a serious problem. Waves of refugees from poor countries and the northeastern US have resulted in a high number of homeless people and panhandlers. What you, as a tourist, should and can do is a very touchy issue. The official Lonely Planet line: Don't encourage them – it only helps to make visitors an easy mark. If you're really concerned, volunteer at a homeless shelter, or donate to homeless-relief programs at local churches and synagogues.

Credit Card Scams

When using phone credit cards, be aware of people watching you, especially in public places. Thieves can memorize the numbers of your card and then make calls without having the actual card. Shield the telephone with your body when punching in your number. Use touch-tone key pads to avoid actually saying your credit card number aloud in a public place. Some walls do have ears.

Try to limit the situations in which you give your credit card number out over the phone. People can charge anything they want if they have your name, card number and expiration date. Destroy any carbons generated by a credit card sale.

Hotels customarily ask for a credit card imprint when you check in to cover incidental expenses. Make certain that this imprint is destroyed if not used.

Enter a '$' sign before, and make certain there's a decimal point in, numbers written in the 'total' box on a credit card slip. You don't want to be charged $1500 for a T-shirt instead of $15.

Bad Service

Miami has arguably the worst service in the USA. Service in some South Beach restaurants can be atrocious. Many waitstaff and others in the 'service' industry are really here to be discovered by a talent agent. When they decide that you're not one, you are of no value to them. Petulant and pouty wannabe models of both sexes can be seen at practically every Ocean Drive restaurant acting as 'hosts.' There's nothing much you can do about it except keep your dignity and remember: Real models don't usually hand out menus.

If you encounter any problems with hotels, restaurants or businesses during your stay, you aren't powerless. For incidents in Miami Beach, contact Michael Aller (☎ 305-673-7010), also known as 'Mr Miami Beach.' He's the city of Miami Beach's lovable Tourism & Convention coordinator.

Sunburn

Use a good sunscreen and take your time. Don't try to become a bronzed demigod or goddess on the first day (or for that matter, the first week). Most doctors recommend sunscreen with a sun protection factor (SPF) of 40 for easily burned areas like your shoulders and nose. Nude sunbathers need to slather the stuff *everywhere*. Besides, no one wants to have sex with someone with bright pink, festering skin who says 'Ouch!' when touched.

Sharks

Shark attacks happen. They happen off Miami Beach a couple of times a year, and there are more sharks out there than you would like to think. But other than staying out of the water, there's not much you can do about it, so, like, don't go see *Jaws* right before you come, OK?

Alligators

It's pretty unlikely that you'll see an alligator in the city, but it's been known to happen. Alligators generally eat only when they're hungry – unless they think they're being attacked. They'll definitely consider eating small animals or things that look like

Don't crouch in a snack-size position.

them (like small children or people crouching down really small to snap a photo). See the boxed text 'Panthers & Gators & Crocs, Oh My!' in the Everglades chapter for more information.

Hurricanes

A hurricane is a concentrated system of very strong thunderstorms with high circulation. The 74mph to 160mph winds created by a hurricane can extend for hundreds of miles around the eye (center) of a hurricane system. Floods and flash floods caused by the torrential rains it produces cause additional property damage. Perhaps most dangerous of all, though, hurricanes can cause a storm surge, forcing the level of the ocean to rise between 4 and 18 feet above normal. The 13- to 18-foot storm surge caused by a cate-

gory 4 hurricane like Andrew would have easily destroyed the entire city of Miami Beach. And, after a hurricane, as if to add insult to injury, conditions become perfect for a tornado.

Every year during hurricane season (from June through November), storms form over the Atlantic Ocean and the Gulf of Mexico and gather strength. Some roll right through the Miami area. Some years see no hurricane activity at all.

Hurricanes are generally sighted well in advance and there's time to prepare. When a hurricane threatens, listen to radio and TV news reports. Give credence only to forecasts attributed to the National Weather Center (short-wave radio listeners can tune to 162.55MHz), and dismiss anything else as rumor.

Plotting a Hurricane

Don't be lulled into a false sense of security (or panic) by TV personalities with complicated Doppler radar charts and satellite imagery. Hurricanes are much like the proverbial 800lb gorilla: They sit down wherever, and whenever, they want.

Scientists and National Weather Center (NWC) meteorologists watch closely as tropical depressions over the ocean and gulf become tropical storms and are finally upgraded to hurricanes. But plotting a hurricane's path is tricky business. In fact, it can't really be done.

Not long ago, Miami television and NWC meteorologists predicted that Hurricane Erin was headed for a touchdown right in the center of the city. Miami and Miami Beach neighborhoods were evacuated, and shelters sent out pleas for volunteers and supplies. Local television news teams ran gleefully around looking for driving rain ('Well, Patricia, it isn't coming down quite yet, but it's looking very ominous indeed…') and waiting for something awful to happen. A mild degree of panic set in among local residents who had not evacuated. And then….

Nothing. At least, nothing in Miami, where it rained a little. That evening, a startlingly clear, star-filled sky, combined with a gentle breeze across the bay, made conditions lovely for a beach stroll.

The storm had suddenly veered due north, catching northern Florida residents totally by surprise – in fact, many South Florida residents who had listened to news reports and evacuated their homes drove into the eye of the storm!

As Erin continued overland, she socked the Florida Panhandle with a wallop that knocked out power, destroyed houses as if they were built out of matchsticks and caused millions of dollars in damage.

About a month later, the second half of the one-two punch slammed the Panhandle as Hurricane Opal came through and flattened almost all of Panama City Beach, ripping down condominiums, and actually tearing up highways, houses and hotels. Pensacola Beach was still under several feet of sand months later.

There are two distinct stages of alert: A Hurricane Watch is given when a hurricane *may* strike the area within the next 36 to 48 hours; a Hurricane Warning is given when a hurricane is likely to strike the area.

If a Hurricane Warning is issued during your stay, you may be placed under an evacuation order. Hotels generally follow these orders and ask guests to leave. The Red Cross operates hurricane shelters, but they are just that – shelter: They do not provide food.

For a full list of tips on preparedness, check the Miami white pages telephone directory. There's a hurricane hot line (☎ 305-229-4483), which will give you information about approaching storms, storm tracks, warnings, estimated time till touchdown...all the things you need to make a decision about if and when to leave.

EMERGENCIES

If you're robbed, report the theft to the police at a nonemergency number. You'll need a police report to make an insurance claim back home.

If your credit cards, cash cards or traveler's checks have been stolen, notify your bank or the relevant company as soon as possible. For refunds on lost or stolen traveler's checks (not cards) call American Express at ☎ 800-221-7282; MasterCard at ☎ 800-223-9920; Thomas Cook at ☎ 800-223-7373; or Visa at ☎ 800-227-6811. See Credit & Debit Cards in the Money section, earlier in this chapter, for numbers to report lost or stolen credit cards.

Foreign visitors who have lost their passports should contact their consulate. Having a photocopy of the important pages of your passport will make replacement much easier.

Dial ☎ 911 for police, fire and medical emergencies. It's a free call from any phone. The inside front cover of the Miami white pages lists a slew of emergency numbers. Some useful ones include the following:

Coast Guard Search	☎ 305-535-4314
Beach Patrol	☎ 305-673-7711

Miami-Dade Police (nonemergency)	☎ 305-595-6263
Miami Beach Police (nonemergency)	☎ 305-673-7900
Poison Information Center	☎ 800-282-3171
Rape Hotline	☎ 305-585-7273
Suicide Intervention	☎ 305-358-4357
Hurricane Hotline	☎ 305-229-4483

LEGAL MATTERS

Florida law tends to be tougher than most states north when it comes to drug possession. At the same time, Miami police are more tolerant than their counterparts in, say, St Augustine, where someone arrested for carrying a pot pipe makes the newspaper. But dozens of people are arrested on minor drug charges each week, and since the late 1990s there's been an increase in police raids on nightclubs. Possession of any amount of marijuana or speed is a misdemeanor and technically punishable by up to one year in prison *and* a $1000 fine.

It's illegal to walk with an open alcoholic drink – including beer – on the street. If you're driving, all liquor has to be unopened (not just sealed, but new and untouched). Technically it must be stored in the trunk of the car.

Driving under the influence of alcohol or drugs in Florida carries a $5000 fine in addition to suspension of your license and possibly some imprisonment.

BUSINESS HOURS

Office hours are generally 9am to 5pm, though these can vary half an hour or so. Many shops are open longer hours and through the weekends, while many food shops and supermarkets are open 24 hours daily. Banks are generally open from about 9am to about 4pm; some have extended hours one day a week and limited hours on Saturday. Banks, offices and many businesses close on public holidays.

PUBLIC HOLIDAYS

If public holidays fall on a weekday or weekend, they are often celebrated on the nearest Friday or Monday, to create a three-day weekend. The following are national public holidays.

New Year's Day – January 1

Martin Luther King Jr Day – third Monday in January

Presidents Day – third Monday in February

Easter – a Sunday in March or April

Memorial Day – last Monday in May

Independence Day – July 4

Labor Day – first Monday in September

Columbus Day – second Monday in October

Veterans Day – November 11

Thanksgiving – fourth Thursday in November

Christmas – December 25

SPECIAL EVENTS

Everyone in Miami likes a good party, and there are plenty of them, though summertime pickings are slim. The Greater Miami Convention & Visitor's Bureau's *What's Happening in Greater Miami & The Beaches* has a complete list of area events, published twice yearly.

Ongoing/Monthly

Farmer's Markets – weekly/seasonal – offerings vary from fresh fruits and veggies (Lincoln Road in South Beach) to gourmet prepared foods (Española Way in South Beach) to handmade crafts (Coral Gables City Hall); see the Things to See & Do chapter for details

Gallery Night – first Friday of the month – a Coral Gables walking and shuttle-bus tour of art galleries (☎ 305-444-4493)

Friday Fest – first Friday of the month – a Homestead festival with music, food and crafts along Krome and Washington Aves (☎ 305-242-4814, W www.homesteadmainstreet.com)

ArtsBeach – second Thursday of the month – a Miami Beach open house of cultural and art institutions (☎ 305-673-7500, W www.2nd thursdays.com)

Coconut Grove Cares Antique and Jewelry Show – every third weekend of the month – over 300 vendors with antiques and jewelry at the Coconut Grove Exhibition Center (☎ 305-444-8454; Map 9)

Cultural Fridays – fourth Friday of the month – music, poetry, dance, theater and visual arts in Little Havana (☎ 305-631-0588)

January

Orange Bowl Festival – early January – a major, classic college football game, played at Pro Player Stadium (Map 2) rather than the actual Orange Bowl (☎ 305-371-4600, W www.orange bowl.com)

Art Deco Weekend Festival – mid-January – a weekend fair from 1st to 23rd Sts, with arts and crafts, food stalls and the usual block party types (☎ 305-672-2014)

Art Miami – mid-January – modern and contemporary works from 100 galleries and international artists displayed at the Miami Beach Convention Center (☎ 305-673-7311; Map 3)

Martin Luther King Jr Parade – mid-January – a parade and festival to honor the slain Civil Rights leader in Liberty City (☎ 305-636-1924)

Taste of the Grove – mid- to late January – an outdoor fundraising spectacle by Coconut Grove restaurants (☎ 305-444-7270)

Key Biscayne Art Festival – late January – since the early 1960s, over 150 artists showcasing their works along Crandon Blvd (☎ 305-361-0049)

Miami Film Festival – late January to early February – sponsored by FIU, a two-week festival (☎ 305-377-3456, W www.miamifilmfestival .com); call for location since it may move from the disastrous 2002 South Beach location back to the mainland

February

Homestead Rodeo – late January to early February – since the late 1940s, a full-fledged rodeo with bull riding, bareback and saddle bronco riding, team roping, steer wrestling and women's barrel racing (☎ 305-247-3515, W www.home steadrodeo.com)

Jazz under the Stars – mid-February – since the mid-1980s, an annual festival at the Miami Metrozoo (Map 1) featuring some of the greatest of the greats (☎ 305-238-1811)

Miami International Boat Show – late February – with over 250,000 attendees, a serious show at the Miami Beach Convention Center (☎ 305-531-8410; Map 3)

March

Asian Cultural Festival – early March – food, music and handicrafts from Asia displayed at the Fruit & Spice Park (☎ 305-247-5727; Map 1)

Grand Prix of Miami – early March – an annual PPG Indy Car World Series opener at the

Homestead Miami Speedway (☎ 305-230-7223; Map 1)

Carnaval Miami – early to mid-March – a nine-day party of festivals, concerts, a beauty contest, an in-line skating contest, a Latin drag queen show and a Calle Ocho cooking contest (☎ 305-644-8888, **W** www.carnaval-miami.org)

Winter Party – early to mid-March – a big gay circuit party bonanza benefiting the Dade Human Rights Foundation (☎ 305-572-1841, **W** www.winterparty.com)

Calle Ocho Festival – mid-March – not for the claustrophobic, since over a million people attend this Little Havana party with 23 blocks of concerts, giveaways, Cuban food and more (☎ 305-644-8888, **W** www.carnaval-miami.org)

Derby Day – mid-March – the most significant preview of the Triple Crown, held at Gulfstream Park, 901 S Federal Hwy in Hallandale (☎ 954-454-7000, **W** www.gulfstreampark.com)

Miami Orchid Show – mid-March – since the mid-1940s, an annual show of flowers from statewide growers at the Coconut Grove Exhibition Center (☎ 305-255-3656; Map 9)

Italian Renaissance Festival – mid-March – period plays, people dressed in traditional Italian costume and period concerts at the beautiful Vizcaya Museum & Gardens (☎ 305-250-9133; Map 9)

South Beach Wine & Food Festival – mid-March – a big and glittery two-day event sponsored by FIU in a big tent at Lummus Park, with over 200 wine producers and seminars and dinners (☎ 877-649-8325, **W** www.sobewineandfood fest.com)

Miami-Dade County Fair & Expo – mid- to late March – an 18-day extravaganza showcasing the area's agricultural roots at the Fair Expo Center, SW 112th Ave at 24th St (☎ 305-223-7060, **W** www.fairexpo.com)

Nasdaq 100 Tennis Open – late March – formerly known as the Lipton and Ericsson Open, top-ranked tennis pros play for millions of spectators (☎ 305-442-3367)

Marine Aquarium Show – late March to early April – since the mid-1960s, at the Miami Museum of Science & Space Transit Planetarium (Map 9), with more than 100 fish tanks on display, as well as lectures on proper lighting and tank maintenance (☎ 305-646-4200, **W** www .miamisci.org)

April

Biltmore International Wine Festival – mid-April – fine wines and gourmet food at the Biltmore Hotel in Coral Gables (☎ 305-445-1926; Map 10)

Great Sunrise Balloon Race – late April – about 40 hot-air balloons racing at Homestead Air Reserve Base to benefit people with disabilities (☎ 305-273-3051)

Miami Gay & Lesbian Film Festival – late April to early May – an annual event with most screenings taking place at the Colony Theatre (☎ 305-534-9924, **W** www.miamigaylesbianfilm.com; Map 3)

May/June

International Hispanic Theatre Festival – late May to mid-June – one of the largest Hispanic theater celebrations in the USA, featuring US, Latin American, Caribbean and European companies (☎ 305-445-8877, **W** www.teatroavante.com)

July

Independence Day Celebration – July 4 – an excellent fireworks and laser show with live music that draws over 100,000 people to Bayfront Park (☎ 305-358-7550; Map 6); there are also good views from Key Biscayne

August

It's too hot and humid to schedule anything; no one would show up.

September

Festival Miami – late September to late October – an annual concert series at the University of Miami Campus in Coral Gables (☎ 305-284-4940, **W** www.music.miami.edu; Map 10)

October

Hispanic Heritage Festival – late October – one of the largest festivals in the country, commemorating the discovery of the Americas with concerts, food, games and folkloric groups; along Sunset Dr between SW 57th Ave and US Hwy 1 (☎ 305-541-5023, **W** www.hispanicfestival.com)

Miami Reggae Festival – late October – since the early 1980s, one of the largest reggae events in the country, held at Bayfront Park (☎ 305-891-2944; Map 6)

November

South Miami Art Festival – early November – since the early 1980s, an annual event with over 150 exhibitors, along Sunset Dr between SW 57th Ave and US Hwy 1 (☎ 305-661-1621)

Winston Cup – mid-November – a NASCAR weekend at the Homestead Miami Speedway

(☎ 305-230-7223, **w** www.homesteadmiami
speedway.com; Map 1)

Miami Book Fair International – mid- to late November – among the most important and well-attended in the USA, with hundreds of nationally known writers joining hundreds of publishers and hundreds of thousands of visitors; don't miss it (☎ 305-237-3258, **w** www.miamibookfair.com)

White Party – mid- to late November – a week-long extravaganza that draws more than 15,000 gays for nonstop partying (☎ 305-667-9296, **w** www.whiteparty.net)

December

Art Basel Miami Beach – early December – one of the most important international art shows, with works from over 150 galleries (☎ 305-674-1292, **w** www.artbasel.com/miami_beach)

Jewish Film Festival – early to mid-December – sponsored by FIU, almost 30 international films and documentaries screened (☎ 305-576-4030, **w** www.caje-miami.org/filmfestival)

King Mango Strut – late December – since the early 1980s, an annual Grove spoof of events and people in the news, along Main Ave and Grand Ave (☎ 305-401-1171)

First Night – December 31 – an alcohol-free New Year's celebration for all ages along Lincoln Road and Convention Center Dr in South Beach (☎ 305-573-2753, **w** www.firstnight miamibeach.org; Map 3) and at Bayfront Park (☎ 305-539-3082; Map 6)

Orange Bowl Parade – December 31 – an annual New Year's Eve blowout since 1940, with an enormous parade, floats, clowns (professional and unintentional), a Folkloric Dance competition, a queen and a whole lot of other stuff. It would seem that all of Miami turns out for it at the Pro Player Stadium, and afterward, the Big Orange celebration at Bayfront Park has a fireworks salute (☎ 305-371-4800, **w** www.orange bowl.com).

DOING BUSINESS

Miami's close physical and cultural proximity to Latin America means that local repre-sentatives of companies throughout the Caribbean and Central and South America set up shop here. And, the multinational flavor of Miami means that there are plenty of resources for Europeans and those who would do business with them.

But Miami is also part of the USA, so things happen quickly and efficiently. Temporary multilingual employees are easy to come by and relatively cheap, certainly by European standards (check under Temporary Employment in the yellow pages).

The nonprofit Beacon Council (☎ 305-579-1300, **w** www.beaconcouncil.com) provides business introductions, research studies and many other business services at no charge. Precision Translating Services (☎ 305-373-7874), 150 W Flagler St, provides translation services. Legal and Technical Translations, Inc (☎ 305-252-0606) specializes in just that.

Registering a foreign company is a matter of dealing with bureaucrats at City Hall. Consult the nearest Chamber of Commerce (see the Tourist Offices section, earlier in this chapter) or the Beacon Council for more information.

WORK

Foreigners cannot work legally in the USA without the appropriate work visa, and recent legislative changes specifically target illegal immigrants, which is what you will be if you try to work while on a tourist visa.

Miami has been ground zero for large numbers of refugees from the Caribbean area, notably Haiti and Cuba, so INS checks are frequent. Local businesses are probably more concerned here than anywhere outside of Southern California and Texas when it comes to verifying your legal status. See Visa Extensions under Documents, earlier in this chapter, for warnings about longer stays.

Getting There & Away

AIR

Because it's isolated at the southern tip of the USA, most visitors end up flying into Miami. The city is also an international gateway for Central and South American travel.

Don't forget to include departure taxes, which vary from airport to airport, in the prices quoted in this section.

Airports

Miami is served by two main airports: Miami International Airport (MIA) and the Fort Lauderdale-Hollywood International Airport (FLL). See the Getting Around chapter for information about getting to and from the airports.

Miami International Airport Commonly called MIA (☎ 305-876-7000/7770, ⓦ www.miami-airport.com), this airport is one of the country's busiest: With about 92,000

people a day passing through, it's third in terms of total international passengers, and 14th in terms of total passengers period. Just 6 miles west of downtown, the airport is open around the clock and is laid out in an open horseshoe design. It's customary for locals to complain about delays and confusion, but if you're a seasoned traveler, it won't feel worse than Chicago, Boston or Los Angeles (which are bad). There's a big capital improvement construction project going on through 2007.

There are plenty of ATMs and information booths throughout the airport. The central information booth is located on Concourse E, in the main lobby on the 2nd floor. Check here for lost and found, too. To page someone, or to answer a page, pick up any white courtesy phone, which will automatically connect you to the central paging office. The 24-hour currency exchange office, at International Arrivals, yields typically awful rates; see Changing Money in the Money section of the Facts for the Visitor chapter for more information. Smoking is prohibited anywhere inside the terminal except in the members-only airline lounges.

Fort Lauderdale-Hollywood International Airport The four-terminal FLL (☎ 954-359-1200, ⓦ www.fll.net), about 30 miles north of Miami just off I-95, is smaller (though undergoing rapid expansion) and friendlier than MIA. Fort Lauderdale serves as a lower-cost alternative to MIA, especially now that the very popular Southwest Airlines services this northern neighbor. There are no courtesy phones or official information booths, but several airline counters may be able to provide help. Other budget carriers include JetBlue, AirTran and Spirit.

If you have some time before your flight, head to the airport meditation room at the south end of Terminal 3 across from the Northwest Airlines ticket counter. Ask at the Concourse F security checkpoint to be let in.

Airlines

Carriers are listed in the phone book under 'Airlines.' However, know that most airlines post better Internet-only fares on their Web sites than you can get by calling them directly. Almost 100 international airlines fly into Miami or Fort Lauderdale (or both), including the following:

US-based airlines

AirTran
☎ 800-247-8726, **W** www.airtran.com

America West
☎ 800-235-9292, **W** www.americawest.com

American
☎ 800-433-7300, **W** www.aa.com

Cape Air
☎ 800-352-0714, **W** www.flycapeair.com

Continental
☎ 800-525-0280, **W** www.continental.com

Delta
☎ 800-221-1212, **W** www.delta.com

Frontier
☎ 800-432-1359, **W** www.frontierairlines.com

JetBlue
☎ 800-538-2583, **W** www.jetblue.com

Midway
☎ 800-446-4392, **W** www.midwayair.com

Northwest
☎ 800-225-2525, **W** www.nwa.com

Spirit
☎ 800-772-7117, **W** www.spiritair.com

Southwest
☎ 800-435-9792, **W** www.southwest.com

Sun Country
☎ 800-359-6786, **W** www.suncountry.com

United
☎ 800-241-6522, **W** www.ual.com

US Airways
☎ 800-428-4322, **W** www.usairways.com

International airlines

Aerolíneas Argentinas
☎ 800-333-0276, **W** www.aerolineas.com

Aeroméxico
☎ 800-237-6639, **W** www.aeromexico.com

Air Canada
☎ 888-247-2262, **W** www.aircanada.ca

Air France
☎ 800-237-2747, **W** www.airfrance.fr

Air Jamaica
☎ 800-523-5585, **W** www.airjamaica.com

Air New Zealand
☎ 800-262-1234, **W** www.airnewzealand.com

Alitalia
☎ 800-223-5730, **W** www.alitalia.it

Bahamas Air
☎ 800-222-4262, **W** www.bahamasair.com

British Airways
☎ 800-247-9297, **W** www.britishairways.com

Cayman Airways
☎ 800-422-9626, **W** www.caymanairways.com

El Al
☎ 800-223-6700, **W** www.elal.co.il

Iberia
☎ 800-772-4642, **W** www.iberia.com

KLM
☎ 800-374-7747, **W** www.klm.com

LanChile
☎ 305-670-9999, **W** www.lanchile.com

LanPeru
☎ 800-735-5590, **W** www.lanperu.com

Lloyd Aéreo Boliviano (LAB)
☎ 800-337-0918, **W** www.labairlines.com

Lufthansa
☎ 800-645-3880, **W** www.lufthansa.com

Mexicana
☎ 800-531-7921, **W** www.mexicana.com

Qantas
☎ 800-227-4500, **W** www.qantas.com.au

Varig
☎ 800-468-2744, **W** www.varig.co.uk

Virgin Atlantic
☎ 800-862-8621, **W** www.virgin-atlantic.com

Buying Tickets

Depending on where you're coming from, your plane ticket could easily be the most expensive item in your budget. It is always worth putting aside a few hours to do research. Start shopping for a ticket early – some of the cheapest tickets must be bought months in advance, and some popular flights sell out early. Note that high season in Miami is mid-November to mid-April. The fares quoted later in this section are only a guide; they do not constitute a recommendation for the carrier. Once you have your ticket, write down its number,

Air Travel Glossary

Cancellation Penalties If you have to cancel or change a discounted ticket, there are often heavy penalties involved; insurance can sometimes be taken out against these penalties. Some airlines impose penalties on regular tickets as well, particularly against 'no-show' passengers.

Courier Fares Businesses often need to send urgent documents or freight securely and quickly. Courier companies hire people to accompany the package through customs and, in return, offer a discount ticket that is sometimes a phenomenal bargain. However, you may have to surrender all your baggage allowance and take only carry-on luggage.

Full Fares Airlines traditionally offer 1st class (coded F), business class (coded J) and economy class (coded Y) tickets. These days, so many promotional and discounted fares are available that few passengers pay full economy fare.

Lost Tickets If you lose your airline ticket, an airline will usually treat it like a traveler's check and, after inquiries, issue you with another one. Legally, however, an airline is entitled to treat it like cash: If you lose it, it's gone forever. Take good care of your tickets.

Onward Tickets An entry requirement for many countries is a ticket out of the country. If you're unsure of your next move, the easiest solution is to buy the cheapest onward ticket to a neighboring country or a ticket from a reliable airline that can later be refunded if you do not use it.

Open-Jaw Tickets These are return tickets that permit you to fly into one place but return from another. If available, these tickets can save you backtracking to your arrival point.

Overbooking Because almost every flight has some passengers that fail to show up, airlines often book more passengers than they have seats. Usually excess passengers make up for the no-shows, but occasionally somebody gets 'bumped' onto the next available flight. Guess who it is most likely to be? The passengers who check in late.

Promotional Fares These are officially discounted fares, available from travel agencies or direct from the airline.

Reconfirmation If you don't reconfirm your flight at least 72 hours prior to departure, the airline may delete your name from the passenger list. Call to find out if your airline requires reconfirmation.

Restrictions Discounted tickets often have various restrictions – for example, they may need to be paid for in advance, or altering them may incur a penalty. Other restrictions include minimum and maximum periods you must be away.

Round-the-World Tickets RTW tickets give you a limited period (usually a year) in which to circumnavigate the globe. You can go anywhere the carrying airlines go as long as you don't backtrack. The number of stopovers or total number of separate flights is decided before you set off, and these tickets usually cost a bit more than a basic return flight.

Transferred Tickets Airline tickets cannot be transferred from one person to another. Travelers sometimes try to sell the return half of a ticket, but officials can ask you to prove that you are the person named on the ticket. On an international flight, tickets are compared with passports.

Travel Periods Ticket prices vary with the time of year. There is a low (off-peak) season and a high (peak) season, and often a low-shoulder season and a high-shoulder season as well. Usually the fare depends on your outward flight – if you depart in the high season and return in the low season, you pay the high-season fare.

together with the flight number and other details, and keep the information somewhere separate. If the ticket is lost or stolen, this will help you get a replacement. If you are buying travel insurance, buy it as early as possible.

Commercial reservation networks offer airline ticketing as well as information and bookings for hotels, car rental and other services. To buy a ticket via the Web, you'll need a credit card; this should be straightforward and secure, as card details are encrypted. Try the following Web sites for good fares:

Atevo Travel	W www.atevo.com
Cheap Tickets	W www.cheaptickets.com
Expedia	W www.expedia.com
Hotwire	W www.hotwire.com
Orbitz	W www.orbitz.com
Priceline	W www.priceline.com
Travel Library	W www.travel-library.com
Travelocity	W www.travelocity.com

Round-the-World Tickets RTW tickets are very popular because they can work out to be no more expensive, or even cheaper, than an ordinary roundtrip ticket. RTW tickets usually combine the services of two airlines: You are permitted to fly anywhere on their route systems as long as you do not backtrack. Read the small print; other restrictions and time limits often apply. Your best bet is to find a travel agent that advertises or specializes in round-the-world tickets. Start with the best by contacting Air Treks (☎ 415-365-1665, W www.airtreks .com) in San Francisco.

Visit USA Passes Many domestic carriers offer Visit USA passes to non-US citizens. The passes are actually coupons that you buy – each coupon equals a flight. You have to book each of these, including your return flight, outside of the US.

Contact the bigger carriers like Continental and American Airlines in your home country. Some will let you fly standby, while others require you to reserve flights in advance (and penalize you if you need to

change the fare). When flying standby, call the airline a day or two before the flight and make a standby reservation. This way you get priority over others who just appear at the airport and hope to get on the flight the same day.

Other Parts of the USA

Check the weekly travel sections of major newspapers like the *New York Times, Los Angeles Times, Chicago Tribune, San Francisco Chronicle,* and *Boston Globe* for discount fares. Scan Miami's *New Times* and *Miami Herald* for advertisements for discounted flights that leave from this area.

Budget travel agents with national repute include Council Travel (☎ 800-226-8624, W www.counciltravel.com) and STA Travel (☎ 800-777-0112, W www.sta.com). While STA and Council cater to students, they happily serve others.

The best deals to Miami are usually from the New York metropolitan area, but this route is also the most crowded: Reserve early, as planes fill up well in advance of the date of departure. Currently, Southwest Airlines has the lowest scheduled airfares between Fort Lauderdale and their metro New York hub, which is actually in Islip on Long Island. With a little luck in winter, you can get a roundtrip fare for as low as $150. On other scheduled airlines departing from JFK and La Guardia, expect to pay at least $225 (roundtrip, advance-purchase); $300 from Los Angeles; and $350 to $450 from San Francisco.

Canada

Travel Cuts (☎ 416-966-2887 in Toronto) has offices in major Canadian cities. Also check the Toronto *Globe & Mail* and *Vancouver Sun,* which carry ads for travel agents. With a little luck and good timing (mid-week, with a 14-day advance purchase and seven-day stay), you might get a roundtrip ticket for C$470 from Toronto and C$625 from Vancouver, regardless of the season.

The UK

Start by perusing the travel sections of *Time Out,* the *Evening Standard* and *TNT.* UK travelers will probably find the cheapest flights advertised by obscure bucket shops. Many are honest and solvent, but some are rogues who will take your money and disappear. If you feel suspicious about a firm, don't give them all the money at once – leave a deposit of 20% or so and pay the balance on receiving the ticket. If they insist on cash in advance, go elsewhere. Once you have the ticket, ring the airline to confirm that you are booked on the flight.

Good, reliable agents for cheap tickets in the UK include Trailfinders (☎ 020-7937-5400, W www.trailfinders.com), 194 Kensington High St, London W8 7RG; Council Travel (☎ 020-7437-7767), 28a Poland St, London W1; and STA Travel (☎ 020-7581-4132), 86 Old Brompton Rd, London SW7 3LQ. The Globetrotters Club (BCM Roving, London WC1N 3XX) publishes the newsletter *Globe,* and can help you find traveling companions.

In January a roundtrip ticket from London to Miami might run UK£135 to UK£275. In July, the same ticket would cost UK£580.

Continental Europe

Most major European airlines service Miami. In January versus June, or high versus low season, expect to pay €500/700 from Amsterdam, €500/765 from Paris, €650/700 from Madrid, and €550/765 from Munich or Frankfurt.

In Amsterdam, NBBS is a popular travel agent. In Germany, contact Council Travel (☎ 211-36-30-30), Graf Adolph Strasse 18, 40212 Dusselford and Council Travel (☎ 089-39-50-22), Adalbertstrasse 32, 80799 Munich 40. Also contact STA Travel (☎ 4969-43-01-91), Bergerstrasse 118, 60316 Frankfurt 1.

In France, contact Council Travel (☎ 01 44 41 89 80), 1 Place de l'Odeon, 75006 Paris.

Australia & New Zealand

There is no direct service from Australia or New Zealand to Miami; you'll have to change planes and/or carriers in Los Angeles, the US hub for Qantas and Air

New Zealand. Most routes fly over Hawaii, so at least the Pacific is covered in one mighty leap. Air New Zealand has the most comfortable coach seats in the sky.

In Australia and New Zealand there are offices for STA Travel (☎ 1-300-733-035 Australia, ☎ 0508-782-872 New Zealand, W www.sta.com) and Flight Centres International (W www.flightcentre.com) in major cities. They sell tickets to everyone, but have special deals for students and travelers under 30. STA's Australian head office (☎ 1300-360-960, 9347-6911) is at 224 Faraday St, Carlton South, Melbourne, VIC 3053; the New Zealand head office (☎ 0800-100-677, 09-309-0458) is at 10 High St, Auckland. To find the Flight Centre International office near you, call ☎ 133-133 in Australia, or ☎ 0800-354448 in New Zealand.

In Australia, don't forget to peruse the Saturday editions of newspapers like the *Sydney Morning Herald* and *The Age.* Kiwis, pick up your *New Zealand Herald.*

The flight from Auckland to Los Angeles takes 12 to 13 hours. On Air New Zealand, expect to spend about NZ$2150 from December to April, but don't forget to add another NZ$670 for the last leg to Miami. The whole trip is only about US$100 less during the US winter.

From Sydney to Los Angeles the trip takes 13½ to 14½ hours. Typical APEX roundtrip fares hover between A$2000 and A$2400 from the Australian east coast, but again, you must add another A$550 to Miami. Since high season in Australia is low season in the USA, flight prices don't change much.

Central & South America

Miami is the main US–Latin American gateway, and MIA is served by everyone and his brother's airlines. You can sometimes get incredible deals through discount brokers in Latin America, but they come and go quickly. The average roundtrip tickets available through Web sites like W www.expedia.com are US$400 to US$450 from major Central American cities.

From Rio de Janeiro, Brazil, economy fares often have to be purchased two weeks in advance and minimum-stay restrictions apply. You can probably find a flight from Rio for around R$1825 *(reais)* in winter.

From Caracas, Venezuela, count on prices of around Bs 362,000 to Bs 500,000 *(bolívares)* in winter.

Asia

Hong Kong is the discount plane ticket capital of the region, but its bucket shops can be unreliable. Ask other travelers for advice before buying a ticket. STA Travel (**W** www.sta.com), which is dependable, has branches in Hong Kong, Tokyo, Singapore, Bangkok and Kuala Lumpur. Many, if not most, flights to the US go via Honolulu, Hawaii.

United, Northwest and Japan Airlines (☎ 0120-25-5971, **W** www.jal.co.jp) all have daily flights to the west coast of the US, where you can get a connecting flight to Miami.

BUS

There are four Greyhound (☎ 800-231-2222, **W** www.greyhound.com) terminals in Miami, which seem to connect to every conceivable Florida town. The main downtown terminal (☎ 305-374-6160; Map 6), 100 NW 6th St, is open from 5am to 11pm daily. Greyhound's airport terminal (☎ 305-871-1810; Map 2), 4111 NW 27th St, is open 24 hours daily. The North Miami terminal (☎ 305-945-0801; Map 2), 16560 NE 6th Ave, is open 5:45am to 12:30am daily. The southern Miami terminal (☎ 305-296-9072), 20505 S Dixie Hwy, at the Cutler Ridge Mall (Map 1), has more limited service. It's open from 9am to 6pm Monday through Saturday and from noon to 6pm Sunday.

There are a few discounts worth pursuing. Seven-day advance tickets are always the way to go. It's always cheaper to travel Monday through Thursday than Friday through Sunday. There are often two-for-one companion tickets. Lastly, students (with identification) get 15% off and seniors get 5% off unrestricted fares.

Since Tampa-St Petersburg to Miami ($35/57 one-way/roundtrip) via Fort Lauderdale ($5) takes between seven and 10

hours, consider renting a car. (You might not even incur one-way drop-off charges.) There are buses at 5:45am, 7am, 9:05am, 12:15pm, 3:20pm and 10:35pm. Orlando ($23/41 one-way/roundtrip) is served by seven to 12 buses a day, and most trips take six to seven hours.

See the Key West and Keys chapters for information on Greyhound buses between Miami and the Florida Keys.

Greyhound service to other parts of the country includes the following: There are four buses daily each to New York City ($113/175 one-way/roundtrip, 27 to 30 hours) and Washington, DC ($110/170, 23 to 25 hours); five to New Orleans ($59/118, 20 to 22 hours); and 10 daily to Atlanta ($59/118, 16 to 18 hours).

TRAIN

Amtrak's main Miami terminal (☎ 305-835-1222, 800-872-7245, **W** www.amtrak.com; Map 2), 8303 NW 37th Ave, connects the city with the rest of continental USA and Canada. If you're coming here by train from anywhere, you will at some point have to connect with Amtrak's No 97 *SilverMeteor,* No 91 *SilverStar* or No 89 *SilverPalm,* which run between New York City and Miami via Tampa or Orlando. Travel time between New York and Miami is a ghastly (or relaxing, depending on your perspective – it's always about perspective, isn't it?) 27 to 30 hours and costs $86 to $235 one-way. It's cheapest to travel Monday to Wednesday. If you want your car when you get there but don't feel like driving it down, inquire about the East Coast Auto Train from Lorton, Virginia, which goes to Sanford, Florida (very close to Orlando).

The trip from Tampa to Miami takes five hours and costs $36 to $71 one-way. Orlando takes six hours and costs $35 to $68. Roundtrip fares are twice the one-way fares.

You can pick up a taxi to your hotel or the airport right outside the Amtrak station. The airport, where you can rent a car, is just 5 miles away; the fare will be about $12 plus tip. Or take the 'L' bus to Miami Beach and No 42 to the airport.

A Free Loaner Car

Want some temporary wheels? Try Auto Driveaway of New York (☎ 212-967-2344), which has locations in major cities around the country. People who want their car moved from city A to city B, but don't have the time or inclination to do it themselves, leave their car with this organization. As long as you're willing to drive from city A to city B in four days and pay for the gas (the first tank's free), the car's yours. To qualify, drivers must be 21 years old, have a valid driver's license and one other form of ID. Non-US citizens can use an international driver's license, but must show a valid entry visa and passport as well. Auto Driveaway requires a $300 refundable deposit (which acts as your collision damage waiver in the event of an accident), and a $15 nonrefundable registration fee. They provide $1 million of insurance. The only downside: Auto Driveaway suggests calling them 10 to 14 days prior to your intended departure date, which will put a damper on trying to get a cheap plane ticket if no car is available.

CAR & MOTORCYCLE

For a particularly rewarding drive from points west of Florida, take I-10, which passes near luscious Pensacola beaches as you cross the Florida Panhandle. I-10 connects with I-95, which runs down the east coast to Miami. From New York, expect a 19-hour trip without stops. Speed limits change from state to state, and some states ban radar detectors. But others don't. Watch yer ass in South Carolina lest coppers slap you with a $150 speeding ticket.

See the Getting Around chapter for regional highway information and rental car agencies.

BOAT

There are very few ways to hop aboard a steamer these days, especially one heading to Miami. The best way to get to Miami by boat is to first get to Fort Lauderdale, as it's America's largest transatlantic yacht harbor.

Every year hundreds of captains look for professional or unpaid crew to help them get their boats from South Florida to wherever they're going. In late spring they're going to Europe; in summer they're heading to New England, the Mediterranean and, less frequently but gaining in popularity, the west coast of the USA, including Alaska. At other times they could be heading just about anywhere. Boats leave for South American, Asian and Australasian destinations year-round. Best of all, it's legal for foreigners to work on a boat that's leaving the USA. Boats also leave from other marinas and ports, of course; check locally for more information.

Getting a slot on a boat is a very interesting way to arrange transportation and perhaps even earn some spending money for wherever you'll end up. Many people have been getting around the world like this for years and don't see any reason to stop. Don't get it wrong – it's hard and serious work that requires concentration, dedication, commonsense and the ability to work and live with others in close quarters. But those who love it wouldn't do anything else.

Crew Information

To get an idea of trends and conditions, start by perusing sailing magazines. Try *Cruising World* and *Sail,* which run ads and classifieds. Blue Seas International has a great Web site (**w** www.jobxchange.com/crew xchange) with postings for crews heading just about everywhere on every type of vessel. Crew placement agencies are located throughout Fort Lauderdale, and they will, for a fee, match up crew hopefuls with boat owners.

The best sources for information are crew houses in Fort Lauderdale, essentially hostels or guest houses for people looking for work. Boat owners call crew houses when they have something coming up. Floyd's Youth Hostel & Crew House (☎ 954-462-0631) is an excellent source of information – see the Places to Stay

Cruises

The Port of Miami (**W** www.co.miami-dade.fl.us/portofmiami/so_cruise.htm), on Dodge Island just south of the MacArthur Causeway, is the largest cruise-ship port in the world, serving more than three million passengers yearly. You can book everything from simple day trips to elaborate round-the-world voyages. The most common are three-day cruises to the Bahamas, and four- and seven-day trips to Caribbean ports of call like San Juan, Puerto Rico, and the islands of St Thomas, St John and St Martin.

Rates fluctuate daily and a number of discounts apply – they're yours for the asking…so ask. The definition of cruise high season (summertime and during school vacations) and cruise low season (winter, with the exception of holidays) varies with each carrier; low season prices can be 15% to 30% less than high season. Port charges and taxes are included in the following high-season prices, which should simply be used as a basis for comparison and are based on double occupancy. Following are the major cruise operators.

The most popular of the bunch, **Carnival Cruise Lines** (☎ 305-599-2600, 800-327-9501, **W** *www.carnival.com*) offers three-night tours (Friday to Monday) on the *Fascination* visiting Nassau, Bahamas. An inside cabin (category four) costs $370 per person, while large suites (category 12) run $790 per person. A four-night cruise (Monday to Friday) on the *Imagination* to Key West and Cozumel, Mexico, runs $510 per person for an inside cabin, $1040 per person for a large suite.

Norwegian Cruise Line (☎ 305-436-4000, 800-327-7030, **W** *www.ncl.com*) is the leader in 'freestyle cruising,' which provides greater flexibility in meal times, dress codes and tipping options. Three-night tours aboard the *Majesty* to the Bahamas run from $290 (category L, the cheapest inside cabin) to $320 (category HH, the cheapest outer cabin with a picture window) per person. Four-night *Majesty* voyages to Key West and Cozumel run from $340 to $395 per person. Note that this ship only sails from mid-November to mid-April.

Royal Caribbean International (☎ 305-539-6000, 800-327-6700, **W** *www.royalcaribbean.com*) offers three-night Bahamas trips on the *Majesty of the Seas*, which run from $375 (category Q, inside) to $1200 (category C, with a verandah) per person. The seven-night Eastern Caribbean cruise aboard the very nice *Explorer of the Seas* is $1175 to $1625 per person.

section of the Fort Lauderdale chapter for more information.

Agencies Smallwood's Yachtware (☎ 954-523-2282), 1001 SE 17th St, in Fort Lauderdale, controls the region's premier unofficial crew agency: a three-ring binder. Owners come here, write their requirements and wait for crew to get in touch. Smallwood's is open 7:30am to 5:30pm Monday to Friday, 9am to 3pm Saturday.

Official agencies charge between $25 and $35 for a listing. In Fort Lauderdale, agencies include Crew Unlimited (☎ 954-462-4624), 2065 S Federal Hwy; Crew Finders (☎ 954-522-2739), 408 SE 17th St; and The

Crew Network (☎ 954-467-9777), 1053 SE 17th St.

When to Go An experienced hand can pick up work within a week or two at any time of the year; in winter, the jobs go to the more experienced workers, but there's plenty of work for everyone. Inexperienced hands looking for volunteer work will also hook up in a couple of weeks. Floyd thinks that about 95% of those coming for work get it if they're serious.

What to Bring Bring as little as possible: Everything you'll need will be provided, except a toothbrush, toothpaste and a hairbrush. You will, of course, need travel documents and, if necessary, visas for your destination country.

Women Crew Members The crew world is a tight one, and both Floyd's and Smallwood's say that they haven't heard in many years of a woman being the subject of unwanted advances from boat owners. But, as with all jobs, it's a possibility. Use your intuition at the first interview to see what services will be required, and if that includes the 'personal' kind. Interview carefully and ask around about the owner before taking on an assignment. Once onboard, your options for recourse are limited.

HITCHHIKING

Hitchhiking in the USA is dangerous, and it's therefore less common than in other countries. Neither Lonely Planet, its attorneys, owners, management, editors, employees, successors or authors recommend hitchhiking. Travelers who decide to hitch should understand that they are taking a small but potentially serious risk.

That said, if you do choose to hitchhike, you will be safer in pairs. Always let someone know where you're planning to go. Officially, hitchhiking is illegal only on interstate highways. But it *is* frowned upon by law enforcement; expect to be hassled if they see you. And as on-ramp signs warn, pedestrians are not allowed on major highways. It helps to look clean cut and to carry a neatly printed sign indicating your destination. Lots of baggage, two or more men, or groups of three of any sex will slow you down substantially. Women should think very carefully about hitchhiking, especially if alone, but even in groups.

Getting Around

TO/FROM THE AIRPORTS
Miami International Airport

MIA is about 6 miles west of downtown, sandwiched between the Airport Expressway (Hwy 112) and the Dolphin Expressway (Hwy 836). If you're traveling with at least one other person, consider renting a car with free drop-off in Miami Beach for one day. It would cost about the same as a taxi or shuttle, and you'd have the added benefit of a car to get your bearings for the first day. See Car Rental, later in this chapter, for more information.

Public transportation from MIA to downtown and Miami Beach is tricky at best, a pain in the rear at worst. Tri-Rail service connects to downtown, where other connections are tricky at best, a pain in the rear at worst. Metrobus service to downtown Miami's Government Center station works in theory but not in practice; connections are tricky at best, a pain in the rear at

From the Airport by Car

All the major car rental companies, as well as some little ones, have offices at MIA (see Car Rental). There's always a traffic jam in front of the terminals.

From MIA to **downtown**, take Hwy 112 (Airport Expressway; small toll) east and I-95 south and follow the signs.

To **South Beach**, take 37th Ave south to Hwy 836 east (Dolphin Expressway) to I-395 east, which leads to the MacArthur Causeway.

For **northern Miami Beach**, take Hwy 112 east directly to I-195 east, the Julia Tuttle Causeway.

For **Coconut Grove**, take Hwy 112 east to I-95 south to US Hwy 1 south and follow the signs.

For **Coral Gables**, head south on NW 42nd Ave, which is also Le Jeune Rd.

worst. You get the idea. Unless you're renting a car, your best bet is a taxi or the SuperShuttle (see below).

Bus Metrobus (☎ 305-770-3131, Ⓦ www.co.miami-dade.fl.us/transit/) departs from the lower level of Concourse E ostensibly every 40 minutes between 5:30am and 9pm weekdays, 6:30am to 7:30pm weekends. Take the No 7 to Government Center (where you can catch a connecting bus to your final destination). The ride takes 35 minutes and costs $1.25. The J bus leaves from the same place, ostensibly every 30 minutes, and takes a circuitous route that ends up in Miami Beach more than an hour later. Ostensibly, there is service from 4:30am to 11:30pm daily, but after 7pm there's only one bus per hour.

Greyhound from MIA is also a pain. I wouldn't bother under any circumstances, but if you want to, here it is: Take a J or No 37 bus (every 30 minutes) or No 42 (one an hour) to the stop at NW 42nd Ave and NW 27th St. Then, walk one block east to the Greyhound Airport Station (☎ 305-871-1810), 4111 NW 27th St, or a take a taxi for about $5. It's 20 minutes from the airport to the downtown station (☎ 305-379-7403), 100 NW 6th St, and the buses ($5) run about 15 times a day between 7am and 9:45pm. That SuperShuttle is looking better still, eh? For more on Greyhound, see the Getting There & Away chapter.

Shuttle At MIA, blue SuperShuttle (☎ 305-871-2000, 800-874-8885, Ⓦ www.supershuttle.com) vans constantly prowl the lower level outside the baggage claim area. Look for the folks wearing yellow shirts or just wave one of the shuttles down. SuperShuttle operates 24 hours daily and takes credit cards. The only drawback is that it makes a lot of stops, letting people off at various hotels along the way. Your hotel could be the closest to the airport or the farthest.

Costs vary depending on destination. From MIA to South Beach, it'll be about $13 to $16 per person; to downtown, it'll be about $11 per person. It's customary to tip the driver a few dollars. If you're going to a residence, the second person in your party is about half the price. For the return trip, call 24 hours in advance of your flight to schedule a pick-up.

If you're traveling solo, it's always cheaper to take a SuperShuttle than a taxi. If you are traveling with one other person, it may be cheaper to take a taxi than a shuttle depending on where you go. Threesomes should definitely always take a taxi.

Taxi There are flat rates between MIA and five zones around the city. It costs $18 to go from MIA to the Port of Miami; $24 to anywhere between Government Cut and 63rd St (zone 4, which includes all of South Beach and takes about 20 to 25 minutes); $29 to anywhere between 63rd St and 87th Terrace (zone 3); $31 to Key Biscayne (zone 5); $34 to anywhere between 87th Terrace and Haulover Beach (zone 2); and $41 to anywhere from Haulover Beach to the Broward County line (zone 1). These rates are per carload, not per person, and *include* tolls and a $1 airport surcharge. Taxis swarm the lower level roadway. It's about $18 from MIA to downtown, $11 to $16 to Coral Gables, depending on the exact location.

Fort Lauderdale-Hollywood International Airport

Many deeply discounted tickets from Europe and from other parts of the USA land in Fort Lauderdale's shimmering new terminal, about 5 miles (10 minutes) south of Fort Lauderdale proper. Even though it's about 30 miles north of Miami, it's still a great choice. Fewer crowds, a slower pace and newer, cleaner and easier-to-use terminals speed you through. You can apply the money you save on airfare to renting a car, which also wipes out the cost (in time and effort) of getting to and from Fort Lauderdale.

Bus & Train Take the Tri-Rail (☎ 800-874-7245, W www.tri-rail.com) shuttle bus or the Broward County Transit (☎ 954-357-8400, W www.broward.org/bct) bus from the airport to the Fort Lauderdale Airport Tri-Rail station (both are free). Then take Tri-Rail to the Metrorail Transfer Station ($3). It's best to call ahead and check the timetable, as service isn't overly convenient at certain times. Get a free transfer at the Transfer Station, and head upstairs for the Metrorail to Government Center, where you can catch a bus to your destination. To Miami Beach, this journey will take about two to 2½ hours. Sounds like another pain in the rear.

Shuttle SuperShuttle (☎ 800-874-8885, W www.supershuttle.com) can take you to, but not from, Fort Lauderdale Airport. From South Beach hotels, the cost is $22 per person.

Car There are almost as many car rental companies here as there are at MIA – see Car Rental, later. Driving is really straightforward: Take I-95 south (there's an airport on-ramp) to I-195 east for northern Miami Beach, I-395 for South Beach, and straight through to downtown Miami. It'll take about 45 minutes.

Taxi Yellow Cab Company (☎ 954-565-5400/8400) is the official airport taxi in Fort Lauderdale. Their cabs are metered and charge $2.75 flagfall for the first mile, and $2 for each additional mile. A taxi ride from Fort Lauderdale Airport to South Beach would run about $60.

BUS
The Wave

For a mere 25¢ per ride, this South Beach electric shuttle bus (☎ 305-843-9283) runs north-south along Washington Ave from 17th St to South Pointe Dr and east-west along 17th St. A second route runs from the Holocaust Memorial over to Collins Ave and up to the Bass Museum of Art. Pick up a copy of the exact route from the Miami Beach Chamber of Commerce

(☎ 305-672-1270, Ⓦ www.miamibeach chamber.com; Map 3), 1920 Meridian Ave.

Along both routes, there are about 30 well-marked stops, many of which are sheltered. Six vehicles run Monday to Wednesday from 8am to 2am, Thursday to Saturday from 8am to 4am, Sunday and holidays from 10am to 2am. The buses are non-polluting, accessible for the disabled, decorated with public art and air-conditioned. It's the best and easiest way to get around South Beach.

Metrobus

First things first, and you can't say we didn't warn you: You'll spend more time *waiting for* a bus than *riding on* a bus and you'll probably describe the experience as 'grueling.' Seriously consider if that's how you want to spend your holiday. Having said that, Metro-Dade Transit's buses cover a healthy amount of the city. They're not the fastest things on wheels, and in most cases they're nowhere near as convenient as a car, but they'll get you there. Each bus route has a different schedule and routes generally run from about 5:30am to about 11pm.

For specific route information or travel planning assistance, call ☎ 305-770-3131 (Ⓦ www.co.miami-dade.fl.us/transit/) from 6am to 10pm Monday to Friday, 9am to 5pm weekends.

To order an advance transit 'map by mail,' call ☎ 305-654-6586 8:30am to 4:30pm Monday to Friday. See the Disabled Travelers section of the Facts for the Visitor chapter for Special Transportation Service (STS) information.

Transit Booths Once in Miami, you will find maps, scheduling information and tokens at transit booths located at Government Center, on NW 1st St, between NW 1st and NW 2nd Aves; at the corner of E Flagler At and E 1st Ave; and at the Omni Metromover terminal, near Biscayne Blvd just south of NE 15th St. The Omni and Government Center terminals are main junction points for buses downtown.

Fares & Passes Pay as you board. Bus fare is $1.25; meters accept dollar bills, coins, or tokens, which are available from transit booths. Transfers from bus-to-Metrorail or bus-to-bus cost 25¢; ask your driver for the transfer slip. A monthly pass is $60, and a monthly rail parking permit bought with the pass is an additional $2.

Routes Some major routes include the following:

bus	between
C, K	Miami Beach and Government Center
S, M	Miami Beach and Omni
S	Omni to South Beach, north on Alton Rd then east on 17th St and north on Collins Ave past the Bass Museum and up to Aventura Mall
8	downtown transit booth and Calle Ocho
17, 6, 22	Government Center and Vizcaya Museum & Gardens/Museum of Science and Space Transit Planetarium and Coconut Grove
B	downtown transit booth and Seaquarium on Key Biscayne
24	downtown transit booth and Miracle Mile in Coral Gables

TRAIN
Metromover

Equal parts bus, monorail and train, the Metromover (Ⓦ www.co.miami-dade.fl.us/transit/; 25¢) offers visitors a great perspective and cheap orientation tour of downtown. For local taxpayers, it's a boondoggle; it loses money hand over fist every single day it starts its proverbial engine. Consider riding it at night, when the city is lit with neon. Besides, the city needs every quarter it can get.

The one- and two-car, rubber-wheeled, computer-controlled vehicles operate on three lines on two 'loops' of elevated track. The Outer Loop's two lines (operational from 6am to 10:30pm), the Omni and Brickell Loops, run between the School Board station, west of the Omni, and the Brickell Financial Center station, at SE 14th St and Brickell Ave. The Omni Loop

GETTING AROUND

starts at School Board station, goes through the Omni, then around downtown and Government Center before heading back north. The Brickell Loop starts at the Brickell Financial Center station, then goes north to Government Center and around downtown, then back south. The Inner Loop (5am to midnight) begins and ends at Government Center and runs around downtown.

You can change between the Metrorail and Metromover at Government Center.

Metrorail

This 21-mile-long heavy rail system (W www.co.miami-dade.fl.us/transit/) has one elevated line running from Hialeah through downtown Miami and south to Kendall/Dadeland. Trains run every 5 to 15 minutes from 6am to midnight. The Metrorail connects with Tri-Rail (at the Tri-Rail/Metrorail Transfer Station, at NW 79th St and E 11th Ave in Hialeah) and the Metromover and Metrobus (at Government Center). The fare is $1.25, or $1 with a Metromover transfer. Transfers to either Tri-Rail or Metromover are free; transfers from Metrorail to Metrobus are 25¢. It costs $2 to park at most stations.

Tri-Rail

Clean and cheap, Tri-Rail (☎ 800-874-7245, W www.tri-rail.com) double-decker commuter trains run along 71 miles of track between Dade, Broward and Palm Beach counties. For longer trips, to Palm Beach, for instance, Tri-Rail is painfully inefficient (it takes four times longer to take Tri-Rail to Palm Beach than to drive). Fares are calculated on a zone basis, and the route spans six zones. The shortest distance traveled will cost $3.50 roundtrip, and the most you'll ever pay is for the ride between MIA and West Palm Beach ($9.25 roundtrip).

Transfers from Tri-Rail to Metrorail are free. From Metrobus, you buy a 25¢ Tri-Rail transfer from the driver, then trade the transfer at the Tri-Rail ticket booth for a $1.50 discount on your Tri-Rail ticket.

The main Tri-Rail station, at 2567 E 11th Ave at NW 79th St in Hialeah, doubles as

Tri-Rail Cops

At first, Europeans using Tri-Rail might be pleasantly reminded of home. But there's one key difference. Tri-Rail's pseudo honor-system isn't easy to beat. Yes, you buy your ticket from the Swiss-made ticket machines (they're the same machines used in U-Bahn throughout Germany) as you wait for the trains. But, while in Europe, inspectors come around at random times to keep everyone honest, on Tri-Rail, an inspector comes around on each train and asks for your ticket. They're armed, and underneath their uniforms lie hearts of stone. Don't bother trying to reason with them. If you don't have a ticket, or if you've pushed the discount-ticket button instead of the regular-fare button, you'll be hit with a $50 fine. Don't mess with Tri-Rail.

the Tri-Rail/Metrorail Transfer station, and there are stations at the Miami and Fort Lauderdale-Hollywood International Airports. For a complete listing of stations, go to the Tri-Rail Web site.

CAR & MOTORCYCLE

The urban sprawl of metro Miami means that most visitors will end up driving. Unless you'll be in South Beach, downtown or Coconut Grove exclusively, get a car. On the interstates, Miami drivers weave in and out of lanes hideously often, and they tend to drive fast. It's a bit unnerving at first, so be prepared for it. Miami drivers are also generally civil. Expect serious rush hour traffic from 7am to 9am and 4pm to 6pm weekdays.

Fuel

Unless you're coming here from Saudi Arabia or Indonesia, US gasoline prices are a gift from heaven: In early 2002 they averaged $1.25 a gallon (a bit less than 4L) in Miami. Always use self-service islands, as full-service pumps cost at least 25¢ more per gallon.

Detail of a mural in Miami's Little Haiti neighborhood

Sculpture at the Bass Museum of Art

Sculpture at the Holocaust Memorial

Relaxing by the largest hotel pool in the continental US, at the posh Biltmore Hotel, Coral Gables

Ancient Spanish monastery, constructed in 1141

Vizcaya Museum & Gardens, Coconut Grove

Rules & Regulations

In the US you drive on the right side of the road and pass on the left. You can make a right turn on a red light, unless otherwise marked, after coming to a complete stop. All passengers must wear seat belts; the fine for not wearing one can be as high as $150. All children under three must be in a child safety seat (rental car companies have them for about $5 a day).

City speed limits are 15mph to 30mph; it's 55mph to 70mph on interstates and turnpikes. Be especially careful in school zones, when the limit is 15mph when the lights are flashing. On causeways, the speed limit is 45mph. Pay attention to these limits, as speeding tickets are outrageously expensive.

Major Arteries

Miami Beach Miami Beach is connected to the mainland by four causeways built over Biscayne Bay. They are, from south to north: the MacArthur (also the extension of US Hwy 41 and Hwy A1A), Venetian (50¢ toll), Julia Tuttle and John F Kennedy.

North-South The most important highway is I-95, which runs north-south until it ends at US Hwy 1 south of downtown. US Hwy 1, which runs from Key West all the way north to Maine, hugs the coastline. It's called Dixie Hwy south of downtown and Biscayne Blvd north of downtown.

The Palmetto Expressway (Hwy 826) makes something of a loop around the city and spurs off below SW 40th St to the Don Shula Expressway (Hwy 874; a toll road). Florida's Turnpike Extension makes the most western outer loop around the city.

Hwy A1A goes by the name of Collins Ave in Miami Beach.

East-West Besides the causeways to Miami Beach, the major east-west roads are Calle Ocho (also called SW 8th St); Hwy 112 (also called Airport Expressway); and Hwy 836 (also called Dolphin Expressway), which slices through downtown and connects with I-395 and the MacArthur Causeway, and which runs west to the Palmetto Expressway and Florida's Turnpike Extension.

Accidents Do Happen

Accidents do happen – especially in such auto-dependent countries as the USA. It's important that you know the appropriate protocol when involved in a 'fender-bender.'

- DON'T DRIVE AWAY! Remain at the scene; otherwise you may spend some time in the local jail.
- Call the police immediately, and give the operator as much specific information as possible (your location, if there are any injuries involved etc). The emergency phone number is ☎ 911.
- Get the other driver's details, including name, address, driver's license number, license plate number and insurance information. Be prepared to provide any documentation you have, such as your passport, international driver's license and insurance documents.
- Tell your story to the police carefully. Refrain from answering any questions until you feel comfortable doing so (with a lawyer present, if need be), and ask for a translator if you need one. That's your right under the law. The only insurance information you need to reveal is the name of your insurance carrier and your policy number.
- Always comply with an alcohol Breathalyzer test. If you opt not to take the test, you'll almost certainly find yourself with an automatic suspension of your driving privileges.
- If you're driving a rental car, call the rental company promptly.

Parking

Except in Coral Gables, South Beach and downtown Miami, parking is pretty straightforward. Regulations are well-signed and meters are plentiful.

Parking downtown can be a nightmare, or at least expensive. Park in the Cultural Center Garage at SW 2nd Ave, just west of the Miami-Dade Cultural Center. If you

A Road by Any Other Name...

As if the traffic volume and sheer sprawl wasn't enough, many streets have multiple names. Calle Ocho has five (count 'em!) names. At various points along the way it's officially called SW 8th St, US Hwy 41, the Tamiami Trail, Calle Ocho and Olga Guillot Way. But Calle Ocho isn't so bad; at least everyone in Miami knows it. It's not that easy with other streets....

You've got the system figured out right? Avenues run north-south and streets run east-west. City addresses (except in Miami Beach) are identified by quadrants, with the axis being Miami Ave and Flagler St.

But Hialeah Gardens and Sweetwater and other communities have their own street names. You can be traveling merrily along your way, trying diligently to find something really worth going out of your way for, and all of a sudden you think you're on the wrong road. Unless you have a really poor sense of direction, it's not you. It's the crazy multi-named signs.

Look carefully at the signs while trying to dodge the traffic and read the map. Better yet, make sure you have a capable copilot or pull over. Driving in Coral Gables has the added problem of ground-level street signs, which are impossible to see at night.

visit the Historical Museum of Southern Florida, Miami Art Museum or main public library in that complex, they'll validate your parking ticket so that parking costs $2.40. Otherwise, you're at the mercy of private lots or full-price public ones.

On Miami Beach there is metered street parking along Washington Ave, Collins Ave and Ocean Drive – and, frankly, on most every other street (except Lincoln Road and residential areas). Meters are enforced from 9am to midnight daily.

There are many municipal parking lots; look for giant blue 'P' signs. Big garages are located at Collins Ave at 7th St; Collins Ave at 14th St; Washington Ave at 12th St; Washington Ave at 16th St; and 17th St across from the Jackie Gleason Theater of the Performing Arts. If you park illegally or if the meter runs out, parking fines are about $20, but a tow could cost $75. Call Beach Towing (☎ 305-534-2128) if you think your car has been towed. If you've kept your rental car agreement in your wallet rather than in the glove compartment, you can tell them your license plate number, though, giving them the specific location might be adequate for identification purposes.

If Miami Beach is tough on enforcement, Coral Gables is positively Orwellian: Metered parking is everywhere that valet

parking is not. If you're even a second late, you'll be hit with varyingly outrageous fines. Depending on how egregious the offense, they may slap two tickets on top of one another.

Meter Cards These magnetic cards are a parker's best friend. Instead of collecting quarters everywhere you go and running back to feed the meter every two to 10 hours, purchase a card from the Miami Beach City Hall (1700 Convention Center Dr, 1st floor; Map 3) or the Historic Old City Hall (1130 Washington Ave, Suite 100; Map 3), both open weekdays; the Chamber of Commerce (1920 Meridian Ave; Map 3), which is open 9am to 5pm Monday to Friday, and 10am to 4pm Saturday and Sunday; or any Publix grocery store (there's one on Dade Blvd at 19th St). Denominations come in $10, $20 and $25. When you're calculating which denomination card is right for you, remember that meters cost $1 per hour.

Coral Gables has a similar cash-key system, but the denominations begin at $25, so it won't be worth it for most people. For details, call ☎ 305-460-5540.

Car Rental

All the big operators, and a host of smaller or local ones, have bases in the Miami area.

If you only want to rent a car for a day or two and are staying in South Beach, ask the agency if they have a location there. Many of the following companies have several locations around town. Advance reservations are always a good idea.

Car rental companies in the Miami/Fort Lauderdale area include the following:

Alamo
☎ 800-327-9633, **W** www.alamo.com
Avis
☎ 800-831-2847, **W** www.avis.com
Budget
☎ 800-527-0700, **W** www.budget.com
Continental
☎ 305-871-4663, **W** www.continentalcar.com
Dollar
☎ 800-800-4000, **W** www.dollar.com
Enterprise
☎ 800-325-8007, **W** www.enterprise.com
Hertz
☎ 800-654-3131, **W** www.hertz.com
Royal
☎ 305-871-6262, **W** www.royalrac.com
Sam's
☎ 877-937-7267, **W** www.samsrentacar.com
Sears
☎ 800-527-0770, **W** www.sears-carrental.com
Thrifty
☎ 800-367-2277, **W** www.thrifty.com

After a spate of terrible carjackings in the early 1990s, car rental agencies removed glaring identification from their cars. But many still have small bar codes on the side or rear windows. There's no way around this, though you might consider renting a car phone if you don't have a cell phone.

Rates Rental rates in Florida tend to be lower than in other places in the country. Rates do fluctuate like the stock market, though; phone around to compare prices. Booking ahead usually ensures the best rates. Expect a typical economy car in Miami to cost $35 a day or $175 a week. With taxes and a host of surcharges the final bill will generally be another $30 to $40 a week higher. Then there's insurance....

Insurance In Florida, liability insurance is not included in rental costs. Some credit cards cover a loss/damage waiver, or LDW, (sometimes also called a collision/damage waiver, or CDW), which means you don't pay if you damage the car. But liability insurance means you don't pay if you hit someone and they sue you. The liability insurance on your car at home may extend to rental cars, but *absolutely* certain before driving on the roads in the litigious USA. Also, if you opt out of the LDW, be *really* certain that your credit card really will cover you for it.

Age, Credit & Mileage Most car rental companies include unlimited mileage at no extra cost. Be sure to check this point so there are no unhappy surprises. Most operators require that you be at least 25 years of age and have a major credit card in your own name. Some will let you get away with the age thing by forking over outrageous surcharges, but renting without a credit card – if you can even accomplish it – will require a large cash deposit, and you'll have to work things out well in advance with the company.

Fuel Costs When you rent the car, you'll probably be offered an opportunity to buy the full tank at a slightly discounted rate. Don't do it. The companies make good profits on the gas that renters leave in the tank. Just remember to return the car with a full tank of fuel. If you forget and they have to fill it, they'll charge you up to $3.99 a gallon.

Motorcycle & RV Rental
American Road Collections (☎ 305-871-1040, 888-736-8433, 1416 18th St; Map 3) rents Harley Davidson motorcycles for $109 to $189 a day, depending on the model and day of the week (weekends are more expensive). Renters must be over 21, have a valid motorcycle license and a major credit card. CDW and liability insurance are each $12 per day. As with car rental, calling ahead is a good idea.

Cruise America (☎ 305-828-1198, 800-327-7799, **W** www.cruiseamerica.com), with several area locations, rents motorcycles and recreational vehicles.

The Motorcycle Training Institute (☎ 877-308-7246, W www.mtii.com) offers complete motorcycle courses that can help get you licensed. The 20-hour courses start at $225, including bike rental.

TAXI

Taxis in Miami have flat and metered rates. The metered fare is $3.25 for the first mile, $2 each additional mile. Regular routes like the South Beach Convention Center to Coconut Grove cost $16. You will not have to pay extra for luggage or extra people in the cab.

Taxis here are in generally bad shape, but they'll get you where you're going. In an effort to provide better service and change the reputation of Miami cabbies, a consortium of drivers has banded together; call their 'Dispatch Service' (☎ 305-888-4444) for a ride.

If you have a bad experience, get the driver's chauffeur license number, name and license plate number and contact the Taxi Complaints Line (☎ 305-375-2460/3677). These folks really do chase down offensive drivers.

Outside of MIA and the Port of Miami where taxis buzz around like bees at a hive, you will use a phone to hail a cab. If the dispatch service above is busy, try these:

Central	☎ 305-532-5555
Diamond	☎ 305-545-5555
Metro	☎ 305-888-8888
Sunshine	☎ 305-445-3333
Yellow	☎ 305-444-4444

BICYCLE

Miami is as flat as a pancake and as smooth as a baby's behind, so biking around the Beach makes a lot of sense. In fact, it makes so much sense that people who don't have bikes will try to steal yours. Use a sturdy U-type bike lock. Mere chains and padlocks do not deter people in Miami Beach, where bike theft rates rival those of Amsterdam.

Bicycles are not allowed on buses, Metrorail or Tri-Rail, but you can bike across the causeways. There are several places in South Beach and on Key Biscayne to rent bicycles; see the Activites section of the Things to See & Do chapter for bike rentals.

ORGANIZED TOURS

More than in most American cities perhaps, Miami's outer layer can be tough to penetrate. Is all that beauty really just skin deep? Not at all and that's where a good historical walking tour with Dr George (see below) or the Miami Design Preservation League comes in particularly handy (see the South Beach section of the Things to See & Do chapter for MDPL tours of the Deco District). It's also worth getting out onto the water, more for the fun of it than for the commentary.

For a really great perspective on many different aspects of the city, call Dr Paul George (☎ 305-237-3723, 305-375-1492), a history professor at Miami-Dade Community College and former head of the Florida Historical Society. He really makes history jump off the page (or in his case, the streets). In conjunction with the Historical Museum of Southern Florida, he leads about 70 different very popular tours of Dade County between September and late June. Tours are conducted by bus and boat (three hours, $37), by foot and bike (two hours, $15) and by public transportation. Tours usually depart at 10am on Saturday and 11am on Sunday; they're always from different locations. Dr George also offers private tours by appointment. A two-hour tour starts at about $100.

For harbor tours, head downtown to Bayside Marketplace (401 Biscayne Blvd; Map 6) and hop aboard the *Island Queen*, *Island Lady* or *Pink Lady* (☎ 305-379-5119). Tickets cost $14/7 adult/child; boats depart hourly from 11am to 7pm. Tours include commentary about the famous folks who live on Star Island and a bit of history, but generally they're alluring because of the skyline views of the dramatic nighttime neon. Only problem with the dusk trip, though, is that you can't see the stars' houses very well. Trade-offs abound.

The M/T *Celebration* (☎ 305-445-8456) runs narrated, hour-long sightseeing tours through Biscayne Bay, the Port of Miami and the Venetian Islands. The tours leave at 1pm, 3pm and 5pm daily, and tickets cost $12 for adults, $10 for seniors and $6 for children.

The well-established Miami Nice Excursions (☎ 305-949-9180) has a wide range of guided excursions to the Everglades, the Keys, Orlando, Fort Lauderdale, the Bahamas and other areas.

Things to See & Do

Miami is a huge, sprawling metropolis. While many attractions and activities are in obviously defined neighborhoods, others are spread out in all directions of Greater Miami. You'll find these latter ones toward the end of the chapter.

Highlights

- Take a walking tour of South Beach's delightful and colorful Deco District.

- Visit the Holocaust Memorial in South Beach for a sobering but stunning reminder of the WWII atrocities.

- Take a refreshing dip in Coral Gables' extraordinarily beautiful Venetian Pool.

- Go hear the New World Symphony (see the Entertainment chapter), an outstanding group of young musicians directed by Michael Tilson Thomas.

- Take a harbor boat tour (see the Organized Tours section in the Getting Around chapter) or hop aboard the Metromover at dusk to fully appreciate downtown Miami's neon buildings at night.

- View the excellent rotating exhibitions at the Museum of Contemporary Art in northern Miami.

- Head to Little Havana to watch old men rolling cigars in little 'factories' or playing dominoes in Domino Park on Calle Ocho.

- Visit downtown's Rubell Family Art Collection for impressive and pioneering contemporary art.

- Drink in the splendor of Coconut Grove's opulent Italian Renaissance–style villa, the Vizcaya Museum & Gardens.

- Enjoy a panoply of outdoor pursuits at Key Biscayne's Bill Baggs Cape Florida State Recreation Area.

- Get all geeked out at the Miami Museum of Science & Space Transit Planetarium.

SOUTH BEACH (MAPS 3 & 4)

Most people come to Miami for beaches, clubs and bars, but there are other compelling attractions within the city of Miami Beach, and specifically the subset of South Beach. Happily, it's a compact area, so a couple of afternoons or mornings of sightseeing will be well spent. From tattoo parlors to tony salons, and from laid-back Larry to high-energy Harry, the Beach has all extremes covered. Yes, the American Riviera is gay, but it also has a heavily Jewish culture and a decidedly Latin flair. In fact, there's even a **Cuban-Jewish Congregation** (☎ *305-534-7213, 1700 Michigan Ave*). From artists to businesspeople to vacationers, everyone has a place in South Beach...except those who call is SoBe (they're instantly labeled tourists). The easiest way to fit in: Attach a cell phone to your ear and start sauntering.

Art Deco District

South Beach's heart is its Art Deco Historic District, one of the largest in the USA on the National Register of Historic Places. In fact, the area's rejuvenation and rebirth as a major tourist destination results directly from its protection as a historic place in 1979. The National Register designation prevents developers from wholeheartedly razing significant portions of what was, in the 1980s, a crime-ridden collection of crumbling eyesores populated primarily by drug-crazed lunatics, Cuban refugees and elderly residents. It's a far cry from that now. Today, hotel and apartment façades are decidedly colorful, with pastel architectural details. Depending on your perspective, the bright buildings catapult you back to the Roaring Twenties or on a wacky tour of American kitsch.

The National Register listing was fought for and pushed through by the Miami Design Preservation League (see Tours, later), founded by Barbara Baer Capitman in 1976. She was appalled upon hearing plans by the city of Miami to bulldoze several historic buildings in what is now the Omni Center. And she acted, forcefully.

MDPL co-founder Leonard Horowitz played a pivotal role in putting South Beach back on the map, painting the then-drab deco buildings in shocking pink, lavender and turquoise. When his restoration of Friedman's Pharmacy made the cover of *Progressive Architecture* in 1982, the would-be Hollywood producers of *Miami Vice* saw something they liked, and the rest is history.

The Deco District is bounded by Dade Blvd to the north, 6th St to the south, the Atlantic Ocean to the east and Lenox Ave to the west. One of the best things about these 1000 or so buildings is their scale: Most are no taller than the palm trees. And, while the architecture is by no means uniform – you'll see streamline moderne, Mediterranean revival and tropical art deco designs – it's all quite harmonious. The 1-sq-mile district feels like a small village.

With more than 400 registered historic landmarks, it's hard *not* to have an interesting walk through the District. And if you know a bit about the architecture, you can follow the Beach boom phases: beginning in the 1930s when 5th St through mid-Beach was developed; moving from the late '30s to early '40s up toward 27th St; and heading north of that into the '50s, when resorts and luxury hotels were interspersed with condominiums (see the 'Art Deco Architecture' special section for a deeper discussion).

Tours The **Miami Design Preservation League** *(MDPL; ☎ 305-672-2014, ⓦ www .mdpl.org)* is still ferociously active protecting and restoring South Beach. They offer first-rate tours that depart from the **Art Deco Welcome Center** *(☎ 305-531-3484, 1001 Ocean Dr; tours $15; building open 9am-6pm daily, tours 10:30am Sat & 6:30pm Thur).* The 1950s building has a space for deco-related exhibits and a gift shop with memorabilia, books and gifts. Volunteer guides of varying strengths illuminate the importance of and reasoning behind certain architecture details on many distinct buildings. Reservations are not required for the

1½-hour walking tours, but you should show up 15 minutes prior to the tour. Tours get crowded during February and March, but otherwise groups usually coalesce with about 15 to 20 people. The morning tour is preferable, since it's difficult to make out building details at night.

For real architecture aficionados, there's also a North Beach tour ($15) that begins at 74th St at the Surf Hotel; it meets at the hotel on the first Saturday of every month.

On the third Sunday of each month, the MDPL also has a two-hour bicycle tour that leaves at 10:30am from the Welcome Center, at 1001 Ocean Dr. It costs $30 including bicycle rental, $15 if you pedal your own wheels.

Ocean Drive

Strolling along Ocean Drive from north to south is a safari through the trendy. On the beach, low-flying planes trail advertisements for nightclubs, restaurants and performances. As the day progresses the clicking, flashing and whirring of high-fashion photo shoots is replaced by rollerbladers and volleyball players. Across from the beach, hotels and sidewalk cafés threaten to spill into the street. Models and wannabes, actors and wannabes, and bedazzled tourists swarm the sidewalks. Vehicular traffic appears to be limited to vintage roadsters, '63 Mustangs and grandiose Harley Davidsons.

The fashion-impaired needn't worry; despite Ocean Drive's undeniable chic, it's definitely a come-as-you-are affair. The minimum requirements are cut-off jeans, a T-shirt and a pair of in-line skates (optional). The first thing to do is get a drink. Dozens of cafés and bistros line the Drive. Grab a sidewalk table if one's available. As the masses strut, sashay, 'blade and groove their way past, order a *café con leche,* keep an eye peeled for famous models and try to look a tad pretentious and self-congratulatory to fit in. It's great fun.

Get your bearings while checking out one of the Beach's finest deco treasures by heading to the roof of **The Park Central** *(640 Ocean Dr).* The seven-story beachfront hotel has a sundeck, and no one seems to mind when visitors just walk past reception, take the elevator to the top floor and gaze out over the city. Visit around 4pm, when luxury cruise ships chug through the channel on their way to the Caribbean.

The hotel's Vampire Lestat room, described in Anne Rice's *Tale of the Body Thief* as the one that the vampire stayed in, is also an attraction of sorts. If you ask nicely at the front desk, and they're not busy and the room's vacant (unlikely in high season), they'll show it to you. You can also stay here; see the Places to Stay chapter.

Casa Casaurina The former residence of slain fashion designer Gianni Versace was built in 1930 with Florida keystone (coral from the Keys), and was originally known as the Amsterdam Palace *(1114 Ocean Dr; no entry)*. The Mediterranean revival house, a three-story Spanish-style palace with exposed timbers, was modeled after the Governor's House in Santo Domingo.

Gianni Versace

'I can spend three million dollars in two hours,' Gianni Versace once declared. Anyone with a couple billion bucks kicking around and residences in New York, Italy and Miami Beach might be able to justify such a shopping spree, but such a statement was typically Versace.

By the time he was 25, Gianni Versace (1947–1997), born to a salesman and a seamstress in Reggio di Calabria, Italy, had moved to Milan to become a designer. His early collaboration with photographer Richard Avedon in 1975 marked Versace's march toward international fame. As his career skyrocketed, Versace designed gowns, dresses and costumes for a gaggle of celebrities including Elton John, the late Princess Diana of Wales, Elizabeth Hurley and scads of others.

Versace's *Miami Vice* designs spawned a look in the 1980s. Celebrities fell over themselves buying his playful, bawdy, revealing and occasionally demure offerings. By the 1990s, Versace had opened shops and studios around the globe, and was Italy's leading ready-to-wear designer. Meanwhile, his more elaborate designs were catching ever more attention in Hollywood, Cannes, London, Paris and Milan. His eye-catching creations oozed – and sometimes shouted at the top of their metaphorical lungs – sex. Everyone referred to the breast-pushing costume created for model/actress Elizabeth Hurley as 'that dress.' While Versace would tone things down for Diana and even Courtney Love, he usually flaunted his playful and sexy side to the hilt.

On July 15, 1997, Versace was shot and killed at the gate of his Miami Beach mansion, Casa Casaurina. Police named a suspect within hours: Andrew Cunanan, a 27-year-old, was already wanted by the FBI in connection with a cross-country murder spree. Earlier, Cunanan was alleged to have killed two Minneapolis men, a Chicago millionaire and a cemetery worker from New Jersey. Police found Cunanan's abandoned red pickup truck in a parking garage near the murder scene and began the most widely publicized manhunt since the OJ Simpson car chase. Miami Beach and the fashion world found themselves at the epicenter of an international media frenzy. Millions watched live on television as, nine days after the murder, police closed in on the houseboat where Cunanan had barricaded himself and already committed suicide. There was wild speculation as to whether Cunanan and Versace had had a relationship. Cunanan, described alternately as a 'prostitute' and a 'kept man,' had apparently boasted to friends that he knew the designer.

Versace was at the height of his career when he was killed. He was universally mourned by the fashion world as a lost star, but he was personally mourned by many in South Beach who knew him as a friend. Since his death, the company has been under his family's control. The House of Versace empire, which the designer ran with his brother Santo and sister Donatella, is still one of the world's largest, with an estimated income of $2 billion a year.

When Versace purchased the property in the early 1980s, poor artists had been living there, and the house was a mess. During Versace's tenure, he renovated the large mahogany front doors, an interior atrium that wraps around a courtyard, and a small copper rooftop observatory; plus, he hired artists to cover every inch of the place with elaborate tile. You'll note that there are actually two buildings on the lot. Since a city ordinance prohibits single-family residences on Ocean Drive, Versace converted the front gate house into a butler's apartment.

The house has always attracted fashion plates, but it's now a morbid destination for ghoulish tourists, who pose for photographs on the very steps where the designer was gunned down in 1997 (see the boxed text). As Versace was unlocking the gate, his murderer shot two bullets through the back of his head.

Versace's villa recently sold for a reputed $35 to $50 million and is in the process of being converted into a *very* high-end place to stay.

The Boardwalk & The Promenade For those who want one last glimpse of the ocean without getting salty prior to their departure, a boardwalk runs from 21st to 46th St.

The Promenade, though, is a wavy concrete ribbon between the beach and Ocean Drive, from 5th to 15th St. If you've ever flipped through a fashion magazine, you've seen it: It's *the* Beach location for photo shoots. If you show up here before 9am, you can watch the glamorous, motor-driven events unfold 1/250 of a second at a time. Other times throughout the day and late into the night, in-line skaters, bicyclists, roller skaters, skateboarders, dog walkers, yahoos, locals and tourists mill about and occasionally bump into each other. Around 8th St, there's a nice shady stretch with a kids' play area.

Collins Avenue
This busy road runs parallel to Ocean Drive and is thick with designer shops between 6th and 9th Sts. Collins has lots of good

hotels that aren't as noisy as those on Ocean Drive.

Washington Avenue
Washington Ave is the Beach's engine room, its main commercial artery. Be as trendy as you like elsewhere, but when you need a quart of milk or a lug wrench, head to Washington. Over the past few years Washington Ave nightclubs, bars and restaurants have gotten decidedly trendier, but a good measure are still small and family-run (often Cuban-run).

Make it a point to mail a postcard at the 1937 **post office** (☎ *305-531-3763, 1300 Washington Ave*). This Depression moderne building was constructed under President Roosevelt's reign with WPA funds, which supported artists who were out of work during the Great Depression. On the exterior, note the bald eagle and the turret with iron railings. The interior dome boasts a painted paper ceiling, beautifully restored in 1996. Sun rays reach out to stars, which in turn stretch toward a wavy ocean and sandy shores.

The imposing **Temple Emanu El Synagogue** (☎ *305-538-2503, Washington Ave at 17th St*) holds services Sunday to Thursday

---

Wiring along the Promenade

If you look up every now and then along the Promenade, you'll see wires, or Erev (**eh**-rev). The Erev accommodate Orthodox Jews who leave their homes for various reasons during the Sabbath (which begins Friday evening at sunset). Very simply put, the Erev function as a connection between the roof of the synagogue and the home. And while Jewish law forbids most manual labor during the Sabbath, when walking within the Erevs' boundaries on the Sabbath, one is allowed a degree of physical labor – such as pushing a baby in a carriage or carrying a talis (prayer shawl). If it sounds easy, imagine trying to avoid the phalanx of joggers and skaters on the Promenade during the Sabbath.

at 8am and 5:30pm, Friday at 8am and 6pm, and Saturday at 9am and 6pm. Farther north, the **Miami Beach Convention Center** *(between Convention Center Dr & Washington Ave)* hosts auto and boat shows and special events. You'll also want to note the Roy Lichtenstein sculpture *Mermaid* gracing the front lawn at the **Jackie Gleason Theater of the Performing Arts** *(1700 Washington Ave)* (see the Entertainment chapter).

Lincoln Road Mall

Ocean Drive may have a firm choke hold on the 'fabulous,' but locals own the Lincoln Road Mall. (OK, let's be realistic; locals have to share Lincoln Road with every single tourist, conventioneer and professional who comes to Miami.) 'The Road' was laid out by designer and architect Morris Lapides in the 1950s; look for his trademark wavy and futuristic sculptures all along Lincoln. After The Road fell into a state of disrepair in the 1970s, it was the recipient of a number of reputation-saving multimillion-dollar facelifts throughout the '80s and '90s. The Beach's cultural epicenter, The Road is a wide, pedestrian-only sidewalk that's hallowed ground for in-line skaters. It's plastered with galleries and outdoor cafés filled with off-duty models trying to relax. It's also lined with lush planters and imposing palms, perfect for a picnic-style late-afternoon snack.

Perhaps inescapably, The Road is morphing into a shopping mall. Gentrification has crept in on the heels of nationally known retailers like The Gap. This, in turn, paved the way for the multiplex Regal South Beach Cinema, which is challenging Lapides' **Colony Theatre**, a deco treasure. Don't miss an opportunity to see something at the Colony or Lapides' other delightful creation, the **Lincoln Theatre**. (See the Entertainment chapter for information on these venues.) You've been gentrified, Bubba.

Be sure to stop in at **Books & Books** *(☎ 305-532-3222, 933 Lincoln Road; open 10am-11pm Sun-Thur, 10am-midnight Fri & Sat)*, the Beach's premier bookstore. It hosts visiting authors and has a nice café, a great travel section and an excellent section on Miami-based and themed fiction.

Nor should you miss the **ArtCenter/South Florida** *(☎ 305-538-7887, 800 Lincoln Road)*. With over 70 artists, this nonprofit collective is fantastic (see the Shopping chapter for more details). It's the most exciting place on Lincoln.

A **farmer's market** *(between Alton Rd & Pennsylvania Ave; held 9am-6pm Sun)* provides a good diversion, with fresh fruits, veggies, juices, breads and more.

The **Antiques & Collectibles Market** *(☎ 305-673-4991, at Washington Ave; held 8am-5pm 2nd & 4th Sun of each month)* offers a fun collection of deco, bric-a-brac, Gothic and 1950s junque.

Española Way

Designed as a Spanish-style village in the early to mid-1920s, Española Way is lined with charming, pink Spanish-style buildings between Washington and Drexel Aves. Originally intended as an artists' colony, it sort of is something of one today, kind of. Little galleries and cafés line the narrow, shaded enclave. A **farmer's market** *(☎ 305-632-8067)* crowds the cafés from 6pm to 10pm Friday, 10am to 1am Saturday and 9am to 10pm Sunday. Look for everything from garage-sale stuff to handmade crafts.

The rambling 1920s Clay Hotel & International Hostel, complete with wrought iron balconies, was formerly the home of Desi Arnaz. The Cuban bandleader, who started the rumba phenomenon, had a conga club here. In its heyday, the ritzy place doubled as a gambling casino. Mobster Al Capone's S&H Gambling Syndicate took over the middle wing (now Rooms 128 to 138).

Ocean Beach Historic District & South Pointe

Since the Deco District boundaries formally extended only to 6th St, the area from there to South Pointe was for years, as the developers like to say, 'in play.' This meant ripping down everything in sight and putting up monstrously tall condominium towers with basement casinos. Fortunately,

Miami Beach voters nixed the casino bill and activists got the city to designate most of the area a historic district in 1996. But by then, several developers managed to get many of their projects 'grandfathered in,' meaning that they were given variances to do whatever they liked. Talk about closing the barn door after the cows have run off.

The Historic District boundaries zigzag from 6th to 1st St and exclude a number of blocks. While construction rumbles, **South Pointe Park** is still a wonderful place to spend a sunny afternoon. It has a nice little playground, a fishing pier from which kids (illegally) dive into Government Cut, a short boardwalk and an excellent stretch of beach that's less crowded during the week than those to the near north. (On weekends it's overrun by families.)

You can't miss the dramatic architecture of **Estefan Enterprises** *(420 Jefferson Ave)*, designed by the internationally renowned firm of Arquitectonia (which has its own offices on Brickell Ave). The dynamic musical duo of Gloria and Emilio Estefan, dubbed 'Miami's Royal Family,' operate their ever-increasing business ventures from here (see Bongos Cuban Cafe under Dance Clubs & Nightclubs in the Entertainment chapter). Latin music is big in Miami, and Sony, EMC, Universal, Warner/Chappell and Island Records all have a serious presence here. South Beach Studios is located right down the road at the Marlin Hotel (see the Places to Stay chapter), and folks like U2, Aerosmith, David Byrne and Prince have recorded here. Industry bigwigs ASCAP and NARAS also have a presence here.

Bass Museum of Art

This museum *(☎ 305-673-7530, Ⓦ www.bass museum.org, 2121 Park Ave; admission $6/4 adult/senior & student; open 10am-5pm Tues, Wed, Fri & Sat, 10am-9pm Thur, 11am-5pm Sun)* was the recent recipient of a greatly heralded expansion, designed by renowned Japanese architect Arata Isozaki. The collection is a wonderful surprise: Permanent highlights range from 16th-century European religious works, to Northern

European and Renaissance paintings, to impressive old masters like Peter Paul Rubens. Look for Albrecht Durer, Toulouse-Lautrec and perhaps the finest Flemish tapestries in an American museum. With visiting exhibitions rotating through other halls, special installations and an outdoor sculpture garden, you could easily spend a few hours here.

Wolfsonian Foundation

It doesn't come as a surprise that this foreboding Mediterranean-style building, which houses the Wolfsonian collection *(☎ 305-531-1001, Ⓦ www.wolfsonian.fiu.edu, 1001 Washington Ave; admission $5/3.50 adult/senior, student & youth 6-18 yrs, admission free 6pm-9pm Thur; open 11am-6pm Mon, Tues, Fri & Sat, 11am-9pm Thur, noon-5pm Sun)*, used to be a storage facility. Over the years, Miami native Mitchell Wolfson, whose family fortune was derived from movie theaters, began storing more and more of his ever-growing collection of art nouveau, Arts and Crafts, and art modern here. One day, it suddenly made sense to turn the building (already outfitted with a great climate-control and security systems) into a 14-room gallery rather than find another permanent home for it. Under the auspices of Florida International University, this fascinating collection of 70,000 pieces (dating from 1885 to 1945) ranges from industrial design to decorative arts to advertising and propaganda. Be sure to check out the tremendous deco 'waterfall' in the lobby. The Wolfsonian also offers free lectures and exhibit-related films (tickets $6/5 adult/senior & student).

Holocaust Memorial

It's impossible to overstate the impact of this memorial *(☎ 305-538-1663, Ⓦ www .holocaustmmb.com, Cnr Meridian Ave & Dade Blvd; admission free; open 9am-9pm daily)*, dedicated to the six million Jews who were killed during the Holocaust. Created through the efforts of Miami Beach Holocaust survivors and dramatically realized by sculptor Kenneth Treister, this elaborate and exquisitely detailed memorial is quite moving. Like the Kaddish, the Jewish prayer for the dead that speaks only of life, the memorial is a testament to humankind's perseverance and the hope for a better world.

There are five main areas, all utilizing Jerusalem stone and marble. Your first glimpse, opposite the Miami Beach Chamber of Commerce, is the *Sculpture of Love and Anguish*. This enormous oxidized bronze arm bears an Auschwitz tattooed number, a number intentionally chosen because it was never issued at the camp. It rises from the depths, symbolizing the last reach of a dying person. Scaling the arm are terrified concentration camp victims attempting to climb out of their hell.

The nearby lily pond and *Garden of Meditation* pays tribute to European culture and the lives of the victims. Follow the path clockwise to reach the *Memorial Wall,* inscribed with the names of Holocaust victims. Continue to the *Dome of Contemplation,* where an eternal flame burns. Note the Star of David, emblazoned with the word *'Jude'* and carved into the wall. A shaft of light pierces the darkness. The *Lonely Hall,* inscribed with major concentration camps' names, leads to the main plaza and the aforementioned *Sculpture of Love and Anguish,* where its full force becomes apparent. The detail in each character's face is haunting.

A terrifyingly powerful collection of statues from the *Beginning* to the *Final Sculpture* surround the arm. As you exit, you'll pass the *Arbor of History,* a vine-covered colonnade of Jerusalem stone. Etched in black granite, captioned photographs summarize the history of the Holocaust.

Miami Beach Botanical Garden

This secret garden (☎ 305-673-7256, *2000 Convention Center Dr; admission free; open 9am-5pm daily*) contains 4 acres of lush plantings that most people don't even realize are here. It's a contemplative place after the Holocaust Memorial.

Sanford L Ziff Jewish Museum of Florida

Jews have been officially 'allowed' to live in Florida since 1763, but evidence suggests that Jews who had converted to Christianity to escape persecution and death were here as early as the 1500s. This museum (☎ 305-672-5044, W *www.jewishmuseum.com, 301 Washington Ave; admission $5/4 adult/senior & student, admission free Sat; open 10am-5pm Tues-Sun except during Jewish holidays),* which is housed in a 1936 Orthodox synagogue (Miami's first congregation), is dedicated to the history of Florida Jews. It tells the stories of immigrants' journeys by way of lectures, exhibits and films. Its mainstay is MOSAIC: Jewish Life in Florida, which features thousands of items, from Russian samovar kettles to photographs, documents and other products of Jewish-owned or -run companies.

NORTHERN MIAMI BEACH (MAP 5)

North of 21st St on Collins Ave, the world of 1950s and '60s Miami Beach comes alive. It's still the kind of place where people say 'love you, kid…and I mean that.' Back then, all the schmoozers, stars and tourists were heading to high-rise hotels lining Collins Ave. With a few notable exceptions (see the Indian Creek Hotel, 2727 Indian Creek Dr, in the Places to Stay chapter), architecture from here to the northern city limits consists of a never-ending string of high-rise condos, hotels and apartments. Officially known as MiMo, or Miami Modern, it's characterized by fancy and glamour.

The iconic 1954 **Fontainebleau Hilton Hotel & Resort** *(4441 Collins Ave)* remains the other architectural highlight. Another brainchild of architect Morris Lapidus, this over-the-top leviathan is unmatched. Just before Collins Ave makes a little jog to the left, note the two magnificent pillars, through which the Fontainebleau's pool is visible. Fooled again. It's actually a spectacular *tromp l'oeil* **mural**, designed by Richard Hass and painted over an eight-week period by Edwin Abreu. It covers 13,016 sq feet of what was, before 1986, a big blank wall.

The enormous **Eden Roc Resort** *(4525 Collins Ave),* another notable '50s-era Lapidus resort (this with a decidedly Caribbean flair), has a fancy pool and indoor rock-climbing facilities (see Activities at the end of this chapter). Try to stop in to both; they are windows to another world.

Backtrack a bit and head west on **41st St**, also called Arthur Godfrey Rd, which is lined with kosher shops, delicatessens and even a kosher pizzeria. It's the 5th Avenue of the Orthodox Jewish South. Head north on **North Bay Rd**, which from 40th to 60th St is lined with mansions belonging to the likes of the Gibb brothers (of Bee Gees fame). Note the road names: Andy Gibb Dr, Ed Sullivan Dr, Ronald Reagan Ave, Brothers to the Rescue Martyr's Blvd and Arthur Godfrey Rd.

As you continue north, you'll pass the community of **Surfside**, a predominately French-Canadian one, and then the ultra-swanky **Bal Harbour Shops** (see the Shopping chapter), which epitomizes a segment of *Lifestyles of the Rich and Famous*. This stretch of northern Miami Beach has a great family-style expanses of sandy beachfront. Perhaps you'll even see former senate majority leader Bob Dole, who lives up here when he's not out of town filming Viagra commercials.

Haulover Beach Park (☎ *305-947-3525, 10800 Collins Ave; admission $4 per car; open sunrise-sunset daily)* has scads of barbecues, picnic tables, and volleyball and tennis courts. You can rent canoes and kayaks nearby at Urban Trails Kayak Co (see Activities, later in this chapter). Thanks to dense plant growth, it's also relatively hidden from the condos. This is also a good beach for surfing and windsurfing, as well as nude sunbathing.

On your way up to the Miami-Dade/ Broward County line, you'll pass through the old-fashioned neighborhoods of **Sunny Isles** and **Golden Beach**, both lined with high-rise condos facing unbroken stretches of fine white sand. Interestingly, it was at **Sheldon's Drugstore** (☎ *305-866-6251, 9501 Harding Ave)* that local resident and internationally known author Isaac Bashevis Singer learned of winning the Nobel Prize for Literature.

As early as 500 BC, the rich Oleta River estuary was home to Tequesta Indians.

Today, the **Oleta River State Recreation Area** (☎ *305-919-1846, 3400 NE 163rd St; admission $2 for 1 person, $4 for 2-4 people, $1 per each additional person over 4; open 8am-sunset daily)*, coming in at almost 1000 acres and certainly the largest urban park in the state, provides a perfect refuge from posing. There are lots of canoe, kayak and bicycle trails (and kayak rentals), a sandy swimming beach and shady picnic areas.

DOWNTOWN MIAMI (MAP 6)

Downtown Miami is not the most exciting American city you'll ever encounter, but if you've never been outside the USA, it will feel more like São Paulo than Seattle. Most streets are lined with shops selling electronics, luggage and clothing to Latin American visitors. Throngs of Brazilians, Colombians and Venezuelans heave bags of electronic goods from shop to shop. But the place dies down quickly after 5pm, when office towers disgorge their worker bees.

Parking can be nightmarish, but public transportation is good, so it definitely pays to park adjacent to the Bayside Marketplace and hop onto the Metromover (most sites are within one or two blocks of the elevated tram); see the Getting Around chapter for more information. Driving can also be nightmarish, since just one or two blocks often separate mildly seedy areas from really seedy areas. Find yourself on the outskirts of downtown, taking the wrong turn off the expressway, and you'll be reliving the opening sequence of *Bonfire of the Vanities*. Highways on stilts and concrete jungle overpasses provide protective cover for communities of homeless people and addicts.

The Waterfront

The enormous *Miami Herald/El Nuevo Herald* **newspaper headquarters** (☎ *305-350-2111,* W *www.miami.com/herald, 1 Herald Plaza; Metromover: Omni)*, houses the flagship of the national Knight-Ridder syndicate – Miami's paper of record and its only major daily.

The barren waterfront **Bicentennial Park** *(Biscayne Blvd; Metromover: Bicentennial*

Park) has an amphitheater with occasional free concerts and events. The adjacent **American Airlines Arena** hosts big concerts and Miami Heat and Miami Sol (WNBA) basketball games. Now that basketball is played in the new AA Arena, the old **Miami Arena** *(NE 7th St; Metrorail: Overtown)* is left to host University of Miami Hurricanes basketball and some touring concerts and shows.

Just south of the American Airlines Arena, the **Bayside Marketplace** *(☎ 305-577-3344, ⓦ www.baysidemarketplace.com, 401 Biscayne Blvd; Metromover: Freedom Tower),* a waterfront pantheon to consumerism, is adored by hordes of tourists and cruise ship passengers who dock nearby. Don't be a mall snob: Order a frozen daiquiri or margarita here and take in the scene. It's vibrant, with small shops, free daily concerts, lots of restaurants and sightseeing boat trips (see Organized Tours in the Getting Around chapter). The *Casino Princesa* is also docked here (see Gambling in the Entertainment chapter).

Bayfront Park *(☎ 305-358-7550; Metromover: Bayfront Park),* a freight port during the first 1920s building boom, is a somewhat calm downtown oasis, with two performance venues. The amphitheater is a great perch for the Fourth of July and New Year's Eve festivities, while the smaller 200-seat South End Amphitheater hosts free springtime performances featuring local talent. Also look for the **JFK Torch of Friendship**, a fountain recognizing the accomplishments of longtime US congressman Claude Pepper, and the **Challenger Memorial**, a monument to the astronauts killed in the 1986 space shuttle explosion.

Miami-Dade Community College

There are two art galleries with rotating exhibitions at the Wolfson Campus of the Miami-Dade Community College *(☎ 305-237-3696, 300 NE 2nd Ave; Metromover: College/Bayside; admission free; both open 10am-6pm Mon-Fri).* Both the 3rd-floor Centre Gallery and the 5th-floor Frances Wolfson Gallery often have photography shows.

Gusman Center for the Performing Arts

Try to see a concert or almost anything being held here *(174 E Flagler St),* since the interior of the former movie palace is stunning. (See the Performing Arts section of the Entertainment chapter for more information.)

Historical Museum of Southern Florida

Within the Mediterranean-style Miami-Dade Cultural Center, this historical museum *(☎ 305-375-1492, ⓦ www.historical-museum.org, 101 W Flagler St; Metromover: Government Center; admission $5/4/2 adult/senior/child 6-12 yrs; open 10am-5pm Mon-Wed & Sat, 10am-9pm Thur, noon-5pm Sun)* celebrates the multicultural roots that nourish South Florida. It's particularly interesting for kids. Covering a whopping 10,000 years of state history, the far-reaching exhibits start with natural habitats, wetlands, coasts and ridges. They then move through prehistoric Florida, the Spanish invaders and a Spanish galleon before continuing on to wreckers, the cigar industry, Indian tribes and the railroad's importance during the Flagler Boom. Exhibits then proceed through the Great Depression, 1930s tourism, WWII and right up to present day. The installations aren't huge, but they're very informative. The museum also has a good gift shop, called the Indies Company, and an admirable program of special events; check the Web site for its Calendar of Events & Programs. Historical tours led by Dr Paul George are in conjunction with this museum (see Organized Tours in the Getting Around chapter).

Miami Art Museum

Also within the Miami-Dade Cultural Center, the adjacent MAM *(☎ 305-375-3000, ⓦ www.miamiartmuseum.org, 101 W Flagler St; Metromover: Government Center; admission $5/2.50 adult/senior & student, child under 12 yrs free; admission free on Sun; open 10am-5pm Tues-Fri, noon-5pm Sat & Sun)* is ensconced in spectacular Philip Johnson–designed digs.

Without a permanent collection, its fine rotating exhibits concentrate on post-WWII international art. Look for good Latin American and Caribbean art, as well as artists in the vein of Jim Dine and Max Beckmann. Themed exhibits, increasingly bold, are explored through a variety of adjunct presentations. Call for a current schedule.

Dade County Courthouse

When Miami's first major post office opened in 1931, it was the tallest building south of Washington, DC. Eventually it was converted into the Dade County Courthouse, to accommodate the needs of US government prosecutors. But as crime increased, the feds outgrew the building and moved to the adjacent **Federal Courthouse** and **Federal Justice Building**. Today, you can visit the old courthouse *(300 NE 1st Ave; Metromover: College North; open 9am-5pm Mon-Fri)* to check out Denman Fink's Law Guides Florida Progress in the main courtroom on the 2nd floor. It depicts 1930s Florida, complete with a Cuba-bound PanAm Clipper. If you visit during winter, you may see turkey vultures roosting here.

Freedom Tower

Designed by the New York architectural firm of Shultz & Weaver in 1925, this tower *(600 Biscayne Blvd; Metromover: Freedom Tower)* is one of two surviving area towers modeled after the Giralda bell tower in Spain's Cathedral of Seville. (The second is at the Biltmore Hotel, discussed in the Coral Gables section, later in this chapter.) The 'Ellis Island of the South,' it served as an immigration processing center for almost half a million Cuban refugees in the 1960s. Placed on the National Register of Historic Places in 1979, it was also home to the *Miami Daily News* for 32 years. Despite being restored, it remains empty, but the Cuban National Foundation does have plans for a museum here.

Seriously Bright Lights, Big City

Downtown Miami, glowing with nighttime neon, easily ranks among the nation's most beautiful and colorful. From buildings and bridges to public transportation rail lines, there's always a colorful distraction luring your eyes from the road. Indeed, lightscaping is just another artistic pastime in a city where art is broadly defined. It's simply your job to notice and appreciate it. Perhaps taking its cue from the bright deco Beach signage, the city's downtown will not be outshone.

Although there are upward of 40 buildings lit up at night, the downtown skyline is dominated by the **Bank of America Tower** *(100 SE 2nd St; Metromover: Knight Center)*. Designed by IM Pei in 1987, this unmistakable symbol is illuminated nightly and for special events. Orange and aqua probably indicates a home game for the Miami Dolphins; snowflakes show up in December. The lights, in fact, are changed every few days. The building's seven faces can be custom lit with a combination of seven colors per face. Unfortunately, there's no observation deck.

Running parallel to the Port of Miami cruise ships, you can't miss the humble **I-395 bridge**, the pilings of which are magnificently awash in fuchsia. When a once-monthly full moon over Miami makes an appearance, it's positively enchanting.

Other funky downtown neon lighting comes courtesy of the Metromover's **rainbow-illuminated 4.4-mile track**, which makes a downtown circuit. It's trippy. It looks like a child took the fluorescent colors from her crayon box and sketched a long ribbon of light beams as far as the eye can see. The ride is spectacular, and spectacularly cheap (25¢), allowing a city tour sans traffic and blaring horns. Several stations have public artwork, such as Brickell's patchwork ceiling celebrating Miami's multicultural 'quilt.'

Lyric Theatre

A local mural depicts prominent black Miamians on the side of this theater (☎ 305-358-1146, 819 NW 2nd Ave). Built in 1913, the 400-seat Lyric used to be a prime venue for silent movies, talkies, vaudeville and live performances by jazz greats like Duke Ellington and his contemporaries. It's the only symbol left of the once-vibrant neighborhood of Overtown (for more information see the Liberty City section, later in this chapter). Over the years, it deteriorated along with the neighborhood and by the 1980s, the building was a shell, a roofless shelter for heroin addicts and homeless people. Then the Black Archives History & Research Center of South Florida (☎ 305-636-2390, 5400 NW 22nd Ave) stepped up to the plate. Kicking in $1.5 million for renovations, they completely overhauled the building. The phoenix reopened its doors in 1999 to appreciative neighbors, civic leaders and entertainers alike. Next up is an expansion project for which they have been awarded a $10 million grant.

Brickell Avenue

An international financial and banking center, Brickell Ave runs south to Coconut Grove along the water. With the newly coalescing Brickell Village, around South Miami Ave between the river and 15th Rd, however, the area isn't just for banking anymore. Developers, knowing that residential downtowns are the key to successful downtowns, are brimming with hope that this area could jumpstart a revitalized 24/7 urban core. It would be a first for Miami.

Crossing the Miami River, the **Brickell Ave Bridge** (Metromover: Knight Center) is more beautiful than ever after a multi-year, $21 million renovation (components for the raising mechanism had to be manufactured from scratch). Both wider and higher, the dimensions certainly seemed to facilitate the speedboat-driving drug runners being chased by DEA agents on the day of the bridge's grand re-opening! Note the 17-foot bronze statue by Cuban-born sculptor Manuel Carbonell of a Tequesta warrior and his family atop the towering *Pillar of History* column.

Miami River

The colorful, seedy riverfront is one of Miami's most fascinating places – but drive: You won't want to walk around here by night *or* day. Much of the shore is lined with makeshift warehouses, where goods are loaded and unloaded onto small tugboats bound for and from the Caribbean and other foreign ports. What exactly is in those containers is best not to ask. But unsavory images of drug smugglers and other rogue elements certainly leap to the imagination. It's all quite alluring and compelling in a mysterious way. Fisherfolk float in with their daily catch, fancy yachts 'slumming it' dock at restaurants, and nonconformists hang out on their houseboats. In order to have an excuse to linger in the neighborhood, where you are bound to get lost, enjoy lunch or dinner at one of the atmospheric seafood restaurants along the shores (see the Places to Eat chapter).

The river, by the way, was fed by the Everglades until the early 20th century. But now it's fed by canals starting at about the 32nd Ave bridge in Little Havana.

The 1897 Flagler **cottage** (66 SE 4th St; no entry), next to Bijan's on the River restaurant, was moved to this location in 1980 from SW 2nd St. It's one of just 14 simple pine houses that were built by railroad magnate and developer Henry Flager. He rented them to workers for $15 to $22 month.

Tobacco Road

Just south of the Miami River Bridge, a small collection of bars line S Miami Ave (Metromover: 8th St). Of these, Tobacco Road (☎ 305-374-1198, 626 S Miami Ave; open 11:30am-5am Mon-Sat, 1pm-5am Sun) is something of a Miami tradition, having received the city's first liquor license. It's been here since the 1920s and was a speakeasy during Prohibition. Stop in for a drink or a listen while you're in the neighborhood. Tobacco Road has live music, too; see the Entertainment chapter for more information.

ART DECO ARCHITECTURE

The end of WWI in 1918 ushers in an era of increased interest in the romance and glamour of travel, which lasts well into the 1930s. There's a giddy fascination with speed and cars, ocean liners, trains and planes. Not coincidentally, the US post-industrial revolution, concerned with mass production, kicks into high gear. New materials like aluminum, polished bronze and stainless steel are utilized in new and exciting ways. Americans begin looking to the future – after everyone else does.

At a 1925 Paris design fair, officially called the Exposition Internationale des Arts Décoratifs et Industriels Modernes (and eventually abbreviated to Arts Deco), decorative arts are highlighted, but the US has nothing to contribute. Europeans are experimenting with repeating patterns in Cubism and influenced by ancient cultures (King Tut's tomb was discovered in 1921), and Americans have to play catch-up.

Back in the States, a mere year later, a devastating hurricane blows through Miami Beach, leaving few buildings standing. The wealthy folks who were living here before the hurricane decamp. The second blow of a one-two punch is delivered by the Great Depression. Eventually, everything is up for grabs.

Hotel rebuilding begins in Miami Beach at the rate of about 100 per year during the 1930s (many architects had 40 to 50 buildings in production at any one time) – until the inception of WWII. This overlaps with a surge in middle-class tourism between 1936 and 1941, when visitors start coming for a month at a time.

Post-depression is an optimistic time, with hopes and dreams pinned on scientific and technological revolutions. Reverence for machines takes on almost spiritual dimensions, finding its aesthetic expression in both symbolic and functional ways.

Top: Art deco frieze detail
(LEE FOSTER)

Right: Floral detail on a fountain

RICHARD CUMMINS

Art Deco Characteristics

What does all this have to do with architecture? Everything. The principles of efficiency and streamlining translated into mass-produced, modest buildings without superfluous ornamentation – at least in the Northeast.

Miami Beach, a more romantic and glamorous resort, developed what came to be known as tropical deco architecture. It organically reflected the natural world around it. For example, glass architectural blocks let bright Florida light in but kept sweltering heat out. They also served a geometric, or Cubist, aesthetic. Floral reliefs, popular during the art nouveau period, appeared here, too. Friezes on façades or etched into glass reflected native flora and fauna like palm trees, pelicans and flamingos. Friezes also took their cues from the uniquely American jazz movement, harmonious and lyrical. Surrounded by water, Miami Beach deco also developed a rhythmic language, with scalloped waves and fountains.

KIM GRANT

Miami Beach needed a large number of rooms, so they ended up being small rooms. With no expectation that they remain standing this long, most hotels were built with inexpensive concrete and with mortar that had too much sand in it. Stucco exteriors prevailed, but locally quarried native keystone (an indigenous limestone) was also used. Except for the keystone, none of this would withstand the test of time with grace, which is one reason the district fell into such a state of disrespect and neglect. It's also why the district remains under a constant state of renovation.

Whereas Northeast deco buildings had socialist overtones, the clean lines of Miami Beach architecture still made room for joyful, playful, hopeful characteristics. Forward thinking, and dreaming about the future, took hold. Space travel was explored through design: Buildings began to loosely resemble rockets, and rooflines embodied fantasies about traveling the universe. Curved walls enhanced aerodynamic principles. Racing stripes,

Left: Palm tree etched in glass, Essex House Hotel

alluding to the new speed of cars and trains, furthered the metaphor of efficiency. Nautical elements from the dawning era of ocean liners found expression through porthole windows and metal railings. Geometric and abstract zigzag (or ziggurat) patterns not only reflected the ancient Aztec and Egyptian cultures, they also symbolized lightning bolts of electricity, which was being harnessed in bigger ways. Sun rays, more imagery borrowed from an ancient culture, were employed as life-affirming elements to counter the dark days of the depression.

RICHARD CUMMINS

Since all hotels were built on the same size lots, South Beach architects began distinguishing themselves from their next-door neighbors through decorative finials and parapets. Neon signage also helped with individualizing buildings. Miami Beach deco relied on 'stepped-back' façades that disrupted the harsh, flat light and contributed to the rhythmical feel. Cantilevered 'eyebrows' jutted out above windows to protect interiors from unrelenting sun. Canopy porches gave hotel patrons a cool place to sit. To reflect the heat, buildings were originally painted white, with animated accent colors highlighting smaller elements. (It was only later, during the 1980s, that interior designer Leonard Horowitz decreed the pastel palette that became the standard.)

With the effects of the depression lingering, ornamentation was limited to the façades; interiors were stripped down. Labor was cheap and readily available. Italians were hired to create terrazzo floors. They'd lay out a patterned grid and pour various colors of terrazzo – crushed stones, shells, marble chips or granite, mixed with concrete – into the grid and then polish it. It's a remarkable marriage of form and function, since terrazzo also cools the feet.

Interestingly, the value of these Miami Beach deco buildings is based more on the sheer number of structures with protected status from the National Register of Historic Places: Individually, the inexpensively constructed houses would be worth far less.

Right: Futuristic discs, Berkeley Shore Hotel

South Beach Deco Highlights

NEIL SETCHFIELD

The **Breakwater Hotel** (built in 1939, by architect Anton Skislewicz, 940 Ocean Dr) boasts a soaring double-faced sign (the tallest in Miami Beach) affixed to a tower-like structure reminiscent of an ancient Mayan temple. In addition to its strong vertical lines, the hotel has horizontal racing stripes. Note the metal railings, evoking the spirit of ocean liners, on the roof.

The **Beach Patrol Headquarters** (1934, Robert Taylor, 1001 Ocean Dr) is whimsy personified. It's a fine example of art imitating a machine (in this case a ship; see opposite page).

The Clevelander Hotel (1937, Albert Anis, 1020 Ocean Dr) typifies most art deco hotels in that it's akin to a horizontally or vertically oriented shoe box. In this case it's tall and thin; others are short and squat. (Remember, they're all built on the same size lots.) It's also typical in its name. Most architects named their hotels after streets, people or towns important to them – in this case, of course, the city of Cleveland. In a way, the Clevelander was the last hurrah for South Beach deco: The pool and outdoor bar glass block (which looks like a flying saucer) were added in the 1950s, during the MiMo (Miami Modern) period.

When it was built, **The Tides** (1936, L Murray Dixon, 1220 Ocean Dr) was the tallest and largest building on the beach. This 'skyscraper,' employing a zigzag design that was ever-present in Manhattan, features porthole windows and fine keystone. The sanded but porous keystone, often dyed, still yields imprinted patterns of fossilized sea creatures. In the lobby, a patch of the original terrazzo floor has been left at the check-in desk. As high-strung guests checked in over the years, they shuffled feet and wore an impression in the soft material.

Epitomizing classic deco style, the **Leslie Hotel** (1937, Albert Anis, 1244 Ocean Dr) is typically rectilinear and boxy, and the architect

Left: Deco signage, Breakwater Hotel

wrapped the eyebrows all the way around the side of the building.

Shuttered more often than not since the late 1980s, and featured prominently in the Robin Williams film *The Birdcage,* the **Carlyle Hotel** (1941, Kichnell & Elliott, 1250 Ocean Dr), with its modernistic and futuristic stylings, easily conjures up images of the Jetsons with their spaceship. The use of a triple parapet makes the building look more imposing and soaring than it really is. It features striking vertical and horizontal lines, and has rounded corners and eyebrow sunshades.

NEIL SETCHFIELD

The graceful **Cardozo Hotel** (1939, Henry Hohauser, 1300 Ocean Dr), named for supreme court justice Benjamin Cardozo and featured in the film *There's Something About Mary,* is now owned by singer Gloria Estefan. It's an outstanding example of streamline moderne, characterized by rounded edges that make the object look like it's made to move fast (think old-fashioned toasters and trains). The windows are framed with lightweight materials developed by a then-burgeoning airplane industry, and the wraparound porch, pillars and balustrades are made of keystone. The renovation was first-rate.

Above: Art deco plays with reality.

Right: Neon of the famous Clevelander

RICHARD CUMMINS

LEE FOSTER

The **Essex House Hotel** (1938, Henry Hohauser, 1001 Collins Ave) features unique glass portholes, original neon signage, octagonal windows, rounded corners and typical racing stripes and eyebrow sunshades. The interior is well-preserved, too. Note the excellent decorative, nostalgic terrazzo and the craftsmanship and artistry employed in laying it; the arrows in the floor point to a tiny bar. How's that for subliminal advertising? The Earl LaPan mural (there were more than a few muralists working in Miami Beach) isn't so subtle. Intending to entice tourists into visiting the Everglades, Earl's mural is conspicuously void of alligators. (He didn't want to scare the tourists.) But when in his 80s he was asked to restore the painting, Earl added a little one. Before leaving, look behind the wooden blinds on the porch side of the lobby for a beautiful etched-glass window with palms and flamingos.

With the exception of the Essex, exteriors have been the focus of discussion, but you can't overlook interior designs – metallic light fixtures, metalwork on doorways and the like. The **National Hotel** (1940, Roy France, 1677 Collins Ave) has a particularly impressive lobby and authentic period murals. Before heading in, don't miss the wacky silver cupola, which tops the building.

Left: Racing stripes grip the curves of the Essex House Hotel.

LEE FOSTER

The roofline of the **Delano Hotel** (1947, Robert Swartburg, 1685 Collins Ave) looks like a spaceship landed on it. Fortunately, the façade of this highly geometrical skyscraper steps back in four planes from the street, making it less imposing.

Nearby, the **Raleigh Hotel** (1940, L Murray Dixon, 1775 Collins Ave) boasts a singularly dramatic 'R' on its tower roof. The asymmetrical parapet reinforces the placement of the masterfully rounded corner and patterned windows.

Over on Washington Ave, the tropically colored **Taft Hotel** (1936, Henry Hohauser, 1040 Washington Ave) has a sweet little façade with serious doses of friezes, stripes and moldings. The doorway features a typical geometric design.

The adjacent **Kenmore Hotel** (1936, Anton Skislewicz, 1050 Washington Ave), linked to the Taft by a wavy concrete wall that runs the length of the city block and has subsumed the city sidewalk, has one of the most severe façades in Miami Beach. The perfectly proportional Bauhaus-influenced design represents the merging of form and **Right:** 'Eyebrows' function. There is no ornamentation; windows are set right into the wrap the classic structure. If you go inside, be sure to check out the exceptional Leslie Hotel.

recessed neon strips in the lobby and stairways, which light the walls rather than the room.

The Governor Hotel (1939, Henry Hohauser, 435 21st St), a mirror image in most ways of the Cardozo, has the added benefit of a stainless-steel flagpole and marquee, which provides a perfect backdrop for the art deco neon lettering. Even the typography during this era was geometrically abstracted, sometimes asymmetrically, just like the buildings themselves.

KIM GRANT

Interestingly, perhaps one-third of the Deco District buildings reflect Mediterranean-revival traditions. Although not true deco, they, like deco architecture, are based in fantasy. The lobby of one of these, the Moorish **Wolfsonian Foundation** (1927, Robertson & Patterson, 1001 Washington Ave), contains a phenomenally theatrical example of a 'frozen fountain.' The gold-leaf fountain, formerly gracing a movie theater lobby (you can bet it wasn't a multiplex!), shoots vertically up and flows symmetrically downward. Once again, these are characteristics that directly enhanced and reinforced the architecture's intent.

Left: Detail of the Wolfsonian Foundation's 'frozen fountain'

KEY BISCAYNE (MAP 7)

Unless you're a humiliated ex-president (the late US President Richard M Nixon had a house here) or a squidgillionaire with a condo, you'll probably be headed for the fun and educational Seaquarium or the fine state park at the end of the key. Basically the city's playground, Key Biscayne is a prime center for windsurfing, swimming, biking, boating, fishing and other outdoor pursuits (see the Activities section, later in this chapter).

The **Rickenbacker Causeway** ($1 toll) links the mainland with Key Biscayne via Virginia Key. The causeway is also a nice place to park under the ironwoods at dusk and watch the sunset. **Virginia Key Beach**, a lovely city park with picnic tables, barbecue grills and relative peace and quiet, is a perfect for families. **Hobie Beach** is great for windsurfing (see the Activities section, later in this chapter). And after a long, hard day of playing, there are lots of waterfront restaurants boasting dramatic skyline views perfect for sunset drinks.

Crandon Park

Definitely worth a visit, this 1200-acre park boasts the **Marjory Stoneman Douglas Biscayne Nature Center** (☎ 305-361-6767, Ⓦ www.biscaynenaturecenter.org, 4000 Crandon Blvd; admission free; open 10am-4pm daily), and **Crandon Park Beach**, a glorious but crowded white-sand beach that stretches for 3 miles. Much of the park consists of a dense coastal hammock and mangrove swamps. Especially fun for children, the nature center, named after the late, beloved environmental crusader, can teach you all about its surroundings. There are weekend hands-on demonstrations and nature talks and walks ($10/5 adult/child) on reef ecology, sea grasses and the like. The sea grass adventure is really fun. Kids get to wade into the water with nets and catch sea horses, sponges, crabs, urchins and other marine life. After discussing them, the sea creatures are released. It certainly offers a more intimate perspective than the Seaquarium. During the week, though, it's mobbed with school groups.

Bill Baggs Cape Florida State Recreation Area

This wildish 494-acre wetland park (☎ 305-361-5811, entrance 1200 S Crandon Blvd; admission $2 per person, $4 for 2 to 8 people; open 8am-sundown daily) is planted with native South Florida species (ever since Hurricane Andrew wiped out every single exotic species, that is). The barrier-island ecosystem is extensive, and there are plenty of walkways, boardwalks, bike trails, relatively secluded beaches, covered picnic areas and a little café selling decent soups and sandwiches. You'll also encounter hungry raccoons who like sandwiches (we don't need to tell you to keep your food to yourself, though, right?). A concession shack rents kayaks, bikes, rollerblades, beach chairs and umbrellas.

At the park's southernmost tip, the 1845 brick **Cape Florida Lighthouse** (☎ 305-361-8779), the oldest structure in Florida, replaces one that was severely damaged in 1836 by attacking Seminole Indians. You can tour it at 10am and 1pm Thursday to Monday (free). Tours are limited to about 12 people, so put your name on a sign up list at least 30 minutes prior to the tour. The lighthouse also boasts an impressive 1st-order lens. What's *that*, you ask? French physicist Augustin Jean Fresnel (1788–1827) devised six different sizes of ingenious beehive-like reflecting lenses. The largest ones, of the 1st order, were stationed on seacoasts and the smallest ones, of the 6th order, were used in harbors.

Miami Seaquarium

This fine 38-acre marine life park (☎ 305-361-5705, Ⓦ www.miamiseaquarium.com, 4400 Rickenbacker Causeway; admission $23/18 adult/child 3-9 yrs; open 9:30am-6pm daily, ticket booth closes at 4:30pm) excels in preserving, protecting and educating us about aquatic creatures. It was one of the country's first dedicated to sea life. There are dozens of shows and exhibits – easily a morning's worth if you're thorough – including a tropical reef; the Shark Channel, with feeding presentations; Faces of the Rainforest, with exotic birds and reptiles;

Manatees' Biggest Threat

Manatees are shy and utterly peaceful mammals. Pollution is a problem, but their biggest killers are boaters, and of those, the worst offenders are pleasure boaters.

Manatees seek warm, shallow water and feed on vegetation. South Florida is surrounded by just such an environment, but it also has one of the highest concentrations of pleasure boats in the world. Despite pleas from environmental groups, wildlife advocates and the local, state and federal governments, which have declared many areas 'Manatee Zones,' some pleasure boaters routinely exceed speed limits and ignore simple practices that would help protect the species.

After grabbing a bite, manatees float up for air and often float just beneath the surface, chewing and hanging around. When speedboats zoom through the area, manatees are hit by the hulls and either knocked away or pushed under the boat, whose propeller then gashes the mammal as the boat passes overhead. Few manatees get through life without propeller scars, which leave slices in their bodies similar to the diagonal slices on a loaf of French bread.

There are several organizations throughout the state that rescue and rehabilitate injured manatees, but they're fighting what would appear to be a losing battle. One of the two largest is the Miami Seaquarium. There are only about 1700 (endangered) West Indian manatees left in the world and the Seaquarium is dedicated to preserving their existence. Divers, animal experts and veterinarians of Seaquarium's Marine Mammal Rescue Team patrol South Florida waters, responding to reports of stranded manatees, dolphins and whales. While the Seaquarium's program has been very successful, pleasure boaters still threaten the manatees survival.

and Discovery Bay, a natural mangrove habitat that serves as a refuge for rehabilitating rescued sea turtles. Check out the Pacific white-sided dolphins or visit the injured West Indian manatees being nursed back to health; some are released.

The three best daily shows feature Lolita, Flipper and Salty. Lolita, a 7000lb killer whale who makes a lot of waves, has *Free Willy* advocates trying to spring her from captivity since her tank isn't nearly big enough. The 'Flipper Dolphin Show,' which stars direct descendants from the original *Flipper* TV series, takes place in the lagoon that was the set for the original 1960s TV series and movie. The 'Sea Lion Show,' headlining the high jinks of Salty the Sea Lion, is always popular, too.

You can also swim in the Flipper Lagoon and interact with the dolphins through Seaquarium's WADE, the Water and Dolphin Exploration program (☎ 305-365-2501; $125; twice daily Wed-Sun).

LITTLE HAVANA (MAP 8)

After the Mariel Boatlift (see the History section in the Facts about Miami chapter), Little Havana exploded with Cuban exiles into a distinctly traditional Cuban neighborhood. Spanish is the predominant language, and you will encounter folks who speak no English; see the Language chapter for some key phrases. The borders of Little Havana are arguable, but for the purposes of this book, they extend *roughly* from W Flagler St to SW 13th St and from SW 3rd

Ave to SW 37th Ave (Douglas Rd). The Miami River also meanders through Little Havana; see the Miami River discussion under Downtown, earlier in this chapter.

The last Friday night of each month is the most happening in Little Havana. From 6pm to 11pm all the shops and restaurants fling their doors open, and café tables and merchandise spill out onto the sidewalks. Artists and craftspeople show their wares. Folks young and old, well-dressed and not, salsa to live and recorded music in the streets, on sidewalks and in shops. While you're in the neighborhood, check to see what's going on at **Tower Theater** (☎ 305-644-3307, 1508 Calle Ocho), a historic theater that shows movies and occasionally holds other events.

Calle Ocho

The heart of Little Havana is Calle Ocho, Spanish for SW 8th St, which runs one-way from west to east. It's teeming with action and lined with Cuban shops, cafés, record stores, pharmacies and clothing stores. Of particular note are the cigar shops and *botánicas* selling Santería-related items like perfumed waters named 'Money' or 'Love Me,' or the more esoteric 'Keep Dead Resting.' See the boxed text 'Calle Ocho: Cigars, Botánicas & More' in the Shopping chapter for details about many of these storefronts.

Little Havana as a tourist attraction is an elusive bugger; in fact, it's not really a tourist attraction at all. It's just a very Cuban neighborhood, which is exactly its attraction. It's real; it's not putting on airs for anyone; and it couldn't care less whether you visit. So, except for the occasional street fair or celebration (see Special Events in the Facts for the Visitor chapter), don't expect Tito Puente leading a parade of colorfully attired, tight-trousered men. More likely you'll see old men wearing boxy *guayaberas* (shirts) arguing politics and playing dominoes.

On your way to a few of the sights discussed below, stop for a *guarapo* (sugarcane juice), *café con leche* or thimbleful of Cuban espresso.

Máximo Gómez Park

Perhaps better known as **Domino Park** (Cnr SW 15th Ave & Calle Ocho; open 9am-6pm daily) because of the scores of elderly Cuban men playing dominoes, this is a highly sensory place to soak in the local scene. The clack-clack-clack sounds of hundreds of black-and-white dominos being slapped on cement tables is downright musical. If you're a brave, older male and speak a little Spanish, join in for yourself. The park's namesake, Máximo Gómez y Baez, was the Dominican-born general of the Cuban revolutionary forces in the late 1800s.

Cuban Memorial Boulevard

The two blocks of SW 13th Ave south of Calle Ocho contain a series of monuments to Cuban patriots and freedom fighters (read: anti-Castro Cubans), including the **Eternal Torch in Honor of the 2506th Brigade**. This one is dedicated to the counter-revolutionaries who died during the botched Bay of Pigs invasion on April 17, 1961 (see the History section in the Facts about Miami chapter). Other monuments include a huge brass map of Cuba, dedicated to the 'ideals of people who will never forget the pledge of making their Fatherland free,' and a bust of José Martí.

Unidos en Casa Elian

The Elian Gonzales house (no ☎, 2319 NW 2nd St; donations requested; open 10am-6pm daily), where his life unfolded before cable news channels on a daily basis, is now a museum. You've undoubtedly seen the little house, on an ordinary street, on television many times. Elian's great-uncle Delfin bought the house in late 2000 and opened it in late 2001 as a shrine honoring Elian's time in the States. The place is filled, floor-to-ceiling, with hundreds of photographs, magazine covers, Elian's toys, his four bicycles, the pedal car he rode around the front yard. His bedroom is a time capsule: Clothes hang in the closet, the inner tube that saved his life at sea hangs on the wall, Spiderman pajamas are laid out on the bed. And then there's the life-size enlargement of the Pulitzer-prize–winning photograph of

José Martí

Havana-born José Martí (1853–1895) was exiled to Spain in 1870 for 'opposition to Colonial rule.' He eventually made his way to North and South America, where his anti-racist writings relentlessly extolled his vision of a free Cuba. He stirred up anti-Spanish sentiment wherever he could, including Florida. Although he was allowed to return to Cuba in 1878, he was quickly booted out by angry Spanish authorities. In 1895, Martí returned to Cuba again, this time to participate in the war for Cuban independence. Considered one of Cuba's leading writers and a hero of its independence, Martí was also one of the first to die in the conflict. **José Martí Park**, between the Miami River and Little Havana at 351 SW 4th St, was dedicated in his honor in 1950.

Elian hiding in the closet and being seized by federal border-patrol agents at gunpoint. The photo hangs right next to the real closet. It's like folks are waiting for him to return one day – the same boy, the same size, with the same impish grin.

Bay of Pigs Museum

This memorial museum (☎ 305-649-4719, 1821 Calle Ocho; open Mon-Fri), also called the Juan Peruyero Museum and Manuel Artime Library, is named after two leaders of the ill-fated Bay of Pigs invasion. The walls are lined with pictures of comrades who were killed during combat and those who participated but have died over the years, without seeing a free Havana. The invasion is documented with memorabilia, flight charts and newspaper clippings. It's all quite personal and moving.

Latin American Art Museum

With 11 rotating exhibits yearly, this museum (☎ 305-644-1127, W www.latinart museum.org, 2206 Calle Ocho; admission free; open 11am-5pm Tues-Fri & 11am-4pm Sat Sept-July) is one of the few in the country dedicated solely to the art and culture of Latinos.

Alpha 66

Also known as the Plaza de la Cubanidad, the Alpha 66 fountain and monument (W Flagler St at NW 17th Ave) is a symbol of hope to Cubans. In the words of José Martí, 'the palm trees are waiting brides.'

COCONUT GROVE (MAP 9)

The Grove has much to recommend it: lots of lush parkland along S Bayshore Dr, including the 28-acre **Kennedy Park**; two great museums and an excellent playhouse; mod, multimillion dollar waterfront homes next to modest cottages; good people-watching in the village center; and a great bicycling route along Old Cutler Rd (see Activities, later in this chapter). At least Madonna and Sylvester Stallone thought so; they chose to live here at one point or another.

Miami's first major settlement dates back to 1834, but it wasn't formally established until 1873, when the population included blacks from the Bahamas, whites from Key West and intellectuals from New England. While the Grove became a big-time bohemian hangout in the 1960s and '70s, its nucleus has morphed into a highly commercialized district. Folks are lured to **Coco-Walk**, a stylized mall with restaurants and a cinema, and the adjacent **Streets of Mayfair**, another upscale shopper's paradise (see the Where to Shop section of the Shopping chapter for more information on both malls). It's really packed on weekends. The **Coconut Grove Exhibition Center** hosts many special events, such as the monthly antique and jewelry show (see the Shopping chapter for more information).

Barnacle State Historic Site

In the center of the village, this 5-acre pioneer residence (☎ 305-448-9445, 3485 Main Hwy; admission $1; house open 9am-4pm Fri-Sun, park open 8am-sundown daily) sits on its original foundations, which date back to 1891. Owned by homesteader Ralph Monroe, often called Miami's first snowbird (a nickname for Northerners who fly south for the winter), the house is open for guided tours at 10am, 11:30am, 1pm and 2:30pm. The guides, by the way, are quite knowledgeable and enthusiastic about the park. Ask about the great once-monthly moonlight concerts.

Vizcaya Museum & Gardens

This opulent Italian Renaissance–style villa (☎ 305-250-9133, W www.vizcayamuseum .com, 3251 S Miami Ave; admission $10/5 adult/child 6-12 yrs; museum open 9:30am-5pm daily, last admission 4:30pm; gardens open 9:30am-5:30pm daily) was built for industrialist James Deering in 1916. Deering employed 1000 people (that was 10% of the local population at the time) for four years to fulfill his desire for a manse that looked centuries old. They did a great job. The villa itself is brimming with 15th- to 19th-century furniture, tapestries, paintings and decorative arts. Although the seaside grounds, which once spread for 180 acres, have been reduced to a mere 30, they're a poetic 30 acres. They feature splendid gardens, beautiful fountains, sculptures, elegant pools, a charming gazebo, canals running everywhere and lots of trails. Movie buffs might recognize the palace; it was the setting for the splendid dinner party in *Ace Ventura: Pet Detective*. Political junkies might recognize the location (dubbed the 'Hearst Castle of the East') as the place where President Clinton hosted the Summit of the Americas, a historic gathering of 34 leaders of the Western Hemisphere.

Although tours of the 1st floor can be inconsistent (since they are led by volunteer guides), they're included with the price of admission, so definitely take one. You'll get to peek into 34 of the 70 rooms. Tours last 45 minutes and run every 15 minutes from 10am to 2pm.

Ermita de la Caridad

The Catholic Diocese purchased some of the bayfront land from Deering's Villa Vizcaya estate and built a shrine (☎ 305-854-2404, 3609 S Miami Ave) here for its parishioners, displaced Cubans. Symbolizing a beacon, it faces the homeland, exactly

---

Pan Am 'Clipper' Air Travel

Pan Am 'Clippers,' big luxurious flying boats really, began taking to the skies off Dinner Key Marina, 3500 Pan American Dr, in 1939. It was a romantic time for air travel, when then-exotic locales like Honolulu and the shores of South America were filled with wonder and newness. It was a time when overnight flights to China carried only 18 passengers, all in first class (the only class). It was a time when, on flights to Cuba and Key West, pilots would bring along carrier pigeons (rather than radios) to notify the terminal if there was trouble during the flight and the plane had to make an emergency landing.

Although originally headquartered in a houseboat, Pan Am built an art deco terminal graced with nautical exterior details on Dinner Key in 1930, when it began flying to South America. It was the talk of the town. Although it has been unceremoniously converted into **Miami City Hall** (open 9am-5pm Mon-Fri), you can still see a 1938 Pan Am dinner menu and models of the clippers and other seaplanes that flew from here. Head into the lobby and turn left, and left again. You'll get a palpable sense of history sitting near the hangars, which are now used for boatyards. The seaplanes stopped flying in 1945, after World War II had fast-forwarded the development of long distance land-based planes. Suddenly the exotic locals weren't so remote, and dare we say, the planet not so lonely.

---

290 miles due south; note the mural that depicts Cuban history. After visiting the Villa or science and space museum (see below), consider picnicking at this quiet sanctuary on the water's edge or at nearby Kennedy Park on S Bayshore Dr.

Miami Museum of Science & Space Transit Planetarium

The highly recommended science and space museum (☎ 305-646-4200, 305-646-4420 *cosmic hot line for planetarium,* W *www .miamisci.org, 3280 S Miami Ave; admission to both $10/8/6 adult/senior & student/child 3-12 yrs; both open 10am-6pm daily)* shares a new affiliation with the Smithsonian Institution for rotating exhibits. The formerly 'very good' attraction just got even better.

The science museum has great hands-on, creative exhibits: from turbulent weather phenomena and the mysterious universe to creepy crawlers and coral reef exhibits. Yes, their virtual reality games are fun, but this museum also shows that gravity can be, too. Even special exhibits like 'microbes: hard to live with, impossible to live without,' which might sound deadly (no pun intended), are interesting. Demos involve fairly engaging audience participation. Kids also tend to love the outdoor Wildlife Center, which features dangerous animals of South Florida and exotic birds of prey.

From outer space to cyberspace, the planetarium shines. On Friday and Saturday nights there are laser shows (the first show, at 7:30pm, is free, but later shows cost $7/4 adult/senior & child) set to the Beatles, Led Zeppelin and Pink Floyd. The planetarium also offers a whole host of informative free lectures and inexpensive telescope viewing sessions. Call for a complete description of what's on when you're in town. Solar system movies, star shows and laser shows are offered throughout the day.

Admission is half-price at 4pm on weekdays, because the last laser show has already begun and at that point, you can only get into the science museum.

Plymouth Congregational Church

From the hand-carved door taken from a monastery in the Pyrenees to the solid masonry work, this 1917 coral mission-style church *(☎ 305-444-6521, 3400 Devon Rd; admission free; office open 8:30am-4:30pm Mon-Fri; ask to take a peek inside)* is striking. The church is set on a lush 11 acres that also contain Dade County's first schoolhouse, a one-room wooden building that

dates to 1887 and was moved here from its original site in 1970.

CORAL GABLES (MAP 10)

This lovely, leafy 'City Beautiful' exudes opulence and comfort, thanks to the vision of developer George Merrick. He took 1600 acres of inherited family land (planted with citrus and avocado trees), purchased 1400 more in 1921 and went on an architect-hiring spree. His goal was simple: Create a planned 'model suburb' with a decidedly Mediterranean theme, magnificent gateways, impressive plazas, fountains and wide, tree-lined streets. The city was in full bloom a mere three years later, and by 1925 it was incorporated. Today, Coral Gables, while exciting to multinational corporations and resident diplomats, is a quiet place with spreading banyan trees, fine restaurants, some very notable sites and an upscale arts scene.

There are really two faces to Coral Gables: the southern neighborhood around the University of Miami, which educates about 14,000 students, and the northern neighborhood along the **Miracle Mile** and off Coral Way (the same street where it's Miracle Mile). A premier shopping street in the 1950s, Miracle Mile (perhaps more accurately called Miracle Half Mile) went through a period of decline, complete with boarded up storefronts, but now it's making a comeback. Just ask Starbucks, always at the fore of resurrection, which has a presence here. There are now about 125 shops and the 1930s Miracle Theatre has been newly renovated.

The winding side streets can be confusing in Coral Gables, but go ahead and get lost. You'll stumble onto some beautiful scenery. A **farmer's market** *(☎ 305-460-5311, 8am-1pm mid-Jan–Mar),* with lots of gourmet picnic-style prepared foods, is held in front of the Coral Gables City Hall, 405 Biltmore Way.

Lowe Art Museum

On the University of Miami campus, the Lowe *(☎ 305-284-3535,* W *www.lowe museum.org, 1301 Stanford Dr; admission $5/3 adult/student; open 10am-5pm Tues,*

Wed, Fri & Sat, noon-7pm Thur, noon-5pm Sun) has one of Dade County's largest permanent collections. Works cover the spectrum, including: Renaissance and Baroque art; Western sculpture from the 18th to the 20th centuries; European paintings by Gauguin, Picasso and Monet; Egyptian, Greek and Roman antiquities; African, pre-Columbian and Asian (textiles, paintings, ceramics) entries; and a collection of Southwestern weavings and Guatemalan textiles. The Central and South American collection reaches from Chile to Mexico in all media. The Lowe also hosts contemporary traveling shows.

The Biltmore Hotel

The city's crown jewel is the 16-story (315-foot) tower of the Mediterranean revival Biltmore *(☎ 305-445-1926, 800-727-1926, Ⓦ www.biltmorehotel.com, 1200 Anastasia Ave)*, modeled after the Giralda bell tower at the Cathedral of Seville in Spain. The history of the 1926 landmark hotel reads like an Agatha Christie novel on speed. Set against an Old World European-style backdrop, the subplots of murder and intrigue spar for attention with strong characters, famous gangsters and inquisitive detectives. Al Capone had a speakeasy here, and the Capone Suite is still haunted by the spirit of Fats Walsh, who was murdered here. More recently, the hotel hosted the 1994 Summit of the Americas, and the 2002 wedding reception of *Sex and the City* star Kyle McLachlan. It's that kind of place. A palpable sense of enormity is also apparent throughout the hotel. The pool is the largest hotel pool in the continental USA.

Don't miss the **guided tour** *(☎ 305-445-1926; free; tours 1:30pm, 2:30pm & 3:30pm Sun)*, run by the Dade Heritage Trust, of the hotel and grounds. Tours leave from the upper lobby concierge desk and include the Capone and Merrick Suites, if they're unoccupied. For in-depth, well-spun yarns about ghosts, visiting celebs and the hotel's construction, check out the fascinating **storytelling** *(☎ 305-445-1926; free; 7pm Thur)*.

Coral Gables Congregational Church

George Merrick's father was a New England Congregational minister, so perhaps that accounts for him donating the land for the city's first church. Built in 1924 and landscaped with stately palms, this lovely church *(☎ 305-448-7421, Ⓦ www .coralgablescongregational.org, 3010 DeSoto Blvd)* holds Sunday services at 8:30am in the chapel, and at 9:15am and 10:45am in the sanctuary.

Venetian Pool

As tons of earth and rock were taken for Merrick's building boom, a very large limestone quarry formed. Then a creative thinker thought: Why not transform this eyesore by letting it fill with water and become an extraordinarily beautiful swimming hole? On the National Register of Historic Places, this 1924 spring-fed pool *(☎ 305-460-5356, 2701 DeSoto Blvd; admission $5.50/2.50 anyone over 13/child 3-12 yrs Nov-Mar, $8.50/4.50 Apr-Oct; open 10am-4:30pm Tues-Sun Nov-Mar; open 11am-5:30pm Tues-Fri, 10am-4:30pm Sat & Sun Apr-May & Sept-Oct; open 11am-7:30pm Mon-Fri, 10am-4:30pm Sat & Sun June-Aug)* boasts coral rock caves, cascading waterfalls, a palm-fringed island, vine-covered loggias and Venetian-style moorings. It was designed by Merrick's uncle Denman Fink. It's large enough to accommodate a big waterfall, a kiddie area (note that toddlers must be over 38 inches tall or parent must have proof that the toddler is at least three years old) and an adults' area for lap swimming. In fact, during its 1920s heyday, it hosted synchronized swimmer Esther Williams and Johnny 'Tarzan' Weismuller, both seen in historic photos at the pool. The free-form pool holds upwards of 825,000 gallons of water and during winter, it's drained and refilled every other night (nightly in summer). Before you get all worked up thinking about the water problem in the Everglades and South Florida, though, you should know that the water is recycled through a natural filtration process. There's a decent snack bar on the premises (you can't bring in your own food) and lockers. The

Master Planner

George Merrick had a dream. He envisioned drawing people into a series of neighborhoods that felt 'old' (today the cynics among us might call it 'Disneyfication') from the start. He wanted to counter the sprawl that was already settling into Miami, with a perfectly designed Mediterranean-style city. So in 1921 he proceeded to hire a gaggle of professionals to realize his vision, including architects Phineas Paist and H George Fink (his cousin), landscaper Frank Button and artist Denman Fink (his uncle). Together they created several very distinct areas. If you were just driving around and stumbled upon them, you'd think you'd entered the twilight zone.

Look for the **Dutch South African Village** *(6612, 6700, 6704 & 6710 SW 42nd Ave and 6705 San Vicente St)* modeled after 17th-century Dutch colonists' farmhouses; a tiny **Chinese Village**, one block between San Sovino Ave, Castania Ave, Maggiore St and Riviera Dr; a **Florida Pioneer Village** *(4320, 4409, 4515, 1520 & 4620 Santa Maria St)*, which looks a lot more like New Hampshire than Miami; the **Italian Village**, on Altara Ave at Monserrate St; and the stunning **French Normandy Village**, on the block between SW 42nd Ave, Viscaya Court, Viscaya Ave and Alesio Ave.

Flush from his early successes, Merrick teamed up with magnate John McEntee Bowman in 1924 to build the $10 million Biltmore Hotel, with its trademark Giralda-style tower visible from anywhere in the city. The red-hot construction boom, though, began to cool in 1926, and a devastating no-name hurricane blew away any remaining embers of development. Merrick went broke in the subsequent real estate crash brought on by the Depression and eventually died a poor man. The city of Coral Gables, only a year old in 1926, also went bankrupt. After the city's finances were sorted out, and it grew with Miami, Coral Gables always remained a bit aloof. It had the good fortune to attract more money and less attention.

Merrick's gorgeous 1925 **Colonnade Building** *(169 Miracle Mile)* served as the headquarters of his Coral Gables Corp. Note the central rotunda, arcades and a lavishly ornamental front entrance. Once the home of Colonnade Pictures, the building was combined with a new tower directly behind it in 1988, and has been converted into the **Omni-Colonnade Hotel** *(☎ 305-441-2600, 180 Aragon Ave)*. It has shops and boutiques and also houses the Coral Gables Chamber of Commerce.

Because of Merrick's vision, Coral Gables is one of the few places in metropolitan Miami that's lovely for walking. Banyan trees shelter the winding streets and provide good relief from the sun. It's also nice for a Sunday drive past the big beautiful homes. (They have homes here, rather than mere houses.) The enclave is also relatively safe; money has a way of insulating things to a certain degree, eh?

water can be a tad chilly in winter. Ever try to heat 825,000 gallons of water?

While you're in the neighborhood, check out the adjacent **DeSoto Fountain**, about four blocks south of Coral Way. Denman Fink also designed this four-faced fountain in the early 1920s.

Merrick House

When George Merrick's father purchased this plot of land sight unseen for $1100 in 1899, it was a rocky plot with a rustic wooden cabin and some guava trees. George and his father certainly developed it, but Merrick's boyhood homestead does not have the same grand style that would later mark his adult vision. Today the modest family residence *(☎ 305-460-5361, 907 Coral Way; admission $5/3/1 adult/senior & student/child 6-12 yrs; open for tours 1pm-4pm Sun & Wed)* looks as it did in 1925, outfitted with family photos, furniture and artwork. While the house is primarily used for meetings and receptions, you can tour it and also see the well-maintained organic garden. King oranges, copperleaf, bamboo and other trees planted at the turn of the century are still thriving.

Coral Gables City Hall

This grand building *(405 Biltmore Way)* has housed city commission meetings since it opened on February 29, 1928. It's impressive from any angle, certainly befitting its importance as a central government building for the City Beautiful. Upstairs, there's a tiny display of Coral Gables Public Transport from the mid-20th century, and rotating photograph and art exhibits are housed here. While you are here check out Denman Fink's *Four Seasons* ceiling painting in the tower, as well as his framed, untitled painting of the underwater world on the 2nd-floor landing.

Entrances & Watertower

Merrick planned a series of elaborate entry gates to the city, but the real estate bust meant that projects went unfinished. Still, there are some worth noting: **Country Club Prado** *(1927; at Calle Ocho & the Prado Country Club);* the **Douglas Entrance** *(1927; at Calle Ocho & Douglas Rd);* the **Granada Entrance** *(Alhambra Circle & Granada Blvd);* the **Alhambra Entrance** *(at Alhambra Circle and Douglas Rd)* and the **Coral Way Entrance** *(at Red Rd & Coral Way).*

The **Alhambra Watertower** (1931), where Greenway Court and Ferdinand St meet Alhambra Circle, looks for all the world like a Moorish lighthouse. The copper dome and frescoes were restored in 1993.

ELSEWHERE IN MIAMI

Just because these sights don't fall within any distinct neighborhood district doesn't mean they aren't worth checking out. On the contrary, some of the following sites are Miami's most intriguing, contemplative, wacky, evocative, historic or fun. Keep in mind, however, that sights within this geographic area are spread out for 20 miles from north to south. Plan your travel time around rush-hour traffic and think carefully about combining sights with visits to adjacent neighborhoods.

Biscayne Bay

Between Miami and Miami Beach there are about a dozen islands, some more exclusive than others, but all visible from the MacArthur, Julia Tuttle and JFK Causeways. Most are accessible by bridges.

Coast Guard Station (Map 4) If you've seen news footage of Coast Guard cutters rescuing Cuban rafters or arresting drug runners, the cutters probably originated from this base. Tours are not generally permitted, though you can sometimes see seized drug boats moored at the pier (hint: drug boats are *not* the ones that say US Coast Guard on them).

Flagler Memorial Monument (Map 4) Accessible only by private boat, this little speck of an island serves as a monument to Henry Flagler, one of Florida's leading pioneers, who, it could be argued, was single-handedly responsible for the development of South Florida. Who ever said no man is an island?

Fisher Island (Map 4) One of the Beach's pioneering developers, Carl Fisher, purchased this glorious little island and planned on dying here. He even built a mausoleum. As is want to happen, though, he got bored with it after a while. When William K Vanderbilt II fell in love with the place, Fisher traded the island for Vanderbilt's 250-foot yacht *and* its crew. Things were like that in those days. Vanderbilt proceeded to build a splendiferous Spanish-Mediterranean-style mansion, with guest houses, studios, tennis courts and a golf course.

Today, this exclusive resort is accessible only by air and private ferry. The condominiums that line the mile-long private beach range from $1 million hovels to the $7-plus-million pad President Clinton once borrowed. It's said that the sun shines over the island even when it's raining in Miami Beach. Perhaps when you play with Nature by importing boatloads of sugary white sand from the Bahamas as they did on Fisher Island, you have some sway over the weather, too. Monied readers can overnight on Fisher Island at the *Inn at the Fisher Island Club* (☎ 305-535-6080, 800-537-3708); see the Places to Stay chapter.

The island is usually open only to paying guests and residents, but you can arrange a tour if you're especially persistent. Ferries leave from the Fisher Island Ferry Terminal off the MacArthur Causeway. The air-conditioned ferries depart every 15 minutes around the clock (yup, that's 24/7) and the trip takes 10 minutes.

Hibiscus, Palm & Star Islands Hibiscus (Map 2), Palm (Map 2) and Star (Map 4) Islands, though far less exclusive than Fisher Island, are three little bastions of wealth. There aren't *as many* very famous people living there now – just very rich ones – although Star Island is home to Miami's favorite star, Gloria Estefan. For a short time Al Capone lived (and died) on Palm Island; ironically, his house is now occupied by a Miami police officer. The islands' circular drives are guarded by a security booth and it's generally hard to get on them. But, the islands' drives are also public, so if you ask politely and don't look like a hoodlum, you should be able to get in. Star Island consists of little more than one elliptical road lined with royal palms, sculpted 8-foot ficus hedges and fancy gates guarding houses you can't see. It will occur to you: So this is how the other .0009% of the population lives. But as one gatekeeper told me: We're probably a lot happier than these folks are and they probably don't even know their neighbors.

Watson Island (Map 2) The island nearest to downtown Miami is the grungiest of the lot and divided in half by the MacArthur Causeway. At press time, **Parrot Jungle & Gardens** (see later in this section) was planning a move to the northern side of Watson Island. The southern side is home to some fishing and air charters. **Action Helicopter Service** (☎ 305-358-4723) runs 10- to 12-minute jaunts above South Beach, Fisher Island, the Port of Miami and Bayside Marketplace for $69 per person (two people minimum). For $114 per person, you can tack on additional flight time over Coconut Grove, downtown and part-time houses of the rich and famous (Ricky Martin, Madonna and Sophia Loren, to name a few). **Chalk's Ocean Airway** (☎ 305-371-8628, 1000 *MacArthur Causeway*) runs a seaplane service to Fort Lauderdale and Bimini.

Port of Miami (Map 2) Miami is the world's cruise capital and when these 14-story floating behemoths are docked at the Port, it's a pretty amazing sight. The traffic jams on Thursday, Friday and Sunday, when the ships are loading and unloading weekend merrymakers, are pretty amazing, too. You also can't help but notice lines of semis hauling containers of goods, stacked like cereal boxes in a supermarket, bound for distant ports.

Pelican Island (Map 5) On weekends you can take a short tootle over to itsy-bitsy Pelican Island on a free ferry from the JFK Causeway west of North Bay Village, about 2 miles west of 71st St in Miami Beach. It's a pleasant little place to unpack a picnic and peer at dozens of congregating pelicans (try saying *that* five times fast).

Parrot Jungle & Gardens (Map 2)

More than just a squawking-parrot show, Parrot Jungle (☎ 305-666-7834, **w** www.parrotjungle.com, 11000 SW 57th Ave; admission $16/14/12 adult/senior & student/child 3-10 yrs; open 9:30am-6pm daily, last admission 5pm) contains lush gardens set in a hardwood hammock, a walk-through aviary and lots of winding trails. With more than 1200 varieties of exotic and tropical plants, the gardens are home to crocodiles, a rare albino alligator, orangutans, chimps, tortoises and very pink flamingos. The bird show is held five times daily; 'highlights' include showy parrots, macaws and cockatoos riding bicycles, roller-skating and playing cards.

Parrot Jungle has been a figure in South Florida kitsch since 1936, but at press time, it was planning a move to Watson Island, off the MacArthur Causeway on Biscayne Bay, by Spring 2003. That 20-acre location (also see Map 2), set in a coral-rock facility, will also have a petting zoo and show area. Check the Web site for updates on the move.

For the time being, to reach the 'old' location, take I-95 south to US Hwy 1 south to SW 57th Ave (Red Rd) south and head 3 miles south to SW 111th St. Just north of Parrot Jungle on SW 57th Ave stop at the **Pinecrest Wayside Market** for a yogurt smoothie or strawberry shake.

Fairchild Tropical Garden (Map 2)

The country's largest tropical botanical garden, the Fairchild (☎ 305-667-1651, W www.ftg.org, 10901 Old Cutler Rd; admission $8/4 adult/child 3-12 yrs; open 9:30am-4:30pm daily) covers 83 acres of lush rain-forest greenery. It has 11 lakes, streams, grottoes, waterfalls and hundreds of varieties of rare and exotic flowers. To simply think of it as a tourist attraction detracts from its serious purpose: the study of tropical flora by the garden's more than 6000 members. In addition to three easy-to-follow self-guided walking tours, there's a good, free 40-minute tram tour of the entire park (on the hour 10am to 3pm). Allow an hour for the Lowland Trail, which runs from the rain forest to the lakes. The other trails take about 30 to 45 minutes each. The park has a good bookstore – a delight to backyard botanists and amateur horticulturists.

To reach the park, take US Hwy 1 south to SW 42nd Ave (Le Jeune Rd), head south and continue south on Old Cutler Rd for 2 miles.

Charles Deering Estate (Map 2)

James' brother Charles created his own 150-acre winter estate (☎ 305-235-1668, 16701 SW 72nd Ave; admission $6/4 adult/child 14 yrs & under; open 10am-5pm daily, last tickets sold at 4pm), although they are much more humble abodes. The grounds, brimming with rare trees and other plant s, contain two houses, which you can to (free with admission). An animal-fossil pit of bones dating back 50,000 years, and the prehistoric remains of Native Americans who lived here 2000 years ago, including a burial ground, were discovered on the grounds. Much of what is appropriate for display can be found at area museums, but some artifacts are on display at the estate. The offshore Chicken Key is also part of the estate, and you can take a three-hour guided **canoe tour** ($20 per person; 10am Sat & Sun) out to the key, mangrove and marsh habitats. Naturalists will elucidate the difference between ibis and egrets, and red and black hammocks, and you can see turtles, sharks, a bird rookery and other seaside life.

To reach the estate, take I-95 south to US Hwy 1 south to SW 57th Ave (Red Rd) south, which turns into Old Cutler Rd. Follow Old Cutler Rd for about 4 miles until you see the estate on your left.

Matheson Hammock Park (Map 2)

This 100-acre county park (☎ 305-665-5475, 9610 Old Cutler Rd; admission $4 per car; open 6am-sunset daily) is the city's oldest and one of the most scenic. It offers good swimming for children in a closed tidal pool, lots of hungry raccoons, dense mangrove swamps, crocodile spotting areas and the notable waterfront restaurant **Redfish Grill** (see the Places to Eat chapter). There's a nice picnic area at the front end of the park, before you to pay to enter.

National Hurricane Center (Map 2)

At press time the center (☎ 305-229-4470, W www.nhc.noaa.gov, 11691 SW 17th St), located on the southwest side of the Florida International University campus, had halted their half-hour tours because of fallout from the events of September 11. But there's no rational reason this place should be closed; it's worth calling to see if the policy has changed. This fascinating center documents the drama of hurricanes and elucidates the intricacies of storm-tracking.

(Map 1)

305-251-0400, W *www
m, 12400 SW 152nd St;
adult/child 3-12 yrs; open
daily; last admission 4pm)*
.imals from more than 200
spec   k for Asian and African ele-
phants, i e and regal Bengal tigers, pyg-
my hippos, Andean condors, cute koalas,
colobus monkeys, black rhinoceroses and a
pair of Komodo dragons from Indonesia.
Less than half of the 740 acres are developed, so you'll see plenty of natural habitats. And keep your eyes peeled for
informative zookeeper talks in front of
some exhibits. At the children's petting
area, kids can play with potbellied pigs,
sheep, ferrets, chickens, lizards and more.
There are also good wildlife shows in the
amphitheater.

For a quick overview (and because the
zoo is so big and can be so tiring), hop on
the Zoofari Monorail for a good orientation; it departs every 20 minutes. If you have
time, take the Behind the Scenes Tram Tour
($2), a 45-minute ride that takes you past

the veterinary hospital, quarantine pens and
brooder and hatchery building. It's wildly
interesting. In general, though, try to visit
the zoo in the morning, when the animals
are more active. This is especially true in
summertime.

Take I-95 south to US 1 south and turn
right on SW 152nd St (Coral Reef Dr); head
west for 3 miles until you see the zoo. It's
about 45 minutes from downtown.

Monkey Jungle (Map 1)

Monkey Jungle (☎ *305-235-1611,* W *www
.monkeyjungle.com, 14805 SW 216th St; admission $15/10 adult/child 4-12 yrs; open
9:30am-5pm daily, last admission 4pm)*
brochures have a tag line: 'where humans
are caged and monkeys run free.' It might
conjure up images from *Planet of the Apes.*
Indeed, you will be walking through
screened-in trails, with primates swinging
freely, screeching and chattering all around
you. But it's not scary, just a bit odiferous,
especially on warm days (read: most days).

In 1933, animal behaviorist Joseph du
Mond released six monkeys into the wild.

I'm bored. Let's go to South Beach.

MARK NEWMAN

Today, their descendants live here with orangutans, chimpanzees and the lowland gorilla. The habitat, a tropical hardwood hammock that contains plants collected in South America, feels like the Amazonian ecosystem. The big show of the day (there are three actually) takes place at feeding time, when crab-eating monkeys and Southeast Asian macaques dive into the pool for fruit and other treats.

Take Florida's Turnpike Ext to exit 11 and head west for 5 miles. It's a long way to come, but if you're all the way out here, go a mile farther to **Bur's Berry Farm** for some of the world's best strawberries (see the Places to Eat chapter for more information).

Fruit & Spice Park (Map 1)

This 35-acre tropical public park *(☎ 305-247-5727, 24801 SW 187th Ave; admission $3.50/1 adult/child; free tours; open 10am-5pm daily)* has more than 100 varieties of citrus, 80 varieties of bananas, 40 types of grapes and a lot more exotic tropical fruits, plants and spices. Many of the plantings are organized by geography: from the Amazon River Basin to the Yucatán to Southeast Asia. In the heart of South Florida's agricultural district, it's the only place like it in the country. In fact, some of the species that grow here can't survive anywhere else. Best of all, while walking along the aromatic paths, you can take anything that falls (naturally) to the ground. Barring that, you can buy the exotic offerings at the **Redland Fruit Store**. Try the pomello, rambutan, lychee, breadfruit and tamarind. And don't forget to check out the poisonous plant area.

To get there, take US Hwy 1 south to SW 248th St west; turn left (south) on SW 187th Ave (Redland Rd). Stop for a cinnamon bun at **Knaus Berry Farm** (see the Places to Eat chapter for more information).

Coral Castle (Map 1)

South Florida has its fair share of strange attractions, half truths, embellishments and wacky stories, and this castle *(☎ 305-248-6345, w www.coralcastle.com, 28655 S Dixie Hwy; admission $9.75/6.50/5 adult/senior &* *student/youth 7-18 yrs; open 7am-8pm daily),* on the National Register of Historic Places, is one if not all of the above. Here's the rumor and legend: After a Latvian was snubbed at the altar by a younger woman, he was so distraught he fled the country and immigrated to the States. He then spent the next 28 years (from 1923 to 1951), using only handmade tools, to single-handedly carve these coral rocks into a monument to unrequited love. The largest stone weighs 29 tons and the swinging gate weighs in at 9 tons. Strangely, no one ever saw him actually building the prehistoric-looking structures. But scholars have come here hoping to unlock the mysteries of how the pyramids were built. It's actually a mistake to refer to it as a castle, since there are no turrets, ramparts or other architectural elements typical of castles.

To reach the site, take the Florida Turnpike Ext south to Homestead. Turn right off Exit 5 (SW 288th St), go 2 miles and turn right onto SW 157th Ave.

Gold Coast Railroad Museum (Map 1)

South Florida would still be a swamp today without the introduction of train service. Primarily of interest to serious train buffs, this museum *(☎ 305-253-0063, w www .goldcoast-railroad.org, 12450 SW 152nd St; admission $5/3 adult/child 3-11 yrs; open 11am-3pm Mon-Fri, 11am-4pm Sat & Sun)* was set up in the 1950s by the Miami Railroad Historical Society. It displays more than 30 antique railway cars, including the Ferdinand Magellan presidential car, which is featured prominently in a famous photograph of newly elected president Harry Truman. He's standing at the rear holding a newspaper bearing the famous erroneous headline 'Dewey Defeats Truman.' The car was also used by US presidents Roosevelt, Eisenhower, and even Ronald Reagan (for whom it was outfitted with 3-inch-thick glass windows and armor plating). On weekends, a 2-mile, 15- to 20-minute train ride ($2) runs at 1pm and 3pm.

Take I-95 south to US 1 south and turn right on SW152nd St (Coral Reef Dr); head west for 4 miles until you see the museum. It's about 45 minutes from downtown.

Wings Over Miami (Map 1)

Air and history buffs will be delighted at this Tamiami Airport museum (☎ 305-233-5197, W www.wingsovermiami.com, 14710 SW 128th St; admission $10/6 adult/senior & child under 13 yrs; open 10am-5pm Thur-Sun), which chronicles the history of aviation. Highlights include a propeller collection, J47 jet engine, a Soviet bomber from Smolensk and the nose section of 'Fertile Myrtle.' An impressive exhibit on the Tuskegee Airmen features videos of the black pilots telling their own stories. The staff is knowledgeable and dedicated.

Take Hwy 836 west to Florida's Turnpike, go south to Exit 19 (120th St), then west on 120th St for about 2 miles to 137th Ave (Tamiami Airport). Turn left (south), enter the airport and follow the signs.

Ancient Spanish Monastery (Map 5)

The Episcopal Church of St Bernard de Clairvaux (☎ 305-945-1461, W www.spanish monastery.com, 16711 W Dixie Hwy; admission $5/2.50/2 adult/senior/child under 12 yrs; open to visitors 9am-5pm Mon-Sat) is a stunning early Gothic and Romanesque building. Constructed in 1141 in Segovia, Spain, it was converted to a granary 700 years later, and eventually bought by newspaper tycoon William Randolph Hearst. He dismantled it and shipped it to the USA in more than 10,000 crates, intending to reconstruct it at his sprawling estate near San Luis Obispo, California. But construction was never approved by the government, and the stones sat in boxes until 1954, when a group of Miami developers purchased the dismantled monastery from Hearst and reassembled it here. It's a lovely, albeit popular, oasis, allegedly the oldest building in the Western Hemisphere. There are nice garden walks around the cloisters, and inside the church you'll want to look for the rare lambskin parchment books and telescopic stained glass windows. Church services are held Sunday at 8am, 10:30am and noon, and a healing service is held Wednesday at 10am.

Museum of Contemporary Art (Map 2)

The MoCA (☎ 305-893-6211, W www .mocanomi.org, 770 NE 125th St; admission $5/3 adult/senior & student; open 11am-5pm Tues-Sat, noon-5pm Sun) features excellent rotating exhibitions of contemporary art done by local, national and international artists. Think along the lines of a Keith Haring retrospective and the first US appearances of Mexican masterpieces by Frida Kahlo and Diego Rivera. The reincarnated MoCA also has a strong permanent collection; look for work by Jasper Johns, Duane Michaels and Roy Lichtenstein. Good films usually accompany and enhance the exhibits. The MoCA is in an unassuming neighborhood, but it's worth going the distance to visit. Definitely call to see what's on tap.

Rubell Family Art Collection (Map 2)

The Rubell family operates a number of top-end hotels on the Beach, but they have also amassed an impressive and pioneering contemporary art collection (☎ 305-573-6090, 95 NW 29th St; admission $5/2.50 adult/senior & student; open 10am-6pm Wed-Sun) that spans the last 30 years. Opened in 1996, the 40,000-sq-foot facility houses works by Cindy Sherman, Keith Haring, Damien Hirst and Jeff Koons. But don't expect just one or two pieces by each artist; the aim is to focus on an artist's entire career. Friendly docents and curators will happily and honestly tell you what they think about a particular piece. The museum is located in an industrial area, in a large yellow building that once served as a former DEA drug- and weapons-confiscation storage facility. It's a pretty unconventional place. There's no sign and you'll have to ring the front doorbell.

American Police Hall of Fame & Museum (Map 2)

A police officer is killed in the USA every 57 hours, and this museum (☎ 305-573-0070,

[W] *www.aphf.org, 3801 Biscayne Blvd; admission $12/9/6 adult/senior/child 12 yrs & under; open 10am-5:30pm daily)* memorializes them. You can't miss the boxy building with a 1995 Chevy Caprice Classic police car glued to the museum wall fronting Biscayne Blvd. In this extraordinarily violent culture we live in, kids seem to be attracted to the gore and execution devices. (Florida recently discontinued the use of the electric chair, as it constitutes cruel and unusual punishment, but the state still enforces the death penalty.) You can play detective and work a crime scene, and check out the holding cell for those presumed innocent until proven guilty. While it has some 'fun' collections, like the cop car from *Blade Runner,* gangster memorabilia, confiscated weapons and restraint devices, it's mainly a tribute to slain officers. Murdered officers' names, ranks, cities and states are engraved in white Italian marble. There's also an inter-denominational chapel.

Bacardi Imports Headquarters (Map 2)
The headquarters for the USA's most popular rum company, Bacardi, has a small museum *(☎ 305-573-8511, 2100 Biscayne Blvd; admission free; open by appointment only 10am-noon & 2:30pm-4pm Mon-Fri)* dedicated to the history of the family company from 1838 to the present. It's filled with mementos, artifacts, artwork, paintings and sculptures by family members.

Liberty City (Map 2)
From the birth of Miami until the 1950s, blacks were permitted to live only in the northwest quarter of downtown, called Colored Town. Since it was 'over the tracks,' the name was later changed to Overtown, and eventually decimated by the construction of freeways and bypasses.

In 1934, a *Miami Herald* series on Overtown's appalling living conditions led to the first federal public-housing project in the southeastern USA. Subsequently, Overtown's residents were shoved into the projects as whites needed the space. The 1950s concrete apartment blocks in Liberty City

were built by white contractors to meet the housing demands of the expanding black community.

Liberty City, north and west of downtown, is a misnomer. Made infamous by the Liberty City Riots in 1980 (see the History section in the Facts about Miami chapter), the area is very poor and crime is higher than in other parts of the city (see the Dangers & Annoyances section in the Facts for the Visitor chapter for more information). And while plans exist to renovate the area by creating a village of cultural and tourist attractions, the prospects of that happening in the near future look doubtful.

Whites, fearing 'black encroachment' on their neighborhoods, actually went so far as to build a *wall* at the then-border of Liberty City – NW 12th Ave from NW 62nd to NW 67th Sts – to separate their neighborhoods. Part of the wall still stands, at NW 12th Ave between NW 63rd and 64th Sts.

For information on Liberty City, Overtown and other areas significant to black history, contact the very helpful **Black Archives History & Research Center of South Florida (Map 2)** *(☎ 305-636-2390, 5400 NW 22nd Ave; open 9am-5pm Mon-Fri, from 1pm-5pm for specific research projects)* in the Caleb Center.

Black Heritage Museum
This museum *(☎ 305-252-3535; call for hours and locations)* is a museum in search of a home. In 1987 teachers Priscilla S Kruize, Dr Paul Cadby and Dr Earl Wells set out to establish a center to celebrate the cultures of African Americans, Bahamians, Haitians and other blacks in Dade County. Since then they have organized rotating exhibitions in different locations, and are trying to raise funds to establish a permanent site.

Little Haiti (Map 2)
As with Little Havana, Little Haiti has absorbed waves of refugees during times of Haitian political strife. Haitians are the third-largest group of foreign-born residents in Florida, after Cubans and (surprisingly) snowbird Canadians. Although Little

Haiti has had limited success in marketing itself as a tourist attraction, check in at the **Haitian Refugee Center** (☎ 305-757-8538, *119 NE 54th St; open 9am-5pm Mon-Fri*), a community center that disseminates information about Haitian life in Haiti and Miami. It's also a good resource for information about community events.

This colorful neighborhood is very roughly bounded by Biscayne Blvd to the east, I-95 to the west, 90th St to the north and 54th St to south. While you're up here, keep an eye peeled for Haitian **botánicas** that sell Vodou-related items. They're worth visiting for beautiful bottles, beads and sequined banners with Vodou symbols. While they may seem pricey at $100 to $200, they're far cheaper here than at galleries around the country, where they sell as art.

Miami City Cemetery (Map 2)

The city of Miami's original cemetery (☎ 305-579-6938, *1800 NE 2nd Ave; admission free; open 7am-3:30pm Mon-Fri, 8am-4:30pm Sat & Sun*) was established in July 1897 and contains over 9000 graves in separate white, black and Jewish sections. Since Julia Tuttle was the 13th burial, she received a gravesite front and center. Mayors and politicians lie alongside about 90 Confederate dead and war veterans from the 20th century. The cemetery still has between 12 and 20 burials a year, though space in the 10½-acre site is dwindling.

Forget Julia Tuttle; Mrs Carrie Miller, who died in 1926, is the highlight of the cemetery. Her husband, William, wrapped her body in a sheet and encased it in a concrete block 6 feet high. 'After the body has gone to dust, her sleeping form will remain,'

Haiti's 1991 Coup

In late September 1991, the Haitian military, led by Lieutenant General Raoul Cedras, overthrew the constitutionally elected government of President Jean-Bertrand Aristide. The US response was economic sanctions, to be lifted only after the return of Aristide to power.

Under Cedras' leadership, Haitian armed forces were given extreme legal and institutional autonomy and were responsible for law enforcement and 'public safety.' As human rights abuses – beatings, torture, executions and 'disappearances' – escalated, refugees began to flee to the relative safety (they thought) of the USA in anything that would float.

For the next three years, the local media was flooded with images of Haitians being rounded up by the US Coast Guard. In the first seven months of 1992 alone, according to the UN High Commissioner for Refugees (UNHCR), the US Coast Guard intercepted and detained at Guantanamo Bay, Cuba, more than 38,000 Haitians fleeing their country. But only about 30% of those were given an INS stamp declaring them 'potentially qualified for political asylum.'

Pressure began mounting from Haitian groups in Miami, who pointed out the historic carte blanche given any Cuban who manages to wash up on US soil. Then the US Supreme Court upheld a detestable Bush (Sr) administration policy that allowed the Coast Guard to return refugees intercepted on the high seas directly to their home country without the benefit of an asylum hearing.

Through a series of maneuvers (including, some say, a covert payment of a cool $1 million by the USA to Cedras), Aristide was returned to power. Cedras resigned, and was granted political amnesty. For the second time in a century, the USA sent troops to Haiti to restore democracy.

This allowed the Clinton administration to say to the remaining Haitians at Guantanamo Bay, in essence, 'please go home now, you no longer have a claim of asylum since your country is once again a model democracy.' Accentuating the divergent treatment of Haitians and Cubans, Clinton announced the policy the day after permitting some 20,000 Cubans at Guantanamo entry to the USA.

Metromover swooping by the IM Pei–designed Bank of America Tower

Miami skyline at night

The Venetian Pool, Coral Gables

SoBe art deco with a little natural decor

This wavy concrete wall and a figure-eight–shaped pool embellish South Beach's Kenmore Hotel.

reads the epitaph. William apparently wanted to join his wife there eventually, but he lost all his money during the Great Depression and died broke. He's buried in an unmarked plot, nearby.

The cemetery is not in the friendliest part of town and you should visit during daylight hours. Take Biscayne Blvd to NE 18th St and turn west to the cemetery to avoid getting lost in the back streets.

ACTIVITIES
Health Clubs

Bronze bods praise the sun, while buff bods bow to free weights. For those who can't go a day or week without flexing some serious muscle, plenty of gyms open their doors for daily and weekly memberships. Some might allow the use of nearby hotel pools; it's always worth asking.

Try **Crunch (Map 3)** (*☎ 305-674-8222, 305-674-0247 class hot line, 1253 Washington Ave; $21/99 day/week)*, a gay fave that's also particularly popular with supermodels, and offers wacky classes such as Rear Attitude and Kardio Kombat. Devotees worship Crunch with the same fervor that others attend Mass.

Idol's Gym (Map 3) (*☎ 305-532-0089, 715 Lincoln Lane; $25/50 three days/week)*, just off Meridian Ave, is typical of South Beach workout emporiums: None of the gym rats ever seem to wear shirts.

Ironworks (Map 3) (*☎ 305-531-4743, 1676 Alton Rd; $15/25/56 day/three days/week)*, popular with locals who size one other up discreetly, offers lots of yoga and aerobics classes. In fact, Gloria Estefan's personal yoga instructor teaches here. Ten visits for $80 is a great deal.

The **Fontainebleau Hilton Spa (Map 5)** (*☎ 305-538-2000, 4441 Collins Ave)* occasionally runs daily and weekly specials for nonguests, but it doesn't really advertise. If you come for a spa treatment and spend at least $65, you get to use the health club and pool.

The **Eden Roc Resort & Spa (Map 5)** (*☎ 305-674-5580, 4525 Collins Ave; hotel guests/nonguests $12/35 per day)* at the Eden Roc Resort (see the Places to Stay

chapter) is a very complete, first-rate sports center with lots of classes and a great indoor climbing wall.

The truly chic head to the ultra stylish **David Barton Gym (Map 3)** (*☎ 305-672-2000, 1685 Collins Ave; $20/75 day/week, 10-visit pass $150)*, on the lower level of the fiercely fashionable Delano Hotel. The nightclub of health clubs, where celebrity-spotting is a frowned-upon sport, delights in dim lighting, designer furniture, loud house music and…oh yes, state-of-the-art exercise equipment. Pumping iron and crunching abs is a bona fide recreational activity. Ask for the pass that gains access to the sexy pool.

Bicycling

The weather's fine and the roads are flat (elevation: sea level). What more could you want? Well, you could call the **Miami-Dade County Bicycle Coordinator** (*☎ 305-375-1647)* for a map highlighting the best metro roads. A leafy canopy lures cyclists in Coral Gables and Coconut Grove, where there's a particularly nice route. Follow the dedicated bike path and lane along S Miami Ave through Coconut Grove and down Old Cutler Rd to Matheson Hammock Park. Key Biscayne and the Bill Baggs Cape Florida State Recreation Area are popular places, as is the Oleta River State Recreation Area. On Key Biscayne you can rent at **Key Cycling (Map 7)** (*☎ 305-361-0061, 61 Harbor Dr)* and **Mangrove Cycles** (*☎ 305-361-5555, 260 Crandon Blvd)*.

Biking in South Beach, especially on the Promenade and the boardwalk along the beach, is an excellent way to get around. Several places rent bicycles, including **Two Wheel Drive (Map 3)** (*☎ 305-534-2177, 1260 Washington Ave; rates $5/15/45 per hour/day/week; open 10am-7pm Mon-Fri, 10am-6pm Sat & 11am-4pm Sun)*. The **Miami Beach Bicycle Center (Map 4)** (*☎ 305-674-0150, 601 5th St; rates $5/20/70 per hour/day/week; open 10am-7pm Mon-Sat, 10am-5pm Sun)* also rents bikes. It's also a nice ride from South Beach over the Venetian Causeway to Bayside Marketplace and back.

For another good biking experience, see the Shark Valley section in the Everglades chapter.

In-Line Skating

In-line skating is the most popular form of South Beach transportation. Everyone seems to have a pair of skates, and most streets are excellent for it. Three caveats for babes on blades: You can't ride on the café and hotel side of Ocean Ave or on the boardwalk that starts on 21st St, and you should use extra caution on Washington Ave. Lincoln Road and The Promenade resemble the Daytona 500 racetrack in sheer volume (if not speed, since riders generally skate at a moderate pace – all the better to see and be seen). Since some shops balk at letting you in with skates on, carry some sandals with you.

For in-line skate rentals, roll over to **Fritz's Skate Shop (Map 3)** (☎ *305-532-1954, 730 Lincoln Road; rentals $7.50/14/ 22.50 hour/6pm-noon/10am-10pm*). Fritz gives free lessons on Sunday morning at 10:30am, when the streets have no name and late-night clubbers have just barely gone to bed.

Beaches

Miami Beach has perhaps the best city beaches in the country. The water is relatively clear and warm, and the imported sand is relatively white. It's wide, firm and long enough to accommodate the throngs. A whopping 12 miles from South Pointe to 192nd St (William Lehman Causeway), the city is said to have an astonishing 35 miles of shoreline when taking into consideration Key Biscayne and the like. (The throngs, by the way, are generally considerate. There's never much litter or broken glass, but do use caution when walking barefoot.) Unless otherwise noted, the beaches discussed are all found on Maps 3 and 4.

Like a large, accommodating restaurant, the Beach is wordlessly zoned to provide everyone with what they want without offending anyone else. So, if you find yourself somewhere where the people around you make you uncomfortable, just move a little and you'll be fine. Perhaps surprisingly, topless bathing is legal in most places, a happy result of Miami Beach's popularity with Europeans and South Americans. In general, skimpy seems to be the order of the day, and you'll see plenty of thongs and other minuscule coverings on the bronzed gods and goddesses. Fear not ye in traditional bathing suits, you won't feel out of place.

The most crowded sections of the Beach are from about 5th St to 21st St. You'll see lots of models preening for photo shoots between 6th and 14th Sts, also known as Glitter Beach. Weekends are usually more crowded than weekdays, but except during special events it's usually not too difficult to find a quiet spot. From 21st St to 46th St, the 1½-mile boardwalk is a nice way to see the beach without getting sand between your toes. Perhaps for a sunset stroll before heading out to an early dinner?

Don't forget to check out the funky, Ken Scharf–designed **lifeguard tower** at 10th St. Other good, locally designed lifeguard towers dot 5th St to 14th St. You'll notice that art deco was not saved just for hotels.

Elsewhere, notwithstanding the weekend traffic snarls (read: crawls) across the Rickenbacker Causeway, Key Biscayne (Map 7) is a key place to go. The 5 miles of Key beaches are relatively undeveloped, commercial-free zones. Joy, ecstasy, delight, rapture.

Family-Fun Beaches

Families head to beaches north of 21st St, especially the one at 53rd St, with a playground and public toilets and the dune-backed one around 73rd St. They also head south to Matheson Hammock Park (Map 2), which has calm artificial lagoons.

Swimming

Water, water everywhere, not a drop to drink. True and not true: These fresh and salty waters are made for swimming, and you can always get a beverage poolside. Plus, sitting poolside sipping a cool drink is a worthy and noble Miami tradition. The spring-fed **Venetian Pool (Map 10)** (see the Coral Gables section, earlier in this chapter) wins hands down.

The excellent T-shaped **Flamingo Park Swimming Pool (Map 3)** (☎ *305-673-7750, 11th St*) has six lanes in its 25-yard lap swimming area and a deep-water area. At press time the pool was closed for reconstruction; call for hours and fees.

The rest of the really good pools belong to hotels, and hotel pools are restricted to hotel guests and club members (see Health Clubs, earlier in this section; you may be able to use some of these pools with a day or week membership). Lonely Planet would *never* suggest breaking hotel policies; the following is simply intended to let you know what you're missing.

The **Raleigh Hotel** (☎ *305-534-6300, 1775 Collins Ave; open 24 hours*) is a class act. Voted most beautiful pool in Florida by

---

Beaches

Gay Beaches

The tides wash up gay sand around 12th St, especially after the clubs close on Friday and Saturday. It's not like there's sex going on (there isn't); it's just a spot where gay men happen to congregate. Though outnumbered, lesbians gather here, too. Sunday afternoon volleyball at 4pm, after everyone has had a decent night's (morning's) sleep, is packed with fun-loving locals.

Surfing & Windsurfing Beaches

First things first: This isn't Hawaii. In Miami Beach, head north to Haulover Beach Park in Sunny Isles (Map 5) or as far south as you can. The breaks between 5th St and South Pointe can actually give pretty good rides (by Florida standards, like 2 to 4 feet). You'll do well with a longboard. Hobie Beach (also called Windsurfing Beach; Map 7) rules for windsurfing. See the individual sections for information on rental, sales and lessons.

Swimming Beaches

What? You actually want to swim? Head to 85th St in Surfside (Map 5), devoid of high-rise condos and safely watched by lifeguards.

Nude Beaches

Nude bathing is legal at Haulover Beach Park in Sunny Isles (Map 5). Head to the northern end of the park between the two northernmost parking lots. The area north of the lifeguard tower is predominantly gay, south is straight. Sex is not tolerated on these beaches and you'll get arrested if you're seen heading into the bushes.

Latino Beaches

Latino families, predominantly Cuban, congregate between 5th St and South Pointe (Map 4). Topless bathing is unwise and can be considered offensive here.

Party-Scene Beaches

Key Biscayne's ever-popular Crandon Park Beach (Map 7) attracts tons of families to its barbecue grills, locals blaring dueling stereos and tried-and-true beach bums. Admission is $2 per carload.

Quiet Beaches

It's pretty low-key up around 53rd St (despite the presence of families; Map 5) and down at Matheson Hammock Park (Map 2).

Life magazine in 1945, it still gets top honors in this book. It's as curvaceous as a 1930s Hollywood vixen. Walk through the posh lobby and straight out to the back. The bar inside makes the best martini on the beach, but there's a bar at the pool, too.

The **Delano Hotel** (☎ 305-672-2000, *1685 Collins Ave*) pool is, like the hotel, swank. Walk through the lobby, through the restaurant, past the back porch to the gardens, where beckoning, bed-like lounge chairs line the lawn. The pool's in the garden; note the table and chairs in the shallow area.

If you've ever seen the movie *Goldfinger*, you've seen the pool at the **Fontainebleau Hilton** (☎ 305-538-2000, *4441 Collins Ave*). Bond, that's James Bond, opens the movie sitting poolside, with a cool drink in his hand, and says 'Now, this is the life.' He's right. Waterfalls, islands and beautiful people abound. Reaching the pool is easier from the beach than the lobby. There's a wet bar and two snack bars (one is beneath the center of the pool, where you can watch the swimmers through a glass wall).

Tennis

The annual 10-day **Nasdaq 100 Tennis Open** (☎ 305-446-2200; *mid- to late March*) is played at Key Biscayne's **Tennis Center at Crandon Park (Map 7)** (☎ 305-365-2300, *6702 Crandon Blvd; open 8am-9pm daily*). It draws such marquee players as the Williams sisters, Hingis, Kuerten, Sampras and Agassi; but you, too, can play in the shadows of the giants. There are two grass, eight clay and 17 hard courts that cost $3 to $6 per person, per hour, depending on the surface and time of day.

The **Flamingo Tennis Center (Map 3)** (☎ 305-673-7761, *1000 12th St; open 7:45am-9pm Mon-Fri, 7:45am-8pm Sat & Sun*) has 19 popular clay courts that are open to the public for $2.50 per person, per hour. On weekends and evenings after 5pm, the place is like a zoo.

Kayaking & Canoeing

Kayaking through mangroves is magical, and you can do it at Haulover Beach Park (Map 5) or Key Biscayne. Equipment rental

is cheap, and you won't even need lessons to make the boat go where you want it to. Make a beeline for **Urban Trails Kayak Co (Map 5)** (☎ 305-947-1302, *3400 NE 163rd St; singles $8/20/25 hour/four hours/day, tandems $12/30/35 including paddles, life jacket & instructions; open 9am-5pm daily, weather permitting*). Add $5 per single and $10 per tandem if you want to keep the kayaks overnight. This friendly outfit can help plan and map your trip to some 19 Intracoastal Waterway islands, many with barbecue facilities. You can even camp on some for nothing. Ask about guided two- to four-hour trips (☎ 305-491-0221) for four or more people ($45 per person).

Sailboards Miami (Map 7) (☎ 305-361-7245, *1 Rickenbacker Causeway; rentals singles/tandem $13/18 hour*) also rents kayaks. See the Windsurfing section, later, for directions. You can also purchase a 10-hour card for $90. To get some exercise for your lower body, you could try renting water bikes, which you sit in a kayak-type boat and rent for the same prices as the kayaks. In either case, if you're goal-oriented and need a destination, head for the little off-shore sandbar.

Canoeing around the 10,000 Islands, or on the Wilderness Waterway between Everglades City and Flamingo, is one of the most fascinating ways to get away into nature; see the Everglades chapter for information.

Running

Running is quite popular, and the beach is very good for jogging as it's flat, wide and hard-packed. The Promenade is the stylish place for both, but more serious runners may appreciate the Flamingo Park running track, just east of Alton Rd between 11th and 12th Sts; the entrance is on the 12th St side at the east end of the fence. Ardent runners can also contact the **Miami Runners Club** (☎ 305-227-1500) for race and special event information. Elsewhere around the city, running is good along S Bayshore Dr in Coconut Grove, around the Riviera Country Club in Coral Gables and anywhere on Key Biscayne.

Surfing

We'll say it again: Offshore Miami bears no resemblance to the Banzai Pipeline. On the Beach, the best surfing is just north of South Pointe Park, with 2- to 5-foot waves and a nice, sandy bottom. Unfortunately, there are a few drawbacks: It's usually closer to 2 than to 5 feet (except, of course, before storms); it can get a little mushy (so longboards are the way to go); and it's swamped with weekend swimmers and surfers. It's better farther north near Haulover Beach Park or anywhere north of, say, 70th St. Call the recorded surf report (☎ 305-534-7873) for daily conditions.

Bird's Surf Shop (Map 5) *(305-940-0929, 250 Sunny Isles Blvd; open 10am-7pm daily)* sells boards.

X-Isle Surf Shop (Map 4) *(☎ 305-673-5900, 437 Washington Ave; rentals from $10/30 hour/day; open 10am-7pm Mon-Fri, 10am-6pm Sat, 11am-6pm Sun)* resembles a T-shirt shop as much as a purveyor of all things surf related. Still, it rents foam boards and sells used boards for about $120 to $275. New ones start at $400.

Windsurfing

Head immediately to Hobie Beach, also known as Windsurfing Beach. For board rentals, try the friendly folks at **Sailboards Miami (Map 7)** *(☎ 305-361-7245, 1 Rickenbacker Causeway; rentals $20-26/hour, lots of multi-hour specials; open 10am-4:30pm daily)*. They offer short and longboard rentals and hold two-hour 'guaranteed-to-learn' windsurfing lessons for $69 (more advanced lessons cost $30/50 half-hour/hour, including equipment). Take the first right turn after the tollbooths for the Rickenbacker Causeway to Key Biscayne, where the water is calm.

Sailing

If you're a bona fide seaworthy sailor, **Sailboats of Key Biscayne (Map 7)** *(☎ 305-361-0328, 4000 Crandon Blvd; rentals $27/81/129 hour/half-day/day for a 22-foot Catalina)* will rent you a vessel.

Wanna buzz down to the Keys, or, say, float over to the Bahamas? **Florida Yacht**

Charters (Map 4) *(☎ 305-532-8600, 800-537-0050, 1290 5th St; open 9am-5:30pm daily)*, at the Miami Beach Marina, rents yachts with and without captains (as long as you pass a little practical test).

Diving & Snorkeling

Miami is not known for great diving, but between offshore wrecks and the introduction of artificial coral reefs, there's plenty to look at if you can part the waters and scratch beneath the surface. Go on a calm day. **Crandon Park Marina (Map 7)** *(☎ 305-361-1281, 4000 Crandon Blvd)* is home to many dive outfits. The *Diver's Dream*, owned by **Bubbles Dive Center** *(☎ 305-856-0565)* is moored at Watson Island (Map 2) and heads out on weekend mornings and afternoons. **South Beach Divers (Map 4)** *(☎ 305-531-6110, 851 Washington Ave)*, a five-star PADI dive center, runs regular diving excursions to Key Largo and around Miami. They also offer three-day self-study classes. For other diving possibilities, see the Keys and Key West chapters, and the Biscayne National Park section in the Everglades chapter.

Fishing

Locals have always fished these bountiful waters and you can, too. You can rent a pricey charter, hop aboard a 'head boat' with 100 or so other fisherfolk (boats are rarely full), or cast a line off numerous piers or bridges. Note that it is illegal to fish off some bridges; look for posted signs. You don't need a license if you're fishing from shore or from a bridge or pier. On your own, drop a line at South Pointe Park (Map 4), off the Rickenbacker Causeway or any Key Biscayne beach or from Haulover Beach Park (Map 5). You can buy equipment and tackle from **Haulover Marine Center (Map 5)** *(☎ 305-945-3934, 15000 Collins Ave; open 24 hours)*. There are lots of fishing charters at the **Crandon Park Marina (Map 7)** *(☎ 305-361 1281; rates $450-500 half day, $600-700 full day)* and at the **Miami Beach Marina (Map 4)** *(☎ 305-673-6000, 300 Alton Rd)*.

Jet Skiing & Motorboating

Jet skis and motorboats kill manatees and fish, rip up sea plants and protected sea grass (destroying the manatees' food supply), scare swimmers, annoy locals and result in several deaths a year. Furthermore, Biscayne Bay and its canals are very shallow and tricky to navigate. Further*most*, many areas are protected Manatee Zones. You can rent these hateful machines around the beach, but we wish you wouldn't. If that's not strong enough for you, consider this: You wouldn't want to take a spill on your wave runner and have it run off without you, leaving you bobbing deep in shark infested waters, would you?

Ultralights & Skydiving

Miami is an aviation center, and hundreds of small planes fill the skies daily. Ultralight aircraft, in fact, became so popular that Dade County built a field specifically for the tiny planes at **Homestead General Aviation Airport** *(HGAA; ☎ 305-247-4883, 28700 SW 217th Ave)*. Ultralights are regulated small aircraft, but you don't need a pilot's license to fly them. **Tony's Ultralight Adven-**

tures **(Map 7)** *(☎ 305-361-3909, Rickenbacker Causeway; open 10am-sundown Sun, by appointment weekdays)* offers lessons and sightseeing flights in its nice, two-seater ultralight seaplane. First come, first served.

At HGAA, **Skydive Miami** *(☎ 305-759-3483; open 10am-4pm Mon & Wed-Fri, 8am-4pm Sat & Sun)* will train you and push you out of a plane on your first jump in one day for $169. Did you see the movie *Drop Zone* with Wesley Snipes? If so, then you've seen these folks in action. One of its former employees trained Snipes for the film, and most of the jumps were filmed here. Call the day before you want to head out.

Rock Climbing

X-Treme Rock Climbing (Map 1) *(☎ 305-233-6623, 13972 SW 139th Court; $12 daily; open 3pm-10pm Mon-Fri, 10am-10pm Sat, 10am-8pm Sun)* boasts over 11,000 feet of climbing surfaces, including beginning routes and expert roof overhangs. Classes ($35) are offered by appointment only.

The Eden Roc Resort's **Spa of Eden (Map 5)** (see Health Clubs, earlier in this section) has a very good indoor climbing wall.

Places to Stay

There are a few visitors who don't sleep much in Miami, but even *they* will need a place to change their clothes. Fortunately, metro Miami is blessed with a range of places to stay. It isn't the ideal place for camping, but there is one unconventional choice: See Urban Trails Kayak Co in the Northern Miami Beach section, later in this chapter. Miami also has a few hostels, so you needn't sleep in the shrubs to save money. You'll also find camaraderie in guest houses and B&Bs. Even though you won't find *many* of these intimate lodgings, the ones that do exist are very good. There are few in South Beach, a lone one in Coconut Grove and another on the Miami River downtown. But that's about it. This is a hotel town, no doubt about it.

There are some safe generalities we can make about South Beach's deco hotels, most of which were built in the 1930s for middle-class vacationers. They have usually been retrofitted with air-conditioning;

rooms and baths are small; and they often look better on the outside than on the inside. Rooms in the boutique hotels (in the upper mid-range and top-end categories) often have Web TV, valet parking, CD players (with CDs!), Internet access, DSL connections, valet laundry and other similar amenities. If some of these are essential to your well-being, don't forget to ask. If we listed them with each entry, this book would look like an American Automobile Association (AAA) directory. As for the more expensive rooms fronting Ocean Ave, consider this: They also face a throbbing nighttime beat of music and relentless conversation; the sun blares in in the morning; and you often can't see much of the beach because of the palm trees blocking the view. But really, don't let that stop you; you wanted to stay on the Beach, didn't you?

The Beach has upwards of 100 hotels with about 8000 beds ranging in price from $13 to $2000 nightly. The hotels listed are categorized based on the price of a room in the wintertime high season; expensive suites skew the practical range. So-called budget rooms are less than $100, mid-range $100 to $200, and top end over $200. But remember, these prices are just guidelines; you should be able to get a room for less, unless you visit during a circuit party or other special event. Once you've arrived, it never hurts to ask to see a room before hauling your bag upstairs. Within the budget and less-expensive mid-range places, some rooms have been renovated, others haven't.

For your dollar, and considering its proximity to the action and neighborhood ambience, you'll do better staying on South Beach than elsewhere, but if you're game, you've got plenty of options (read on). No matter where you stay, you'll have to swallow hard to absorb the 12.5% room tax. A few places even tack on an obligatory 15% service charge; ask before making a reservation. Hotel parking costs extra, but at least it includes in-and-out privileges.

SOUTH BEACH (11TH TO 23RD ST; MAP 3)

From rock bottom to top dollar, South Beach booms with choices. There are still a few places where you can pay less than $75 a night, but you'll sacrifice quality. Shop the budget places carefully and check the rooms before committing. Even at the height of high season, you'll have a choice. Don't let anyone convince you otherwise. Also note that true deco style is compact by modern standards, so the more 'landmark' deco a hotel is, the smaller its rooms are likely to be. Unless otherwise noted, assume all South Beach hotels are two- to four-story low-rise hotels.

Budget

Banana Bungalow (☎ 305-538-1951, 800-746-7835, fax 305-531-3217, **W** www.bananabungalow.com, 2360 Collins Ave) Dorm beds $15-19; singles/doubles $45-99/56-102 off-season, $84-116/91-130 Dec-Apr. That the fun Bungalow has a big canalside pool surrounded by a concrete slab doesn't deter a bevy of bathing beau-

ties. Perhaps that's because of the loud music as well as the adjacent happening bar with a seriously rowdy international crowd. The office was formerly a gas station, but that's about the extent of the kitschy '50s feel. There are 60 spartan private rooms and 30 dorm rooms (most with six beds each), a borderline inadequate communal kitchen and two Internet terminals.

Clay Hotel & International Hostel (☎ 305-534-2988, 800-379-2529, fax 305-673-0346, **W** www.clayhotel.com, 1438 Washington Ave) Dorm beds $15-18, singles/doubles $40-54/42-60 off-season, $42-64/46-76 mid-Dec–mid-Apr. Perhaps the country's most beautiful HI hostel, this 100-year-old Spanish-style villa is also the Beach's most established. The Clay has an array of clean and comfortable rooms, from single-sex dorms with four to eight beds, to spacious VIP rooms with balconies to family rooms and decent private rooms with TV, phone, bath and air-con. Many are located in a medina-like maze of adjacent buildings. The excellent kitchen is large, but very warm in summer. While the staff might be a little harassed due to sheer volume, they're friendly and helpful. Internet access is readily available ($1 for seven minutes).

Tropics Hotel & Hostel (☎ 305-531-0361, fax 305-531-8676, **W** www.tropicshotel.com, 1550 Collins Ave) Dorm beds $16, private rooms $50/63/75 double/triple/quad Apr–mid-Feb, $75/88/100 high season. The surprisingly nice Tropics sports an Olympic-sized swimming pool, spacious brick patio, barbecue area and a full kitchen. Its clean dorms have four beds and attached bath, while the nice private rooms have firm mattresses, TV and phone. Some have great views of the pool. Lockers and Internet access ($1 per five minutes) are available.

San Juan Hotel (☎ 305-538-7531, fax 305-532-5704, **W** www.sanjuanhotelsouthbeach.com, 1680 Collins Ave) Rooms $59-99. The San Juan doesn't initially look appealing, and the reception doesn't exactly make up for that with charm, but its 80 rooms are surprisingly clean and they all have a fridge and microwave. Although there's barely enough room to lounge around the pool, it's better than soaking in your bathtub.

Fairfax Hotel (☎ 305-538-3837, fax 305-673-9408, Ⓦ www.hotelfairfax.com, 1776 Collins Ave) Rooms $69 off-season, $89 mid-Dec–Apr. This older hotel, with 86 rooms, is fairly clean. Speaking of which, try for a room with tiled floors instead of carpeting; it's easier for the staff to clean. Kitchen sizes vary, so if you plan on eating in, ask for a room with larger facilities. Try to ignore the dark hallways and tiny breakfast room.

Mid-Range

The Governor Hotel (☎ 305-532-2100, 800-542-0444, fax 305-532-9139, Ⓦ www.governorsouthbeach.com, 435 21st St) Rooms $69-89 off-season, $95-125 mid-Oct–Apr. This is what unrenovated, old-fashioned deco hotels look like: Old ceiling fans line the long, narrow hallways, which have exposed pipes, and bathroom ceilings peel. But these 121 rooms are fairly inexpensive for South Beach.

Beachcomber Hotel (☎ 305-531-3755, 888-305-4683, fax 305-673-8609, Ⓦ www.beachcombermiami.com, 1340 Collins Ave) Rooms $75 off-season, $98 mid-Dec–Apr. Inquire about weekly rates. For the price, you could overlook soft mattresses and torn upholstery. I didn't mind the overwhelming odor of disinfectant; the housekeeping staff had obviously been working. At press time, a little more than half the 29 simple rooms had been renovated; try to get one of these. When deciding, factor in friendly service, free local calls and Continental breakfast.

Brigham Gardens Guesthouse (☎ 305-531-1331, fax 305-538-9898, Ⓦ www.brighamgardens.com, 1411 Collins Ave) Rooms $70-110 off-season, $100-145 mid-Nov–May. Weekly discounts. This charming guest house, built around a lush garden that attracts tropical birds, feels like a sanctuary. Perhaps it's the bamboo, hammocks, fountains and patio chairs. Or perhaps it's the attention paid by the hosts to ensure you a restful respite. Choose from among 23 large and airy guest rooms (most with kitchens and bathrooms), studios and apartments.

Some have convertible futon sofas; all rooms enjoy bright tropical colors and decor. As if that's not enough, there's a barbecue area and laundry. Pets are accepted.

Aqua Hotel (☎ 305-538-4361, fax 305-673-9109, Ⓦ www.aquamiami.com, 1530 Collins Ave) Rooms & suites $75-295 off-season, $95-395 Oct-May. Renovated in 2001, this hip place utilizes wood and concrete for flooring, and marble and stainless steel in the bathrooms. Mod kitchenettes and Web TV are also appealing. At press time, the penthouse was one of Miami's best bargains. Giant palms and teak furnishings surround the pool and courtyard, off which all 50 rooms are located. A second-story patio, where you can bring your Continental breakfast buffet goodies, overlooks the street. Pets are welcome.

The Dorchester (☎ 305-531-5745, 800-327-4739, fax 305-673-1006, Ⓦ www.dorchesterhotel.net, 1850 Collins Ave) Rooms/suites $89/219 off-season, $115/269 late Dec–mid-Apr. Even though these 94 rooms are clean, they could stand some renovating, and the squeaky beds could be a bit firmer. Still, for the price, they're a good value. As for the 35 nicely renovated one-bedroom suites, they boast bona fide full kitchens and separate living rooms; some have sofa beds. The staff is very nice.

Abbey Hotel (☎ 305-531-0031, fax 305-672-1663, Ⓦ www.abbeyhotel.com, 300 21st St) Rooms $95-165 off-season, $120-185 Dec-Mar. Insulated from the partying throngs, these 50 rooms manage to make timeless deco feel contemporary and warm. For the price, they're a very good value. Renovated in 1999, rooms feature touches of burnished chrome, platform beds and an earth-tone color scheme. There's no pool, but there is a nice garden. (A rooftop solarium is in the works.)

Villa Paradiso (☎ 305-532-0616, fax 305-667-0074, Ⓦ www.villaparadisohotel.com, 1415 Collins Ave) Studios $79-115 off-season, $125-135 late Dec–mid-Apr. Similar in its upscale style and friendly personality to its neighborly competitor (Brigham Gardens), Villa Paradiso is another very good choice for studios and one-bedrooms with kitchens.

The Carlton Hotel (☎ 305-538-5741, 800-722-7586, fax 305-534-6855, ⓦ www.carlton miamibeach.com, 1433 Collins Ave) Rooms/suites $95/205-250 off-season, $139/250-350 Nov-Apr. The Carlton offers clean rooms with soft platform beds, huge fridges, ceiling fans and small, older bathrooms. Some of the 70 rooms have kitchenettes, and all have covered, louvered doors, which might make one wary about room noises traveling far and wide. Draws include a big swimming pool and helpful staff.

Marseilles Hotel (☎ 305-538-5711, 800-327-4739, fax 305-673-1006, ⓦ www .marseilleshotel.com, 1741 Collins Ave) Rooms/suites $95-115/169-189 off-season, $139-189/199-229 Jan–mid-Apr. This ocean-front property has eight very nicely renovated suites and 104 comfortable regular rooms. For the money, they're a very good deal. At press time there was a small ocean-front pool and cabana in need of a renovation (fortunately, the hotel is in agreement with this assessment and has plans to work on it).

Kent Hotel (☎ 305-531-6771, 800-688-7678, fax 305-531-0720, ⓦ www.thekent hotel.com, 1131 Collins Ave) Rooms $130 off-season, $145 Oct-May. Owned and operated by Island Outpost, the hipster Kent was one of the Beach's best values at press time. Completely gutted in 2000, these 54 rooms have warm-wood floors, blonde-wood furnishings and stainless steel accents. You'd better like lilac if you stay here, though: The walls, bedspreads and robes are all lilac. It'd also help if you like comic strips, too, since the elevator is papered with them. Besides the funky lobby, other common space includes a side garden with Indonesian-style tables, bamboo and hammocks.

Crest Hotel Suites (☎ 305-531-0321, 800-531-3880, fax 305-531-8180, ⓦ www.crest hotel.com, 1670 James Ave) Rooms/suites $115-140/145-195 off-season, $155/195-235 Dec-Apr. This family-owned place, with 61 rooms in two buildings, is an excellent choice. Studios and one-bedroom suites feature custom galley-kitchens, combo

living/dining areas, modern bathrooms and small work spaces. Don't overlook the added value of a pool and rooftop solarium.

Betsy Ross Hotel (☎ 305-531-3934, fax 305-531-5282, ⓦ www.betsyrosshotel.com, 1440 Ocean Dr) Rooms/suites $120-180/180-340 off-season, $160-230/230-350 Nov-Apr. With a unique blend of deco and colonial styles, the Betsy Ross surely like the most out-of-place hotel in Miami. This solidly moderate place has 61 refurbished rooms featuring traditional furnishings. Luckily its rooftop deck overlooks the beachfront promenade, as the pool is smallish.

Greenview (☎ 305-531-6588, 877-782-3557, fax 305-535-8602, ⓦ www.rubell hotels.com, 1671 Washington Ave) Rooms/suites $95-150/175-230 off-season, $160/260 late Dec–Apr. With only 40 rooms, this delightful find is at once homey and elegant. Furnishings are spare, with black-and-white photos on the walls and piles of white bedding. A Continental breakfast is included, as are the pool facilities at its sister hotel, the Albion (see Top End).

The Penguin Hotel (☎ 305-534-9334, 800-235-3296, fax 305-672-6240, ⓦ www .penguinhotel.com, 1418 Ocean Dr) Rooms $115-170 off-season, $160-250 late Nov–mid-Apr. The sweet 44-room Penguin has quite pleasant, largish rooms with mini-fridges and a nice staff. Pricey oceanfront rooms have big louvered windows. But for a real splurge, the penthouse rooms ($250 in high season) have private rooftop terraces. A small wading pool is set in a similarly small but tropical patio.

Cavalier Hotel (☎ 305-534-2135, 800-688-7678, fax 305-531-5543, ⓦ www.cavalier hotel.com, 1320 Ocean Dr) Rooms/suites $130-160/250-275 off-season, $175-210/350-395 Oct-May. Got deco-overdose jitters? The Cavalier offers a decidedly refreshing change of pace. Another Island Outpost property, the excellent Cavalier has 45 sophisticated rooms decorated with Afro-Caribbean influences, batik fabrics, tile floors and wood accents. In addition to upscale amenities, the hotel offers passes to 'certain' clubs.

Holiday Inn South Beach Resort (☎ 305-779-3200, 800-356-6902, fax 305-532-1403, **w** *www.holidayinnsouthbeach.com, 2201 Collins Ave*) Rooms $149 off-season, $189 late Dec–Mar. You probably didn't come to South Beach to sleep here, but the Holiday Inn has 355 rooms, which you can probably get for less than the rack rate. The massive, impersonal building sidles up to a few barren and unrenovated blocks, but it's also on the beach. Amenities include tennis, a fitness center and heated pool.

Top End

Nassau Suite Hotel (☎ 305-532-0043, 866-859-4177, fax 305-534-3133, **w** *www .nassausuite.com, 1414 Collins Ave*) Suites $150-260 off-season, $190-300 Nov-May. All of these 22 homey, contemporary pads feature shellacked hardwood floors, comfy pull-out sofas, fully equipped kitchens and walk-in closets. The rooms also have DSL connections and entertainment centers. You could easily imagine living here a while.

Cardozo Hotel (☎ 305-535-6500, 800-782-6500, fax 305-532-3563, **w** *www.cardozo hotel.com, 1300 Ocean Dr*) Rooms/suites $150-285/300-400 off-season, $195-310/395-450 Nov-May. The leopard-patterned hallway carpet sets the tone for singer Gloria Estefan's hotel, which looks every bit as distinctive and pricey as it is. Many of its 43 large, elegant rooms have dark hardwood floors and handmade furniture. Triple sheeting is but one of the typically luxurious amenities. The small bathrooms are outfitted with cool porcelain sinks and lots of glass and marble. Yessiree, this place is nice indeed.

Hotel Ocean (☎ 305-672-2579, fax 305-672-7665, **w** *www.hotelocean.com, 1230 Ocean Dr*) Rooms/suites $179-250/275-345 offseason, $200-270/300-400 mid Nov–May. This intimate, Mediterranean-style hotel isn't pompous or exclusive, but the renovated waterfront suites (expensive but not outlandish when you consider what you get) have every right to be. Most of the hotel's 27 large rooms have ocean views and lots of light streaming in; some have a private terrace. In these, you'll also enjoy fine fabrics, finer furnishings and the finest aesthetics. Other rooms are merely 'fine.'

Hotel Impala (☎ 305-673-2021, 800-646-7252, fax 305-673-5984, **w** *www.hotel impalamiamibeach.com, 1228 Collins Ave*) Rooms/suites $185-220/250-340 off-season, $225-250/300-400 Oct-May. Accessed through its lush courtyard, this lovely European-style hotel features 17 rooms with oversize bathtubs, and the requisite VCR, stereo with CD player etc. The friendly staff has managed to create atmospheric elegance without arrogance. Rates include Continental breakfast.

Albion (☎ 305-535-8606, 877-782-3557, fax 305-535-8602, **w** *www.rubellhotels .com, 1650 James Ave*) Rooms/suites $155-220/200-265 off-season, $245-265/320-390 late Dec–Apr. This sexy, sleek hotel bills itself as the nexus of cutting edge design and deco, where the patron saints are Monica and Bill, and the best minibar items are condoms and Red Bull. That's about right. The vibe is cool at the pool, too. As for the 96 rooms, they feature white bedding, gray carpeting, blonde-wood furnishings and stainless steel accoutrements.

Roney Palace (☎ 305-531-8811, 800-432-4317, fax 305-604-6535, **w** *www .roney-palace.com, 2301 Collins Ave*) One-bedroom apartments $249-329 off-season, $289-379 Jan-Mar. This massive all-efficiency hotel occupies an entire city block and cuts off the beach from the rest of the world. If you like shiny marble, the anonymity of high-rises and super-spacious accommodations, the 585-room Roney will rock your world. But if you've got a backpack rather than luggage that rolls, you're going to be singing the blues.

National Hotel (☎ 305-532-2311, 800-327-8370, fax 305-534-1426, **w** *www.national hotel.com, 1677 Collins Ave*) Rooms $255-355 off-season, $315-450 Oct-May. (Suites are about twice the room rate.) This completely renovated deco landmark doubles as a super-chic South Beach hangout. While the rooms aren't as mod as the lobby, they're lovely, with wood furnishings and shiny bathrooms. About a quarter of the 152 guest rooms in this mid-rise are more tropical than the rest, and have balconies overlooking the pool. One palm-lined pool, a spectacular 250 feet long, leads to another, which in turn leads to a beachside tiki bar. If you've got bucks, consider spending them here.

Raleigh Hotel (☎ 305-534-6300, 800-848-1775, fax 305-538-8140, **W** www.raleigh hotel.com, 1775 Collins Ave) Rooms $209-359 off-season, $319-499 Oct-May. If not at the National, then drop some of your hard earned cash here. A hands-down fave, the mid-rise Raleigh is high-style deco luxe all the way. The bar is excellent; the pricey dining room is romantic; the fitness equipment is al fresco; pets are permitted; and the closets are cedar-lined. The 107 rooms have a host of contemporary amenities such as three separate phone lines. Low platform beds make rolling out of bed in the morning very easy. We won't bother saying the pool is 'arguably' the best in town because no one would argue. It's swanky; you'd better suit up with self-confidence to bare your skin here. (If you have to ask how much the suites are, you can't afford to stay here.)

Marlin Hotel (☎ 305-604-5000, 800-688-7678, fax 305-673-9609, **W** www.themarlin hotel.com, 1200 Collins Ave) Rooms & suites $325-415 Oct-May, negotiable in summer. If you've got a fat wad of cash and commensurately thin thighs, access to these 11 Caribbean-style rooms are worth the steep price tag. And the service is superb if you've got the attitude that often accompanies sculpted cheekbones. Home to the Elite Modeling Agency and South Beach Studios (where Aerosmith and U2 have recorded), Marlin rooms are all unique, right down to beds and couches on wheels. Where do they think you're going anyway? Rooms have good work spaces, stainless steel kitchens, plush bathrobes, entertainment centers and evening turndown service. Dogs are welcome but, surprisingly, there's no pool.

Loews Miami Beach (☎ 305-604-1601, 800-235-6397, fax 305-531-8677, **W** www.loews hotels.com, 1601 Collins Ave) Rooms $249-399 off-season, $339-499 mid-Sept–May, suites up to $4000. New in late 1998 and geared toward conventioneers, this mon-strous monolith boasts an incredible 800 rooms and 20 butler-serviced oceanfront cabanas. The palatial marble lobby sets a tone that suggests you could be in any metropolitan locale.

Delano Hotel (☎ 305-672-2000, 800-555-5001, fax 305-674-6499, **W** www.ianschrager hotels.com, 1685 Collins Ave) Rooms $205-475 off-season, $325-575 Jan-Apr. To enter this fiercely fashionable sanctum, you must confidently stride past two hyper-tanned doormen dressed in white. Once inside, the self-congratulatory staff will politely rent you one of their 208 slick, sparse and mini-mally appointed rooms. This being South Beach, the Delano is in demand (Madonna had a birthday party here and used to own the Blue Door restaurant downstairs – see the Places to Eat chapter), so reserve early. A theater-set designer clearly worked the lobby: A Euro dance beat pulses, and floor-to-outrageously-high-ceiling curtains billow around enormously round pillars. Get into the groove.

The Tides (☎ 305-604-5070, 800-688-7678, fax 305-605-5180, **W** www.thetideshotel.com, 1220 Ocean Dr) Rooms/suites $475/575 off-season, $525/625 mid-Dec–May, penthouses up to $3000. Everything's chic and chichi at The Tides, where service is ultra-cool but surprisingly gracious. The lobby is awash in Latin jazz, equally soft lighting and over-stuffed couches. Guest rooms – all 45 of which face the ocean – are wonderfully soothing, decorated in a rich (yes, rich) palette of beige, cream and a paler shade of white. They all have telescopes for planetary or Hollywood stargazing. The excellent pool is open around the clock. Are you surprised this is another Island Outpost hotel?

SOUTH BEACH (1ST TO 11TH ST; MAP 4)
Budget
Miami Beach International Travelers Hostel (☎ 305-534-0268, 800-978-6787, fax 305-534-5862, **W** www.sobehostel.com, 236 9th St) Dorm beds $13-15 year-round, private rooms $32-59 off-season, $49-89 Jan-Apr. This 9th St hostel, not an HI member, has a little less of everything than the

Best Beds on the Beach

Best Cheap Digs	Clay Hotel & International Hostel
Best Value	Kent Hotel; Crest Hotel Suites
Best Intimate Hideaway	Hotel Leon
Most Low-Key Luxe	Whitelaw Hotel
Expense-Account Faves	Cardozo Hotel; The Tides
Best Deco Delight	National Hotel; Raleigh Hotel
Best Relief from Deco	Cavalier Hotel; Nassau Suite Hotel
Best Guest House	Brigham Gardens Guesthouse
Most Family-Friendly	Hideaway Suites
Most Attitude	Delano Hotel
Best Grande Dame	Eden Roc Resort
Best Je Ne Sais Quoi	Hotel Astor

PLACES TO STAY

competition, but that applies to the digits on the prices as well. Rooms are a tad worn, but security is good and the staff friendly. Half the 100 rooms are private; dorms have four beds. The kitchen is big, the video rental library decent and the Internet access speedy. You'll need an out-of-state university ID, HI card, US or foreign passport with a recent entry stamp, or an onward ticket to get a room, but these rules are only enforced when it's crowded.

Mid-Range

The Clevelander Hotel (☎ 305-531-3485, fax 305-531-3953, Ⓦ www.clevelander.com, 1020 Ocean Dr) Rooms $80-105 off-season, $95-120 Jan-May. You've seen the façade hundreds of times; it shows up in all the deco Beach photos. Justifiably famous for its glass-and-neon bar, it's better to belly up to the bar for a beer than lay your head here – unless you don't plan on sleeping.

Wave Hotel (☎ 305-673-0401, 800-501-0401, fax 305 531-9385, Ⓦ www.wave hotel.com, 350 Ocean Dr) Rooms $95-115 off-season, $129-350 late Dec–Mar. Renovated in 2000, this groovy low-key hotel ably employs the blue-wave motif in the lobby with curvy couches, a blue ceiling and a back-lit azure bar. The 66 rooms feature Italian platform beds, white-noise machines and entertainment centers. The shaded front porch and interior courtyard are relaxing. A full breakfast is included in packages.

Kenmore Hotel (☎ 305-674-1930, 888-424-1930, fax 888-972-4666, 1050 Washington Ave) Rooms $85 off-season, $125 Dec-Apr. In early 2002 Best Western was renovating and managing the Kenmore and its adjacent three properties (Park Washington, Taft and Belaire), which collectively take up an entire block. The Kenmore has a distinctive deco look, with a wavy concrete wall and a figure-eight–shaped pool. You'll appreciate the relative remoteness of these 1930s establishments, close enough to the scene but just beyond the demarcation line for partiers.

Lily Guest House (☎ 305-535-9900, 305-535-3341, fax 305-535-0077, Ⓦ www.south beachgroup.com, 835 Collins Ave) Rooms for 1-6 people $85-185 off-season, $125-300 Feb-Mar. This charming Euro-deco inn with 19 rooms and friendly service has bright, impeccably decorated rooms with kitchenettes, marble bathrooms and hardwood floors. The sundeck is nice, as are the complimentary drinks served from 6pm to 10pm.

Hideaway Suites *(☎ 305-538-5955, 888-881-5955, fax 305-531-2464,* **w** *www.hideawaysuites.com, 751 Collins Ave)* **Units** $99 off-season, $128-158 Dec-May. These 10 spotless apartments, tucked away in a little courtyard insulated from street noise, feature a washer/dryer, full kitchens, free local calls, daily maid service and a very friendly staff. One wish would be that the units had more than one window.

Deco Walk Hotel *(☎ 305-531-5511, 888-505-5027, fax 305 531-5515,* **w** *www.decowalk.com, 928 Ocean Dr)* **Rooms** $79-89 off-season, $135-150 Dec-Feb & June-July. Set just back from the street, this unrenovated hotel is a blast from the past. The platform bed frames and couches reek of retro vinyl. Service is nice but slow, rooms reasonably clean and large. If the 10 rooms weren't across from the beach, the prices would rightfully be lower. Free local calls, beach towels and Continental breakfast add value.

Hotel Leon *(☎ 305-673-3767, fax 305-673-5866,* **w** *www.hotelleon.com, 841 Collins Ave)* **Rooms/suites** $100/145-195 off-season, $145/185-245 Oct-May. This 18-room Mediterranean hideaway is a hands-down fave for its friendly service and impeccable attention to detail. The hotel boasts (actually, it's too understated to boast, but we will) refreshing features like in-room fireplaces, deep bathtubs, *saltillo* tiles, exposed rafters, rattan furnishings, high ceilings and textured walls. The eclectic artwork feels chosen by an individual rather than a designer. Oh, and choose the non-junior suite if you want to have a dance party with 20 of your closest friends; it's big enough. The warmth continues into a communal buffet-breakfast room (add $7 per person). Pets are welcome.

Waldorf Towers Hotel *(☎ 305-531-7684, 800-933-2322, fax 305-672-6836,* **w** *www.waldorftowers.com, 860 Ocean Dr)* **Rooms** $89-199 off-season, $139-249 Nov-Apr. A very good value, the Waldorf was renovated

in early 2002. The 42 crisp but warm rooms feature blonde hardwoods, shellacked floors, platform beds and big windows.

Hotel Shelley *(☎ 305-531-3341, 800-414-0612, fax 305-674-0811,* **w** *www.hotelshelley.com, 844 Collins Ave)* **Rooms** $119 off-season, $149 Nov-May. This 49-room hotel offers lots of amenities for the money, including free airport pick-up, Continental breakfast, open bar (6pm to 10pm), gym passes, morning newspapers and fresh flowers. The bathrooms feel glamorous, with big white towels. The only thing out of whack is the smoky, moldy smell in some of the rooms. Ask for a non-smoking room.

Avalon Majestic Hotel *(☎ 305-538-0133, 800-933-3306, fax 305-534-0258,* **w** *www .southbeachhotels.com, 700 Ocean Dr)* **Rooms** $89-210 off-season, $159-240 late Dec-Mar. In a gorgeous 1941 streamline building, this hotel is perhaps known more for its trademark white-and-yellow 1955 Lincoln convertible parked out front than for its 64 rooms, which are pleasant and clean. Although renovated, style must not have been a consideration. A Continental breakfast buffet is included.

Essex House Hotel *(☎ 305-534-2700, 800-553-7739, fax 305 532-3827,* **w** *www.essexhotel.com, 1001 Collins Ave)* **Rooms/suites** $129/189 off-season, $175/239 Nov-Apr. The lovingly restored Essex, with its ever-so-authentic deco lobby, is a friendly place with a helpful staff, a small pool and large rooms furnished with soft, subdued colors. The side verandah, filled with rattan furnishings, is a particularly pleasant place to people-watch. A Continental breakfast is included with the 58 rooms and 18 suites.

Royal Hotel *(☎ 305-673-9009, 888-394-6835, fax 305-673-9244,* **w** *www.royalhotelsouthbeach.com, 763 Pennsylvania Ave)* **Rooms/suites** $152/250 off-season, $190/290 Nov-May. The Royal is time-warp central, but it's unclear whether past or future. Somehow I suspect that the Jetsons would feel right at home, though, with oddly shaped molded-plastic end tables and beds (with cup holders). The 42 renovated rooms have ultra-white bedding, lavender and lime walls, shag throw rugs, refrigerators and modern tiled bathrooms. Note that the front door is on Washington Ave.

Top End

The Park Central (☎ 305-538-1611, 800-727-5236, fax 305-534-7520, W www.thepark central.com, 640 Ocean Dr) Rooms/suites $95-165/145-195 off-season, $185-250/295-350 Nov-Apr. This 1937 art deco classic is a consummate SoBe hot spot; its pool is fabulous (if small) and its rooftop deck is a must-see even if you're not staying here. The 127 guest rooms and bathrooms are small but first-rate. The Vampire Lestat Room (No 419; see the Things to See & Do chapter), while heavily booked, isn't any more expensive than other similar rooms. To reach the roof, walk past reception, take the elevator to the top floor and walk out to the right. Go around 4pm, when cruise ships chug down Government Cut, or on any weekend night for a great view of the Drive's action.

Century Hotel (☎ 305-674-8855, 888-982-3688, fax 305-538-5733, W www.century southbeach.com, 140 Ocean Dr) Rooms/suites $99-150/200 off-season, $190/300 Jan-Mar. Sporting the coolest hotel logo on the beach – sort of a lizardy thing – the 31-room Century is a darned nice hotel located far enough south to keep things quiet, even on weekends.

Whitelaw Hotel (☎ 305-398-7000, fax 305-398-7010, W www.whitelawhotel.com, 808 Collins Ave) Rooms $95 off-season, $195 Nov-Apr. The brochure promises 'clean sheets, hot water, stiff drinks,' but the 49-room Whitelaw goes a tad beyond that. The crisp bedding is Belgian, the bathrooms marble, and the alcohol complimentary from 8pm to 10pm. After white sheets, white robes, billowy white curtains and white pickled floors, the sea-blue bathrooms come as a welcome shock. (To be fair, the blinds are chrome.) Airport pick-up and Continental breakfast are included. Oh, and could the retro vinyl lobby furniture get any whiter?

Beacon Hotel (☎ 305-674-8200, fax 305-674-8976, W www.beacon-hotel.com, 720 Ocean Dr) Rooms $145-215 off-season, $190-315 Nov-May. This nicely restored deco hotel has 79 truly spic-and-span rooms, with warm wood furnishings (are you tired of vinyl and chrome yet?) that contrast nicely with sheer sea-colored curtains and white down comforters. The small courtyard rooms, which overlook an outside hallway rather than any greenery, are kinda depressing compared to other Beacon rooms.

Hotel Astor (☎ 305-531-8081, 800-270-4981, fax 305-531-3193, W www.hotel astor.com, 956 Washington Ave) Rooms/suites $110-230/220-600 off-season, $195-290/390-900 Jan-Mar. An easy favorite, these 40 oh-so-inviting rooms are done in soothing earth tones. Note that 'regular' rooms are indeed small. But the bathrooms, with plenty of marble and mirrors, are bigger than most. The Astor has a small pool with a very cool 'water wall' surrounded by lots of comfy chaise lounges and a low-key bar with funky music. The intimate lobby is classic, with paddle fan ceiling, terrazzo floors and overstuffed chairs.

Pelican Hotel (☎ 305-673-3373, 800-773-5422, fax 305-673-3255, W www.pelican hotel.com, 826 Ocean Dr) Rooms/suites $135/230-310 off-season, $180-200/300-400 Nov-May. Theme rooms rule here like nowhere else on the Beach. When the owners of Diesel jeans purchased the hotel in 1999, they scoured garage sales looking for just the right stuff. They found it – in spades. From 'born in the stars and stripes' and Western motifs to 'some like it wet' and psychedelic themes, all 30 rooms are completely different and fun. One particularly nice touch: The typically small but renovated bathrooms have cut-out windows.

Casa Grande Hotel (☎ 305-531-8800, 800-688-7678, fax 305 531-5543, W www .casagrandehotel.com, 834 Ocean Dr) Suites & one-bedrooms $195-325 off-season, $295-450 Oct-May. Set back from the street, off a lobby redolent with flowery incense, the Casa Grande offers big bang for admittedly big bucks. Service is refined, with plenty of perks like nightly turndown service and flowers on your pillow. The 34 beautiful suites, replete with Indonesian furniture and warm fabrics, also have full kitchens.

The Hotel (☎/fax 305-531-2222, W www .thehotelofsouthbeach.com, 801 Collins Ave) Rooms/suites $255-295/395 off-season, $275-325/425 Jan-May. Another fine boutique hotel, with only 48 rooms and four suites, this Todd Oldham–designed accommodation boasts the best rooftop pool in South Beach, with cabanas, a fitness facility and showers. The casually elegant guest rooms feature handmade and artisanal detailing, like mosaic doorknobs and shower stalls, stylishly lush fabrics, and wood furnishings, along with modern amenities like data ports. Formerly The Tiffany Hotel, look for the neon sign of that name when trying to find The Hotel.

Inn at the Fisher Island Club (☎ 305-535-6080, 800-537-3708, fax 305-535-6003, W www.fisherisland.com) Rooms $325-1135 off-season, $395-1735 Oct-May. The only way to glimpse exclusive Fisher Island (see the Things to See & Do chapter) is to stay at this luxurious resort. Whether on 'simple' rooms or four-bedroom units, your money will be well spent. Spa packages include two Swedish massages or aromatherapy treatments, one fitness assessment or seaweed body wrap, two island salt-glow or aromatherapy herbal wraps, a hydromassage or target massage, one deep pore cleansing facial *and* one manicure.

NORTHERN MIAMI BEACH (MAP 5)

Many hotels here are converted into condos at a clip that would outpace a roadrunner. But the following are fairly safe bets for standing their ground into the foreseeable future. These are also convenient to South Beach.

Budget

Urban Trails Kayak Co (☎ 305-947-1302) This is a rare inner-city treat: You can camp for free on a myriad of little uninhabited intracoastal islands. But how to reach them? The airline wouldn't check your kayak as legit luggage? Luckily, this facility (see the Activities section in the Things to See & Do chapter) rents kayaks overnight, and they'll show you the way.

Mid-Range

Suez Oceanfront Resort (☎ 305-932-0661, 800-327-5278, fax 305-937-0058, W www .suezresort.com, 18215 Collins Ave) Rooms $65-125 off-season, $82-135 mid-Dec–mid-Apr. Who said there wasn't truth in advertising? This family-friendly 200-room motel would have to be underwater to be closer to the ocean. A throwback to an earlier era, the hotel boasts two pools, tennis courts and a tropical patio with lots of tables, umbrellas and palm trees. Spring for a room overlooking the patio rather than annex rooms on the parking lot. PS: Look for the deliberately tacky pyramid and sphinxes in front; you'll know you've arrived.

Dezerland Beach Resort Hotel (☎ 305-865-6661, 800-331-9346, fax 305-866-2630, W www.dezerhotels.com, 8701 Collins Ave) Rooms $89-139. The common areas of this 10-story hotel are mired in the past, too. The fabulous '50s roar to life in the form of rumble seats, oversized antique gas station signs and fin-backed cars that have been converted into dining tables. But while the hotel lobby-as-theme-park is decidedly retro, the 225 largish guest rooms are newly renovated, with tile floors. Some have a balcony and all are adjacent to a 50-acre park. The hotel provides a convenient shuttle to South Beach.

Bay Harbor Inn & Suites (☎ 305-868-4141, fax 305-867-9094, W www.bayharbor inn.com, 9660 E Bay Harbor Dr) Rooms $89-99 off-season, $119-139 mid-Dec–mid-Apr. Operated by earnest Johnson & Wales University students as an integral part of their hands-on hospitality training, this upscale small hotel has 45 rooms and suites on and off the Intracoastal Waterway. Friendly service keeps this place from being too stuffy. A complimentary Continental breakfast is served on the waterfront deck.

Best Western Oceanfront Resort (☎ 305-864-2232, 800-327-1412, fax 305-864-3045, W www.bwoceanfront.com, 9365 Collins Ave) Rooms $89-139 off-season, $119-169 late Dec–early Apr & mid-June–mid-Sept. This renovated 93-room chain motel has a prime oceanfront location. Because the suites have kitchens and can accommodate up to five people, this could be considered a bargain.

Indian Creek Hotel (☎ *305-531-2727, 800-491-2772, fax 305-531-5651,* **w** *www .indiancreekhotelmb.com, 2727 Indian Creek Dr)* Rooms/suites $90/150 off-season, $140/240 Oct-Apr. The rustically civilized lobby and tropical courtyard here are delightfully serene places to wile away a few hours. Mix in a friendly staff, a cool pool and a location just far enough from the madness, and you've got a recipe for a restful retreat. The 61 deco-style rooms are a tad dark, but you won't be in them during the day anyway.

Top End

Eden Roc Resort (☎ *305-531-0000, 800-327-8337, fax 305-674-5555,* **w** *www.edenroc resort.com, 4525 Collins Ave)* Rooms starting at $189 off-season, $259 late Dec–mid-Apr. The gloriously renovated Eden Roc Resort is giving the Fontainebleau Hilton (see next) a run for its money. With extras such as an indoor rock-climbing complex, an Olympic-sized pool and an oceanfront spa and health club, it's a great place to get away. There are 349 rooms from which to choose.

Fontainebleau Hilton Hotel & Resort (☎ *305-538-2000, 800-548-8886, fax 305-673-5351,* **w** *www.fontainebleau.hilton.com, 4441 Collins Ave)* Rooms starting at $189 off-season, $239 late Dec–May. Probably the Beach's most recognizable landmark, the 1200-room Fontainebleau opened in 1954 and was purchased by Hilton in 1978. It could be a bit more stylish, even though it has every conceivable amenity, including restaurants and bars galore, beachside cabanas, seven tennis courts, a kids' activity program, grand ballroom, business center, marina, shopping mall and an ab-fab swimming pool. The Towers Level, a separate building with keyed entry, has a concierge service and even more extras. Otherwise, the rooms leave a bit to be desired for the money.

DOWNTOWN MIAMI (MAP 6)

Downtown isn't the most exciting or beautiful place to stay, but the neighborhood might be centrally located for those exploring the farther reaches of the city with a car. With one noteworthy exception, accommodations consist of big chains catering to businessfolk and some cheap hotels. Note that much of downtown gets downright desolate after the white-collar business crowds flee their office cubicles.

Budget

Miami Sun Hotel (☎ *305-375-0786, 226 NE 1st Ave)* Singles $39, doubles $45. This centrally located hostelry, adjacent to the courthouses and an undeveloped city block, is clean. Yup; that's about it. Oh, there are 80 rooms.

Leamington Hotel (☎ *305-373-7783, fax 305-536-2208, 307 NE 1st St)* Doubles $46. Not a bad option, this decent place has 90 rooms and features an old-fashioned elevator. Whoopi.

Howard Johnson (☎ *305-358-3080, 800-654-2000, fax 305-358-8631, 1100 Biscayne Blvd)* Doubles $89-99 Jan-Apr, $10 less off-season. In a trafficked location just off I-395 and the AIA Hwy, which leads directly to the Beach (five minutes by car), this standard chain motel best serves those who want a quick getaway in their cars. There are 115 rooms.

Everglades Hotel (☎ *305-379-5461, 800-327-5700, fax 305-577-8390,* **w** *www.miami gate.com/everglades, 244 Biscayne Blvd)* Doubles $99, less in summer. This 300-room behemoth looks like a three-star tourist hotel in post-embargo Havana: The lobby is suitably dark, the staff suitably morose, the decor suitably clunky. As you might expect, the rooms are below average. Still, it's a worthwhile budget option in the heart of downtown.

Mid-Range

Miami River Inn (☎ *305-325-0045, 800-468-3589, fax 305-325-9227,* **w** *www.miami riverinn.com, 119 SW South River Dr)* Doubles $69-129 off-season, $109-199 Dec-Mar. This necessarily gated complex across from the river, in the middle of a colorful nowhere (see the Things to See & Do chapter), has charming New England–style rooms with wicker, brass and antiques. In addition to friendly service and fluffy comforters, you'll enjoy the lushly landscaped pool and Continental breakfast. There are 40 rooms, including a couple of apartments, within four wooden buildings from the early 20th century. Check out the treasure trove of Miami books in the guest library.

Clarion Hotel & Suites (☎ 305-374-5100, 800-252-7466, fax 305-381-9826, W www .clarionmiaconctr.com, 100 SE 4th St) Doubles $79-119 off-season, $129-189 Jan-Mar. Alongside the river in a location that can be maddeningly difficult to find, this 150-room Clarion has large, well-appointed rooms and suites. Some have microwaves and fridges. The hotel is adjacent to the Knight Center Metromover station.

Miami Downtown Plaza Hotel (☎ 305-374-3000, fax 305-374-4263, W www.miami downtownplaza.com, 200 SE 2nd Ave) Doubles $69-99 off-season, $139 Jan-May. This former Holiday Inn has 258 standard rooms.

Hyatt Regency (☎ 305-358-1234, 800-233-1234, fax 305-679-3294, W www.hyatt.com, 400 SE 2nd Ave) Doubles $140-250. These 612 rooms are geared toward business travelers. The price differential between a weekday and weekend stay is enormous: $250 versus $140 for the same room. You'll be able to get a room on a summer weekend for much less.

Sheraton (☎ 305-373-6000, 800-325-3535, fax 305-374-6619, W www.sheraton.com, 495 Brickell Ave) Doubles $119-164 off-season, $169-209 Jan-Mar. A dependable and predictable option, the Sheraton has typical business-hotel amenities and a whopping 598 rooms.

Top End
Mandarin Oriental Miami (☎ 305-913-8288, 866-888-6780, fax 305-913-8317, W www .mandarinoriental.com, 500 Brickell Key Dr) Doubles starting at $395 off-season, $550 Dec-May. This premier Asian hotelier always takes top honors in my books and this exclusive, extravagant Miami location is no exception. Don't worry about the sticker shock; with 324 rooms, you'll rarely have to

pay rack rates. You might be able to get an entry-level $550 room with a balcony and breakfast for about $269. The full service spa is outstanding.

KEY BISCAYNE (MAP 7)
Seriously consider staying on the sandy shores of Key Biscayne.

Silver Sands Beach Resort (☎ 305-361-5441, fax 305-361-5477, W www.silver sandsmiami.com, 301 Ocean Dr) Rooms/cottages $129-149/279 off-season, $169-189/329 mid-Dec-late Apr; weekly rates available; kids free under age 14 when sharing a room with their parents. Hidden in a quiet neighborhood just steps from the beach, this 60-room single-story motel is a quiet gem. The simple rooms, half of which spill out onto a garden courtyard (they're worth the extra $20), have clean bathrooms, tile rather than carpeting, firm mattresses and mini-kitchens. Of course there's a pool.

Sonesta Beach Resort Key Biscayne (☎ 305-361-2021, 800-766-3782, fax 305-361-3096, W www.sonesta.com, 350 Ocean Dr) Rooms $195-330 off-season, $295-425 late Dec-Apr. On a wide stretch of powdery sand, this 295-room mid-rise hotel works hard and successfully to make you never want to leave the property. It's a really fine place to relax, and boasts an oceanfront pool, a kids' activity program, bicycle rentals, plenty of bars and restaurants, contemporary rooms, tennis courts and a fitness center.

COCONUT GROVE (MAP 9)
A waterside neighborhood with lots of options, Coconut Grove offers a couple of distinct alternatives.

Budget
Hampton Inn (☎ 305-448-2800, 800-426-7866, fax 305-442-8655, W www.hampton inn.com, 2800 SW 28th Terrace) Rooms $89 off-season, $129 late Dec-late Apr. This modest 136-room hotel, easily accessible off US Hwy 1, but not within walking distance of the Grove, includes a Continental breakfast buffet in its rates. Many rooms have

refrigerators and microwaves. Will wonders never cease: They also offer free local calls.

Mid-Range

Coconut Grove Bed & Breakfast *(☎ 305-665-2274, 800-339-9430, fax 305-666-1186, ⓦ www.kwflorida.com/coconut.html, Douglas Rd)* Rooms $115-175 off-season, $135-210 mid-Dec–mid-Apr. Highly recommended, this two-story house has only three rooms, but they're nicely decorated with the pottery, textiles and paintings of owner Annette Rawlings. Her family has been in South Grove for decades, and was among a legendary group of starving artists who set out to make names for themselves in the late '60s – and did. Rates include a spectacular homemade breakfast. Ann doesn't take walk-ins and prefers not to be on our map; so you'll have to get directions when making reservations.

The Mutiny Hotel *(☎ 305-441-2100, 888-868-8469, fax 305-441-2822, ⓦ www.mutiny hotel.com, 2951 S Bayshore Dr)* Suites $149-325 mid-June–Sept, $199-399 mid-season, $219-429 Jan-Mar. This small luxury hotel, with 120 one- and two-bedroom suites, featuring balconies, boasts an indulgent staff, luxe bedding, gracious appointments, fine amenities and a small heated pool. Although it's on a busy street, you won't hear the traffic noises once inside. Firmly smitten in the understated finery, no guests have been known to jump ship here.

Doubletree Hotel *(☎ 305-858-2500, 800-222-8733, fax 305-858-5776, ⓦ www.double treecoconutgrove.com, 2649 S Bayshore Dr)* Rooms $129 July-Aug, $259 Sept-June (prices fluctuate greatly). The 192 rooms here attract business travelers, but that doesn't mean that you can't find pleasure in their upscale accommodations.

Top End

Sonesta Hotel & Suites Coconut Grove *(☎ 305-529-2828, 2889 McFarlane Rd)* Rooms $165-185 off-season, $175-295 late Dec–mid-Apr; one-bedroom suites are more expensive. Opened in March 2002, this 300-room hotel is the excellent sister prop-

erty to the one on Key Biscayne (see that entry, earlier).

Mayfair House *(☎ 305-441-0000, 800-433-4555, fax 305-441-1647, ⓦ www.may fairhousehotel.com, 3000 Florida Ave)* Rooms $169-209 off-season, $289-329 late Dec–mid-Apr. Tucked behind the Shops at Mayfair, this exclusive all-suite hotel has 179 units overlooking a central courtyard. The large Mayfair, Executive and Deluxe suites (there are even more expensive categories) feature Japanese hot tubs, marble bathrooms, separate sitting areas and private terraces. Need three telephone lines? Opt for the Deluxe suite; the other suites only have two lines.

CORAL GABLES (MAP 10)

A tony and leafy neighborhood, Coral Gables offers a little of everything.

Budget

Terrace Inn *(☎ 305-662-8845, fax 305-662-5562, 1430 S Dixie Hwy)* Rooms $59 off-season, $69-89 Nov-Apr. This bi-level place, just far enough off US Hwy 1 to make it quieter than its competitors, used to be a Howard Johnson. You'll recognize the trademark hotel roofline. The 80 rooms are modest.

Mid-Range

Holiday Inn *(☎ 305-667-5611, 800-465-4329, fax 305-669-3151, 1350 S Dixie Hwy)* Rooms $99-129 off-season, $119-169 mid-Dec–mid-Apr. A gargantuan chain hotel with 155 standard-issue rooms, Holiday Inn has newly renovated rooms near the university. You'll find the requisite kidney-shaped pool and a fitness center on the premises.

Hotel Chateau Bleau *(☎ 305-448-2634, 888-642-6442, fax 305-448-2017, ⓦ www.hotel chateaubleau.com, 1111 Ponce de León Blvd)* Rooms $69 off-season, $89-109 Dec-Mar. Although the name has grander aspirations than the rooms deliver, this is still a commendable lodging choice. Operated by Best Western, this low-rise motel has a friendly staff and 120 newly renovated rooms, most of which overlook a parking lot. For what it's worth, though, there are balconies and a small pool. A few rooms have kitchenettes.

Hotel Place St Michel *(☎ 305-444-1666, fax 305-529-0074,* W *www.hotelplace stmichel.com, 162 Alcazar Ave)* Rooms/suites $125/160 off-season, $150-165/185-200 Nov-Apr. The first things you'll notice at this charming Old World, European-style hotel are the vaulted ceilings, fancy tile work and inlaid wood floors. With only 27 rooms, though, the hotel's hallmark is excellent service. You can also expect amenities like Continental breakfast, a morning newspaper and evening turndown service. The plush furnishings are a welcome relief from the omnipresent, stark deco look.

Top End

Hyatt Regency Coral Gables *(☎ 305-441-1234, fax 305-441-0520,* W *www.hyatt .com, 50 Alhambra Plaza)* $139/229 weekday/weekend mid-June–mid-Sept, $119/315 weekday/weekend mid-Sept–mid-June. Pricier than its downtown sibling, these 242 upscale rooms are everything you'd expect from a Hyatt. Business-plan rooms, with a fax machine and access to the business center, plus other perks, are cheaper than so-called standard rooms.

The Biltmore Hotel *(☎ 305-445-1926, 800-727-1926, fax 305-913-3159,* W *www .biltmorehotel.com, 1200 Anastasia Ave)*

Doubles starting at $359 Jan-Mar (with four seasonal price changes throughout the year), suites a heck of a lot more. The brochure buzzwords here are apt and do not overstate the hotel's case: splendor, glamour, opulence, bygone era, exquisite style, pampered luxury. You get the idea. This 1926 National Historic Landmark, built in a Mediterranean style, also has the largest hotel pool in the country. But do you dare swim in it? Promise to stop by even if you haven't packed in high-style. There are 280 rooms. The popular Capone Suite (see the Things to See & Do chapter) is priced according to availability, but it hovers in the $1000 to $2000 range.

GREATER MIAMI (MAP 1)

Miami-Homestead-Everglades KOA *(☎ 305-233-5300, 800-562-7732,* W *www.miami camp.com, 20675 SW 162nd Ave)* Tents/hookups $26/30, 'kamping kabins' $45 (2-4 people), 1-/2-room lodges $59/89. The area's only KOA has almost 300 sites (only 13 of which are specifically for tenters), a pool, game room, shuffleboard, bike rentals, laundry facilities etc. Cabins have bunk beds, a porch and barbecue grills. Lodges sleep four to eight people and have almost-full kitchens. If you intend to 'commute' to Miami from here, note that it's 25 miles south of downtown.

Places to Eat

Miami restaurants enliven the palate and the eyes. From authentic hole-in-the-wall Cuban joints to haute New World fusion that'll knock your sockless sandals off, there is something for every budget and trendy taste bud. Cuisine can be as sophisticated as you are, as lowbrow as Uncle Mike or as campy as Aunt Mildred. Certainly, the experience of dining out can be as much about being seen as it is about being nourished. You decide. Miami eateries benefit from a cultural connection to Latin America and the Caribbean that's simply not matched elsewhere in the country. Take advantage of it. And if you haven't been to Miami in 15 years, forget what you thought you knew about Miami dining. Miami chefs are playing a whole new ball game – enjoy the indulgent feast.

Establishments are categorized according to the restaurant's average main courses at dinner: budget (up to $10), mid-range ($10-19) and top end ($20 and up). A general rule of thumb for calculating the price of a full meal with a glass of wine, tax, tip and an appetizer *or* dessert is to double the entrée price. Don't rule out the top-end places just because you're budget conscious. Consider getting a couple of appetizers and sharing an entrée. You don't think rail-thin models *ever* eat full meals, do you? In an effort to draw folks in, many restaurants offer early specials. Don't be demure about asking. While you'll find plenty of cheap and wildly pricey places, it's not that easy to find great moderate places (although there is a very admirable selection here). Reservations are essential at many of the top-end restaurants; call ahead. In the off-season, many restaurants close on Monday, so it's always a good idea to call ahead.

SOUTH BEACH (MAPS 3 & 4)

Simply put, South Beach restaurants cater to every style and budget. Although there are still a few home-style Cuban joints and Jewish delicatessens, creeping gentrification has generally pushed out the mom-and-pop joints in favor of fast-food chains and chic eateries. That said, some bargains can still be found. Many Italian eateries offer homemade pasta and a glass of wine for a price that won't bust your budget. Many restaurants also have early specials. Rest assured, though, that South Beach's fashionable bistros can compete with the trendiest in New York or LA. Most upscale restaurants showcase 'Floribbean' cuisine, a fusion of New American with Caribbean ingredients and cooking styles.

The restaurant scene in South Beach is so varied that this section has been organized by the type of food served, for example, Mexican, Italian, seafood etc, then price sub-categories where necessary. Most Beach restaurants serve brunch from 10am to 3pm on weekends. Generally speaking, you can get a huge breakfast and a Bloody Mary or mimosa for about $10 a person.

Yes, South Beach service can be poor if you're not a VIP, or at least a VBP (very beautiful person), but in the wake of the September 11 tragedy, when folks stopped traveling and the travel industry was left high and dry, service has also become somewhat solicitous. Remember that many places – such as the News Cafe – include the tip automatically. Be vigilant and don't tip twice!

Markets

Hit Alton Rd for moderately priced picnic fixings of extraordinary delights.

Wild Oats Community Market *(☎ 305-532-1707, 1020 Alton Rd)* **Map 4** Open 7am-11pm daily. This has got to be the best natural-food market on earth, and grazing is the order of the day here. With aisles and aisles of wonderful stuff, it's South Beach's primo place to assemble a fantastic and healthy meal. There's also a magnificent salad bar and pre-made vegetarian, vegan, organic and even meat entrées. Get the food at the deli counter and sit at the tables in front, where there's even free spring water. Or, belly up to the juice bar, where the tonics will cure whatever ails you.

South Beach Coffee Bars

This is not Seattle, or even Atlanta, when it comes to the coffeehouse scene. But while most small coffee bars on the Beach have fallen victim to Starbucks, there are alternatives to the super sugary, high-octane joe served at Cuban places around town.

Segafredo Zanetti Espresso (☎ 305-673-0047, 1040 Lincoln Road; Map 3) is an honest-to-goodness bona fide Italian café, serving Italian sweets and heavenly espresso drinks. It's open 11am to midnight Sunday to Thursday, until 1am on Friday and Saturday.

Kafka Kafé (☎ 305-673-9669, 1464 Washington Ave; Map 3) has Internet access and a bookish, coffeehouse vibe. It's open 8:30am to midnight daily.

Joffrey's Coffee Co (☎ 305-445-5116, 660 Lincoln Road; Map 3), a newer chain than Starbucks, is trying to give them a run for your coffee dollars. The digs are still unpretentious and the staff is friendly. It's open 11am to midnight Sunday to Wednesday, until 2am Thursday to Saturday.

Starbucks has rolled into town in a big way, with South Beach branches at 1451 Ocean Dr (☎ 305-674-0074), 749 Lincoln Road (☎ 305-538-5906), and 1570 Alton Rd (☎ 305-538-0958).

If you blink you'll miss **Van Dyke News** (☎ 305-534-3600, 846 Lincoln Road; Map 3). Around the corner from the busy hubub of the Van Dyke Cafe, this little convenience store-cum-newsstand-cum-sidewalk-espresso bar is frequented by locals hanging out, reading the paper and sipping cappuccino in peace.

Epicure Market (☎ 305-672-1861, 1656 Alton Rd) **Map 3** Dishes $5-8. Open 10am-8pm Mon-Fri, 10am-7pm Sat, 10am-6pm Sun. Head to the kosher deli counter for excellent prepared salads and pasta dishes, which can be heated if you want.

Apple A Day Food Market (☎ 305-538-4569, 1534 Alton Rd) **Map 3** Open 8am-11pm Mon-Sat, 8am-10pm Sun. In addition to prepared foods and a juice bar, the smaller-but-still-well-stocked Apple A Day has good oils and homeopathic cures.

There are only a couple of real American-style supermarkets in the area. Look for **Publix** (☎ 305-538-7250, 1045 Dade Blvd; Map 3) on Miami Beach; **Publix** and **Winn-Dixies** markets are scattered all over the area.

Bakeries & Delicatessens

Pan D'Oro (☎ 305-531-8100, 1080 Alton Rd) **Map 4** Dishes $4-6. This bakery features an impressive array of gourmet pastries, sandwiches, salads and smoothies.

5th Street Deli (☎ 305-604-0555, 458 Ocean Dr) **Map 4** Dishes $5-7. Open 8am-8pm Mon-Thur, 8am-9pm Fri-Sun. Another purveyor of tasty deli-style sandwiches, 5th Street features Boar's Head meats, as well as some vegetarian options like roasted vegetables, avocado and brie.

Le Chic (☎ 305-673-5522, 1043 Washington Ave) **Map 4** Sandwiches $5-7. Open 6:30am-7:30pm Mon-Sat, 6:30am-2:30pm Sun. This authentic French bakery serves sandwiches on fresh baguettes or croissants. Treat yourself to a delectable pastry, unless you model in your spare time.

Neam's Gourmet (☎ 305-538-3500, 300 Alton Rd) **Map 4** Dishes $6-8. Open 7am-7pm daily. On the other side of the Beach from the 5th Street Deli, the hot and cold deli case at this gourmet shop also features Boar's Head meats. Neam's also has good salads.

Wolfie's (☎ 305-538-6626, 2038 Collins Ave) **Map 3** Dishes $9-15. Open 24 hrs daily. Established in 1938, this is the Beach's reigning classic Jewish delicatessen. Most agree that the place has declined, but could it simply be that tastes have changed? Both the food and atmosphere harken to a bygone South Beach era, that's for sure. Still, if you have a hankering for deli-style diner chow, a corned beef and cabbage or pastrami sandwich from Wolfie's will satisfy your craving. Everything comes with a bowl of pickles. Early bird specials are very popular among the older set.

Seafood

Mid-Range *Les Deux Fontaines (☎ 305-672-7878, 1230 Ocean Dr)* **Map 3** Breakfast mains $5-10, dinner dishes $10-20. Open 7:30am-midnight daily. Open for breakfast, light lunches and more substantial dinners, this restaurant, at the Ocean Hotel, has its terrace perfectly perched above Ocean Drive – just close enough to people-watch but far enough to keep the 'riffraff' from your food. Seafood is the specialty, but don't expect fancy preparations. It's a nice spot to nibble tuna carpaccio and sip a midday glass of wine. Prices shoot upward at dinnertime, although it's not as expensive as it looks or feels. A decent wine list features French and American bottles.

South Beach Stone Crabs (☎ 305-538-5888, 723 Lincoln Road) **Map 3** Stone crabs $25 & up, mains $12-34. Open noon-midnight daily. An alternative to the interminable line at Joe's, this sidewalk eatery offers the same crustaceans, with a prime view of the Lincoln Road *passagiato*. When crabs are out of season, feast on other seafood and pasta specials.

A Fish Called Avalon (☎ 305-532-1727, 700 Ocean Dr) **Map 4** Mains $15-22. Open 6pm-11pm nightly. The menu here will please seafood fanciers. While terrace tables afford a nice view of the Ocean Ave cavalcade, sidewalk tables leave one feeling a bit trampled upon. From 6pm to 7pm the three-course fixed-price menu ($19.50) is a steal. The dining room features nightly live music.

Grillfish (☎ 305-538-9908, 1444 Collins Ave) **Map 3** Mains $13-22. Open 6pm-11pm Sun-Thur, 6pm-midnight Fri & Sat. Grillfish has a wonderful atmosphere. Greek? Mediterranean? 'Gay,' said the cute waiter. It's elegant, but tuxedos are fortunately forbidden. The mainly Italian-inspired seafood dishes are very good, but they also do chicken. Try the salmon or rainbow trout served over pasta. If you have an appetite, the mussels and shrimp scampi 'apps' are tasty, too.

Jeffrey's (☎ 305-673-0690, 1629 Michigan Ave) **Map 3** Mains $15-27. Open from 6pm Tues-Sat, from 5pm Sun. Jeffrey's – not to be confused with Joffrey's, the coffee place – is romantic and graced with artwork, candles, lace curtains and Tiffany lamps. Appetizers feature artichokes, a chicken salad plate and stuffed mushrooms. Mains include a nice vegetarian plate, crab cakes and veal cutlets.

Top End *Monty's Seafood & Stone Crab Restaurant (☎ 305-673-3444, 300 Alton Rd)* **Map 4** Lunch mains $6-30, dinner mains vary according to market prices. Lunch served at the downstairs raw bar from 11:30am daily, dining room open 6pm-10pm Sun-Thur, 6pm-11pm Fri-Sat. Overlooking the marina, Monty's is pleasantly casual, airy and bright. The real draw during stone crab season is the all-you-can-eat 'select' size crabs ($45). The open-air raw bar, located next to a swimming pool, is particularly popular from 4pm to 8pm weekdays.

Joe's Stone Crab Restaurant (☎ 305-673-0365, 227 Biscayne St) **Map 4** Open 11:30am-2:30pm Tues-Sat & 5pm-10pm daily mid-Oct–mid-May (stone crab season); closed mid-May–mid-Oct. As close as Miami Beach gets to a world-famous restaurant, Joe's has been around since 1913. No reservations are accepted and the line is a mile long – tip the maître d' or be prepared to wait and wait, and wait some more. The quality and high profile come at a price: Medium-sized stone crab claws cost $20 (eight per order), 'selects' $27 (seven per order) and large ones $37 (five per order). If your appetite and wallet are robust, you can easily polish off two orders per person. Other dishes, like broiled swordfish steak or fried chicken, are tasty and cheaper. Save room for the Key lime pie. You can call ahead for takeout (☎ 305-673-4611). Addicts can even arrange overnight air shipment (☎ 800-780-2722, **w** www.joesstonecrab.com).

PLACES TO EAT

Tantra (☎ *305-672-4765, 1445 Pennsylvania Ave*) **Map 3** Mains $32 & up (market price for seafood). Open 7pm-1am daily. One of South Beach's coolest celebrity hot spots also serves some of its most creative and exciting cuisine. Based on the premise that all senses are to be awakened, Tantra delivers in the visual, aural and taste departments. Large portions of eclectic cuisine like Thai spiced duck confit with an orange-scented cucumber salad share the stage with Moroccan spiced lamb with mint and mango. The lobby features freshly cut grass, while the bar pulses to tantric music as sweet somethings wander around offering aphrodisiac cocktails. Their martinis and desserts are very worthy.

American
Budget There are lots of great places to get a quick sandwich.

La Sandwicherie (☎ *305-532-8934, 229 14th St*) **Map 3** Dishes $5-9. Open 9am-5am daily, delivery available until 10pm. Despite its faux-French name, baguettes and pretentious translations *(cornichons* = French pickles), La Sandwicherie is as American as

SoBe Dining on the Cheap

With the sheer volume of good restaurants, some excellent bargains can get lost in all the ink. Despite some fierce competition, these are the top bargains. Feel free to let us know what you think.

San Loco (Map 3)	Large burritos
Spris (Map 3)	'Beat the Clock' specials
Nexxt Cafe (Map 3)	Huge portions
Lincoln Road Café (Map 3)	Hearty breakfast
Sport Café (Map 4)	Anything
Wild Oats Community Market (Map 4)	Salad bar
Pizza Rustica (Maps 3 & 4)	Slices of gourmet pizza
The Terrace (Map 3)	The café menu

a sex scandal over nothing. This means that it has great – and great-big – sandwiches. The fruit juices, smoothies and shakes are also good. Located in an alley (which smells a bit ripe now and then), the shop has about four stools and a small sandwich bar.

Ice Box Cafe (☎ *305-538-8448, 1657 Michigan Ave*) **Map 3** Open 11am-11pm Tues-Thur & Sun, 11am-midnight Fri & Sat. This catering operation-cum-ultra-chic-café serves beautifully prepared sandwiches and salads and luscious desserts in an intimate storefront setting. You can eat in or take out.

Van Dyke Cafe (☎ *305-534-3600, 846 Lincoln Road*) **Map 3** Dishes $6-15. Open 8am-2am daily. One of Lincoln Road's most touristed spots, the Van Dyke serves adequate food in a cool setting. It's usually packed to the rafters and takes over half the sidewalk. Service is very friendly, even efficient, and if you could just avoid the models preening and posing, it would be a far better place to enjoy the burgers, open roast beef sandwiches and eggplant parmigiana (a house specialty). There's also nightly jazz upstairs.

Mid-Range *News Cafe* (☎ *305-538-6397, 800 Ocean Dr*) **Map 4** Dishes $9-12. Open 24 hrs daily. It's worth spending part of an afternoon at this painfully trendy South Beach landmark. The food almost rivals the street-side perch. It has terrific salads, plain omelets and pasta dishes, but is perhaps more well known for tomato bruschetta. Pair it with an iced tea, while watching the skaters wiggle and glide down Ocean Drive. A 15% tip is added to all checks, but if you're really unhappy with the service, they'll remove it upon request.

11th Street Diner (☎ *305-534-6373, 1065 Washington Ave*) **Map 4** Dishes $5-15. Open 24 hrs daily. This original art deco diner, trucked down from Wilkes-Barre, Pennsylvania, has been renovated and serves really good three-egg omelets, sandwiches and down-home favorites like fried chicken and meatloaf. The service is leisurely but cheery.

Front Porch Cafe (☎ *305-531-8300, 1418 Ocean Dr*) **Map 3** Lunch mains $8-9, dinner mains $11-14. Open 8am-10:30pm daily.

Since 1990 (eons by South Beach standards), the Front Porch has been noteworthy for its low-key, pleasant atmosphere and its good sampler salads and sandwiches. It's a quiet place to meet for a fashionable breakfast without the side order of attitude.

Big Pink (☎ 305-532-4700, 157 Collins Ave) **Map 4** Dishes $7-20. Open 9am-1am Sun-Thur, 9am-2am Fri & Sat. Big Pink is big fun '50s style. What can you say about a place whose signature dish is an authentic, American-style 'TV dinner' served on a six-compartment steel tray? Burgers, sandwiches, pizza, meal-sized salads, nacho platters, buckets of fries and chicken wings are served in a cavernous, convivial atmosphere. Breakfast is available all day. Dine inside or at sidewalk tables. Either way, save room for the Key lime pie.

Balans (☎ 305-534-9191, 1022 Lincoln Road) **Map 3** Mains $8-18. Open 8am-midnight Sun-Thur, 8am-1am Fri & Sat. This chic, British-owned, oh-so-Soho bistro has a modern-yet-comfortable atmosphere. The menu fuses Mediterranean and Asian cuisines; their signature lobster club sandwich is worth every penny. Sidewalk seating appeals to those who prefer open-air people-watching.

Café Cardozo (☎ 305-695-2822, 1300 Ocean Dr) **Map 3** Breakfast & lunch $3-12, dinner mains $10-18. Open 8am-midnight Sun-Thur, 8am-2am Fri & Sat. This offshoot of the popular News Cafe features tasty appetizers like conch fritters and black-bean cakes, as well as burgers, sandwiches, salads, pizza, grilled fish and pasta dishes. Breakfast is served until 4pm. On warm days, a cooling mist falls from the terrace above to gently spritz the diners at sidewalk tables. Sounds like a cooling idea, but on breezy days, the cars driving down Ocean Dr get most of the benefit.

Nexxt Cafe (☎ 305-532-6643, 700 Lincoln Road) **Map 3** Mains $12-20. Open 11am-11pm Mon-Thur, 11:30am-midnight Fri-Sun. You can not go wrong with the wide-ranging salads, pastas, grilled fish and meat dishes here. And the immense menu mirrors equally immense servings; entrées are big enough to share. It's a struggle, but

leave room for a luscious dessert. Sidewalk seating provides a full view of the Lincoln Road parade.

Top End *The Terrace* and *1220 Restaurant* (☎ 305-604-5130, 1220 Ocean Dr) **Map 3** Terrace mains $11-26. Open 11:30am-11pm daily. The Tides Hotel has two upscale restaurants. The ultra chic '1220' serves an exquisite, if pricey, dinner nightly. The same kitchen prepares a café menu (lunch and dinner) served at The Terrace, overlooking Ocean Drive. From this lovely perch, above the maddening crowds, you can dine on watermelon gazpacho, gourmet sandwiches and salads, or elegantly prepared and presented fish dishes like grilled blue marlin with shiitake-citrus risotto.

Joe Allen Miami Beach (☎ 305-531-7007, 1787 Purdy Ave) **Map 3** Mains $15-25. Open 11:30am-11:30pm daily. South Beach's hidden gem is located in an underdeveloped bayside neighborhood. This hip and decidedly low-key restaurant serves outstanding food to an upbeat, unpretentious crowd. Great steaks, fresh fish, salads, pizza and smooth service keep everyone well fed and happy.

Pearl Restaurant & Champagne Lounge (☎ 305-538-1111, 1 Ocean Dr) **Map 4** Mains $17-37. Open 7pm-midnight Wed-Sun. This upscale, groovy eatery is orange. You can't avoid it and you'll soon be basking in it. Just give into it and enjoy the fun. Perhaps you'll head straight to the centerpiece of the lounge/club/restaurant, a champagne bar with high-backed, sculpturally molded chairs. I highly recommend seeing it for yourself. As for the first-rate creative cuisine, it ranges from miso-marinated Chilean sea bass to garlic-and-herb–crusted rack of lamb. Save room for dessert. The whole experience is peppered with little touches that really set the place apart, as if orange somehow wasn't enough. Months later, after months of dining out, I still remember Pearl vividly; you will, too.

Tiger Oak Room (☎ 305-534-6300, 1775 Collins Ave) **Map 3** Mains $18-34. Open 7am-3:30pm Mon-Thur, 7am-10pm Fri-Sun. Lunch at the Raleigh Hotel's romantic New

PLACES TO EAT

American restaurant is surprisingly reasonable considering the FQ (Fabulous Quotient). Try roasted vegetables Provençal, a tuna burger with ginger soy sauce, or grilled jumbo shrimp gazpacho. Sunday brunch is a wonderfully chichi affair; dine simply on a wild mushroom omelet with fresh herbs and goat cheese. The fun bar, if you haven't heard yet, makes the best martini on the Beach (it's huge, dry and made with Bombay Sapphire).

Wish (☎ 305-531-2222, 801 Collins Ave) **Map 4** Breakfast $8-15, dinner mains $23-34. Open 7am-11pm Sun-Thur, 7am-midnight Fri & Sat. Put Wish on the top of your wish list for a quiet, romantic dinner spot. Within the Todd Oldham–designed 'The Hotel,' highly acclaimed chef Michael Reidt takes contemporary French-Brazilian cuisine to the next level, emphasizing fresh fish, savory flesh and fancy fowl. Look for innovative mains like marinated tuna served over a jicama-quinoa salad on spicy charred watermelon, or coriander-crusted lamb leg, smoked black bean couscous, mint and pineapple. The elegantly understated dining room is lovely, with Persian-inspired decor, but the adjoining candlelit courtyard may be the Beach's most romantic dining spot. Wine-pairing is a house specialty. Desserts are a bit heavy relative to the delightfully sophisticated flavor pairings in the mains and apps, but perhaps that's just my taste.

Blue Door (☎ 305-674-6400, 1685 Collins Ave) **Map 3** Lunch mains $13-22, dinner mains $29-46. Open 11:30am-4pm & 7pm-11:30pm daily. The Delano Hotel's very chic Blue Door restaurant has very nice service and it's surprisingly very democratic when it comes to getting a table. Maybe it's possible that everyone assumes it's outrageously expensive and difficult to get into. Neither is overly true. Complement your experience with a generous martini or cosmopolitan.

Smith & Wollensky (☎ 305-673-2800, 1 Washington Ave) **Map 4** Lunch mains $6-30, dinner mains $20-35. Open noon-2am daily. For the view, S&W can't be beaten. Grab a seat at the clubby bar or on the patio in the afternoon and watch the ships gliding into the channel. Beyond the view, the traditional American steak house emphasizes just that – steak, steak and more steak.

Astor Place (☎ 305-672-7217, 956 Washington Ave) **Map 4** Mains $26-36. Open 7pm-11pm Sun-Thur, 7pm-midnight Sat & Sun. Chef Johnny Vinczecz' menu features dishes like sliced aged New York striploin with lobster mashed potatoes, grilled asparagus and enoki mushrooms. Servings are enormous. The subterranean dining room, with high ceilings and a glass atrium, is surprisingly open and airy, giving the place a breezy elegance. Check out the Sunday Jazz Gospel Brunch (mains $8-15; seatings at noon and 1pm).

Mark's South Beach (☎ 305-604-9050, 1120 Collins Ave) **Map 3** Lunch mains $15-17, dinner mains $25-38, five-course tasting menu $65. Open noon-3pm & 7pm-11pm daily. The most innovative kitchen in South Beach lies within the chic Nash Hotel. Chef-owner Mark Militello, one of the original trio of chefs known as the Mango Gang, is forever pushing the proverbial envelope. He works magic on dishes like Oregon black-truffle risotto with pappardelle, red grapes, marsala and crisp pancetta. Although the menu, which changes nightly, tilts toward seafood, meat eaters will be intrigued, too. Desserts are as beautiful as the clientele. The subterranean dining room is cozy and elegant, the service helpful and assured.

Cuban

David's Cafe (☎ 305-534-8736, 1058 Collins Ave) **Map 4** Dishes $3-6. Open 24 hrs daily. The round-the-clock *café con leche* market has been cornered by this storefront diner. It has counter service, not-awesome Cuban food and OK breakfasts. It's mainly mentioned as an emergency stopgap for when you're starving at 3:15am and don't want pizza.

David's Cafe II (☎ 305-672-8707, 1654 Meridian Ave) **Map 3** Dishes $3-6, buffet lunch $7.50. Open 7am-11pm daily. Most folks come for a quick shot of Cuban coffee from the take-out window, but the place is also popular for cheap breakfasts, taken at bar stools, and a bountiful lunch buffet, served in the dining room.

Lincoln Road Café (☎ *305-538-8066, 941 Lincoln Road)* **Map 3** Dishes $3-6, buffet lunch $7.50. Open 8am-1am daily. This long-time, famous Cuban spot is known for infuriatingly slow service and reliably decent food (the poultry dishes are very good). Unless you want to send yourself into diabetic shock, skip the incredibly sweet *tres leches* (literally, 'three milks'; figuratively, 'three-milk pudding-cake'; actually, 'three hundred parts sugar, one hundred parts milkfat') in favor of the *arroz con leche* (rice pudding).

Pollo Tropical (☎ *305-672-8888, 1454 Alton Rd)* **Map 3** Dishes $7-13. Open 11am-midnight daily. The most nutritious fast food in the country is served here. Yes, it's fast food in fast food surroundings, but it's great. Since the name means 'tropical chicken,' the poultry has been marinated in fruit juices and spices and then flame grilled. The bird is served with delicious Cuban home-style side dishes like black beans, rice, plantains, and *yuca* with garlic sauce.

El Viajante Segundo (☎ *305-534-2101, 1676 Collins Ave)* **Map 3** Dishes $7-11. Open 24 hrs daily. This diner serves authentic family-style Cuban food popular with locals and tony tourists alike. You won't find anything fancy here, just good solid food for a good value. Eat at the bar or at tables in the dark dining room.

Puerto Sagua (☎ *305-673-1115, 700 Collins Ave)* **Map 4** Dishes $6-25. Open 7:30am-2am daily. An anomaly on this stretch of Collins Ave – it's neighbors are the Gap and Benetton – this authentic Cuban diner and restaurant serves humongous portions at reasonable prices. Try the black bean soup, *arroz con pollo* (rice with chicken) or *ropa vieja* (shredded beef), or specialties like *filete de pargo grillet* (grilled red snapper). Stick to the low-end and moderately priced dishes; this is not the place to drop $25 on an entrée. If you haven't had Cuban café con leche yet, this is the place to do it because they serve the espresso and steamed milk in separate cups and let you add the sugar. Breakfasts, however, can be a tad greasy.

Lario's on the Beach (☎ *305-532-9577, 820 Ocean Dr)* **Map 4** Dishes $10-30. Open 11am-3am daily. This Cuban-themed restaurant and salsa club, co-owned by singer Gloria Estefan, draws folks more for the atmosphere than the food (which is good but not outstanding). Still, if you are into the scene, it's definitely worth a visit. Try the paella (for two people; it takes 45 minutes) or the less expensive fish Creole. Otherwise, a couple can squeak out for $25 or so by sharing three or four appetizers (like a huge Cuban sandwich) and getting one drink apiece.

Yuca (☎ *305-532-9822, 501 Lincoln Road)* **Map 3** Lunch mains $13-30, dinner mains $22-40. Open noon-11pm Mon-Sat, noon-10pm Sun. Reviews are mixed: When it opened, Yuca was the Beach's best Cuban Nouveau place (actually it was and remains the *only* one, but let's not get picky). Folks loved the marvelous food, chic European decor and youthful vibe. But then its star chef decamped for Manhattan and he may have taken a good deal of the magic with him. The menu still features Cuban-inspired dishes like plantain-coated dolphin fish with tamarind tartar, and baby back ribs with spiced guava sauce served with yuca shoestring fries and chipotle cole slaw. And certainly, it still has its admirers, but others simply head upstairs to the chic lounge for drinks and live music.

Other Caribbean

Tap Tap (☎ *305-672-2898, 819 5th St)* **Map 4** Dishes $9-13. Open 11am-11pm Mon-Fri, 4pm-midnight Sat & Sun. No doubt about it: Tap Tap's tropical fruit and vegetable salads and dishes like stewed goat and pumpkin soup should be experienced. It's also fun for a drink; try anything with Haitian Barbancourt rum, which is available in several grades. The atmosphere is charming and vibrant, the decor colorful, with handmade Haitian furniture and murals throughout. Live music and other entertainment rotates through quite often – check the *New Times* or call for information.

6 Degrees (☎ 305-538-2212, 685 Washington Ave) **Map 4** Mains $13-20. Open 7pm-2am Sun-Thur, 7pm-5am Fri & Sat. Executive chef Jason Strom's inviting menu features tasty appetizers like crab cakes and coconut-crusted shrimp. The entrées and desserts are downright lovingly prepared. His pork tenderloin signature dish cures for 18 hours in a mixture of salt, brown sugar, *mirepois,* and juniper berries and is then grilled to perfection and served with parsnip puree, caramelized apples and fried onions. The bar, which runs the length of the deep red dining room, attracts an increasingly bustling crowd as the night progresses.

Asian
Budget There are surprisingly few good, cheap choices.

Maiko (☎ 305-531-6369, 1255 Washington Ave) **Map 3** Dishes $4-15. Open noon-midnight Sun-Thur, noon-2:30am Fri & Sat. The prices are reasonable and the sushi, teriyaki and tempura are great. If only the decor matched the food.

Thai House (☎ 305-531-4841, 1137 Washington Ave) **Map 3** Dishes $7-13. Open noon-3pm & 5pm-midnight Mon-Fri, 2pm-midnight Sat & Sun. This family-run place features friendly service and a number of veggie dishes, tasty pad Thai and higher-priced specialties.

Mid-Range *Toni's Sushi Bar* (☎ 305-673-9368, 1208 Washington Ave) **Map 3** Mains $13-25. Open 6pm-midnight Sun-Thur, 6pm-1am Fri & Sat. Sushi starts simple and runs to an extravagant sushi boat here. On the scene for a long time, Toni's remains wildly popular, though some think the quality has slipped as Toni has extended his empire. Cooked seafood shares the stage with sushi.

Sushi Rock Café (☎ 305-532-2133, 1351 Collins Ave) **Map 3** Dishes $8-12. Open noon-midnight Sun-Thur, noon-1am Fri & Sat. With decent service and slightly higher prices for à la carte sushi and slightly lower for combinations and rolls, Sushi Rock is known mainly for its loud music in the evenings. If you don't need to hear yourself

think or if you're a raw fish and classic rock aficionado tired of conversing with your companion, come on by.

World Resources Café (☎ 305-535-8987, 719 Lincoln Road) **Map 3** Mains $13-22. Open noon-11:15pm Sun-Thur, 11am-12:15am Fri & Sat. For years this place was known as a funky world-music and gathering spot. After being taken over by Miami's Southeast Asian–fusion king, Toni Takarada, all that's left of the old place is the name. Sushi and Southeast Asian cuisine rule the menu, with curries and more expensive fare. There's a definite upscale vibe.

Thai Toni's (☎ 305-538-8424, 890 Washington Ave) **Map 4** Mains $10-20. Open 6pm-11:30pm daily. Renowned for pricey seafood specialties, chic clientele and a dramatically lit and understated open dining room, Thai Toni's has indisputably very good food – especially the soups. Curry dishes also share the stage with a good selection of vegetarian meals. The more exotic palates can munch on basil or garlic frog's legs.

Sushi Samba (☎ 305-673-5337, 600 Lincoln Road) **Map 3** Starters $7-12, dinner mains $17-29. Open noon-2am daily. New in late 2001, this wildly different eatery successfully blends Japanese with Brazilian and Peruvian flavors in a mod setting that emphasizes the sensual rhythms of samba music. For sure, it's a very fun restaurant with a novel cuisine that's highly evolved and well executed. Definitely try the sashimi seviche, one-of-a-kind sushi rolls, *tiradito,* a Peruvian-inspired dish similar to seviche, blue-cornmeal–crusted calamari, and a *saketini* (martini with saki) or *sakegria,* made with plum sake.

Top End *Nemo* (☎ 305-532-4550, 100 Collins Ave) **Map 4** Lunch mains $10-19, dinner mains $21-32. Open noon-3pm & 7pm-midnight Mon-Fri, 7pm-midnight Sat, 11am-3pm & 6pm-11pm Sun. Foodies love Nemo, where culinary wizard Michael Schwartz conjures up a Mediterranean-inspired pan-Asian menu featuring appetizers like crispy duck confit with cauliflower mash and wilted greens and pear-raisin chutney. Entrées range from wok-charred salmon and grilled Indian-spiced pork chops to pan-roasted chicken with garlic mashed potatoes. The dining room is perhaps a bit too cozy; the most sought-after tables are in the lovely courtyard. Dress to kill.

Pacific Time (☎ *305-534-5979, 915 Lincoln Road*) **Map 3** Mains $21-32. Open 6pm-11pm Sun-Thur, 6pm-midnight Fri & Sat. Chef-owner Jonathan Eismann's time-tested favorite dazzles with Pacific Rim–inspired food served in a chic and bustling (noisy) setting. Seafood dishes are consistently dynamite; try any preparation featuring locally caught dolphin fish. The wine list spans the world.

China Grill (☎ *305-534-2211, 404 Washington Ave*) **Map 4** Lunch mains $22-35. Open noon-midnight Sun-Thur, noon-1am Fri & Sat. The southern outpost of Manhattan's famed grill sports the same flash and panache as its older sibling. Dishes, *slightly* cheaper at lunchtime, are served family-style (well, *wealthy*-family–style) in large bowls intended to be shared. Try the dry-aged and grilled Szechuan beef, spicy sizzling whole fish, lobster with ginger, curry and crispy spinach or wasabi mashed potatoes. Don't come expecting to enjoy an intimate conversation; the room is cavernous and the music loud. Instead, come for the scene; when it's full, the sensory input can be overwhelming.

Italian (& Pizza)

Budget *Spris* (☎ *305-673-2020, 731 Lincoln Road*) **Map 3** Dishes $7-15. Open noon-1am daily. Spris' innovative early bird special, known as 'Beat the Clock,' begins at 5:30pm and ends at 7:30pm sharp. Here's how it works: The price you pay is determined by the time you place your order for one of three specials. Order at 6:15pm, pay $6.15. Specials consist of individual-sized, wood-oven-baked pizzas and a beverage (wine, beer or soda). Adding a delicious salad won't add much to the bill, but it will sure round out your meal. Spris is a great addition to the al fresco Lincoln Road scene.

Rosinella (☎ *305-672-8777, 525 Lincoln Road*) **Map 3** Dishes $8-11. Open 11:20am-midnight Sun-Thur, 11:30am-1am Fri & Sat. Under the same ownership as Sport Café, this small, cozy place has wonderful organic soups and vegetarian dishes. The fresh pastas and sauces taste like they were made by the Italian grandmother of your dreams. The antipasti and salads are assembled with beautiful produce and imported gourmet ingredients. As if that wasn't enough, you'll be greeted warmly, in Italian, by a friendly staff.

Paninoteca (☎ *305-538-0058, 809 Lincoln Road*) **Map 3** Dishes $4-9. Open 11am-11:30pm daily. An Italian sandwich bar with salads and individual-sized focaccia pizzas

Gelato & Ice Cream

It's warm and humid. Forget about the calories and pick one of the following places.

Gelateria Parmalat (☎ *786-276-9475, 670 Lincoln Road*) **Map 3** Open noon-midnight Sun-Thur, noon-1:30am Fri & Sat. The specialty here is authentic Italian gelato, served up in ultra-cool surroundings.

Frieze Ice Cream (☎ *305-538-0207, 1626 Michigan Ave*) **Map 3** Open noon-midnight Sun-Thur, noon-1am Fri & Sat. This is the real thing: high-fat, creamy and delicious. If you're watching your waistline, indulge in tropical sorbets.

Coco Gelato (☎ *305-538-1179, 1434 Washington Ave*) **Map 3** Open 11am-1am daily. You can't avoid the 52 flavors of Italian-style gelato ranging from traditional Italian (tiramisu) and American (rum raisin) to Caribbean (tamarindo).

Ben & Jerry's (☎ *305-673-8895, 760 Ocean Dr*) **Map 4** Open noon-11pm daily. Now part of a worldwide commercial empire, Ben & Jerry's can no longer be considered homemade, even in Vermont. Still, as the pioneer of American-style gourmet ice cream, it continues to earn its due. Grab a cone, park yourself on a bench across Ocean Drive and enjoy the show.

PLACES TO EAT

(pizzini), Paninoteca also has hot and cold sandwiches *(pannini)* with tasty toppings, fillings and spreads like black olive, onion confit and sun-dried tomatoes.

Pizza wars are in full swing. The only decisions are: by the slice, by the pie, take-out, delivery or eat-in.

Pizza Rustica *(☎ 305-538-6009, 1447 Washington Ave)* **Map 3** *(☎ 305-674-8244, 863 Washington Ave)* **Map 4** Slices $2.50-3.50. Open 11am-6am daily. South Beach's favorite pizza bar has two locations to satisfy the demand for Roman-style crusty/chewy slices topped with an array of exotic offerings. A slices is a meal unto itself. There's free delivery from the lower Washington Ave location only.

Pucci's Pizza *(☎ 305-674-1110, 1608B Alton Rd)* **Map 3** Slices $3, pies $10-25. Open 'until we close,' usually 11am-3am Sun-Thur, 11am-5am Fri & Sat. This popular pizza bar serves thin-crust New York–style pizzas with all the traditional toppings.

Au Natural Gourmet Pizza *(☎ 305-531-0666, 1427 Alton Rd)* **Map 3** Dishes $5-10. Open 11am-11pm Sun-Thur, 11am-midnight Fri & Sat. You can't get slices here, but the whole-wheat, multi-grain crusts are sized to feed from one to four. Toppings range from traditional (pepperoni) to nouveau (soy cheese, sautéed spinach and sun-dried tomatoes) to off-beat (pineapple and cherries). Pasta dishes, submarine sandwiches and salads are also available. Since most of the service is take-out, there are only a few tables, inside and out.

Bella Napoli *(☎ 305-672-1558, 1443 Alton Rd)* **Map 3** Pies $8-13. Open 11am-11pm daily. If you're after good, cheap pizza rather than chichi atmosphere, Bella Napoli serves it in a no-nonsense, Formica-tabled, family-style eatery.

Master's Deli Pizza *(☎ 305-672-2763, 1720 Alton Rd)* **Map 3** Medium pies $7. Open 10am-1am daily. Master's serves honest-to-goodness New York–style pizzas in a no-nonsense storefront eatery.

Ciccio's Pizza *(☎ 305-534-7155, 1405 Washington Ave)* **Map 3** Slices $2.50-3.50. Open 11am-6am daily. Another entry in the slice-joint wars, Ciccio's is popular with late-night revelers.

Mid-Range *Sport Café (☎ 305-674-9700, 560 Washington Ave)* **Map 4** Specials $7-16. Open 11:30am-1am daily. The name of this unpretentious and comfortable café disguises its true nature. The family-run place feels more like a Roman café – not a slicked-up American version of a Roman café, but a real one! Freshly baked bread with a dipping plate of spiced extra-virgin olive oil starts the evening off right. Try any of the excellent homemade pastas, and of the daily specials, don't miss the crab ravioli in pink cream sauce topped with freshly ground Romano cheese and black pepper. The first-rate Roman-style pizza boasts a perfectly thin crust. There's suave and attentive service, a good and inexpensive wine list and live music on weekend evenings.

Carnevale *(☎ 305-672-3333, 607 Lincoln Road)* **Map 3** Lunch mains $8-9, dinner mains $11-22. Open noon-1am daily. Serving pastas, pizza, sandwiches and salads at lunchtime, this Venetian-style café features more serious Italian meat dishes, chicken and risotto at dinner.

Spiga *(☎ 305-534-0079, 1228 Collins Ave)* **Map 3** Mains $12-19. Open 6pm-11:30pm. The lovely, intimate dining room is an oasis of elegant tranquility on bustling Collins Ave. The menu features homemade tagliolini pasta and endive with a light gorgonzola sauce, as well as veal scaloppini with prosciutto and sage in a white-wine sauce.

Da Leo Trattoria *(☎ 305-674-0350, 819 Lincoln Road)* **Map 3** Mains $9-21. Open 10am-11pm daily. Known for generous portions of home-style pasta dishes, Da Leo is no longer the only or the best Italian on Lincoln Road. Still, it has its partisans and has demonstrated its staying power. You could do a lot worse.

Osteria del Teatro *(☎ 305-538-7850, 1443 Washington Ave)* **Map 3** Mains $16-42. Open 6pm-11pm Mon-Thur, 6pm-midnight Fri & Sat. Considered Miami's best Italian restaurant by many, Osteria offers pricey but very delicious northern Italian meals and gracious service. If you arrive between 6pm and 7pm or after 10pm, the three-course fixed-price dinner with a glass of wine is worth every penny.

Top End *Escopazzo (☎ 305-674-9450, 1311 Washington Ave)* **Map 3** Mains $18-28. Open 6pm-midnight Sun-Thur, 6pm-1am Fri & Sat. Head here for the best value in this price range. The authentic Italian restaurant earns its reputation nightly with delectable dishes and friendly service. The homemade pasta dishes are exceptional. Reservations are a must – the dining room only seats 70 or so.

Tuscan Steak (☎ 305-534-2233, 433 Washington Ave) **Map 4** Mains $19-43. Open 6pm-midnight Sun-Thur, 6pm-1am Fri & Sat. The lovingly prepared Florentine dishes here are served family-style and intended for sharing. Dine as Italians do by starting with a salad, moving to a pasta or risotto and following it with a meat or fish dish. Grilled to perfection, the signature steak is garnished with roasted garlic puree; it's big enough to feed a hungry family. The handsome and sophisticated dining room is firmly controlled by the maître d' – be prepared for a weekend wait unless you're a long-lost pal.

French
Cafe Papillon (☎ 305-673-1139, 530 Lincoln Road) **Map 3** Dishes $6-11. Open 8:30am-11pm daily. For a real bargain, make a beeline here. Try the lunch plate ($7.50) with soup and a large (half) sandwich or quiche. The French *tartines* (grilled open-face sandwiches with marinated artichokes, grilled eggplant or roasted peppers in pesto sauce) are also quite tasty. It's even harder to beat the dinner special ($30), which includes two entrées and a bottle of house wine. Papillon has sidewalk tables and a casual, if small, French country dining room, plus newspapers for your perusal.

La Terrasse (☎ 305-695-9191, 639 Lincoln Road) **Map 3** Dishes $10-23. Open noon-midnight daily. This authentic French bistro meshes seamlessly among Lincoln Road's sidewalk cafés. One bite of the *tarte tatin* (upside-down caramelized apple tart) and

Places to Eat 24/7

When hunger strikes in the middle of the night, after clubbing or a bad dream, you have options. These places are open 24 hours a day, seven days a week.

El Viajante Segundo	Map 3
Wolfie's	Map 3
David's Cafe	Map 4
11th Street Diner	Map 4
News Cafe	Map 4
Rascal House	Map 5
La Carreta **(in Little Havana)**	Map 8

you'll think you're on the Left Bank. At times la Terrasse offers a three-course dinner menu ($17.50).

L'Entrecote de Paris (☎ 305-673-1002, 419 Washington Ave) **Map 4** Mains $16-26. Open 6pm-midnight Sun-Thur, 6pm-1am Fri & Sat. This authentic French brasserie and bar is known for its steak and all-you-can-eat *frites*, as well as simple salads and a reasonable wine list.

Mexican
The bout for best South Beach burrito has several worthy contenders.

Texas Taco Factory (☎ 305-535-5757, 1608 Alton Rd) **Map 3** Dishes $1.50-5.50. Open 7am-11pm daily. This Tex-Mex joint features fresh ingredients and rock-bottom prices. The 'fat boy' burrito has beans, cheese, lettuce, tomatoes, sour cream and guacamole; add meat for an extra 75¢. Fajita platters (half a pound of grilled meat and all the accompaniments) are big enough to share.

San Loco (☎ 305-538-3009, 235 14th St) **Map 3** Dishes $2-7. Open 11am-5am Sun-Thur, 11am-6am Fri & Sat. San Loco still has the Beach's best burrito, hands down. The restaurant also makes enchiladas, tacos, nachos (free of bushels of cilantro) and really excellent taco salads. The lovely staff will take good care of you.

Mrs Mendoza's Tacos al Carbon (☎ 305-535-0808, 1040 Alton Rd) **Map 4** Dishes

$3-5. Open 11am-10pm Sun-Thur, 11am-11pm Fri & Sat. This slightly-out-of-the-way option serves up even bigger burritos, with less garlic and heaps more cilantro. Of course you can also get tacos, chips and salsa, guacamole and rice and beans. The atmosphere is more 'fast food' than San Loco, but Mrs M is not kidding about her salsa: It's not just hot, it's head-blowing, ulcer-slammin' *hot!*

El Rancho Grande (☎ *305-673-0480, 1626 Pennsylvania Ave)* **Map 3** Lunch mains $5-7, dinner mains $9.50-18. Open 11:30am-11pm daily. This comfortable and cozy restaurant, where dishes are served in terra-cotta dishware, is more formal than its competition. While burritos come smothered with two types of melted cheese and sour cream, and rice, beans and guacamole, salads are a bit skimpier. Lunch specials and margaritas are key. If you love cilantro, you'll love El Rancho; they put it in everything they serve (except the margaritas).

And the heavyweight medal goes to whom?

German

Dab Haus (☎ *305-534-9557, 852 Alton Rd)* **Map 4** Dishes $7-13. Open 4pm-'closing' daily. Beyond the drab exterior lies a quick trip to Munich, with excellent German dishes like bratwurst, *currywurst, knoblauchwurst, sauerbraten* and pork and chicken schnitzel. It also has crêpes with mushrooms, potatoes, red cabbage and cheese. Don't miss the honey-garlic brie. Wash it all down with a hearty Bavarian ale, preferably when there's live music and a lively crowd.

Israeli

Pita Loca (☎ *305-673-3388, 601 Collins Ave)* **Map 4** Dishes $4-9. Open noon-11:45pm Sun-Thur, noon-4:30pm Fri, 8pm-1am Sat. This Israeli shawarma-and-falafel joint is perfect for a quick bite, but service can be a bit brusque. Note the hours (closed during Shabbat.)

NORTHERN MIAMI BEACH (MAP 5)

Not to be confused with North Miami Beach, which is a distinct entity, these places

lie east of the Intracoastal Waterway, in the communities of Surfside, Bal Harbour and Sunny Isles.

Rascal House (☎ *305-947-4581, 17190 Collins Ave)* Dishes $7-15. Open 24 hrs daily. Wolfie Cohen's nostalgic 1954 Miami eatery has sassy service, classic swivel stools at the counter and Naugahyde booths. It bustles with older patrons, Northeastern snowbirds and curious tourists who relish roast brisket, latkes, blintzes, beet borscht and Lake Erie whitefish salad. The grilled salmon and Reuben sandwiches are also reliable. Every single thing is homemade and it's all available for take-out. But you're coming for the atmosphere, right? A parking lot attendant meets you in a golf cart to whisk you to the front door. Expect to wait a bit (for a table, not the cart).

Arnie & Richie's (☎ *305-531-7691, 525 41st St)* Dishes $4-24. Open 6:30am-8:45pm Mon-Fri, 7am-4pm Sat & Sun. Smoked whitefish, corned beef and other Jewish deli staples rule the roost at this authentic deli.

Oasis Cafe (☎ *305-674-7676, 976 41st St)* Lunch dishes $7-10, dinner mains $7-16. Open 11am-10pm Mon-Sat, 5pm-10pm Sun. Tired of all the South Beach hype? This Mediterranean vegetarian café will treat you right, right down to the healthful dolmas (stuffed grape leaves), eggplant salad and hummus. Try the grilled fish on focaccia for more substance.

DOWNTOWN MIAMI (MAP 6)

Most downtown places cater to 9-to-5ers, but an increasing number are also attracting a burgeoning pleasure-seeking crowd. You'll find some surprising choices worth searching out.

Budget

Food courts (SE 1st Ave between E Flagler St & SE 1st St; Biscayne Blvd between NE 1st St & E Flagler St) Dishes $1-6. Open weekdays. Chinese, Mexican and Indian food, as well as pizza, sandwiches, and other fast foods, fit the bill at these two food courts.

Panini Coffee Bar (☎ *305-377-2888, 16 NE 3rd Ave)* Dishes $4-7. Open 8:30am-6pm

Neon-lit Port of Miami bridge

Buildings along Ocean Drive, South Beach

The wavelike roof of this art deco lifeguard tower displays a common deco theme.

RICHARD CUMMINS

Tile detail of coffee and a cigar against the Cuban flag in Miami's Little Havana

LEE FOSTER

See and be seen at places like busy Van Dyke Cafe, on Lincoln Road in South Beach.

LEE FOSTER

Miami cuisine highlights seafood, especially during stone crab season (mid-October to mid-May).

Mon-Fri, 9am-4:30pm Sat. This indoor/ outdoor café, Frenchish and trendy by downtown standards, has requisite coffee and pastries. But they also have sandwiches on French bread, salads and soup by the cup and bowl.

S&S Restaurant (☎ 305-373-4291, 1757 NE 2nd Ave) Dishes $4-10. Open 5:30am-6pm Mon-Fri, 6am-2pm Sat & Sun. Step back into the past at this classic '40s-style diner with downright sassy service ('Keep yer shirt on, hon!') and great old-fashioned choices that define 'comfort food.' You'll be happy with humongous burgers, meatloaf and baked macaroni and cheese, or more adventurous entries like shrimp Creole. It's no wonder the small horseshoe-shaped linoleum lunch counter is always very crowded, especially with cops.

Granny Feelgood's (☎ 305-377-9600, 25 W Flagler St) Breakfast $3-7, lunch $4-12. Open 7am-4pm Mon-Fri. A neighborhood staple since the mid-1970s, this health-food emporium has great chicken, fish and veggie dishes. If you 'feel good' after your meal (and you will), consider purchasing some of Granny's vitamins and herbal goods next door.

Café Nash (☎ 305-371-8871, 37 E Flagler St) Dishes $7-10. Open 8am-4pm Mon-Fri, 9am-4pm Sat. Within the Seybold Building Arcade, Nash is a fairly small place that appeals to businessfolk. The fare ranges from omelets and salads to sandwiches and combo platters.

Tobacco Road (☎ 305-374-1198, 626 S Miami Ave) Dishes $7-11. Open 11:30am-5am daily (kitchen stops serving at 2am). Miami's oldest bar, on the scene since the 1920s, Tobacco Road is primarily a blues and jazz joint, but it also has excellent burgers, with toppings ranging from mundane (cheese) to strange (eggs). During the Friday happy hour, it is indeed a happy place to be ($5 cover). But Tuesday nights are even better, when the Road has lobsters for $11 from 5:30pm until they run out (about 7:30pm).

Mid-Range

Cacique's Corner (☎ 305-371-8317, 100 W Flagler St) Dishes $6-7. Open 5am-7pm

Bagels

Greater Miami is the New York–Jewish capital of the southern USA, and bagels are everywhere. A bagel, for the uninitiated, is a doughnut-shaped bread product made from heavy dough that has been boiled and then baked. The result is a substantial and chewy roll with a uniquely textured coating – the closest comparison would be a real Bavarian brez'n, but that's not really it. Just eat one.

Originally ethnic Jewish, the bagel has insinuated itself into the American menu and can now be bought in big cities from coast to coast. They are usually offered plain or rolled in sesame seed, poppy seed, onion, garlic, combinations of the previous or, more rarely, salt. They're available in any diner and in most restaurants that serve breakfast.

daily. This classic Cuban place ladles out meal-sized portions of *bistec de pollo* with rice, beans and plantains.

Hard Rock Cafe (☎ 305-377-3110, Bayside Marketplace) Dishes $8-20. Open 11am-10pm Sun-Thur, 11am-midnight Fri & Sat. In the waterfront Bayside Marketplace, this middle-of-the-road eatery is known more for the gigantic rotating electric guitar on its roof than for its food, which is perfectly fine. A fun place to take the kids or a tourist trap – it's your call. In lieu of a main dish, try an enormous sandwich like the VLT (veggie, lettuce and tomato) or smoked barbecued beef on a pretzel roll.

Fishbone Grille (☎ 305-530-1915, 650 S Miami Ave) Lunch mains $9-16, dinner mains $9-25. Open noon-4pm & 5:30pm-10pm Mon-Fri, 5:30pm-10pm Sat. Arguably Miami's best cheap fish house, this casual place with an open kitchen features grilled, blackened, sautéed, baked or *française* seafood preparations. Prices fluctuate with the market; check the long chalkboard list for the prime catches of the-day. The seafood gumbo is interesting, the jalapeño cornbread a killer, and the pizzas justifiably renowned. But you didn't come for pizza, right? The wine list is reasonably priced, too.

Bubba Gump Shrimp Co (*☎ 305-379-8866, Bayside Marketplace*) Dishes $10-19. Open 11:30am-10:30pm daily. You'll dine at picnic tables under thousands of white lights and outstretched banyan tree limbs at this open-air eatery. Feast on large portions of shrimp cooked every which way and described with the wackiest names and by the wackiest waiters you'll ever have to affectionately endure. True fans of the movie *Forrest Gump* (on which this themed chain restaurant is based) won't overlook the gift store, which rivals the size of the restaurant section.

Garcia's (*☎ 305-375-0765, 398 NW North River Dr*) Dishes $11–market price. Open 11:30am-6:30pm Mon-Sat, 11am-4:30pm Sun. Another reliable choice for inexpensive, fresh seafood on the banks of the seedy Miami River, Garcia's has indoor counter service and outdoor tables.

Los Ranchos (*☎ 305-375-8188, Bayside Marketplace*) Dishes $11-market price. Open 11:30am-11pm daily. A meat eater's utopia, this Nicaraguan eatery loads up its lean entrées with excellent sides of beans and rice. Unlike the bottom-feeders swimming in the huge, centrally located fish tank, you'll enjoy your perch in the glassed-in waterfront restaurant.

Perricone's (*☎ 305-374-9449, 15 SE 10th St*) Lunch mains $8-9, dinner mains $12-20. Open 7am-10pm Sun-Wed, 7am-11pm Thur-Sat. Ensconced in a huge Vermont barn trucked down for a new lease on life, Perricone's has a winning formula in its combo deli-restaurant. Purchase some wine from the market and they'll uncork it (for a fee that's much less than the normal markup on wine) at the restaurant. Sandwiches, pastas and grilled dishes are popular. The outdoor terrace, offering much-appreciated relief from the downtown bustle, attracts more suits than travelers, but don't let that stop you. The all-you-can-eat Sunday buffet ($15), with pasta, omelets and fruit, is a bargain.

Provence Grill (*☎ 305-373-1940, 1001 S Miami Ave*) Lunch mains $5-12, dinner mains $13-20. Open 11:30am-3pm & 5:30pm-10:30pm daily. Ooh-la-la! If you didn't get to France this year, no worries, mate. One bite of the Grill's mussels in garlic, or one whiff of the lavender-laced crème brûlée and you'll be transported across the Atlantic before you can say *mais oui*. The setting, complete with a lush outdoor bar (where you'll wait since service at this popular restaurant breezes by slower than an escargot), is surprisingly countrified for the locale. *C'est bon.*

Gordon Biersch Brewery (*☎ 786-425-1130, 1201 Brickell Ave*) Lunch mains $9-13, dinner mains $18-22. Open 11:30am-11pm Sun-Thur, 11:30am-midnight Fri & Sat (bar open until 2am Fri & Sat). This cavernous brewpub, with great German-style beer, has an eclectic menu. Stick to the brick-oven pizzas, burgers and garlic-laden french fries rather than trying the more elaborate offerings. Friday afternoon happy hour resembles Ivy League fraternity parties, which will bring back fond memories for some.

Joe's Seafood (*☎ 305-374-5637, 400 NW North River Dr*) Lunch specials $8, lunch mains $14-25, dinner mains $14-36. Open 11am-10pm Mon-Thur, 11am-11pm Fri-Sun. To fully appreciate the colorful Miami River atmosphere, you'll want to eat on the deck of this rustic establishment. Since it's a combo fish market and restaurant, you're practically guaranteed fresh fish. The service is slow but perfectly good-natured.

Top End

Big Fish (*☎ 305-373-1770, 55 SW Miami Ave*) Lunch mains $8-20, dinner mains $11-35. Open noon-3pm & 6:30pm-11:30pm Mon-Fri, noon-11:30pm Sat & Sun. It's got riverfront competition, but the big fish on the block grills some tasty denizens of the deep. (Some dependable Italian dishes grace the menu, too.) Waiting at the congenial bar for dramatic skyline views and a funky atmosphere won't be difficult, but you will have to do it. It's a little tough to find, with all the one-way streets, but don't give up.

Café Sambal (*☎ 305-913-8251, 500 Brickell Key Dr*) Lunch mains $12-20, dinner mains $18-30. Open 6:30am-11pm daily. Located within the luxe Mandarin Oriental Miami hotel on Brickell Key, this nouveau Asian bistro pairs exceptional food (including crab cakes) with 'relaxed' service. But who cares? You can still savor the skyline while you sip a martini and drink in the view.

Capital Grille (☎ 305-374-4500, 444 Brickell Ave) Lunch mains $12-25, dinner mains $25-35. Open 11:30am-3pm & 5pm-10:30pm Mon-Fri, 6pm-11pm Sat, 5pm-10:30pm Sun. This posh carnivore's paradise boasts steak, more steak and great big steaks. Service is hushed and reverent as it's frequented by suited expense-accounters who appreciate chandeliers, marble floors and dark wood paneling as much as steak, steak and more steak. The bar is equally hush-hush and handsome, the perfect perch for a secret rendezvous and a dry martini.

Porcão (☎ 305-373-2777, 801 Brickell Bay Dr) $33 per person. Open noon-midnight daily. You'd better come with an appetite. This excellent Brazilian *churrascaria* features an elaborate *rodízio*, a traditional endless feast of skewered, flame-broiled meats. Waiters circulate with the flaming skewers and describe exactly what's what. There are something like 30 different kinds of salad at the buffet. Someone sure named this restaurant right; you'll feel like a stuffed pig by the end.

KEY BISCAYNE (MAP 7)

Peckish at the Seaquarium? Need a post-beach pick-me-up? Or a sunset drink? Or picnic fixings for a lighthouse excursion? Few of these places win 'best of' awards, but they're all respectable.

Farmer's Market (☎ 305-361-1300, 91 Harbor Dr) Open 9am-8pm Mon-Fri, 8am-8pm Sat & Sun. This upscale market carries smoked salmon, hot and cold prepared foods, Old World cheeses, olives and luscious pastries and breads.

Lu Curreta (☎ 305-365-1177, 12 Crandon Blvd) Dishes $4-5. Open 7am-11pm daily. For quick, no-frills Cuban-style snacks, this Miami chain offers dependably filling and cheap choices – from big breakfasts to sandwiches.

Oasis (☎ 305-361-5709, 19 Harbor Dr) Dishes $4-12. Open 6am-9pm daily. From blue-collar workers to blue-blood pols, socioeconomic barriers come tumbling down at this Cuban coffee oasis. More aptly described as a hole-in-the-wall with a take-out coffee window, Oasis serves dishes like sandwiches, paella and the like.

Stefano's (☎ 305-361-7007, 24 Crandon Blvd) Mains $11-29. Open 5pm-11pm Sun-Thur, 5pm-5am Fri & Sat. Surf-and-turf, pastas and good Italian specialties lead the menu, but Stefano's is much more than a menu. It's a wacky place to hang out, if you don't mind hopping into a time machine and going back to the 1980s. Firstly, it attracts an older local crowd in the early evening. Then, at 10pm or so, a DJ starts with the pop tunes. You gotta give Stefano's credit; they have staying power. Check out their adjacent wine shop, with caviar, foie gras and salmon.

Sunday's on the Bay (☎ 305-361-6777, 5420 Crandon Blvd) Mains $15-24. Open 11am-11pm Mon-Thur, 11am-3am Fri, 11am-5am Sat & Sun. The bountiful Sunday buffet ($24 per person) draws crowds, but then again so do the tropical bar, marina views and large outdoor terrace. Drinks are fun anytime, but Sundays on the bay are better than any other day on the bay. The predictable seafood dishes are just that: predictable, but fine.

Rusty Pelican (☎ 305-361-3818, 3201 Rickenbacker Causeway) Lunch mains $8-19, dinner mains $18-25. Open 11:30am-4pm & 5pm-11pm Mon-Thur, 11:30am-4pm & 5pm-midnight Fri & Sat, 10:30am-3pm & 5pm-11pm Sun. Panoramic skyline views, perhaps the best in Miami, draw the faithful and romantic to this airy, tropical restaurant. Come for a sunset drink, then head into the sunset somewhere else for dinner. The average surf-and-turf menu is nothing to scream hysterically (positively or negatively) about. Don't worry if you have a few too many drinks and stay for dinner; I's nothing to be embarrassed about in the morning.

LITTLE HAVANA (MAP 8)

Cuban, Cuban and more Cuban. Only Fidel's island nation has more authentic eateries, none of which will strain your budget. If you don't speak Spanish, bring a Spanish-English dictionary with you – many places have only Spanish menus and monolingual waitstaff.

Budget

Karmen Bakery (☎ 305-642-7171, 1854 Calle Ocho) Open 5am-8pm Mon-Sat, 6am-3pm Sun. There's a reason there's always a line here: It's impossible to pass up the aromatic, tasty pastries.

Versailles Bakery (☎ 305-441-2500, 3501 Calle Ocho) Open 8am-10pm daily. This bakery, where rum cake is a favorite, adjoins the famed restaurant (see later).

El Rey de las Fritas (☎ 305-858-4223, 1177 Calle Ocho) Sandwiches $2-4. Open 9am-10:30pm Mon-Sat. The self-proclaimed King takes fried fast food to new heights – of cholesterol (in)tolerance. El Rey specializes in sandwiches with fried fillings (potatoes come inside sandwiches, not alongside). Unless you're friends with the counter workers, the service bounces between inattentive and grumpy. Don't be shy; sit yourself down at a barstool and let the illuminated photo menu on the wall be your guide.

Calle Ocho Marketplace & Cafetería (no ☎, 1390 Calle Ocho) Sandwiches $3. Open daily. Almost everyone stops by this combination lunch counter/laundry/food market/coffee stand eventually, for something.

Taquerías el Mexicano (☎ 305-858-1160, 521 Calle Ocho) Dishes $5-10. Open 9am-11pm daily. This casual, friendly joint serves tasty Mexican food; a number of choices are vegetarian. For a Mexicano-style breakfast of champions, order *chilaquiles* – tortilla chips simmered in green sauce mixed with scrambled eggs and covered with cheese and sour cream, and rice and beans. Wash your dinner down with a decent Mexican beer like Bohemia or Negra Modelo.

Exquisito Restaurant (☎ 305-643-0227, 1510 Calle Ocho) Dishes under $7. Open 7am-midnight daily. For cheap coffee, casual atmosphere and home-style food, this place is exquisite! Order any combination of steak, french fries, sausage, ham, eggs, toast and café con leche for under $4. The full breakfast *(desayuno)* will keep you going all day.

El Pescador (☎ 305-541-9224, 1543 Calle Ocho) Dishes $4.50-13. Open 10:30am-10pm Tues-Sun. This little storefront eatery is bright and cheerful and the service friendly. It's a real winner for seafood lovers. Daily specials might include grilled dolphin fish and shrimp Creole accompanied by rice and black beans, fried plantains or potatoes.

La Esquina de Tejas (☎ 305-545-0337, 101 SW 12th Ave) Dishes $4-14. Open 8am-5pm daily. There's no escaping this restaurant's claim to fame: US President Ronald Reagan ate here in 1983. The evidence is everywhere, from the shrine to the Presidential Seal and autograph reproduction on the menu. In spite of the Reaganmania, the place serves some of the best Cuban food in Little Havana. The wide-ranging menu features numerous sandwiches, and daily and house specials like *arroz con calamares con maduros* (squid and rice with fried sweet plantains) or roast chicken in sherry sauce. Breakfast is a bargain.

Versailles (☎ 305-444-0240, 3555 Calle Ocho) Dishes $8-10. Open 8am-2am Mon-Thur, 8am-3:30am Fri, 8am-4:30am Sat, 9am-2am Sun. Don't be fooled by the name; there's nothing French here but the chandeliers (and those aren't really either). The cavernous and glitzy (in a 1980s *Scarface/Miami Vice* kind of way) restaurant is a landmark. And since it's a favorite among Cuban power brokers and families alike, you might want to go out of your way to eat here. It can be fun with a group and a pitcher of (weak) sangria. Service is fine but the food barely reaches average. Live with it. Order *palomilla* (Cuban steak) with fries or *vaca frita* (shredded beef grilled with onions) and plantains.

Islas Canarias (☎ 305-649-0440, 285 NW 27th Ave) Dishes $8-10. Open 7am-11pm daily. Many Cubans think Islas Canarias has Miami's best Cuban food. Bring a hearty

Cuban Cuisine

There's nothing delicate about Cuban cooking; it's hearty and hefty. The most common ingredients are pork, beef, rice, beans, eggs, tomatoes, lettuce, lemons and oranges. Cuban food isn't generally spicy either. Garlic and onions, rather than chili peppers, are used for seasoning. Floridian Cuban cuisine utilizes *mojo*, a garlic-citrus sauce.

The most common dishes are *carne asada* (roasted meat), *puerco asado* (roast pork), *carne de cerdo* (pork), *bistec* (steak), *arroz con pollo* (chicken and rice), *filete de pescado* (fish filet) and *ropa vieja* (literally 'old clothes,' but actually shredded skirt-steak stew served up with rice and plantains).

Other meat and poultry dishes include *bistec de res* (beefsteak), *cabra* (goat), *cabrito* (kid goat), *chorizo* (spicy pork sausage), *cordero* (lamb) and *jamón* (ham). Seafood dishes include *ceviche* (raw seafood, marinated in citrus juice), *calamar* (squid), *camarones* (shrimp), *jaiba* (small crab), *langosta* (lobster), *mariscos* (shellfish) and *ostiones* (oysters).

Common side dishes include *arroz* (rice); *moros y christianos* (literally 'Moors and Christians,' gastronomically black beans and rice); *frijoles negros o rojos* (black or red beans); *yuca* (manioc or cassava), a starchy root vegetable that's boiled, baked or fried, like french fries; and *maduros* (fried plantains), a larger cousin of the banana. When done right, fried plantains are crispy outside and sweet and starchy inside.

Sandwiches

Cuban sandwiches from *loncherías* (snack bars) are in a class of their own. They're made by slicing Cuban loaves lengthwise, filling them with ingredients and toasting (also known as smashing) them in a *plancha* – a heated press. The most popular ones include the *cubano* (pork or ham and cheese, sometimes with mustard and pickles, depending on how much you look like a gringo), *pan con lechón* (extra crispity-crunchity pork and mojo), *palomilla* (steak with fried onions) and *medianoche* (literally 'midnight'; actually with ham, cheese and roast pork).

Desserts

Desserts *(postres)* include *arroz con leche* (rice pudding), *crepa* (thin pancakes or crêpes), *flan* or *crème caramel* (custard), *galletas* (cookies or biscuits), *gelatina* (jello), *helado* (ice cream) and *pastel* (pastry or cake). Watch out for *tres leches* (literally 'three-milk' cake), which is actually a glucose-tolerance test disguised as pudding.

Tea & Coffee

The big players are *café con leche* (half coffee and half hot steamed milk); *café con crema* (coffee with cream served separately); *cafecito* (espresso served in thimble-size shots); *té de manzanilla* (chamomile tea); and *té negro* (black tea). When ordering coffee don't expect a Seattle-style look-alike. The Cuban version is an industrial-strength, over-sweetened beverage (they pour, really pour, in the sugar for you unless you specifically request they don't). Non-Cuban palates may find it ghastly.

Fruit & Vegetable Drinks

Pure fresh juices *(jugos)*, where the nectar is squeezed right in front of you, are popular and readily available. Every fruit and many vegetables are used. Ever tried pure beetroot juice? Another local favorite is *guarapo* (sugarcane juice). *Licuados* blend fruit or juice with water and sugar. *Licuados con leche* use milk in lieu of water. Consider adding raw egg, ice, and flavorings like vanilla and nutmeg. *Aguas frescas* or *aguas de fruta* combine fruit juice or a syrup made from mashed grains or seeds with sugar and water.

PLACES TO EAT

appetite and order one of the daily specials, like *ropa vieja* (shredded beef stew) or *bacalao* (salted codfish). It's located in a strip mall and the decor is strictly Formica, but the service is friendly.

Guayacan (☎ *305-649-2015, 1933 Calle Ocho*) Dishes $7-15. Open 11am-10pm Sun-Thur, 11am-11pm Fri & Sat. For Nicaraguan cooking, served by friendly folks in a pleasantly homey atmosphere, you'll like Guayacan. Along with the hearty specialty soups, you could make a meal of the *antojitos* (appetizers) like *chorizo de cerdo* (pork sausages) and Nicaraguan tamales. Or order the house special: *pescado a la Tipitapa* (whole red snapper, de-boned and deep fried, served with a zingy pepper-and-onion sauce). All specials come loaded with sides: salad, rice and beans, plantains, french fries, corn tortillas, bread. You certainly won't leave hungry.

Hy Vong Vietnamese Restaurant (☎ *305-446-3674, 3458 Calle Ocho*) Dishes $8-15. Open 6pm-10:30pm Tues-Sun; closed mid–late Aug. Little Havana's culinary anomaly rocks Miami's food world. Hy Vong really does serve some of the best Vietnamese food in the USA. Favorites include *bun* – thin sliced meat with vermicelli – and the squid salad marinated in lime juice and onions. Most dishes are quite spicy and portions are generous. Get to the tiny storefront eatery early; it may look like a dive, but it's no secret.

Mid-Range
Casa Panza (☎ *305-643-5343, 1620 Calle Ocho*) Tapas $3.50-6, mains $12-15. Open 11:30am-10pm Sun & Mon, 11:30am-2am Tues-Sat. Dark and cozy and more than a little kitschy, Cafe Panza serves authentically prepared and presented dishes. Order a glass of sherry and start with a bowl of *caldo gallego* (white-bean soup with pork sausage). Then order some tapas like *tortilla de patatas* (potato and onion omelet, served at room temperature), *gambas al ajillo* (shrimp in garlic sauce) and *boquerones en vinagre* (fresh anchovies in vinaigrette). End your meal with the sweet and silky *crema catalana*. Casa Panza also has live flamenco music and dance shows (see the Entertainment chapter).

La Carreta (☎ *305-444-7501, 3632 Calle Ocho*) Dishes $5-20. Open 24 hrs daily. The original link in a Cuban chain, La Carreta features all the traditional Cuban dishes you'll find at Versailles. The decor is a little less glaring and in-your-face, though no less kitschy in its country farmhouse way. Open around the clock, it's popular for *medianoches* (Cuban-style grilled ham and cheese sandwiches) and *café cubano*. If you just need a caffeine and sugar fix, order from the take-out window in the back.

COCONUT GROVE (MAP 9)
The Grove can satisfy every conceivable culinary desire, from cheap Middle Eastern to authentic French to Miami's best Indian.

Budget
The Oak Feed (☎ *305-448-7595, Oak Ave at Mary St*) Open 9am-10pm daily. Miami's first natural-foods store is still going strong. Instead of serving 1960s flower children, though, the Oak Feed's clientele is yuppies and boomers.

Bacio (☎ *305-442-4233, 3462 Main Hwy*) Open noon-11pm Sun-Wed, noon-midnight Thur, noon-1am Fri & Sat. What's an evening *passagiato* without a scoop of Italian gelato?

Daily Bread Marketplace (☎ *305-856-5893, 2400 SW 27th St*) Dishes $3-6. Open 9am-8pm Mon-Sat, 11am-5pm Sun. Essentially a small grocery store with tables, this family-run Middle Eastern deli has superb lentil soup, lamb kebabs, spanakopita, falafel and gyro sandwiches. Otherwise, assemble a picnic with olives, baba ghanoush, baklava and homemade pita bread. There are a few outdoor tables.

Johnny Rockets (☎ *305-444-1000, 3036 Grand Ave*) Dishes $4-6. Open 11am-midnight Mon-Thur, 11am-2am Fri & Sat, 11am-midnight Sun. This 1950s-style chain hamburger joint, with a soda fountain and old-fashioned Coca-Cola glasses, is cramped inside but has plenty of sidewalk tables. The No 12 cheeseburger (with red sauce, pickles, lettuce and tomato) is terrific, but get the red sauce on the side before committing. The chicken breast sandwiches are also good.

Mid-Range

Cafe Tu Tu Tango (☎ *305-529-2222, Coco-Walk*) Dishes $4-10. Open 11am-midnight Sun-Wed, 11am-1am Thur, 11am-2am Fri & Sat. This wacky second-floor theme restaurant resembles an artist's studio or garret, deliberately cluttered with half-finished paintings. While munching on eclectic Spanish tapas, have a tarot-card reading and watch the artists painting at their easels.

Green Street Cafe (☎ *305-567-0662, 3110 Commodore Plaza*) Breakfast $4-7, lunch & dinner $10-17. Open 7:30am-11pm Sun-Thur, 7:30am-midnight Fri & Sat. People-watching takes precedence over the food at this longtime corner café. But still, you can get good American-style breakfasts until 3pm. Pizza, salads, elaborate pasta dishes and salmon filets are offered at lunch and dinner.

Paulo Luigi's (☎ *305-445-9000, 3324 Virginia St*) Lunch mains $7-9, dinner mains $10-30. Open 11:45am-2:35pm & 5pm-11pm Mon-Thur, 11:45am-2:35pm & 5pm-1am Fri, 5pm-1am Sat & Sun. Practically obliterated by CocoWalk, this now-hidden family-friendly (and all-around friendly) Italian restaurant has been a local favorite since the mid-1970s. Why? It offers decent pizza and creative pasta dishes for reasonable prices, in a homey environment. Geeze. It's a rarity.

Anokha (☎ *786-552-1030, 3195 Commodore Plaza*) Veg dishes average $11, other mains average $14. Open 6:30pm-10:30pm Tues, Wed & Sun, 6pm-11:30pm Thur-Sat. Perhaps Miami's best Indian restaurant, this family-run phenom goes beyond excellent vindaloos, curries and tandooris. It's small in size but huge in my estimation.

Cheesecake Factory (☎ *305-447-9898, CocoWalk*) Dishes $13-24. Open 11:30am-11:30pm Sun-Thur, 11:30am 1am Fri & Sat. The hefty menu reads like a glossy magazine, thick with advertisements; you'll work up an appetite just getting through it.

Luckily the large portions are pretty good *and* the menu is wide-ranging – from burgers and Thai chicken to pastas and pizza topped with roasted pepper, ricotta and sun-dried tomatoes. There are over 30 kinds of cheesecake ($5-6) for dessert; save some room. Expect to wait at this popular nationally known chain.

Top End

Le Bouchon du Grove (☎ *305-448-6060, 3430 Main Hwy*) Lunch mains $12-20, dinner mains $15-25. Open 9:30am-3pm & 5pm-11pm daily. Francophiles unite. The atmosphere is authentic but unpretentious, the staff friendly and heavily accented. Although tables are crammed close together and huge antique signs are plastered everywhere, it feels cozy rather than claustrophobic, since the tables spill onto the sidewalk. Try the beef filet in peppercorn sauce or the excellent, traditional onion soup.

CORAL GABLES (MAP 10)

Most Coral Gables restaurants are clustered near 'Restaurant Row,' on Giralda Ave between Ponce de León Blvd and Miller Ave, but that's not the only game in town. You'll want to cruise Miracle Mile, too. In all, there are dozens of places serving dozens of types of cuisine from Italian to bistro-style French. The upscale ones are worth every penny.

Budget

Starbucks (☎ *305-443-6620, 200 Miracle Mile*) has helped enliven the late-night scene on Miracle Mile.

Allen's Drug Store (☎ *305-665-6964, 4000 Red Rd*) Dishes $3-6. Open 6am-8pm Mon-Fri, 6am-5pm Sat, 6am-3pm Sun. For drug-store chic and retro cheesiness, Allen's 'Picnics Cafe' boasts cheap and reliably good burgers, meatloaf, diner specials and a cool jukebox. Since the actual drug store caters to elderly patrons, you'll be chowing down next to walkers and other paraphernalia that aids seniors. It's a trip, a fun one.

Miracle Mile Cafeteria (☎ *305-444-9005, 147 Miracle Mile*) Dishes $4-6. Open 11am-8:30pm daily. It's astonishing that some national retailer hasn't invaded this space, full of kitsch, Formica and a friendly staff. They're deservedly proud of their old-fashioned Southern fare, like brisket of roast beef and barbecue ribs. Enjoy a slice of history with a slice of pie; one day they'll both be gobbled up for good.

Café Demetrio (☎ 305-448-4949, 300 Alhambra Circle) Dishes $4-7. Open 7:30am-9pm Mon-Thur, 7:30am-midnight Fri & Sat. Decidedly European, from Spanish omelets and Italian coffee to Greek salads and Linzer tortes, this unpretentious place is a breath of fresh air in Coral Gables. Sandwiches and salads are menu mainstays.

Mid-Range

Miss Saigon Bistro (☎ 305-446-8006, 148 Giralda Ave) Lunch mains $7-10, dinner mains $10-16. Open 11:30am-10pm daily. For great soups, noodle dishes and other Vietnamese food, you can't beat this solid family-run place. Portions are hefty. Since it's small, there are always people waiting to feast here.

Taisho (☎ 305-441-1217, 2522 Ponce de León Blvd) Lunch buffet $11, dinner buffet $13. Open noon-2:30pm & 5:30pm-9:30pm Mon-Fri (until 10:30pm Fri), 5:30pm-10:30pm Sat, 5:30pm-9:30pm Sun. This serviceable place offers a midday sushi buffet, while the evening one expands to include tempura and other Japanese goodies.

Top End

Caffe Abbracci (☎ 305-441-0700, 318 Aragon Ave) Lunch mains $14-16, dinner mains $16-24. Open 11:30am-3:30pm Mon-Fri, 6:30pm-11:30pm daily. The most reasonably priced of these pricey restaurants, Abbracci embraces you warmly, from the time you make a reservation to the moment you're walking out the door a satisfied customer. The dark, elegant and upscale eatery is decidedly trendy, but it serves some of the best northern Italian food in the city. Pastas are fresh, antipasti plentiful, veal a specialty and the tiramisu a delight. The daily lunch special of pasta and fish is a bargain at $15.50.

Meza Fine Art Gallery & Cafe (☎ 305-461-2733, 275 Giralda Ave) Lunch mains $6-12, dinner mains $16-29. Open 11:30am-2:30pm & 6pm-'who knows' Mon-Sat. Tired of fussy food but still want the dining room to have an energetic buzz? This artful place puts as much creativity on the plates as it does in the sleek space, which doubles as a performance space and gallery. The cuisine blends Mediterranean, Cuban and Mexican flavors in dishes like guava-chili sirloin and salmon with a mango ginger sauce. The bar scene picks up with a younger crowd later in the evening, when there is often live music.

Restaurant St Michel (☎ 305-446-6572, 162 Alcazar Ave) Lunch mains $8-12, dinner mains $17-30. Open 11am-10pm daily. One of Miami's most romantic and charming restaurants, this Mediterranean-looking place serves eclectic international cuisine. The menu offers hearty and lighter dishes. Try the Australian lamb, aged meats, wild game, or sautéed Florida Keys yellowtail with a citrus beurre blanc, or filet mignon in cabernet sauce with caramelized red onion marmalade and chipotle mashed potatoes. The desserts are just as excellent.

La Dorada (☎ 305-446-2002, 177 Giralda Ave) 'Executive lunch special' $19, dinner mains $18-27. Open 11:30am-3:30pm & 6:30pm-11:30pm Mon-Sat. For inventive and classic Spanish presentations of fresh seafood, this place is a treat. Try the special sampler plate. Dorada, by the way, is a wonderful Mediterranean fish that's not served at very many places.

Ortanique on the Mile (☎ 305-446-7710, 278 Miracle Mile) Lunch mains $11-16, dinner mains $20-27. Open 11:30am-2:30pm & 6pm-10pm Mon-Wed, 11:30am-2:30pm & 6pm-11pm Thur & Fri, 6pm-11pm Sat, 5:30pm-9:30pm Sun. This contemporary and upscale Caribbean restaurant serves dishes like grilled grouper and double jerk pork chops that burst with tropical flavors. By all means, don't miss the specialty pumpkin soup. Ortanique, by the way, is a rare tropical fruit.

Norman's (☎ 305-446-6767, 21 Almeria Ave) Mains $20-40. Open 6pm-10:30pm

Mon-Sat. The hype about chef-owner Norman Van Aken's restaurant – that it's *the* best restaurant in Miami and perhaps the best in the southeastern US – is no hyperbole. If you're gong to blow some bucks, this is the right place (as long as you have reservations). With gracious service, handsome surroundings, an open kitchen and creative New World cuisine that fuses Caribbean, Asian, Latin and North American, Norman's delights the senses. Look for something delectable like pecan-crusted Louisiana catfish with fried green tomatoes and mashed sweet potatoes. The wine pairing is exceptional.

GREATER MIAMI

You might not go out of your way to eat at these places (except one!), but if you're in their neighborhoods at lunch or dinner, you'll appreciate knowing they're there.

Laurenzo's Italian Supermarket (☎ 305-945-6381, 16385 W Dixie Hwy) **Map 5** Open 8:30am-7:30pm Mon-Fri, 8am-7pm Sat, 8am-6pm Sun. After visiting the Ancient Spanish Monastery, pop into this bustling Italian grocery for fresh ravioli, excellent cheeses, farm fresh produce and everything else Italian and edible. It's kept the local *paisanos* happy since the early '60s. A wood-fired oven churns out tasty pizzas, but there are also daily specials, like eggplant parmigiana, and salads. Before heading back to South Beach, check out their great wine selection.

JD's Pizza & Subs (☎ 305-652-4455, 1620 NE 205th Terrace) **Map 2** Open 11am-10pm Mon-Sat. If you're heading to Fort Lauderdale and feeling a hole in your stomach, stop at JD's, on the west side beneath the I-95 overpass at Ives Dairy Rd. It doesn't look like much, but the pizza is great ($2 per slice) and it'll tide you over nicely.

Cafe Buena Vista (☎ 305-573-5521, 3622 NE 2nd Ave) **Map 2** Dishes $5-7. Open 8am-5pm Mon-Fri, 9am-3pm Sat. This Design District coffeehouse and lunch place serves daily specials like grilled chicken with coconut sauce and a stir-fry veggie platter with tofu. True to their word, sandwiches are piled high.

5061 Eaterie (☎ 305-756-5051, 5061 Biscayne Blvd) **Map 2** Dishes $4-20. Open 6:30am-10:30pm daily. New in late 2001, this Morningside neighborhood meeting place is a combination takeout deli, upstairs bookstore/café and restaurant. The food is charmingly uncomplicated, perfect when you tire of haute cuisine's vertical presentation. The industrial chic loft-like surroundings bridge the gap between urban and cozy, while the menu runs from eggs Benedict and country omelets at breakfast, to sandwiches and salads at lunch, to quiches, pastas, raw-bar items and fish prepared however you like it and paired with whatever sauce you like at dinner.

Chef Allen's (☎ 305-935-2900, 19088 NE 29th Ave) **Map 5** Mains $26-40. Open 6pm-'until the last guest leaves' daily. Welcome to his world, and thus by extension yours: Chef Allen was dubbed James Beard's 'Best American Chef in the Southeast' in 1994. Master of his universe (which clearly reaches far beyond this Aventura neighborhood), Allen Susser reigns with New World–Floribbean cuisine, which pairs fresh local ingredients with tantalizing global flavors. If you splurge just once, Susser will not disappoint. A special trek here will reward you with a mountain of memories. Speaking of mountains, save room for Susser's trademark soufflé.

The following are *way* out but worth the trip, especially if you're visiting the Monkey Jungle, the Fruit & Spice Park, Fairchild Tropical Gardens, Matheson Hammock Park or the Miami Metrozoo.

Bur's Berry Farm (no ☎, 12741 SW 216th St, Goulds) **Map 1** Open 9am-5:30pm daily Dec-May. This berry farm surely has the country's best strawberries: fist-sized, sumptuously sweet, breathtakingly fresh, unbelievably satisfying strawberries. People come from miles around – a *lot* of miles (there's a private air strip out back for well-known customers who – yes – *fly* there for these berries!) – to stand in line to buy pints and quarts of 'em. Bur's also makes a killer strawberry shake.

Knauss Berry Farm (☎ 305-247-0668, 15980 SW 248th St) **Map 1** Only open late

Nov–Apr. This farm has similarly heavenly cinnamon rolls that create similarly long lines, especially on Saturday. It also has lush strawberries and luscious breads, cakes and brownies. Sugar high, anyone?

Shorty's BBQ *(☎ 305-670-7732, 9200 S Dixie Hwy)* **Map 2** Dishes $6-16. Open 11am-10pm Sun-Thur, 11am-11pm Fri & Sat. This South Dade institution has enjoyed buckets of fame since the early 1950s. Long before deco became de riguer, and probably long after the vibe settles over South Beach, this rustic place will still be dishing out sweet baby back ribs ($16), cobbed corn, barbecued spare ribs ($9)

and tender chicken ($6), on picnic tables. Look for the branch at 11575 SW 40th St (☎ 305-227-3196; Map 2) when you're heading back into the city from the Everglades.

Redfish Grill *(☎ 305-668-8788, 9610 Old Cutler Rd)* **Map 2** Mains $15-25. Open 6pm-10pm Tues-Fri, 5pm-10pm Sat & Sun. In peaceful and off-the-beaten path Matheson Hammock Park, Redfish Grill enjoys a marvelous outdoor beachfront setting. It's perfect for drinks and appetizers or perhaps some fresh fish. Mains center around seafood, but there are also a few chicken, steak and pasta dishes.

Entertainment

Calling Miami a trendy nightspot is a little like calling New York a fairly large city. Miami Beach is one of the most fashionable places in the country for clubbing. But nightlife encompasses far more than just nightclubs, bars and lounges. The New World Symphony is a delightful treat, and legitimate theater is also very active. The fine arts scene has evolved from a handful of grungy studio-galleries into a driving force in the American art world. Sports fans go nuts in a city with professional football, baseball, basketball and hockey, plus jai alai, NASCAR and horseracing.

BARS

There are perhaps more bars than street corners in Miami Beach. Note that all the restaurants along Ocean Drive have outdoor seating, and unless it's very crowded, you can usually sit outside with a drink without having to order food. Remember to bring photo identification, because if you look under 30 you will be asked for ID. The strictly enforced drinking age in Florida is 21.

Hotel Lounges, Lobbies & Bars

Some hotels offer complementary cocktails to their guests for a limited period each night. Inquire to find out if your hotel is among them.

Marlin Hotel (☎ 305-604-5000, 1200 Collins Ave,) **Map 3** Open 5:30pm-2am daily. This bar rocks the martini world with incredible beachside Bombay Sapphire martinis (yeah, they're pricey, but they're worth every penny). The tropical, chic atmosphere, smooth service and occasional live music are included at no extra charge. There's something different each night, from DJs who spin deep house, R&B and hip-hop, to karaoke and 'smokin' words' open mic night.

Raleigh Hotel (☎ 305-534-6300, 1775 Collins Ave,) **Map 3** Open 5pm-midnight daily. Martinis are the drink of choice in this intimate bar just off the landmark deco lobby.

Delano Hotel (☎ 305-672-2000, 1685 Collins Ave,) **Map 3** Open noon–2am Sun-Thur, noon-3am Fri & Sat. The ultra chic Rose Bar at this elegant hotel is a watering hole for beautiful creatures. If you don't count yourself among that set, bring a healthy ego. Regardless of your physical attributes, you'll need a hefty wallet to drink here.

National Hotel (☎ 305-532-2311, 1677 Collins Ave,) **Map 3** Open 9am-1am daily. Martini Mondays are a hot ticket with two-for-one drinks at the Deco Bar from 5pm till 8pm.

The Tides (☎ 305-604-5070, 1220 Ocean Dr,) **Map 3** Open 7pm-1am daily. Elegant and understated, this bar feels like a breezy oasis above and beyond the Ocean Drive throngs. At press time, tropical vodka popsicle martinis were the house drink currently in vogue.

Chelsea Hotel (☎ 305-534-4069, 944 Washington Ave) **Map 4** Open 8pm-10pm daily. Particularly popular with locals in the know (and now with Lonely Planet readers), the Wednesday night party features free sushi and vodka (from 8pm to 10pm).

The Clevelander Bar (☎ 305-531-3485, 1020 Ocean Dr) **Map 4** Open 11am-5am daily. This open-air glass and neon bar, adjacent to a wet T-shirt kind of pool and overlooking the Ocean Drive tourist parade, is a casual scene. The inside sports bar, with multiple TVs, is a Bud and Bud Lite kind of place.

Pubs

Mac's Club Deuce Bar (☎ 305-673-9537, 222 14th St,) **Map 3** Open 8am-5am daily. The oldest bar in Miami Beach, established

What'll Ya Have?

Miami bars serve the standard cocktails you'd find in any major international tourist destination. The specialty, however, is cool and colorful tropical drinks. Top shelf liquor and fresh fruit juice make all the difference. Most bartenders have a signature concoction; ask the maestro for something special (you might want to inquire about the price beforehand…).

Cuba Libre
Rum and Coca-Cola with a splash of lime juice, served on the rocks.

Daiquiri
Rum, lime and sugar. Variations include the addition of all manner of tropical fruit, but mango and papaya are particularly popular. Frozen daiquiris, the equivalent of a grown-up Slurpee, are standard; you'll have to specifically indicate if you want yours on the rocks.

Margarita
Tequila, orange liqueur (triple sec or Grand Marnier) and fresh lime juice. The key is fresh, not re-constituted, lime juice. Order it on the rocks, not frozen, and ask for a salted glass. When it's made well, this is a cool refreshing drink. When it's not, it's a sickly sweet disaster.

Martini
Vermouth and top-shelf vodka or gin, shaken or stirred until it's ice cold, accented with olive, cocktail onion or a twist of lemon (whatever your preference). Martinis remain the classic for sophisticated palates with hefty wallets. Many bars have come up with signature variations.

Mojito
Rum, sugar, club soda, lime juice and fresh mint – it's a true Miami cocktail.

Piña Colada
Tropical milk shakes with a kick – rum, pineapple juice and coconut milk blended with ice and served frozen thick: It's more Caribbean than Miamian.

in 1926, 'the Deuce' is a real neighborhood bar and hype-free zone. There's no posing here, and the atmosphere, though seedy, feels *real*. The clientele defies categorization. Every conceivable affiliate of the South Beach community hangs here, from transvestites to construction workers, stars to star-gazers, hipsters to yupsters to bikers. The dark but friendly and welcoming room has a pool table, jukebox, reasonably priced beer and no-nonsense service.

Irish House Bar & Grill (☎ *305-534-5667, 1430 Alton Rd)* **Map 3** Open 11am-5am daily. This comfy bar is another local fave, featuring half-price weekday happy hours (4pm to 7pm), pool tables, video games, dart boards and a jukebox. Pitchers (depending on the brew) cost $12 to $16.

The Playwright (☎ *305-534-0667, 1265 Washington Ave)* **Map 3** Open 11am-5am daily. This authentic Irish pub features a large selection of imported beers, a big screen TV for sporting events, live music and weekday happy hours from 4pm to 7pm. Down $6 pitchers from Sunday to Thursday.

Lost Weekend (☎ *305-672-1707, 218 Española Way)* **Map 3** Open 5pm-5am daily. An aptly named place to while away some weekend hours, this good neighborhood bar has pool tables, a comfy upstairs loft and Wednesday ladies' night.

See also *Churchill's Hideaway* under Live Music, later in this chapter.

Restaurant & Theme Bars
Laundry Bar (☎ *305-531-7700,* **w** *www .laundrybar.com, 721 Lincoln Lane N)* **Map 3**

Open noon-5am daily. This bar/billiards parlor/coin Laundromat is a hoot. As they say, 'get sloshed while you wash.' The place has a decidedly gay (and lesbian) vibe, but it's certainly relaxed and welcomes all. In addition to two-for-one drinks daily until 9pm, they offer different nightly specials and themes.

Blue (☎ 305-534-1009, 222 Española Way,) **Map 3** Open 10pm-5am daily. Everything is blue but the patrons at this ultra-chic cocktail bar and lounge. Even the music is a bluesy mix of deep house and sultry soul.

Tantra (☎ 305-672-4765, Ⓦ www.tantra restaurant.com, 1445 Pennsylvania Ave) **Map 3** Open until 1am nightly. This slightly out of the way, exotic restaurant (see the South Beach section of the Places to Eat chapter) is also a great place to hang out after dinner, when it becomes a late-night lounge. Guest DJs spin music to complement the sensual, candlelit ambience and aphrodisiac cocktails.

Tap Tap (☎ 305-672-2898, 819 5th St), **Map 4** Open 11am-11pm Sun-Thur, 11am-midnight Fri, 5pm-midnight Sat, 5pm-10pm Sun. This Haitian restaurant and bar (see the South Beach section of the Places to Eat chapter) is a cool and colorful place to hang out drinking Haitian Babencourt rum or African Ngoma beer. There is often live Haitian and Caribbean music. The restaurant also exhibits art and hosts community meetings.

Dab Haus (☎ 305-534-9557, 852 Alton Rd) **Map 4** Open 4pm-11pm Sun-Thur, 11am-midnight Fri & Sat. This honest-to-goodness German pub has the area's best German beer, wine and schnapps. Try the Dortmunder pils, Alt Tucher hefe weizen, dark hefe weizen, Kristall weizen, Königs pils and/or Hacker-Pschorr. They also have wine by the glass, but that's not why you came. It's a darned serviceable German restaurant, too – see the South Beach section of the Places to Eat chapter.

Pearl Restaurant & Champagne Lounge (☎ 305-538-1111, Ⓦ www.penrods.com, 1 Ocean Dr) **Map 4** Open 7pm-5am daily. Champagne sippers recline on fur-trimmed designer chairs, while enjoying a variety of bubblys by the glass, complemented by caviar hors d'oeuvres. DJs spin lounge classics and R&B at this decadent, deep-orange haven situated within Penrod's Entertainment Complex; see also the South Beach section of the Places to Eat chapter.

Microbreweries

Abbey Brewery (☎ 305-538-8110, 1115 16th St) **Map 3** Open 1pm-5am daily. Abbey Brewery makes really good beer, including Abbey Brown, Oatmeal Stout, Porter Christmas and India Pale Ale (all are $4.25 a pint). But it also has some dozen more beers on tap and a little pub grub.

Titanic Brewery & Restaurant (☎ 305-667-2537, Ⓦ www.titanicbrewery.com, 5813 Ponce de León Blvd) **Map 10** Open 11:30am-1am Sun-Thur, 11:30am-2am Fri & Sat. Titanic has a happy hour from 4pm to 8pm nightly, featuring six handcrafted ales. Live music (there's rarely a cover) ranges from jazz and blues jams to national touring acts; karaoke is featured on Sunday.

See also Tobacco Road under Live Music, later in this chapter.

Cigar Bars

Unlike the rest of the country, most Miami restaurants allow cigar smoking.

Condal & Peñamil (☎ 305-604-9690, 741 Lincoln Road) **Map 3** Open noon-1am daily. In addition to serving a full range of alcoholic drinks and coffee, the staff at this handsome cigar bar will help you select just the right stogie to complement them.

LIVE MUSIC
Latin/Tropical

Mango's Tropical Cafe (☎ 305-673-4422, 900 Ocean Dr) **Map 4** Cover $10-20. Open 11am-5am daily. You can play it safe by simply joining the curious crowd gathering around Mango's entrance. From the street you can feel the spicy beat and catch a glimpse into the open-air courtyard. Or you can shed your inhibitions, make your way in and join the bumping, grinding and booty-shaking. Live bands play salsa, reggae and merengue into the early morning hours. The first band starts at

The Ever-Changing Scene

The club and entertainment scene changes faster than a chameleon facing imminent danger. Although I've tried to primarily include venues that have withstood the test of time, it is ironically the very nature of time that can imperil these very same venues. Longevity can kill, can breed boredom. A buzz is created by newness, not oldness. Today's hot club is tomorrow's closed club. Replacing one kind of logic for another, clubs thrive on reinventing the wheel. Reinvention is paramount, just look at Madonna (the singer, not the club).

So, for up-to-date info on the ever-changing entertainment scene, pick up the *New Times*, a weekly fave published on Thursday, and *Wire*, the weekly gay bible that comes out on Thursday. Also look for the *Miami Herald's* Friday 'Weekend' section and the free weekly, *The Street*.

Also, consider cruising the Internet before cruising the clubs. Check these sites for daily listings of what's going on:

City Search	w www.miami.citysearch.com
Entertainment News & Views	w www.entnews.com
Miami Night Guide	w www.miami.nightguide.com
New Times	w www.miaminewtimes.com
Street	w www.streetmiami.com
SunPost	w www.miamisunpost.com

6:45pm nightly, and the last one goes on at 2am on weekends.

Club Tropigala *(☎ 305-541-2631, 305-538-2000, 4441 Collins Ave)* **Map 5** Cover $20. Open 7pm-'till the last person leaves' Wed-Sun. The Fountainbleu Hotel houses this '50s era, kitschy Cubano supper club featuring highly produced dance shows at 8pm or 8:30pm. Put yourself in a Desi Arnaz frame of mind and ba-ba-loo the night away.

Gil's Cafe *(☎ 305-867-0779,* **w** *www .gilscafe.com, 216 71st St)* **Map 5** Cover $5 after 8pm. Open daily. Live Brazilian jazz, R&B, Latin, reggae and blues are on tap Wednesday to Sunday, while a gospel brunch praises the Almighty on Sunday. Professional tango instruction is offered on Monday, salsa on Tuesday.

Hoy Como Ayer *(☎ 305-541-2631, 2212 Calle Ocho)* **Map 8** Cover $5-10. Open 8pm-5am Wed-Sun. This hot spot, with authentic Cuban music and a small dance floor, is enhanced by Cuban memorabilia and cigar smoke. A house band is often complemented by other musicians who stop in to jam. The café also plays vintage Cuban music videos and film clips.

Casa Panza *(☎ 305-643-5343, 1620 Calle Ocho)* **Map 8** Open 11:30am-10pm Sun & Mon, 11:30am-2am Tues-Sat. This atmospheric Spanish taverna (see the Little Havana section in the Places to Eat chapter) hosts lively and popular flamenco music and dance shows. If you are so inspired, you too can dance around dinner tables with the other patrons. There are evening shows Tuesday, Friday and Saturday (but always call ahead).

Jazz & Blues

Les Deux Fontaines *(☎ 305-672-7878,* **w** *www.lesdeuxfontaines.com, 1230 Ocean Dr)* **Map 3** Music during dinner nightly. This French restaurant (see the South Beach section of the Places to Eat chapter) features jazz.

Van Dyke Hotel Lounge *(☎ 305-534-3600,* **w** *www.thevandyke.com, 846 Lincoln Road)* **Map 3** Cover $5. Open nightly. Local and nationally known jazz musicians play to a sophisticated audience nightly in this intimate 2nd-floor hotel bar.

A Fish Called Avalon *(☎ 305-532-1727, 700 Ocean Dr)* **Map 4** Open 6pm-11pm daily. Live nightly jazz gets top billing at this restaurant and lounge in the Avalon Hotel.

Sport Café (☎ 305-674-9700, *560 Washington Ave*) **Map 4** This restaurant (see the South Beach section of the Places to Eat chapter) dishes up Latin jazz Thursday to Saturday.

Jazid (☎ 305-673-9372, *1342 Washington Ave*) **Map 3** Cover $10 Fri & Sat, free Sun-Thur. Open 9pm-5am daily. Live jazz, soul and funk bands play in this sophisticated and intimate candlelit lounge. It's smooth.

Wallflower Gallery (☎ 305-579-0069, W *www.wallflowergallery.com*, *10 NE 3rd St*) **Map 6** Open Thur-Sat (generally). This gallery hosts a variety of programs; it's always best to call ahead.

Tobacco Road (☎ 305-374-1198, W *www .tobacco-road.com*, *626 S Miami Ave*) **Map 6** Cover about $5, after 9pm only. Open 11:30am-5am daily. This venerable bar and live music venue serves several of its own microbrews in addition to jazz, blues and classic-rock bands. The kitchen satisfies cravings with bar food until 2am (see the Downtown Miami section of the Places to Eat chapter). Friday night happy hours are popular.

See also Gil's in the Latin/Tropical section, earlier, and Astor Place in the South Beach section of the Places to Eat chapter.

Rock

Churchill's Hideaway (☎ 305-757-1807, W *www.churchillspub.com*, *5501 NE 2nd Ave*) **Map 2** Cover $10-15. Open 11am-3am Mon-Sat, noon-3am Sun. A rockin' English pub in Little Haiti, Churchill's Hideaway has been around since the 1950s. This place feels like an authentic English bar, not some gussied up tourist trap. It features satellite TV broadcasts of UK football and rugby, dozens of beers and local rock and punk bands on weekend nights.

See also Titanic Brewery & Restaurant under Microbreweries, earlier, and Tobacco Road under Jazz and Blues.

DANCE CLUBS & NIGHTCLUBS

Clubs rise and fall like the Nasdaq composite after a tech bubble bursts. It's like on *The Jetsons* when the daughter tells her father, 'No, Daddy, that band was groovy *last* week!' Indeed, in a matter of a few months spent researching this edition, some very popular and fashionable spots shuttered their doors and disappeared. Celebrities grace clubs with their presence, then leave for the next place others will then declare as cool. If it isn't obvious already, the information in this section is the most volatile in the book.

Drugs are illegal and the law is strictly enforced by undercover narcotics cops who pose as barflies. That said, never leave your drink unattended; you never know who might slip what into it.

The club scene gets going late and doesn't wind down until the wee hours of the morning. Arriving when the doors open at 11pm tags you a dreaded early bird, but it may help you get in. To increase your chances of going the distance, take a 'disco nap' in the evening, and as you hop from club to club, refuel with a *cafecito* or two or three.

South Beach nightclubs are generally a healthy mix of gay, lesbian and straight, though several are more exclusively gay. We list the mixed and straight ones together, as the lines are very blurry. If a place is predominantly gay, they'll politely let you know.

There is a club to suit every taste, and some clubs change their ambience and musical style on a nightly basis; for an idea of what's available see the boxed text 'The Ever-Changing Scene.'

Straight & Mixed

Rain (☎ 786-295-9540, 305-674-7447 *guest list*, *323 23rd St*) **Map 3** Cover $20. Open 10pm-5am Tues, Fri & Sat. Far from the maddening crowds, but not too far, the stage is set at Rain with white couches, multihued ceilings and energetic dance music. A beautiful crowd dances up a storm on indoor and outdoor dance floors. It's a very dancey place.

Billboardlive (☎ 305-538-2251, W *www .billboardlive.com*, *15th St & Ocean Dr at Ocean Steps*) **Map 3** Cover $20. Open

Don't You Know Who I Am?!?

For reasons best left to psychology, the more offensively and breathtakingly rude a doorman, and the more ruthlessly exclusive a club, the larger the clamoring hordes of short-skirted women and big-tipping men trying to gain entry.

When the average nightclub cover charge on the Beach is about $20 (except when it's free), why anyone would lay out cold hard cash or certain parts of their warm bodies to get into a place where drinks cost $10 a pop is beyond reason. But there it is.

To get into some of the more popular clubs, ask the concierge or bellperson at your hotel to get you on the guest list. Or try calling and putting yourself on the guest list. Or try one or more of the following strategies:

Be polite: Don't be meek, but don't act as if you're Sean Penn.

Have attitude: You're a lean, mean, partying machine, and no one's gonna mess with you. Oh yeah, you're gorgeous, too.

Be cool: When the competition is as fierce as it is here (think gigantic sale at a department store two days before Christmas), a nanosecond of hesitation will keep you milling about on a crowded sidewalk filled with wannabes.

Dress properly: Standard Miami nightclub garb mirrors New York, Paris or any other fashion center: look expensive, but understatedly so. Dress in black, unless it's a White Party. Or at least dress interestingly – drag queens and other outrageously dressed people get in as well.

Get there early: Yeah, we know; cool people are not the first ones in line. But do you want to be cool or do you want to get in?

Know someone

Be famous

None of the above worked last night? This is only a hint, but you could try 'Hi, this is – [your name here] – with South African *Vogue;* I'm in town doing a piece on....' Don't say you're from Lonely Planet.

Fri-Sun. As a general rule, this three-story space starts the evening slowly, with ambient lounge music, building the tempo and volume as the night progresses. The club often reaches its 1500 person capacity for the Sunday afternoon tea dances (doors open at 5pm). Local and nationally known DJs and bands are booked.

Crobar (☎ 305-531-5027, Ⓦ *www.crobar miami.com, 1445 Washington Ave*) **Map 3** Cover $25. Open 10:30pm-5am Thur-Sun.

This Chicago import has breathed new nocturnal verve into the renovated art deco Cameo Theatre. You may need an actual crowbar to get past the doormen, but once in you'll be part of the hottest scene on South Beach. The sound and light show alone is worth the price of admission. 'Anthem' Sunday nights are gay and feature local superstar DJ Abel.

Level (☎ 305-532-1525, Ⓦ *www.level nightclub.com, 1235 Washington Ave*) **Map 3**

Cover $20. Open 10pm-5am Mon, Thur-Sat. This art deco palace is a clubland smorgasbord – too huge and sprawling to be truly exclusive. With 40,000-plus sq feet of space spread out over three floors, you can take your pick of dance floors, VIP lounges (if you can gain admittance) and bars. Themes vary from room to room and the crowd is young and exuberant. Friday nights are gay.

Liquid (☎ *305-531-9411*, W *www.liquid nightclub.com, 1532 Washington Ave)* **Map 3** Cover usually $10. Open 11pm-5am Tues-Sat. Liquid has stayed fluid, reincarnating itself through new ownership and retaining its much-vaunted exclusivity in new digs. Unless you are dressed very smartly, forget it. Once admitted, however, the vibe is pretty democratic: Everyone is assumed to be worthy. Thursday nights are gay, as is the after hours party on Sunday morning (from 8am until 'whenever everyone's left or passes out'). Yes, you read that correctly; the party *starts* at 8am on Sunday morning.

Lola (☎ *305-695-8697*, W *www.lolabar .com, 247 23rd St)* **Map 3** No cover. Open 11pm-5am Tues, Thur-Sat. A little off the beaten path, Lola rewards those in the know with a cozy atmosphere with comfy lounge chairs, pool tables and great music. The DJ spins music you can actually dance to, not just pose to. Tuesdays are quite popular. What you save with free admission, you'll no doubt spend on overpriced bar drinks. You can't win 'em all.

Mynt (☎ *786-276-6132, 1921 Collins Ave)* **Map 3** Cover $20 for men Fri & Sat. Open 10pm-5am Wed-Sat. Whatever you do, don't wear something that will clash with the mint-green palette. Likewise, since the air conditioning system doubles as an aromatherapy conduit (guess the scent), wear perfume that complements a minty-fresh ambience. Chocolate perfume might be in order. To carry the theme to its natural conclusion, order a *mojito* and try not to go green with envy while drinking in all the beautiful people. Be forewarned: Green is also the color of American greenbacks (money). You may need to 'mynt' your own to afford an evening here.

Kiss South Beach (☎ *305-695-4445, 301 Lincoln Road)* **Map 3** No cover. Open 7pm-4am Mon-Sat. Within the Albion Hotel, this club aims to titillate with red decor and red accents. The pervasive atmosphere is sex, sex, sex. Actually, when it was still a design concept waiting to be fulfilled, the place was meant to be even racier, with topless dancers and female waitstaff trained to suggest service of a more personal variety. Even though the original plan was nixed, Kiss still closes the gap between Miami's dance and sex clubs with DJs and dancers.

Rumi (☎ *305-672-4353, 330 Lincoln Road)* **Map 3** No cover. Open 7pm-5am Tues-Sun. Named for the 13th-century Sufi mystic whose poetry is currently in vogue, Rumi is like a scene out of the Arabian Nights. Its numerous dining rooms, decorated in dark, rich red and earth tones, are transformed into intimate lounges and dance areas as the night wears on (after 11:30pm or so).

Touch (☎ *305-532-8003, 910 Lincoln Road)* **Map 3** No cover. Open 7pm-'whenever' daily. This restaurant is transformed into a spicy nightclub nightly around midnight when it features DJs.

Opium Garden (☎ *305-531-5535, 136 Collins Ave)* **Map 4** Cover $20. Open 11pm-5am Fri-Sun (and sometimes Thur). This decadent den is not for the faint-of-ego. If you are either drop-dead gorgeous or up for a challenge, sashay to the velvet ropes and try to gain *entrée*. Once in, strike your most disinterested pose and glide through the various levels until you find a perch that suits you. Dancing and drinking take second and third place to watching people who are watching people who are people-watching.

Nikki Beach (☎ *305-538-1111*, W *www .penrods.com, 1 Ocean Dr)* **Map 4** Cover $20 after 10pm Fri & Sat and after 4pm Sun. Open 11am-5pm Mon-Thur, 11am-5am Fri-Sun. Part of Penrod's Entertainment Complex, this beach-blanket-bimbo-themed beach party is for adults reliving their college spring break experiences – assuming, that is, that any memories survived the drunken haze of yore. If you can gain entrance to the semiprivate stretch of sand, you can party with the glamorous throngs in thongs. On Monday night an open-air movie screening is followed by the infamous Beehive Party. Friday night happy hour features discount cocktails, a buffet and free champagne for the ladies (5pm to 7pm). A bonfire at 7:30pm.

BED (☎ *305-532-9070, 929 Washington Ave)* **Map 4** No cover. Open 8pm-5am Wed-Sun; reservations open at 10am (call early!). What will they think of next? Anything to get a little press between the sheets, eh? Everything but dancing is done here while comfortably ensconced on an actual bed. Take off your shoes and stay awhile. Drop by on Thursday for 'dream girls dinner theater,' a drag cabaret show.

Bongos Cuban Cafe (☎ *786-777-2100,* W *www.bongoscubancafe.com, 601 Biscayne Blvd)* **Map 6** Cover $10 before midnight, $20 after. Nightclub open 11pm-5am Fri & Sat. Singer Gloria Estefan's family-style Cuban-themed restaurant transforms itself into a hot-hot-hot salsa club. For the price of the cover, you get the liveliest show in town. It's packed, and once the joint starts jumping, the rhythm is gonna get ya (if claustrophobia doesn't first).

Clubspace (☎ *305-375-0001,* W *www .clubspace.com, 142 NE 11th St)* **Map 6** Cover $20. Open 10pm-10am Fri & Sat. This gargantuan warehouse, located in a former no-man's-land downtown, is the current late-night/early morning club of choice. With 30,000 sq feet to fan out, dancers really have room to strut their stuff. An around-the-clock liquor license redefines the concept of after-hours.

Gay & Lesbian

The gay South Beach club scene, according to an infamous local quip, can be summed up as men who 'look like Tarzan, walk like Jane and talk like Cheetah.' Note to lesbians: When it comes to the club scene, gay means male. There are no exclusively lesbian clubs in Miami. Although lesbians (and straight women, generally) are welcome in most gay clubs, the vibe in these places is decidedly driven by high-octane testosterone.

For up-to-date club and event listings, check out *Wire,* or log onto the Internet and peruse the following Web sites: Express (W www.expressgaynews.com), Wire (W www.thewireonline.com), and Weekly News (W www.twnonline.org).

Traveling Tuesdays Martini Club (W *www .sobesocialclub.com)* 9pm-midnight Tues. This group of local gay professionals meets at a different upscale place every week; you're welcome to join them. Check the SoBe Social Club Web site for this week's listing.

Cactus (☎ *305-438-0662,* W *www.thecactus .com, 2041 Biscayne Blvd)* **Map 2** Cover $3 on Sat. Open 4pm-2am Sun-Thur, 4pm-3am Fri & Sat. With different themes, happy hours and drag shows nightly, Cactus boasts seven gay clubs in one. One size fits all? Check out the popular Latin-themed 'Ay Papi!' show on Saturday night, complete with male go-go dancers.

Club 1771 (☎ *305-673-6508, 1771 West Ave)* **Map 3** Cover varies depending on when you arrive. Open 10pm-4am Sat. These warehouse digs are mammoth, yet somehow this club manages to fill to the brim on Saturday night, when groovy professional dancers entertain the throngs upstairs, and nationally known DJs spin downstairs. If you don't mind being unfashionably early, there are free drinks from 10pm to 11pm.

Twist (☎ *305-538-9478, 1057 Washington Ave)* **Map 4** Never a cover, always a groove. Open 1pm-5am daily. Twist has more depth than the other flavor-of-the-month clubs; it has staying power. This two-story club has six different bars, including a rooftop bar and patio, a lively and fun place to hang out. Themes change nightly.

Pump (☎ *305-538-7867, 841 Washington Ave)* **Map 4** Cover $15-20. Open 4am-'whenever' Sat & Sun morning. Yes, you read that right. Ready for bed? NOT. Only true nocturnal creatures need apply to this antidote for insomnia.

See also Laundry Bar (under Restaurant & Theme Bars, earlier), and Crobar, Level and Liquid (under Straight & Mixed, earlier).

Circuit Parties

Not since ancient Rome have so many men gathered together for a common purpose (or so it appears on the streets of South Beach). In case you didn't know, Miami boasts two huge circuit parties – extravagant annual affairs saturating weeks (and longer). And, hallelujah, it's raining men.

With buns far tighter than anything you'd see at the supermarket bread aisle, buff knights dressed in white descend for The White Party (**w** www.whiteparty.net), a lavish 10-day spectacle held mid- to late November. Why white? As Frank Wagner, the event's co-founder, says, 'White stands for purity. White is elegant, nonpolitical, noncombative and makes people look just plain beautiful.' Known as the 'Jewel of the Circuit Parties,' the main event is held on the Sunday after Thanksgiving at Vizcaya Museum & Gardens (see the Coconut Grove section of the Things to See & Do chapter). Tickets can be very hard to come by – the sophisticated event attracts upwards of 3000 people. They pour in to support a very vital cause: Care Resource, South Florida's oldest and largest HIV/AIDS service organization. Renowned around the world, the actual party sees folks arriving in yachts, and there's plenty of live music. Ancillary parties at hotels and clubs attract gays by the tens of thousands, and the atmosphere is wild. Let the rhythm move you.

Dancing queens, leave your tambourine at home during the Winter Party (**w** www.winterparty.com), a weeklong dance fest in early March benefiting the Dade Human Rights Foundation. Growing out of a response to statewide gay and lesbian civil rights threats in 1993, the party's unofficial mantra: 'Dance till you can dance no more.' Venues and events, from the well-known Ice Palace Party and Miami Light Project show to tea dances and film festivals, are held around South Beach and Miami. If the idea of pink palm trees and 5000 nearly naked men dancing on the beach gets you all sizzling and steamy, make your reservations right this minute. You'll return home bronzed and boozy after having a blast givin' it up for nationally known DJs and supporting a good cause. Enjoy.

STRIP JOINTS

Sex is a large part of Miami's allure: The city is packed with young, beautiful and half-naked people partying and posing through the long sultry nights. Spoken or unspoken, Miami promises sex with a fine degree of sleaze. Whether you're straight, gay or bi, there's a pervasive atmosphere of dangerous sensuality and untold passion. Most idle curiosity can be satisfied at a safe distance through interaction in clubs, bars and on the beach, but there are more than a couple of venues where nakedness and suggestive dance performance is the featured attraction. The clubs mostly do not feature actual sex acts, but they do offer a particularly masochistic form of entertainment. A totally nude woman rubs herself along a customer's legs and presses her flesh in his face while neckless goons stand by waiting to see if he makes a move to reciprocate. If he makes the slightest move in that direction, he's thrown out. As you might guess, these places, though ostensibly open to all, are strictly oriented to male heterosexuals.

We'll give you one and let you find the rest on your own.

Club Madonna (☎ *305-534-2000,* **w** *www .clubmadonna.com, 1527 Washington Ave)* **Map 3** Cover $20. Open 6pm-6am daily. This is the club that the pop star sued, not the one she owns or frequents. On Tuesday the club holds striptease contests.

CINEMAS

Every major shopping mall has a standard, googolplex-type cinema; call the main mall numbers under Where to Shop in the Shopping chapter. For general information on what's playing where and when, call ☎ 305-888-3456. At big megaplexes it's always cheaper to see afternoon movies;

ENTERTAINMENT

students and seniors usually get discounts with identification.

Regal South Beach Cinema (☎ 305-674-6766, 1100 Lincoln Road) **Map 3** This mod, state-of-the-art, 21-screen theater anchors the western end of Lincoln Road. It shows foreign and independent films, as well as critically acclaimed mass-appeal movies.

Tower Theater (☎ 305-644-3307, ⓦ www.thetowertheater.com, 1508 Calle Ocho) **Map 8** This 1926 renovated city-owned movie theater, on the National Register of Historic Places, shows Spanish-language films and dubbed English-language films for just $2.50/2 adult/child. There are special events held the last Friday ('Cultural Fridays') of every month, some of which might include art exhibits.

Absinthe House (☎ 305-446-7144, 235 Alcazar Ave) **Map 10** Ah, the good old days…this art house has only one screen for independent and foreign films.

IMAX (☎ 305-663-4629, ⓦ www.IMAX.com, 5701 Sunset Place) **Map 10** This way-larger-than-life virtual-reality screen with surround sound shows dramatic, almost educational footage that takes advantage of its large screen. But then again, they also show films like *Beauty and the Beast*.

Bill Cosford Cinema (☎ 305-284-4861, ⓦ www.miami.edu/cosford, Memorial Classroom Building, Second Floor, off University Dr) **Map 10** On the UM campus, this newly renovated art house was launched in memory of the *Miami Herald* film critic. Catch something here if you can; they always deliver a good lineup of international films, as well as host the Cuban Film Festival. Be sure to call to see what's playing; the chatty film descriptions are enthusiastic and informative.

Film Festivals
Miami Gay & Lesbian Film Festival (☎ 305-534-9924, ⓦ www.miamigaylesbianfilm.com) This annual event, held late April to early May, is organized by Robert Rosenberg, the Emmy Award filmmaker of the classic documentary *Before Stonewall*. Most screenings occur at the Colony Theatre (see Venues below).

Miami Film Festival (☎ 305-377-3456, ⓦ www.miamifilmfestival.com) For two weeks in late January to early February this vibrant festival bursts to life with extravagant galas and premieres, plus dialogues with directors and screenwriters. International films and Spanish-language films are at the fore. Newly sponsored by Florida International University, the venue may change, so call for the location.

Jewish Film Festival (☎ 305-576-4030, ⓦ www.caje-miami.org/filmfestival) Also sponsored by Florida International University, this early to mid-December festival screens upwards of 30 films at various locations.

PERFORMING ARTS
Purchasing tickets to upcoming shows at specific venues around Miami is not the most efficient way to spend your holiday. Consider buying direct through the venue's Web site or contact the following agencies.

Ticketmaster (☎ 305-358-5885, ⓦ www.ticketmaster.com), an omnipotent force in the ticketing world, sells tickets to practically everything as long as you have a credit card. But you always have to pay a service fee for the convenience.

Ticket Madness (☎ 800-249-2787, ⓦ www.culturalconnection.org) offers discounted tickets through this 24-hour arts and entertainment hot line.

Venues
You'll see a huge 'coming soon' billboard on the downtown side of the MacArthur Causeway promoting a gigantic, $250 million performing arts center. Someday it will house the city's homeless (but resident) performing arts companies. It's been in the works since the early 1990s.

Miami-Dade County Auditorium (☎ 305-547-5414, 2901 W Flagler St) **Map 2** On the western edge of Little Havana, this 2500-seat venue with excellent acoustics hosts opera and classical music.

Colony Theatre (☎ 305-674-1026, 1040 Lincoln Road) **Map 3** A stunning deco showpiece, this small 1934 performing arts center has 465-seats with great acoustics. It's a treasure. And it hosts everything from movies and an occasional musical to theatrical dramas, ballet and off-Broadway productions.

Lincoln Theatre (☎ *305-531-3442, 555 Lincoln Road*) **Map 3** The Beach's theatrical jewel hosts a wide variety of performances from local groups to visiting artists. It's somewhat intimate, with only 785 seats.

Jackie Gleason Theater of the Performing Arts (☎ *305-673-7300,* W *www.gleason theater.com, 1700 Washington Ave*) **Map 3** Built in 1951, the Beach's premiere showcase for touring Broadway shows, orchestras and other big musical productions has 2700 seats and very good acoustics. They were so good, in fact, that Jackie Gleason chose to make the theater his home for the long-running 1960s television show.

Gusman Center for the Performing Arts (☎ *305-374-2444,* W *www.gusmancenter.org, 174 E Flagler St*) **Map 6** This ornate venue, within an elegantly renovated 1920s movie palace, services a huge variety of performing arts – film festivals, symphonies, ballet and touring shows. The acoustics are excellent and the fresco ceiling is covered in twinkling stars and clouds. Even though the 1700-seat center isn't as fully booked as it should be, if you get a chance to attend something here, by all means, do.

Tower Theater (☎ *305-644-3307, 1508 Calle Ocho*) **Map 8** This renovated, historic theater screens English films with Spanish subtitles. It's an easy way to practice your Spanish. Besides, tickets are a mere $2.50/2 adult/senior & child.

Theater

Gable Stage (☎ *305-445-1119,* W *www.gable stage.org, 1200 Anastasia Ave*) **Map 10** Tickets $32/28/15 adult/senior/student. Adjacent to the Biltmore Hotel, this company performs an occasional Shakespeare play (which harkens back to their roots), but mostly contemporary and classical pieces. Currently in an intimate 154-seat theater, look for their new digs in fall 2003.

New Theatre (☎ *305-443-5909,* W *www .new-theatre.org, 4120 Laguna St*) **Map 10**

Tickets $20-25; student $10 half-hour before show Fri-Sun, free half-hour before show Thur (tickets are usually available). Performances Thur-Sun. This genuinely strong company primarily performs contemporary pieces and modern classics that fall squarely between the conventional and alternative. You'll be up close and personal with the actors since there are only 70 seats in this theater.

Actors' Playhouse (☎ *305-444-9293,* W *www.actorsplayhouse.org, 280 Miracle Mile*) **Map 10** Tickets $30-32. Performances Wed-Sun. Within the 1948 deco Miracle Theater, this 600-seat venue stages well-known musicals and comedies. Their smaller venue is perfect for children's theater.

Jerry Herman Ring Theatre (☎ *305-284-3355,* W *www.miami.edu/ring, 1321 Miller Dr*) **Map 10** Tickets $14/10 adult/senior. This University of Miami troupe stages musicals, dramas and comedies from September to May. Alumni actors include Sylvester Stallone, Steven Bauer, Saundra Santiago and Ray Liotta. One-act 'summer shorts' from June to August are fun.

Coconut Grove Playhouse (☎ *305-442-4000,* W *www.cgplayhouse.com, 3500 Main Hwy*) **Map 9** Tickets $40-45/15 adult/youth under 24 yrs, day-of-performance $15 off when paying with cash (they rarely sell out). This lovely state-owned theater, anchoring the Grove since 1956, gained fame from the moment it opened by premiering Samuel Beckett's *Waiting for Godot*. The main stage, with 1100 seats, features highly regarded earnest and experimental productions by local and international playwrights. The smaller Encore Room features theater-in-the-round cabaret.

Spanish-language theater comes and goes; check in the Spanish-language press.

Classical Music

Concert Association of Florida (☎ *305-532-3491,* W *www.concertfla.org, 555 17th St*) Founded in 1967, this association is run by dedicated folks who bring world-class classical music (and an occasional dance production) to Miami.

Florida Philharmonic Orchestra (☎ 305-476-1234, 800-226-1812, W www.florida philharmonic.org) Tickets prices vary greatly, students $5 on same day when there are extra tickets (call same day and arrive one hour prior to show). Performances Nov-May. Appealing to large audiences with its popularized classics, this orchestra plays all over the state. It also performs a few family programs.

New World Symphony (☎ 305-673-3331, 800-597-3331, W www.nws.org) **Map 3** Tickets $24-70, students half-price, $20 standby tickets for any age (one hour prior to performance; take any empty seat). Performances Oct-May. Sometimes described as 'America's training orchestra,' the deservedly heralded NWS serves as a three- to four-year preparatory program for very talented musicians who've already graduated from prestigious music schools. Founded in 1987, the NSW is led by artistic director Michael Tilson Thomas, who still conducts performances for 12 weeks a year despite his national fame and fortune. A host of guest conductors and artists also appear. There are an astonishing number of inspiring and original performances, held at the Lincoln Theatre, many of which are free.

Miami Chamber Symphony (☎ 305-858-3500) Tickets $12-30, students half-price. Performances Nov-May. Performances are held at the Gusman Concert Hall (1314 Miller Dr; Map 10), not to be confused with the downtown Gusman Center for the Performing Arts, and feature world-renowned soloists.

University of Miami School of Music (☎ 305-284-6477, W www.music.miami.edu) Performances Oct-May. Also held at the Gusman Concert Hall, as well as Clark Recital Hall (5501 San Amaro Dr), these free concerts are a bargain, highlighting university students. Seek out their long-running international Festival Miami (☎ 305-284-4940), late September to late October, featuring symphonies, chamber music and jazz.

Opera

Florida Grand Opera (☎ 305-854-1643, W www.fgo.org) Tickets $19-135. Performances Dec-May. Founded in the 1940s, this highly respected opera performs five nights a week. Even though they stage the operas in their original languages, don't worry: English subtitles are projected. Two of the famed 'three tenors,' Placido Domingo and Luciano Pavarotti (who made his American debut here in 1965), have graced their stage. The FGO moves to a new headquarters and auditorium in fall 2003. Currently, they perform at the Miami-Dade County Auditorium (Map 2), and the Broward Center for the Performing Arts in Fort Lauderdale.

Dance

Florida Dance Festival (☎ 305-867-7111, W www.fldance.org) Tickets $10-20. Held at the New World School of the Arts (500 71st St), this two-week festival, held in mid- to late June, consists of classes, workshops, special events and performances. It's a treat.

Performing Arts Network and *Ballet Flamenco La Rosa (☎ 305-672-0552, W www.panmiami.org, 13126 NW Dixie Hwy)* **Map 2** This professional flamenco, salsa and merengue dance company performs on a very loose schedule. Call for performance dates and prices. PAN instructors will teach beginners (6:30pm Thursday) and intermediates (7:30pm Thursday) how to salsa for $8 per class, and flamenco (Tuesday, Thursday and Saturday; call for class time) for $12 per class. You can dance if you want to, but can you dance well? The red-hot dancers will make sure you can.

Miami City Ballet (☎ 305-929-7010, 877-929-7010, W www.miamicityballet.org, 2200 Liberty Ave) **Map 3** Tickets $19-59. Performances Sept-Mar. Formed in 1985, this resident troupe is guided by artistic director Edward Villella, who studied under the great George Balanchine at the New York City Ballet. In fact, Balanchine works dominate the repertoire. In addition to performing in Fort Lauderdale and West Palm Beach, the company has a national and international road show. It also gives holiday performances of *The Nutcracker* at several area venues. In early 2000 they moved into a $7.5 million three-story headquarters, designed by the famed local architectural firm Arquitectonica. You can buy tickets there (from 10am to 5pm Monday to Friday) and watch the dancers rehearsing through big picture windows. The Ballet also offers DanceTalks – talks hosted by Villella before each new repertory program that touch on 20th-century dance and choreography.

The company runs **Ballet for Young People**, an introduction for children to the ballet and its dancers. Excellent dance performances are preceded by a talk by the director and the opportunity for children to meet ballet dancers. Tickets to these shows cost $12 to $27 for adults and children.

BOOK READINGS

There are free book readings held regularly at both branches of **Books & Books** (See the What to Buy section of the Shopping chapter). **Meza Fine Art Gallery & Cafe** (☎ 305-461-2733, 275 Giralda Ave; Map 10) also has occasional readings.

CABARET & COMEDY

People in South Beach aren't here to laugh; they're here to look good, and the paucity of cabaret and comedy acts confirms it. For cabaret, see the **Coconut Grove Playhouse**, in the Performing Arts section, earlier in this chapter.

Improv Comedy Club (☎ 305-441-8200, 3390 Mary St) **Map 9** Tickets $15-18. Open Tues-Sun. Part of a national chain, this 3rd-floor club doesn't have scouts for Jay Leno or David Letterman in the audience, but it'll do if you feel like laughing.

GAMBLING

The casino initiative that would have undoubtedly turned South Beach into a nightmare failed, so until the developers and high rollers can figure out a way to bribe officials or dupe the public (and they probably will manage both at some point), gamblers are rather limited in their choices. While gambling is illegal in Florida, it thrives just offshore in international waters, on 'cruises to nowhere.' It also still lives at jai alai matches, dog tracks (which we don't endorse) and horse tracks.

Casino Princesa (☎ 305-379-5825, W www .casinoprincesa.com, 100 S Biscayne Blvd) **Map 4** Tickets $6. Docked adjacent to the Hard Rock Cafe in the Bayside Marketplace, this big, upscale yacht departs on 4½-hour voyages (at 12:30pm weekdays, 7:30pm weekends) that head 3 miles offshore. There's an additional, free sailing at 1am on Saturday morning. The boat has two decks of gaming tables (blackjack and craps are big), slot machines and bars.

See also Miccosukee Resort & Gaming in the Along the Tamiami Trail section of the Everglades chapter.

SPECTATOR SPORTS
Professional Sports

Football Miami Dolphins (☎ 305-620-2578, W www.miamidolphins.com) Tickets $20-54. Season Aug-Dec, with home games about twice a month. Attending an American football game may be one of the most intense experiences in spectator sports, and 'Dol-fans' get more than a little crazy when it comes to their Miami Dolphins. Even though their franchise quarterback Dan Marino retired in 2000, and a Superbowl win has evaded them since 1985, and the 1972 glory days of Coach Don Shula taking his team to 17-0 are long since over (it's still an NFL record though), games are wildly popular and the team quite successful.

The Dolphins play at **Pro Player Stadium** (2269 NW 199th St; Map 2), a mile south of the Dade-Broward county line. On game days there is bus service between downtown Miami and the stadium (contact Metrobus at ☎ 305-770-3131 or check www.co.miami-dade.fl.us/transit/). If you're a real football fanatic, you can watch preseason practices near Fort Lauderdale. Take I-95 or Florida's Turnpike to I-595 west to the University Drive exit. Turn left at SW 30th St and make another left. The training facility's half a mile down on the right.

Basketball Miami Heat (☎ 786-777-4328, W www.nba.com/heat) Tickets $33-100. Season Nov-Apr. Since 1996, the Armani-clad celebrity coach Pat Riley has led the Miami Heat. In fact, the Heat has been the reigning NBA team from the 1996–97 season to the 2000–1 season, winning four straight titles. They play at the *American Airlines Arena (601 Biscayne Blvd; Map 6)*, where Madonna and other elusive stars have been sited courtside.

Miami Sol (☎ 786-777-4765, Ⓦ *www .wnba.com/sol)* Tickets $6-52. Season June-Aug. This women's team also plays pro hoops at the American Airlines Arena in downtown.

Baseball *Florida Marlins* (☎ 305-626-7400, Ⓦ *www.marlins.mlb.com)* Ticket $4-55/2-55 adult/child. Season May-Sept. Founded in 1993, the Florida Marlins are the fastest franchise in the history of baseball to win a World Series (1997). The triumph disgusted baseball purists, who loudly shouted that their hallowed series had been bought – a reference to the team's then outlandish payroll. As if to prove them right, the owner sold the star players immediately after winning the World Series. Tickets are easy to come by since it's hot down here in the summer and since the Marlins are once again doormats, losing quite often at *Pro Player Stadium (Map 2)*.

Hockey *Florida Panthers* (Ⓦ *www.florida panthers.com)* Tickets $14-67. Season mid-Oct–mid-Apr. The Panthers, who picked up the Stanley Cup in 1996, play National Hockey League games at the *National Car Rental Center* (☎ 954-835-8000, *2555 Panther Pkwy)*, in Sunrise, Florida. From Miami, take the Palmetto Expressway (SR 826) or Florida's Turnpike to I-75 north, to the Sawgrass Expressway (toll road 869). After the toll plaza stay in the far right lane and take exit 1B.

College Sports

University of Miami Hurricanes (☎ 800-462-2637, Ⓦ *www.hurricanesports.com)* The UM Hurricanes dominates college area sports, especially the football squad (tickets $25 to $45). Watch these 'Canes at the famed *Orange Bowl Stadium (1145 NW 11th St; Map 1)*.

Hurricane baseball (tickets $7 to $15) is played at *Mark Light Stadium (Map 10)*. Hurricane basketball (tickets $15 to $20) is played at the *Miami Arena (Map 6)*.

Auto Racing

Homestead Miami Speedway (☎ 305-230-7223, Ⓦ *www.homesteadmiamispeedway .com, 1 Speedway Blvd)* **Map 1** This $50 million racing center built in 1995 hosts NASCAR and Winston Cup races. The *New York Times* once quipped that it would be hard to imagine anyone in Homestead wanting to see something coming at them at 200mph after Hurricane Andrew, but people do.

Horse Racing

Calder Race Course (☎ 305-625-1311, Ⓦ *www.calderracecourse.com, 21001 NW 27th Ave)* **Map 2** Entrance $2. Live races May-Dec. This 1971 track hosts the Festival of the Sun Derby and always has simulcasts (TV broadcasts) of national races.

Jai Alai

Miami Jai Alai (☎ 305-633-6400, *3500 NW 37th Ave)* **Map 2** Tickets $1-5. Matches noon-5pm Wed-Mon, 7pm-midnight Mon, Fri & Sat. Jai alai (**high** aligh), which roughly translates as 'merry festival,' is a fascinating and dangerous game. Something of a cross between racquetball and lacrosse, it originated in the Basque region of the Pyrenees in the 17th century, and was introduced to Miami in 1924. The fronton where the games are held is the oldest in the States, having been built just two years after the game was introduced. What *is* the game? Well, players hurl a *pelota* (very hard ball) at more than 170mph to their opponents, who try to catch it with a *cesta,* or woven basket, attached to their glove. Audiences wager on the lightning fast games, said to be the fastest on earth. No kidding. Bus No 36 stops right in front of the arena.

Shopping

Conspicuous consumption, a favored American pastime, is alive and well in Greater Miami. It appears most readily in sprawling mega-malls, modern pantheons that inhabit every city neighborhood. From the Dolphin Mall outlets to the exclusive Bal Harbour Shops, these malls have the allure of one-stop shopping, food courts and 'attractions' for the kids. As for quirkiness and one-off shops, South Beach boutiques and Little Havana have the most independent personalities. Shopaholics, clotheshorses and wannabe interior designers shouldn't miss the Design and Fashion Districts (see the Where to Shop section, later in this chapter).

WHAT TO BUY
Accessories
SEE (☎ *305-672-6622, 921 Lincoln Road*) **Map 3** Open noon-10pm Mon-Thur, noon-11pm Fri, 11am-11pm Sat, noon-6pm Sun. Do you see what they see? Considered by some to be a discount designer shop, all glasses (including prescription) start at $169.

Sunglasses Hut (☎ *305-672-7788, 673 Collins Ave*) **Map 4** This chain offers all the usual suspects, but if you lost your glasses or are blinded by the light, feel your way here for some shades.

Liliblue (☎ *305-538-7431, 760 Ocean Dr*) **Map 4** Open 11am-8pm Mon-Thur, 11am-10pm Fri & Sat, noon-7pm Sun. Specializing in fashion jewelry, this shop sells gorgeous baubles and bangles.

Seybold Building (☎ *305-374-7922, 36 NE 1st St*) **Map 6** Open 9am-5:30pm Mon-Sat. Upwards of 300 independent stores offer a lively array of glittery diamonds, gold pendants, rings and other trinkets.

Antiques & Art
Lincoln Road and the Design District (see the Where to Shop section, later in this chapter) offer a plurality of pursuits. As for individual shops, they're all over the map.

Barbara Gillman Gallery (☎ *305-759-9155, 5582 NE 4th Court*) **Map 2** Open noon-6pm Tues-Sat. From unknown local painters, to Rauschenberg and Warhol, to a tried-and-true collection of black-and-white jazz photography by Herman Leonard, this gallery has staying power. It's been around since the early 1980s.

ArtCenter/South Florida (☎ *305-538-7887, 800 Lincoln Road* **Map 3** Open 11am-10pm Mon-Wed, 11am-11pm Thur-Sun (the gallery, as opposed to studios, opens at 1pm). The most exciting starting place on the Road, the nonprofit ArtCenter collective hosts regular openings and events. Tour the more structured gallery, as well as the maze of working studios where dozens of diverse artists pursue their inner demons and outer expressions of spirituality. It's great fun to peer down into their minimal spaces, trying to understand their creative processes.

Britto Central (☎ *305-531-8821, 818 Lincoln Road*) **Map 3** Open 10am-11pm Mon-Thur, 10am-midnight Fri & Sat, noon-10pm Sun. This neo-pop shop exhibits the work of Brazilian painter Romero Britto, who is either the current Andy Warhol or a vibrant caricature. You decide.

Carel Gallery (☎ *305-534-4384, 922 Lincoln Road*) **Map 3** Open 11am-6pm

Mon-Sat. The Road's first gallery (1963) is a serious one; 19th- and 20th-century post-impressionist oil paintings are shown.

Bettcher Gallery (☎ 305-758-7556, 919 Collins Av) **Map 4** Open noon-7pm Mon-Thur, noon-10pm Fri & Sat, 2pm-5pm Sun. One of the more affordable galleries in the area, Bettcher shows individual and group shows of photography, painting and sculpture.

Wallflower Gallery (☎ 305-579-0069, 10 NE 3rd St) **Map 6** Open 10am-8pm Tues-Fri. Put this funky, cool gallery on your short list of places to check out. Between performance pieces, live music and 'regular' art shows featuring local talent, this cultural oasis is worthy of your support. The staff is also particularly friendly. Wandering around the upstairs space with a drink is not at all intimidating. Special events are held on most Thursday, Friday and Saturday nights.

Meza Fine Art Gallery & Cafe (☎ 305-461-2733, 275 Giralda Ave) **Map 10** Open 11:30am-3pm & 6pm-'who knows' daily. Unless there's an opening, you visit between lunch and dinner or you're dining; otherwise, it's a bit awkward to wander around and check out the Latin and contemporary canvases. But as the host says, 'Come on over, have a glass of water, use the bathroom, get some affection, you have the right to be happy all the time.' He really believes this. There are also concerts and poetry readings, making Meza a delight.

Coral Gables Gallery Night (☎ 305-444-4493) Held 7pm-10pm the first Friday of every month. Even if you come for the complimentary refreshments (read: wine), you'll leave with a greater appreciation for Latin American and contemporary paintings, works on paper and photography. A minibus shuttles visitors between 10 participating galleries, including Books & Books (see Books, below), which is a good place to start.

Architectural Antiques (☎ 305-285-1330, 2500 SW 28th Lane) **Map 9** Open 10am-6pm Mon-Sat, noon-4pm Sun. Since much of the merchandise comes from mansions, there's treasure in them there piles of furni-

ture, paintings and other household items. It's a salvage warehouse, in essence, and you'll end up on a scavenger hunt.

Antique and Jewelry Show (☎ 305-444-8454, S Bayshore Dr) Third weekend of each month. This Coconut Grove Exhibition Center show attracts dealers from all over the country. Proceeds assist Coconut Grove Cares, a laudable social organization that provides summer jobs and runs after-school youth programs and day camps.

Books

Borders (☎ 305-935-4712, 19925 Biscayne Blvd) **Map 5** Open 9am-11pm Mon-Sat, 9am-9pm Sun. This Aventura megastore has a café and an enormous Florida selection. There's also a branch (☎ 305-447-1655) at the Streets of Mayfair complex (Map 9; see Where to Shop, later) in Coconut Grove.

Lambda Passage (☎ 305-754-6900, 7545 Biscayne Blvd) **Map 2** Open 11am-9pm Mon-Sat, noon-6pm Sun. Since the mid-1980s, this bookstore has been a fixture and meeting place for gays and lesbians.

Kafka Kafé (☎ 305-673-9669, 1464 Washington Ave) **Map 3** Open 8:30am-midnight daily. In addition to 24 computer terminals, Kafka sells thousands of used books. Their magazine selection is good, too.

Books & Books (☎ 305-532-3222, 933 Lincoln Road, ☎ 305-442-4408, 296 Aragon Ave) **Map 3 & 10** Lincoln Road location open 10am-11pm Sun-Thur, 10am-midnight Fri & Sat; Coral Gables open 9am-11pm daily. Long live the independents! The best locally owned bookstores, Books & Books hosts visiting authors, discussions and poetry readings. Both branches have a café, excellent fiction and Florida-related sections. The South Beach location is a bit heavier on gay titles, but the Coral Gables location has an outstanding department with rare books and first editions and frequent (small) photography exhibits. Open poetry readings (7:30pm-closing) are held on the last Friday of the month, and alternate between Coral Gables and South Beach.

Barnes & Noble (☎ 305-446-4152, 152 Miracle Mile) **Map 10** Open 9am-11pm daily. With the nearby university influencing the store vibe and selection, this B&N is a relaxing place to hang.

One of the best places to go for Spanish-language books is **Cervantes Book Store** (see the boxed text 'Calle Ocho: Cigars, Botánicas & More').

Collectibles & Gifts

Kitsch in Miami is like mountains in Alaska, steak in Texas and jazz in New Orleans. It's everywhere you look. Cheezoid '50s and '60s Americana and martini-chic rule. Then again, cigars make a nice gift for that perfect someone, too (see the boxed text 'Calle Ocho: Cigars, Botánicas & More').

Miami Twice (☎ 305-666-0127, 6562 SW 40th St) **Map 2** Open 10am-7pm Mon-Sat, noon-6pm Sun. Collectibles, accessories, jewelry and clothes…it's all here at a veritable one-stop department store for old Florida stuff on the '30s, '40s and '50s.

Gotta Have It (☎ 305-446-5757, 4231 SW 71st Ave) **Map 2** Open 8am-5pm Mon-Fri. For you celebrity-autograph hounds who just 'gotta have it,' these folks can get it for you if they don't have it. From Marilyn and JFK paraphernalia to James Dean and Babe Ruth signatures, they've seen and sold it all.

Senzatempo (☎ 305-534-5588, 1655 Meridian Ave) **Map 3** Open 11am-7pm Mon-Sat. Offering a myriad of timepieces, Senzatempo is trying to tell you something: It's time to go to their shop. You'll have fun searching for retro decorative stuff and furniture from the 1930s to the 1960s.

Beatnix (☎ 305-532-8733, 1149 Washington Ave) **Map 3**. Open noon-midnight daily. This shop has a monstrous collection of kitsch, including clothes, coasters, postcards, glasses and the like.

Pop (☎ 305-604-9604, 1151 Washington Ave) **Map 3** Open noon-10pm daily. Dare we say that kitsch doesn't get more collectible than at Pop? From George Jetson and his nuclear family to Ken and Barbie, the traditional household unit is covered.

Mike's Cigars (☎ 305-866-2277, 1030 Kane Concourse) **Map 5** Open 8am-6:30pm Mon-Fri. Although Little Havana hosts the bulk of cigar shops (see the boxed text 'Calle Ocho: Cigars, Botánicas & More'), Mike's offers sweet tobacco from Jamaica, Honduras and the Dominican Republic. He's just off 96th St.

Indies Company (☎ 305-375-1492, 101 W Flagler St) **Map 6** Open 10am-5pm Mon-Wed, Fri & Sat, 10am-9pm Thur, noon-5pm Sun. The gift shop at the Historical Museum of Southern Florida thrives on Florida, Florida and more Florida: Think faux alligators and tacky postcards. Actually, the shop has fine souvenirs and a great collection of Miami and South Florida books, too.

The **Art Deco Welcome Center** (see the South Beach section of the Things to See & Do chapter) has a gift shop with memorabilia, books and deco-related gifts.

Cosmetics

South Beach Make-Up (☎ 305-538-0805, 439 Española Way) **Map 3** Open 11am-8pm daily. This place has mostly natural makeup, essential oils and kindly soaps; it's sort of a less-activist Body Shop.

Brownes & Co Apothecary (☎ 305-532-8703, 841 Lincoln Road) **Map 3** Open Mon-Sat 10am-8pm, noon-6pm Sun. Expensive or not, this casually chic shop has *the* best selection of soaps, cosmetics and beauty and skin products from around the world. Having a bad hair day? They also analyze skin and hair problems and offer makeup lessons. Their newly expanded 'Some Like it Hot' salon is justifiably famous for Dead Sea–salt foot baths, hot-rock massages and a two-hour 'Beyond the Realm' treatment, with a variety of massages.

MAC (☎ 305-604-9040, 650 Collins Ave) Open 11am-9pm Mon-Thur, 10am-10pm Fri & Sat, noon-7pm Sun. In anticipation of a particularly special night on the town, why not get a particularly special makeover ($40) using this cosmetic line. Spokespeople KD Lang and Lil' Kim have them in common. Who-da-thunk-it?

Essentials

Compass Market (☎ 305-673-2906, 860 Ocean Dr) **Map 4** Open 8am-11pm daily. Normally, this kind of market, packed to the gills with cheap sandals and umbrellas, wouldn't make it into a guidebook. But on South Beach, the shop is unorthodox and we bet you'll stop in here for something.

Fashion

Fashion and South Beach stroll arm in arm. Upmarket chain stores and designer boutiques saturate Collins Ave between 6th and 9th Sts. It's a veritable ground zero for fashionistas.

Absolutely Suitable *(☎ 305-604-5281, 1560 Collins Ave)* **Map 3** Open 9am-5pm daily. For looking your best on the Beach, peruse these fine racks for swimming trunks and tankinis. Check out the sale rack, too.

Ritchie Swimwear *(☎ 305-538-0201, 106 8th St)* **Map 4** Open 9am-9pm Mon-Sat, 10am-7pm Sun. Ritchie comes through for every woman who needs a separate size top and bottom.

Whittall & Shon *(☎ 305-538-2606, 1319 Washington Ave)* **Map 3** Open 11am-8:30pm Mon-Thur, 11am-10:30pm Fri-Sun. When the disco beat here gets your gay blood pumping, shake your gay booty while flipping through gay tank tops. (What makes a tank top gay, you ask? Only what's inside it.) Don't get us wrong, heterosexuals are certainly welcome, but they'll be in the minority for once.

Recycled Blues *(☎ 305-538-0656, 1507 Washington Ave)* **Map 3** Open 1am-9pm daily. Got budgetary blues? South Beach is actually a great place to buy used clothing. These folks have Levi's for $12, shorts for $8 and jackets for $20.

Rags to Riches *(☎ 305-891-8981, 12577 Biscayne Blvd)* **Map 2** Open 10am-5:30pm Mon-Sat. Although this consignment shop is a ways up Biscayne, it's worth the trip. Your personal sleuthing skills will have a decided effect on whether you walk away with riches or rags, though. While you're in the area, consider popping into some other thrift store neighbors along this stretch.

Versace Jeans Couture *(☎ 305-532-5993, 755 Washington Ave)* **Map 4** Open 10am-9pm Mon-Sat, noon-7pm Sun. With the help of a friendly staff, fashion plates can select

$430 bathrobes or $155 blue jeans. Don't let the price tags scare you.

A!X Armani Exchange *(☎ 305-531-5900, 760 Collins Ave)* **Map 4** Open 10am-9pm Mon-Thur, 10am-10pm Fri & Sat, noon-8pm Sun. Not to be outdone, Armani has similarly priced merchandise to Versace.

Betsey Johnson *(☎ 305-673-0023, 805 Washington Ave)* **Map 4** Open 11am-7pm Mon-Fri, 11am-8pm Sat, noon-6pm Sun. This hugely popular line of women's clothing has a few pieces of clothing so revealing that they may as well be ribbons with pockets. But one particular Lonely Planet editor swears by her clothes, ribbons and all.

Deco Denim *(☎ 305-532-6986, 645 Collins Ave)* **Map 4** Open 10am-10pm daily. For Levi's from $20 and Ray Bans for about $60, this shop delivers (well, not literally).

Miami Surf Style *(☎ 305-532-6928, 421 Lincoln Road)* **Map 3** Open 9am-midnight daily. Dude, cheap jeans, hats and T-shirts rule this roost.

See also the boxed text 'Calle Ocho: Cigars, Botánicas & More.'

Liquor

SoBe Liquor *(☎ 305-674-1212, 1609 Alton Rd)* **Map 3** Open 10am-10pm Mon-Thur, 10am-11pm Fri & Sat, noon-8pm Sun. Can't rouse yourself? Rather just slip in a video and enjoy a glass of wine or beer in bed with your sweetie? SoBe Liquors delivers seven days a week.

Music

With regards to the recording industry, Miami is right up there with LA, New York and Nashville these days. All the major labels have offices here. And it would be embarrassing for *any* music store to have anything less than a wide selection of imports, as well as listening stations. They won't disappoint. From jazz to hip-hop to house, music connoisseurs young and old can find what they're looking for in Miami.

Yesterday & Today *(☎ 305-468-0311, 7902 NW 36th St)* **Map 2** Open 11am-7pm Tues-Thur, 11am-8pm Fri & Sat, noon-4:30pm Sun. This being Miami, Y&T has vinyl (records, that is, not the distant cousin to fabric) and every other format recorded. The very helpful and knowledgeable staff specializes in '50s, '60s and '70s tunes and little 45s (singles).

Spec's Music (☎ *305-534-3667, 501 Collins Ave*) **Map 4** Open 10am-midnight Sun-Thur, 10am-1am Fri & Sat. Spec's, the Tower Records of Miami, has almost 20 supershops around town (for a list, check **w** www.fye.com). This location has a café, lots of listening booths and Latin dance tunes for their clientele: dancing queens.

Virgin Megastore (☎ *305-665-4445, 5701 Sunset Place*) **Map 10** Open 10am-midnight Mon, 10am-11pm Tues-Thur, 10am-midnight Fri & Sat, 11am-11pm Sun. You'll find the standard wide selection and de rigueur listening stations at this Miami branch of the chain.

See also the boxed text 'Calle Ocho: Cigars, Botánicas & More.'

Periodicals

News Cafe Store (☎ *305-538-6397, 800 Ocean Dr*) **Map 4** Open 24 hrs daily. Look for the separate 24-hour newsstand between News Cafe's restaurant and bar. It has a good selection of international and domestic papers.

Piercings & Tattoos

Everyone in Miami Beach and their dog seems to have a tattoo. And while piercings aren't as popular here as they are in some other large cities, Beach piercers can put a pin through it with the best of them – from eyebrows and tongues to nipples and navels.

Tattoos by Lou (☎ *305-532-7300, 231 14th St*) **Map 3** Open noon-1am Mon-Thur, noon-2am Fri & Sat, noon-midnight Sun. Not surprisingly, the most famous Beach tattoo parlor has been here the longest. Since you must be at least 18 years old, bring your ID. Lou's has three other Miami locations (9820 S Dixie Hwy, 456 NE 167th St, and 1193 W 37th St).

Art Attack (☎ *305-531-4556, 1344 Washington Ave*) **Map 3** Open 11am-midnight Mon-Thur, 11am-2am Fri-Sun. Same as Lou's, these friendly folks have a state-of-the-art studio for tattooing and piercing.

South Beach Tattoo (☎ *305-538-0104, 861 Washington Ave*) **Map 4** Open 11am-2am daily. From body piercing and tattoos for a minimum of $50 to a good selection of T-shirts for $15, this place covers your skin one way or another.

Sex Stuff

Given the amount of sexual openness on South Beach, it may be surprising that real sex shops are few and far between.

Pleasure Emporium (☎ *305-538-6434, 1671 Alton Rd*, ☎ *305-673-3311, 1019 5th St*) **Maps 3 & 4** Alton Rd open 9am-2am daily, 5th St open 24 hrs daily. Out of two convenient locations, this company sells boatloads of videos and fetish wear.

New Concept Video (☎ *305-674-1111, 1671 Meridian Ave*) **Map 3** Open 1am-midnight Mon-Thur, 11am-2am Fri-Sun. Check out this selection of gay, lesbian, foreign and XXX movies. New Concept rents video players sometimes.

Fetish Factory (☎ *954-563-5777, 855 E Oakland Park Blvd, Fort Lauderdale, www.fetish-factory.com*) Open 11am-9pm Mon-Sat, noon-6pm Sun. Hard core masters of their universe make a bee line to Fort Lauderdale to peruse this enormous selection of leather, PVC and rubber clothes, masks, bondage accessories and adult toys.

WHERE TO SHOP

No matter what the neighborhood, Miami offers plenty of choices.

Flea Markets

Opa-Locka/Hialeah Flea Market (☎ *305-688-8080, 12705 NW 42nd Ave*) **Map 2** Open 6am-7pm Mon-Fri, 8am-5pm Sat & Sun. With about 1200 vendors, this is a biggie.

Antiques & Collectibles Market (☎ *305-673-4991, Lincoln Road at Washington Ave*) **Map 3** Held 8am-5pm second & fourth Sun of each month. All the bases are covered with deco, Gothic and 1950s junque. If the timing is right with your holiday, it's fun.

Española Way (*between Washington & Drexel Aves*) **Map 3** Held 7pm-midnight Fri, 9am-midnight Sat, 11am-9pm Sun. This hippie-style market has handcrafted items, clothing, food vendors and Latin music. On Friday and Saturday evenings, it turns more artsy.

Malls

There are a dozens, but these are two of the biggest and best.

Dadeland Mall (☎ 305-665-6226, **W** www .shopsimon.com, 7535 N Kendall Dr) **Map 2** Open 10am-9:30pm Mon-Sat, noon-7pm Sun. In addition to 175 or so other stores, this Kendall mall boasts Florida's first and largest Burdines department store, plus another Burdines solely devoted to home furnishings. The Spanish-challenged should note that many store employees here speak limited English.

Dolphin Mall (☎ 305-365-7446, **W** www .shopdolphinmall.com, Florida's Turnpike & Dolphin Expressway) **Map 2** Open 11am-10pm Mon-Sat, noon-8pm Sun. The largest discount-outlet center within city limits, this bargain mall boasts an Off Saks Fifth Ave,

Marshall's Megastore, a big sporting goods store, a 28-screen movie theater, a huge food court and a roller coaster to keep the kids occupied – it's fun for the whole family. Mall developers expect you to make a day of it.

Design District (Map 2)

Just north of our downtown map borders, between N Miami and NE 2nd Aves and NE 37th and 42nd Sts, the Design District (**W** www.designdistrict.com) has long been poised to become the new South Beach. Why? Because conditions here mimic those prior to the SoBe Boom, when higher rents in more fashionable neighborhoods forced creative people to relocate. The Buena Vista neighborhood, in which the Design District is located, is home to artists, studios, film companies, photographers and dancers – basically, anyone who needs lots of space and little overhead. Billed in the 1960s as 'the Square Mile of Style' and visible from I-95, the District is Miami's

RICHARD CUMMINS

Actors take the stage? Nope. Shoppers enjoy the storefront of a Design District business.

epicenter for the interior decorating and design industry. It's an amalgam of international showrooms for antiques, tiles, furniture and art. If it has to do with outfitting or redesigning a home or office, you name it, it's here. Start your exploration at NE 2nd Ave and NE 40th St.

Fashion District (Map 2)

Also just north of our downtown borders, along NW 6th Ave between 23rd and 29th Sts, the less fashionable Fashion District has outlets for about 30 of the 500 or so garment manufactures in the Miami area. From holes-in-the-wall with handbags to a few chic boutiques, patient shoppers will enjoy the adrenaline rush that comes with finding a bargain. Since the neighborhood is a bit seedy, less adventurous bargain hunters might head out to the Dolphin Mall instead (see Malls, earlier). Most stores are open 9am to 5pm Monday to Saturday.

South Beach (Maps 3 & 4)

Lincoln Road, a long pedestrian- and rollerblade-friendly byway, attracts both models and conventioneers. It's lined with cafés frequented by locals and primed for people-watching. In addition to a mega-cineplex that anchors the western end, The Road (as it's known locally) is crowded with Williams-Sonoma, Pottery Barn and the like. But it also has its share of independent clothing boutiques, cool gift stores, galleries and artsy lighting stores. We don't include many specific ones because they change all the time or are gobbled up by the next Gap lookalike. The nearby *Burdines* (☎ 305-674-6311, 1675 Meridian Ave) belongs to the empire of grand Southern department stores. It's the most convenient department store in South Beach.

Collins Ave, between 6th and 9th Sts, is the undisputed Fifth Avenue of South Beach. But, unavoidably, it has its share of ubiquitous chain stores, from Urban Outfitters to the Gap to Armani. *Washington Ave* is a mixed bag; some blocks are lined with galleries and shops, while others are bare. *Alton Rd* caters to more utilitarian needs.

Northern Miami Beach (Map 5)

Aventura Mall (☎ 305-935-1110, W www.shopaventuramall.com, 19501 Biscayne Blvd) Open 10am-9:30pm Mon-Sat, noon-8pm Sun. This upscale granddaddy of a mall, which attracts families with an enormous indoor playground, has a Macy's, Lord & Taylor, Burdines, Bloomingdale's and a 24-screen movie theater with new-fangled stadium seating. Look for South Beach shuttles from many hotels (including Loews Miami Beach).

Bal Harbour Shops (☎ 305-866-0311, W www.balharbourshops.com, 9700 Collins Ave) Open 10am-9pm Mon-Fri, 10am-7pm Sat, noon-6pm Sun. This exclusive and lush Bal Harbour mall boasts tony shops like Chanel, Tiffany, Louis Vuitton, Hermés and Zhiguli. No, you only think you're on Rodeo Drive.

Downtown Miami (Map 6)

The heart of downtown, especially along *Flagler St*, is crammed with dozens and dozens of shops selling…well, selling export-ready electronics mainly to Latin American visitors. Additionally, you'll see truckloads of luggage, watches, cameras (without warranties) and leather. You'll probably have to bargain your heart out to get a deal equivalent to one at *Circuit City* (☎ 305-933-8616) – where you get a 30-day money-back guarantee, a better selection and fixed prices. Circuit City has several Miami locations selling a decent range of electronics, computers, appliances and other gizmotronics. Nevertheless, head downtown if you're up for haggling and you speak a modicum of Spanish. Cuban coffee windows will keep the buzz up as you wing it.

Bayside Marketplace (☎ 305-577-3344, W www.baysidemarketplace.com, 401 Biscayne Blvd) Open 10am-10pm Mon-Thur, 10am-11pm Fri & Sat, 11am-9pm Sun. This touristy bayfront mall has entertainment, restaurants, bars, tour-boat docks, push-cart vendors and name-brand shops. There are no surprises, except for the nice views.

There's a downtown branch of *Burdines* (☎ 305-577-2312, 22 E Flagler St), a grand Southern department store.

Calle Ocho: Cigars, Botánicas & More (Map 8)

Little Havana's main thoroughfare, filled with tiny shops you will not find anywhere else in the States, is certainly distinct. Check it out.

Cigars

Although it's illegal to import cigars (and anything else) from Cuba, shops still market Cuban cigars. How can they do that? Simple: They use tobacco that comes

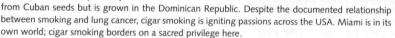

from Cuban seeds but is grown in the Dominican Republic. Despite the documented relationship between smoking and lung cancer, cigar smoking is igniting passions across the USA. Miami is in its own world; cigar smoking borders on a sacred privilege here.

According to an article in *Cigar Aficionado*, Ernesto Curillo, the owner of **El Crédito Cigars** (☎ 305-858-4162, *1106 Calle Ocho; open 8am-6pm Mon-Fri, 8am-4pm Sat*), is one of the leaders of the Cigar Renaissance. The store, supplied by perhaps Miami's most successful cigar factory, offers several lines, one of hottest of which is La Gloria Cubana. Peer into the store's picture windows to watch a dozen or so Cuban *tabaqueros* hand-rolling cigars on well-worn wooden benches, then cutting and pressing them. Or go inside to flex your olfactory senses (tobacco smells heady and sweet) and purchase some fat stogies either in bulk or singles. The folks are nice about letting people take photos; ask if you want one.

Padron Cigar (☎ 305-643-2117, *1566 W Flagler St*) Open 9am-5pm Mon-Fri, 9am-noon Sat. Off Calle Ocho, but still in the neighborhood, Padron also offers visitors the chance to watch the process of rolling cigars.

La Tradición Cubana (☎ 305-643-4005, *1894 Calle Ocho*) Open 9am-5pm Mon-Fri, 10am-2pm Sat. This little cigar factory is the real thing, not some gussied up showroom for tourists. You can watch workers roll the cigars you are about to buy. The cigars made here are known for their robust aroma and taste.

To sample some stogies before committing to a box, head to **Condal & Peñamil** (Map 3), on Lincoln Road; see Cigar Bars in the Entertainment chapter.

What? Don't know how to smoke a cigar? Cut off the end closest to the band with a sharp knife and light that end so that it burns evenly. Draw, but don't inhale the smoke; let it roll around your mouth before exhaling. By all means don't gnaw or suck on the cigar. Don't take more than one or two puffs per minute; if it burns too quickly it'll taste sour. Practice a studied, conversational look.

Botánicas

The spiritual shops of Santería, *botánicas* sell a variety of lotions, potions, sprays, candles and soap to assist in worship and prayer. Bad news coming? Try 'Door Evil Stopper.' Tighten the lips of loose-mouthed relatives with a bath using 'Stop Gossip' soap. Friend on trial? Pick up some 'Court Case.' Keep Miami's finest at bay with 'Law: Stay Away' candles. Kids won't listen? You need 'Do As I Say' floor wash. Botánicas also sell books, incense, good luck charms and other Santería and related items.

Everything in these religious supply shops is taken very seriously, so treat them with the same respect and reverence you would in a Christian Science Reading Room or, say, a bible shop. The following are some of the better known Calle Ocho botánicas.

Botánica El Camino (☎ 305-643-9135, *1896 Calle Ocho*) is the place to stock up on candles and aerosol sprays; it's delightfully welcoming to browsers from out of town. **Botánica Las Mercedes** (☎ 305-631-0606, *2742 Calle Ocho*), located in a little strip mall, is run by Mercedes, who speaks English and is warmly welcoming to anyone with a genuine interest in her craft. **Botánica La**

[Continued on page 161]

Bridge, Interrupted: The Old Seven Mile Bridge now serves as a fishing pier. Florida Keys

Brown pelican, Florida Keys

Bonefishing at sunset, Florida Keys

LEE FOSTER

When in Key West, one *must* watch the sunset.

LEE FOSTER

Galleon treasures are on display at the Mel Fisher Maritime Museum in Key West.

Calle Ocho: Cigars, Botánicas & More (Map 8)

[Continued from page 160]

Negra Francisca (☎ 305-860-9328, 1323 Calle Ocho) stocks the usual array of candles, but also has plants, flowers and exotic birds.

Music
Power Records (☎ 305-285-2212, 1419 Calle Ocho) Open 9:30am-8:30pm Mon-Thur, 9:30am-9pm Fri & Sat, 11am-7pm Sun. Follow your ears for a huge selection of Latin, salsa, rumba, South American and Cuban music at decent prices.

Do Re Mi Music Center (☎ 305-541-3374, 1829 Calle Ocho) Open 10:30am-8pm Mon-Sat. In addition to carrying musical instruments, this outlet has a good selection of Latin cassettes, records and CDs.

Casino (☎ 305-856-6888, 1208 Calle Ocho) Open 9am-9pm Mon-Sat, 10am-5pm Sun. Cuban musicians have a friend in Casino. You can find Cuban music here that can't even be purchased in Havana. Knowledgeable salespeople oversee a hefty Latin selection.

Books
Cervantes Book Store (☎ 305-642-5222, 1898 Calle Ocho) Open 9:30am-5:30pm Mon-Sat, noon-4pm Sun. This is *the* place to purchase Spanish-language books.

Guayaberas
La Casa de las Guayaberas (☎ 305-266-9683, 5840 Calle Ocho) Open 10am-7pm Mon-Sat. You, too, can dress like the legendary musicians in the Buena Vista Social Club. Handmade *guayaberas,* traditional Cuban dress shirts for men, start at $15 for a cotton-poly blend and go up to $130 for linen.

Piñatas
La Casa de Piñatas (☎ 305-649-4711, 1756 Calle Ocho) Open 11am-7pm Mon-Sat. For those unfamiliar with them, piñatas are hollow papier-mâché figures (usually of animals) filled with candy, small toys and trinkets. At children's birthday parties, games are devised to get at the treasure hidden inside. The Mexican tradition usually involves smashing the piñata with a stick until it breaks open. The Cuban tradition is less violent; Cuban piñatas are intended to yield their contents when the children pull a ribbon. This small showroom has a number of ready-made piñatas, but you can also custom order one.

Souvenirs
Havana-To-Go (☎ 305-857-9720, ⓦ www.littlehavanatogo.com, 1442 Calle Ocho) Open 10:30am-6pm Mon-Sat, noon-4pm Sun. Little Havana's official souvenir store is not as cheesy as you might think. They actually have some cool authentic stuff and the folks who work here are very friendly and helpful.

Other
Los Pinareños (☎ 305-285-1135, 1334 Calle Ocho) Open 8am-7:30pm Mon-Sat, 7:30am-2pm Sun. This open-air fruit-and-flower market has a great tropical-juice bar.

La Casa de los Trucos (☎ 305-858-5029, 1343 Calle Ocho) Open 10am-6pm Mon-Sat. The House of Tricks has costumes, fake blood, trick gum, sex toys and unrippable toilet paper – just what you needed, right? Still, if you are planning to attend a theme night at an exclusive club, this place may have just what you need, from wigs and feather boas to makeup.

Coconut Grove (Map 9)

With a few exceptions, individual shops have given way to the following two upscale outdoor malls.

CocoWalk (☎ 305-444-0777, Ⓦ *www .cocowalk.com, 3015 Grand Ave)* Open 11am-10pm Sun-Thur, 11am-midnight Fri & Sat. In the heart of a formerly charming neighborhood, this open-air mall has a Gap, Victoria's Secret, Banana Republic and a 16-screen AMC cinema (☎ 305-448-6305).

Streets of Mayfair (☎ 305-448-1700, Ⓦ *www.streetsofmayfair.com, 2911 Grand Ave)* Open 10am-10pm daily. While the Streets of Mayfair shopping mall has many fashionable shops, plus several restaurants and galleries, many people don't even know the large complex exists because of the more obvious CocoWalk, which lies adjacent to it.

Coral Gables (Map 10)

Miracle Mile This broad and shady street runs from dowdy discount shops to bridal shops for the ladies-who-lunch set. With the arrival of Starbucks and Barnes & Noble, the street continues its march toward mass 'Gapification.' Shops become more high end as you head farther west.

Merrick Park Under construction at press time, this new upscale mall between Le Jeune Rd and Ponce de León Blvd, is scheduled to open Fall 2002.

The Shops at Sunset Place (☎ 305-663-0482, Ⓦ *www.shopsimon.com, 5701 Sunset Place)* Open 10am-10pm Mon-Fri, 11am-10pm Sat, 11am-9pm Sun. This mall-as-theme-park features faux trees and waterfalls and bird sounds, an IMAX theater, the virtual-reality Gameworks emporium, Nike-Town, FAO Schwarz, a teen skating ramp and a 24-screen movie complex.

Key West

The capital of the Conch Republic, Key West has a well-earned reputation as a tropical paradise with gorgeous sunsets and raucous nightlife. Yes, it's overrun by tourists and its Conchs have become cynical, but if you look carefully, you'll find fleeting images of the former Key West. Walking through narrow side streets away from Truman Ave or Duval St, you'll see lovely Keys architecture and get a sense of how the locals live (at least, those who aren't there to sell you a T-shirt or a seat on a glass-bottom boat).

History

The area's first European settlers were the Spanish, who upon finding Indian burial sites, named the place Cayo Hueso (kah-ya **way**-so) – Bone Island, a name that was later Anglicized into Key West. Purchased from a Spaniard by John Simonton in 1821, Key West was developed as a naval base in 1822. It then served as the naval base for David Porter's Anti-Pirate Squadron, which by 1826 had substantially reduced pirate activity in the region. From then on, Key West's times of boom and bust were closely tied to a military presence.

The construction of forts at Key West and on the Dry Tortugas brought men and money. As well, the island's proximity to busy and treacherous shipping lanes (which attracted the pirates in the first place) created a wrecking industry – salvaging goods from downed ships.

In the late 1800s, the area became the focus of mass immigration and political activity for Cubans, who were fleeing oppressive conditions under Spanish rule and trying to form a revolutionary army. Along with them came cigar manufacturers, who turned Key West into the USA's cigar manufacturing center. That would end when workers' demands convinced several large manufacturers, notably Vicente Martínez Ybor and Ignacio Haya, to relocate to Tampa in southwest Florida.

During the Spanish-American War, Key West may have been the most important staging point for US troops, and the military buildup lasted through WWI. All of the Keys began to boom when Henry Flagler's Overseas Highway – running over a series of causeways from the mainland to Key West – was constructed.

In the late 1910s, with Prohibition on the horizon, Key West became a bootlegging center, as people stocked up on booze. To make matters worse, after the city went bankrupt during the Great Depression, a 1935 hurricane depleted what little enthusiasm remained (even though writer Ernest Hemingway resided here between 1931 and

KEY WEST

The Conch Republic

Conchs (pronounced 'conk' as in 'bonk,' not 'contsh' as in 'paunch') are people who were born and raised in Key West. It's a rare and difficult title to achieve. Even after seven years of living here, residents only rise to the rank of 'Freshwater Conch.' You will hear reference to, and see the flag of, the Conch Republic, and therein lies an interesting tale.

In 1982, the US border patrol and US customs erected a roadblock at Key Largo to catch drug smugglers and illegal aliens. As traffic jams and anger mounted, many tourists disappeared. They decided they'd rather take the Shark Valley Tram in the Everglades, thank you very much.

To voice their outrage, a bunch of fiery Conchs decided to secede from the USA. After forming the Conch Republic, they made three declarations (in this order): Secede from the USA; declare war on the USA and surrender; and request $1 million in foreign aid.

Every February, Conchs celebrate the anniversary of those heady days with nonstop parties.

KEY WEST

PLACES TO STAY
5 Jabour's Camp & Lodge
21 Curry House
24 Frances St Bottle Inn
31 Holiday Inn La Concha
33 Marrero's
34 Big Rubys Guesthouse
36 Pegasus Hotel
40 The Gardens Hotel
45 Merlin Guesthouse
47 Andrews Inn
49 Wicker Guesthouse
54 Conch House Heritage
     Inn
56 Chelsea House
57 The Mermaid & The
     Alligator
58 La Pensione
63 Pearl's Rainbow
64 Best Western Hibiscus
65 Key West Youth Hostel
     & Seashell Motel
67 Atlantic Shores Resort
69 Wyndham Casa Marina
     Resort & Beach House

PLACES TO EAT
2 Turtle Kraals Restaurant
     & Bar
4 Java Lounge; Key West
     Lime Shoppe
6 Waterfront Market;
     Schooner Wharf Bar
7 BO's Fish Wagon
8 Pepe's Cafe
9 PT's Late Night
27 Kelly's
41 Mangoes
51 The Deli Restaurant
55 Cafe des Artistes
59 El Siboney
61 Alice's; La Te Da
62 Camille's
68 Louie's Backyard

ENTERTAINMENT
17 Captain Tony's Saloon
18 Rick's/Durty Harry's;
     Upstairs at Rick's
19 Sloppy Joe's Bar
35 Margaritaville Café
38 Green Parrot
39 Bourbon St Pub
43 801 Bourbon Bar

OTHER
1 Yankee Freedom II
3 Key West Aloe
10 Parking
11 Key West Chamber of
     Commerce
12 Old Town Trolley Tours
13 Key West Shipwreck
     Historeum
14 Key West Cigar Factory
15 Mel Fisher Maritime
     Museum
16 Audubon House &
     Tropical Gardens
20 Curry Mansion
22 Helio Gallery
23 Flaming Maggie's

25 Haitian Art Co
26 Little White House
28 Wreckers' Museum/
     Oldest House
29 Public Library
30 Post Office
32 Key West Island Books
37 Bank of America
42 Key West Business Guild
44 Pandemonium
46 Key West Lighthouse
48 Hemingway House
50 Keys Mopeds & Scooters
52 Truman Medical Center
53 Moped Hospital
60 Gay & Lesbian
     Community Center
66 Southernmost Point
70 West Martello Tower

Key West Bight

Land's End
Marina

Historic
Seaport

Gulf of

Mexico

Pier B

*Submarine
Basin*

*Truman
Annex*

Mallory
Square

Front St
Ann St
Simonton St
Greene St
William St
Duval St
Dey St
Caroline St
Elizabeth St
Bahama St
Eaton St
Fleming St
Southard St
Angela St
Whitehead St
Olivia St
Thomas St
Emma St
Julia St
Howe St
Covington Ave
Dekalb Ave
Fort St
Wall St

*Harry S Truman
US Naval Reservation*

**Fort Zachary
Taylor State
Historic Site**

Whitehead Spit

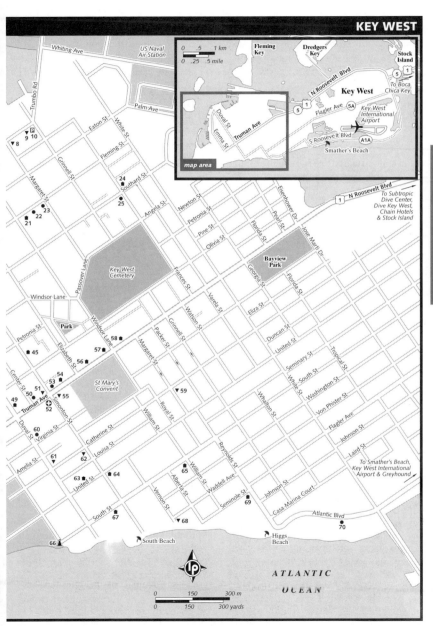

KEY WEST

Whiting Ave

US Naval Air Station

Fleming Key

Dredgers Key

Stock Island

0   .5   1 km
0 .25 .5 mile

N Roosevelt Blvd

Key West

To Boca Chica Key

Trumbo Rd

Palm Ave

5

Flagler Ave

5A

Key West International Airport

Eaton St

White St

Duval St

Emma St

Truman Ave

S Roosevelt Blvd

A1A

Fleming St

9 10

8

Smather's Beach

map area

Margaret St

Grinnell St

Southard St

24

25

Angela St

Newton St

Petronia St

Eisenhower Dr

Pearl St

1   N Roosevelt Blvd
To Subtropic Dive Center, Dive Key West, Chain Hotels & Stock Island

23

22

21

Pine St

Olivia St

Florida St

Jose Marti Dr

Key West Cemetery

Passover Lane

Frances St

Varela St

Georgia St

Bayview Park

Florida St

Windsor Lane

Windsor Lane

Eliza St

Petronia St

Park

Elizabeth St

58

57

Packer St

Grinnell St

Duncan St

United St

45

56

Margaret St

Seminary St

Tropical St

Center St

54

53

St Mary's Convent

White St

South St

Washington St

49

50

51

55

52

Truman Ave

Simonton St

Royal St

Whalton St

Von Phister St

60

Virginia St

William St

Flagler Ave

Duval St

Catherine St

Johnson St

61

62

Louisa St

Reynolds St

Laird St

To Smather's Beach, Key West International Airport & Greyhound

Amelia St

63

64

65

Waddell Ave

Johnson St

United St

Alberta St

William St

Seminole St

69

Casa Marina Court

South St

67

Vernon St

68

Atlantic Blvd

70

66

South Beach

Higgs Beach

ATLANTIC OCEAN

0   150   300 m
0   150   300 yards

1940). WWII, though, breathed new life into Key West when the naval base once again became an important staging area. And everyone in Washington was certainly happy about that presence when the Bay of Pigs crisis unfolded in 1961 (see the History section of the Facts about Miami chapter for more).

Key West has always been a place where people bucked trends. A large society of artists and craftspeople congregated here at the end of the Great Depression because of cheap real estate, and that community continues to grow (despite today's pricey real estate). While gay men have long been welcomed, the gay community really picked up in earnest in the 1970s. Today it's one of the most renowned and best organized in the country.

While Key West is home to hundreds of hotels, restaurants and bars geared to all desires and tastes, it isn't a resort, and it isn't a 'gay' destination any more than Miami's South Beach is. 'All welcome' means just that. Despite cynicism and some price gouging, visitors find Key West to be almost as good as they'd imagined.

Orientation

The island of Key West is roughly oval shaped, with most of the action taking place in the west end. The main drags are Duval St and Truman Ave (US Hwy 1). Downtown streets are laid out in a grid, with street numbers (usually painted on lampposts) in a hundred-block format counting upward from Front St (100) to Truman Ave (900) and so on. Mallory Square, at the far northwestern tip, hosts nightly sunset celebrations.

Information

Tourist Offices The Key West Chamber of Commerce (☎ 305-294-2587, 800-527-8539, W www.keywestchamber.org), 402 Wall St, Mallory Square, is an excellent source of information, brochures, maps and advice. It's open 8:30am to 6:30pm Monday to Saturday, until 6pm on Sunday.

Coming into town on US Hwy 1, you pass the Key West Welcome Center (☎ 305-296-4444, 800-284-4482), 3840 N Roosevelt Blvd, which sells discounted attraction tickets and helps with accommodations. It's open 8am to 7:30pm Monday to Saturday, 9am to 6pm Sunday.

Gay & Lesbian Organizations Representing many gay-owned and -friendly businesses, the 2nd-floor Key West Business Guild (☎ 305-294-4603, W www.gay keywestfl.com), 728 Duval St, is a very helpful organization. Then again, so is the Gay & Lesbian Community Center (☎ 305-292-3223, W www.glcckeywest .org), 1075 Duval St. Pick up the free weekly *Celebrate* (W www.celebratekey west.com), the 'voice' of Key West's gay and lesbian community.

Bookstores & Libraries This town of 28,000 souls is very literary. Key West Island Books (☎ 305-294-2904), 513 Fleming St, has an excellent selection of works by Key West writers, from the famous dead ones to the still-alive-and-soon-to-be-famous ones.

Flaming Maggie's (☎ 305-294-3931), 830 Fleming St, is a great gay bookstore cum art and coffee shop.

South Florida's first public library (☎ 305-292-3535), 700 Fleming St, was founded in 1892.

Media The semi-weekly *Key West Keynoter* (W www.keynoter.com) and weekly *Key West: The Newspaper* are the local rags of record. *Solares Hill* (W www.solareshill .com) is the local radical newspaper (though far less than it was in the '70s), focusing on community interest.

National Public Radio (NPR) is at 91.3 FM.

Medical Services Lower Keys Medical Center (☎ 305-294-5531, 800-233-3119), 5900 College Rd, Stock Island, near MM 5, has a 24-hour emergency room. For less-critical problems, Truman Medical Center (☎ 305-296-4399), 540 Truman Ave, is open 9am to 4:45pm Monday to Friday, 9:30am to noon Saturday.

THINGS TO SEE & DO
Mallory Square
This cobblestone square hosts Key West's famous nightly sunset celebration, the uniquely Key West carnival featuring jugglers, acrobats, well-trained parrots and artisans. The atmosphere seems designed to get as many people as possible near the bars, restaurants, trinket shops and sidewalk stalls. But despite the cynicism, the event *is* interesting – once. Show up an hour beforehand to get the full effect.

Hemingway House
One of Key West's great attractions, this lovely Spanish-colonial house (☎ *305-294-1575,* w *www.hemingwayhome.com, 907 Whitehead St; admission $9/5 adult/child 6-12 yrs; open 9am-5pm daily)* was Hemingway's house from 1931 to 1940. It was here that he wrote *The Short Happy Life of Francis Macomber, A Farewell to Arms, Death in the Afternoon* and *To Have and Have Not,* and where he began *For Whom the Bell Tolls.* But he didn't just write here; he procrastinated by installing Key West's first saltwater swimming pool in a kind of romantic garden. The construction project set him back so much that he pressed 'my

last penny' into the cement on the pool's deck. It's still there today. Hemingway retained ownership of the house until his death in 1961; the descendants of his famous six-toed cat still rule the house and grounds. Tours, departing every 15 minutes and lasting about 30 minutes, include fun stories about his wives, the chandeliers and the old overgrown gardens.

Key West Cemetery
One of the country's more fascinating cemeteries contains tombstone epitaphs like 'I told you I was sick' and 'At least I know where he is sleeping tonight.' You'll have to hunt for them, but that's the fun of it. Guided tours are available on Tuesday and Thursday at 9:30am (☎ *305-292-6829; tours $10 per person)* from the main gate at Margaret and Angela Sts.

Curry Mansion
This 100-year-old Victorian mansion (☎ *305-294-5349,* w *www.currymansion.com, 511 Caroline St),* with extraordinary woodwork and Tiffany sliding-glass doors, was built by Milton Curry, one of Florida's first millionaires; it's now a guest house. On most days you can take a self-guided tour of the antique-packed rooms from 8:30am to 5pm; it's $5 for adults, $1 for children. If you're impressed enough that you want to stay, rooms range from $150 to $250 nightly off-season, $240 to $325 from mid-January to mid-April. Be careful, though; only four rooms are in the main house (16 more are out back and eight others are across the street). Note that Curry Mansion is not Curry House (see the Places to Stay section).

Wreckers' Museums
Two small museums are dedicated to study of the wreckers. The home of Confederate blockade-runner Francis B Watlington's house, the **Wreckers' Museum/Oldest House** (☎ *305-294-9502, 322 Duval St; admission $5/1 adult/child; open 10am-4pm daily),* is filled with period antiques and has enjoyable, volunteer-led tours.

The **Key West Shipwreck Historeum** (☎ *305-292-8990, 1 Whitehead St; admission*

'Papa' Hemingway

$8/4 adult/child 4-12 yrs; open 9:45am-4:45pm daily) is more interesting. A narrated film portrays the lives and times of the wreckers and knowledgeable volunteers explain how Key West developed as a port. Allow about 30 to 45 minutes to see and do everything.

Southernmost Point

An official marker at the corner of South and Whitehead Sts indicates the southernmost point in the continental USA (technically there's land farther south, but it's within the naval base, which is private property and therefore doesn't count) and draws hundreds of photo-seeking tourists. You gotta be able to prove 'I was there,' after all.

Key West Lighthouse

This functioning lighthouse (☎ *305-294-0012,* W *www.kwahs.com, 938 Whitehead St; admission $8/6/4 adult/senior/student over 7 yrs; open 9:30am-4:30pm daily)* is farther inland than you might expect for two reasons. First, the navy filled in about 2000 yards between here and Fort Taylor. Second, lighthouse placement isn't all that important when you consider that it sits at the high point (10 feet above sea level) on a flat island in the middle of the ocean. Lighthouses are designed so boats know that if they're lined up with the lighthouse's red lens, they're in trouble. The adjacent keeper's house contains a little museum, but visitors can also climb the 88 steps to the top of the lighthouse.

Audubon House & Tropical Gardens

This lovely early-19th-century house (☎ *305-294-2116,* W *www.audubonhouse .com, 205 Whitehead St; admission $8.50/ 7.50/3.50 adult/senior/child 6-12 yrs; open 9:30am-5pm daily)* was built by ship's carpenters for Captain John H Geiger, whose family lived here for about 120 years. In 1958 it became Key West's first restored building and was named after John James Audubon, who painted in the garden in 1832 before the house had been built.

Take a free, self-guided, half-hour tour with narration supplied courtesy of a CD player. The rooms are furnished with authentic 19th-century Key West furniture and many Audubon lithographs. The tropical gardens are especially nice, rife with birds of paradise, star-fruit trees, fishtail ferns and palms, hibiscus and jasmine.

Mel Fisher Maritime Museum

This fascinating museum (☎ *305-294-2633,* W *www.melfisher.org, 200 Greene St; admission $7.50/3.75 adult/child 6-12 yrs; open 9:30am-5pm daily)* exhibits the rich 17th-century galleon treasures of Spain's Santa Margarita and the Atocha, discovered by the late Mel Fisher in 1980–85 (he started his galleon search in 1969). Various jewels, tools, coins and navigational pieces are displayed on the ground floor, along with a world map showing shipping routes that the boats took. The 2nd floor features a slave ship and interesting changing exhibits. Mel, whose motto was 'Today's the day,' took walks through the museum until just months before he died in 1998.

Little White House

President Harry S Truman's former vacation house (☎ *305-294-9911, 111 Front St; admission $10/5 adult/child 5-12 yrs; open 9am-5pm daily),* with restful, lush and lovely grounds, is open only for guided tours. You'll see Truman's piano, lots of original furnishings and a 15-minute video about Truman's life. The knowledgeable guides rattle out trivia and fun facts for everyone from children to serious history buffs. It's located in the Harry S Truman Annex (in which you can wander around by yourself).

East Martello Tower

This Civil War citadel (☎ *305-296-3913, 3501 S Roosevelt Blvd; admission $6/4/2 adult/ senior/child; open 9:30am-4:30pm daily),* across from Key West Airport, houses a gallery with local artwork and an interesting Key West history museum. Diehards can climb the central tower to a watchtower with horrible airport views and unimpressive beach views. Metal sculptures, originally stored within the tower for lack of space elsewhere, have turned into an attraction in and of themselves.

Fort Zachary Taylor State Historic Site

Fort Zachary Taylor (☎ *305-292-6713; admission $2.50 for one person in a car, $5 for two, plus 50¢ for each additional person in a car, $1.50 per pedestrian; open 8am-sunset daily)*, at the southwestern end of the island, operated from 1845 to 1866 and defended against blockade-running Union ships during the Civil War. Today the state historic site and park has showers, picnic tables, a very good beach and the deepest, clearest water on the island – it's great for swimming. Ranger-led tours depart at noon and 2pm.

ACTIVITIES
Beaches

All three city beaches on the southern side of the island are narrow, with calm and clear water. **South Beach** is at the end of Simonton St. **Higgs Beach**, at the end of Reynolds St and Casa Marina Court, has barbecue grills, picnic tables and a long wooden pier that draws gay sunbathers. **Smathers Beach**, farther east off S Roosevelt Blvd, is more popular with jet skiers, parasailers, teens and college students. Don't forget Key West's best beach, at Fort Zachary Taylor (see above), favored by gay locals.

Diving & Snorkeling

Dive opportunities aren't as plentiful as elsewhere in the Keys, but they are definitely here. Because of pollution and activity, there's no snorkeling to speak of on Key West beaches. Most dive companies take you west, to sites including Cottrell, Barracuda, Boca Grande, Woman, Sand, Rock and Marquesas Keys. At some dive sites – especially around the Marquesas – nondivers can go along and snorkel. Don't touch the coral.

The best opportunities for diving (and the skill levels required to dive them) include the following:

Cayman Salvage Master (advanced) – 67 to 90 feet; a coral- and plant-covered fish farm

Eastern Dry Rocks (beginner) – 20 to 25 feet; there's snorkeling here, too

Joe's Tug (intermediate) – a submerged tugboat, at a depth of about 65 feet

Western Dry Rocks (beginner) – massive coral and mounds of brain

Dive companies set up at kiosks around Mallory Square and other places in town, notably the corner of Truman and Duval Sts. Shop around carefully as prices vary greatly. Check these well-established places: **Subtropic Dive Center** (☎ *305-296-9914, 800-853-3483, 1605 N Roosevelt Blvd)* and **Dive Key West** (☎ *305-296-3823, 800-426-0707, 3128 N Roosevelt Blvd)*.

ORGANIZED TOURS

Old Town Trolley Tours (☎ *305-296-6688; tours $20/10 adult/child 4-12 yrs)* runs 90-minute narrated tram tours starting at Mallory Square and making a large, lazy circle around the whole city (both the old and new town), with nine stops along the way. You can get on and off, going in the same direction, as often as you want for one rotation. Trolleys depart every 15 to 30 minutes from 9am to 4:30pm daily. Narration is hokey and touristy, but you'll get a good overview of Key West, its history and gossipy dirt about local issues and people in the news.

PLACES TO STAY

Key West is packed with rooms, but picking the right one takes some forethought.

Camping

There's a $20 difference between staying right in town as opposed to just outside of town.

Boyd's Key West Campground (☎ *305-294-1465, 6401 Maloney Ave)* Sites $35/41 non-waterfront/waterfront off-season, $41/48 mid-Nov–mid-Apr; water and electricity $10. Just outside town on Stock Island (turn south at MM 5), Boyd's has upwards of 300 sites. There's a bus stop for downtown practically at their front door.

Jabour's Camp & Lodge (☎ *305-294-5723, 223 Elizabeth St)* Sites $46 off-season, $60 mid-Dec–mid-Apr, 4- to 6-person motor homes $57 off-season, $75 winter. The only campground actually in Key West is near Key West Bight.

Hostels
Key West Youth Hostel & SeaShell Motel (☎ 305-296-5719, W www.keywesthostel.com, 718 South St). Dorms $19.50/22.50 members/nonmembers, motel rooms $75 off-season, $110-150 Dec–mid-Apr. At the cheapest place in town, rates include sheets and use of the communal kitchen, but the hostel also sells cheap breakfasts and dinners. Alcohol is prohibited. Since a taxi between here and the main Greyhound station costs $7 per person, you'd be better off getting off at the downtown Key West stop (at Caroline and Grinnell Sts) and then calling a taxi for about $4 per carload.

Motels & Hotels
Chain hotels include **Courtyard By Marriott** (☎ 305-294-5541, 3420 N Roosevelt Blvd); **Best Western Hibiscus** (☎ 305-294-3763, 1313 Simonton St at United St); **Days Inn** (☎ 305-294-3742, 3852 N Roosevelt Blvd), one of the cheapest places in town; **Radisson** (☎ 305-294-5511, 3820 N Roosevelt Blvd); and **Holiday Inn La Concha** (☎ 305-296-2991, 430 Duval St).

Pegasus Hotel (☎ 305-294-9323, fax 305-294-4741, W www.pegasuskeywest.com, 501 Southard St) Rooms $95-129 off-season, $139-199 late Dec–late Apr. Well situated, clean and friendly, this hotel has 25 guest rooms, and the added benefit of a nice rooftop pool, deck, Jacuzzi and limited free parking.

Wyndham Casa Marina Resort & Beach House (☎ 305-296-3535, 800-949-3426, fax 305-296-4633, W www.wyndham.com, 1500 Reynolds St) Rooms $169-359 off-season, $169-409 late Dec–Mar, suites more. Next to Higgs Beach, this first-rate 311-room resort was built in the 1920s by railroad magnate Henry Flager. Of course he chose the prime location; the present-day resort has the Key West's largest private beach. Look for three oceanside pools, every recreational pursuit imaginable, a kid's program, daily activities and plenty of dining and entertainment,

choices. Guest rooms and suites have private balconies or terraces.

B&Bs
Unless otherwise noted, a Continental breakfast is included in the rates; it's usually served pool or gardenside.

The Mermaid & The Alligator (☎ 305-294-1894, 800-773-1894, fax 305-295-9925, W www.kwmermaid.com, 729 Truman Ave) Rooms $88-168 off-season, $118-228 late Dec–Apr. Casually elegant, this early-20th-century Victorian house has nine individually decorated rooms, lots of character, off-street parking, full breakfast, complimentary evening wine and a small pool surrounded by tropical plantings and a charming brick patio. It's a very good choice.

Chelsea House (☎ 305-296-2211, 800-845-8859, fax 305-296-4822, W www.chelseahousekw.com, 707 Truman Ave) Rooms $79-190 off-season, $160-255 late Dec–Apr. With an atmosphere more akin to a college dorm than a traditional Victorian mansion, this 1870 house defies a 'gay' or 'straight' categorization. The majority of guests on any given day may be gay or straight – the Chelsea House welcomes all at this 18-room complex. Rooms have TV, air conditioning, fridge and bath. There's a clothing-optional sundeck, paperback library, free parking and brick paths that lead to a small pool and tropical garden.

Wicker Guesthouse (☎ 305-296-4275, 800-880-4275, fax 305-294-7240, W www.wickerhousekw.com, 913 Duval St) Rooms $85-98 off-season, $130-150 mid-Dec–May, studios & suites $105-135 off-season, $185-235 winter. Despite a location in the middle of everything, this modern 18-unit guest house complex has a secluded garden, nice pool and off-street parking. Wicker and wood furnishings abound. While some rooms have a kitchenette, there's also a shared kitchen. Rates for two-bedroom suites include four people.

Merlinn Inn (☎ 305-296-3336, 800-642-4753, fax 305-296-3524, W www.merlinnkeywest.com, 811 Simonton St) Rooms $89-109 off-season, $135-169 late Dec–mid-Apr, suites & cottages $119-225 off-season, $169-300 late Dec–mid-Apr. Set in a secluded garden with a pool and elevated wooden walkways, this 20-room B&B boasts airy, light and very tidy guest rooms. Everything is made from bamboo, rattan and wood; many rooms have high ceilings or exposed rafters.

Frances St Bottle Inn (☎ *305-294-8530, 800-294-8530, fax 305-294-1628,* **w** *www .bottleinn.com, 535 Frances St)* Rooms $80-135 off-season, $139-169 mid-Dec–Apr. Gay-friendly and with a welcoming staff, this small inn has eight updated rooms, very tidy and clean bathrooms, a two-story verandah and a small patio with hot tub. Cheaper rooms have a shared bath across the hall. Rental bikes are available.

Conch House Heritage Inn (☎ *305-293-0020, fax 305-293-8447,* **w** *www.conch house.com, 625 Truman Ave)* Rooms $98-168 off-season, $148-228 Jan-Apr. Built in 1875 and family-owned since 1889, this six-room place with a small pool is very clean and nice. While the inn is gay- and lesbian-friendly, kids under 12 are a bit iffy.

La Pensione (☎ *305-292-9923, fax 305-296-6509,* **w** *www.lapensione.com, 809 Truman Ave)* Rooms $108-138 off-season, $168 Jan–mid-May. A very good value for

Gay Accommodations in Key West

Again, unless otherwise noted, a Continental breakfast is included in the rates; it's usually served pool or gardenside.

Pearl's Rainbow (☎ *305-292-1450, 800-749-6696,* **w** *www.pearlsrainbow.com, 525 United St)* Rooms & suites $69-199 off-season, $109-249 mid-Dec–Apr. Key West's only women-only place (gay or straight) is welcoming and well-maintained. The 38 rooms range from small third-floor cubbies to deluxe poolside suites with balconies. In addition to a popular bar (see the Entertainment section, later in this chapter), look for two sun/shade decks, two pools and two hot tubs. Double the fun, eh?

Atlantic Shores Resort (☎ *305-296-2491, 800-526-3559, fax 305-294-2753,* **w** *www .atlanticshoresresort.com, 510 South St)* Rooms $80-145 off-season, $110-250 Jan–late Apr. Defying a sexual-orientation categorization, all are welcome at this clean, motelish, faux–art-decoish place. It boasts a clothing-optional pool, popular tea dances (see the Entertainment section, later in this chapter) and an adjacent liquor store, which pretty much sums up the emphasis at this resort. No breakfast here, folks.

Marrero's (☎ *305-294-6977, 800-459-6212, fax 305-292-9030,* **w** *www.marreros.com, 410 Fleming St)* Rooms $90-170 off-season, $120-210 mid-Dec–Apr. This late-19th-century mansion, once owned by a prominent cigar manufacturer, has 13 rooms and suites. All are decorated quite differently, but you can expect high ceilings, antiques, wood floors and modern amenities like refrigerators and phones. Two verandahs and a large pool (clothing-optional area) are nice.

Curry House (☎ *305-294-6777, 800-633-7439, fax 305-294-5322, 806 Fleming St)* Rooms $85-140 off-season, $140-190 mid-Dec–Apr. Key West's oldest exclusively gay male guest house is housed in a 100-year-old, Victorian-style, three-story mansion. Two of the nine rooms have shared bath. Rates include a full hot breakfast and daily happy hour; there's a clothing-optional pool and Jacuzzi.

Big Rubys Guesthouse (☎ *305-296-2323, 800-477-7829, fax 305-296-0281,* **w** *www .bigrubys.com, 409 Appelrouth Lane)* Rooms $85-187 off-season, $145-255 mid-Dec–Mar. Upscale and sleek, in an *Architectural Digest* sort of way, this impeccable 17-room complex has a lagoon pool area with elegant decking and tropical palms, luxuriously full breakfasts, fine linens and lots of privacy. Low-key luxe sums it up.

the price, this elegant 1891 revival mansion has nine well-kept rooms and a friendly staff. A very full breakfast buffet taken on the verandah or in the communal dining room will stand you in good stead, as will the pool and off-street parking.

Andrews Inn (☎ *305-294-7730, fax 305-294-0021,* Ⓦ *www.andrewsinn.com, Zero Whalton Lane)* Rooms $115-149 off-season, $169-189 late Dec–Apr. Draws include a tranquil backyard, small pool, friendly hosts, lots of cats and a tropical feel; some of the six wicker-filled rooms have decks. Evening cocktails are included for inn guests.

The Gardens Hotel (☎ *305-294-2661, 800-526-2664, fax 305-292-1007,* Ⓦ *www.gardens hotel.com, 526 Angela St)* Rooms $155-285 off-season, $265-355 mid-Dec–Apr, suites at least $100 more. Occupying almost an entire city block, this walled, private and chichi enclave was formerly Key West's largest private residence. It boasts botanical-garden–quality grounds, a kidney-shaped pool and plantation-style houses. The 17 guest rooms are romantic, elegantly furnished, understated with floral motifs and filled with indulgent amenities. A full breakfast is included.

PLACES TO EAT

Even though Key West cuisine often takes a backseat to drinking, you'll find more than a few culinary delights here. Most restaurants offer reliably good food, fresh seafood and decent portions. Interestingly, a good percentage of that 'local' seafood comes from somewhere other than the Keys.

Budget

Java Lounge (☎ *305-296-7877, cnr Greene & Elizabeth Sts)* Referring to it as a lounge is a stretch; it's only big enough for a few patrons to order at a time. Still, for strong espresso and sweet treats, make a beeline here.

Waterfront Market (☎ *305-296-0778, 201 William St)* Open 7am-6pm Sat-Thur, 7am-8pm Fri. Not simply a breakfast place, this market has bagels, coffee, sandwiches, organic produce, health foods, wine, beer and a juice bar. The dockside entrance doors open before the front entrance.

BO's Fish Wagon (☎ *305-294-9272, 801 Caroline St)* Dishes $8-10. Open 11am-8pm Mon-Sat, 11am-5pm Sun. For fried fish, catch of the day, grilled sandwiches and a cool atmosphere, BO's is your place.

Mid-Range

The Deli Restaurant (☎ *305-294-1464, 531 Truman Ave)* Lunch $5-10, dinner mains $7-20. Open 7:30am-10pm daily. For friendly service and well-prepared 'comfort food' head to this biscuit-and-cornbread sort of place. A local hangout, operated by the same family since 1950, it serves killer breakfasts, filling seafood dishes and meatloaf. Vegetarians can pile on side dishes like mashed potatoes, rice and beans, zucchini, carrots and other veggies.

Camille's (☎ *305-296-4811, 1202 Simonton St)* Breakfast $3-7, lunch $6-12, dinner $14-25. Open 8am-3pm, 4pm-10:30pm daily. An island fave since forever, Camille's is packed all day because of good, friendly service and creative dishes. Breakfast is particularly renowned; lunchtime salads are refreshing; dinner specials are always fresh. During the afternoon happy hour (4pm to 6pm daily) you can only get light fare like burgers and sandwiches.

PT's Late Night (☎ *305-296-4245, 920 Caroline St)* Lunch $7-9, dinner mains $9-16. Open 11am-3am daily. When they say late night, they mean it, eh? When you're finished drinking and have worked up a good appetite, PT's serves hearty portions of diner fare, salads and nachos. As much sports bar as eatery, burger aficionados will nonetheless be quite pleased.

El Siboney (☎ *305-296-4184, 900 Catherine St)* Dishes $5-13. Open 11am-9:30pm Mon-Sat. Sure, authentic Cuban cuisine can be found in Miami's Little Havana, but in Key West? Yup. Ignore the unstylish environs to dine on large portions, with locals, at this family-style place. Catch some Old Key West flavor while it's still here.

Turtle Kraals Restaurant & Bar (☎ *305-294-2640, 1 Land's End Village)* Lunch dishes $6-11, dinner mains $10-18. Open 11am-10:30pm Mon-Fri, noon-11pm Sat &

Sun. A rustic marina-front eatery housed in an open-air warehouse, Turtle Kraals specializes in fish prepared with a Cuban-Caribbean-Southwestern twist. It's popular with locals as well as tourists. Try the excellent mango crab cakes with fried plantains, mojo grilled shrimp or lobster chili rellenos. Lunch is more simple, with, perhaps, a char-grilled fish sandwich.

Kelly's (☎ 305-293-8484, 301 Whitehead St) Lunch dishes $6-11, dinner mains $12-23. Open noon-4pm & 5pm-10pm daily. Kelly's is a cool bar and grill owned by actress Kelly McGillis (who sometimes works here). The restaurant is housed in the former home of Pan American Airways. The first Pan Am flight (001) departed to Havana, Cuba, from here on October 27, 1927. It has prime outdoor tables, its own brewery, decent lunch specials, a raw bar and a tapas-style menu. Yeah, it's a bit touristy, but it'll admirably satisfy most everyone.

Pepe's Cafe (☎ 305-294-7192, 806 Caroline St) Lunch dishes under $10, dinner mains $17-20. Open 6:30am-10:30pm daily. Key West's oldest restaurant dates back to 1909. It's a rustic institution with a great local's bar and outdoor patio – perfect for margaritas made with fresh-squeezed lime juice. As for the food, the barbecue specials on Sunday night are primo, as are the oysters, burgers and steaks. Lunch revolves around soups, sandwiches, chili and conch chowder. The breakfasts are huge.

Top End
Consistency tops the attributes of these fine places.

Mangoes (☎ 305-292-4606, 700 Duval St) Lunch mains $8-15, dinner mains $15-30. Open 11am-3:30pm & 5:30pm-11pm daily. At first glance, you might expect the brick patio on Duval to be Mangoes' best feature; it could probably get away with it. But Mangoes is far better than that. It delivers upscale, creative Florida cooking with a sprinkling of Caribbean influence. The wood-fired pizzas served at dinner are very good, too.

Alice's (☎ 305-296-6706, 1125 Duval St) Mains $20-27. Open 6pm-11pm daily. Chef-owned Alice's restaurant wins rave reviews hand over fist for its creative, eclectic menu. Patrons have been singing her praises for years and follow her to the ends of the earth (ie, around Key West). You will too.

Louie's Backyard (☎ 305-294-1061, 700 Waddell Ave) Lunch mains average $15, dinner $30. Open 11:30am-3:30pm & 6pm-10:30pm daily. Started by a Conch in his house, Louie's is one of Key West's most popular places, as much for its romantic location, location, location as its excellent and highly creative Caribbean-American cuisine. In fact, the setting is as much a feast for the eyes as the seafood is for the stomach. If your wallet can't take it, though, at least have a drink at the waterfront bar (it closes at 2am). You'll remember it for years.

Cafe des Artistes (☎ 305-294-7100, 1007 Simonton St) Mains $25-35. Open 6pm-9pm daily. Tired of seafood, however flawlessly prepared, in rustic surroundings? A treat for serious foodies, this longtime nouveau French restaurant is arguably the best in Key West. Daily specials are always creative and often tropically influenced; perhaps you'll find sautéed yellowtail snapper with shrimp and scallops or raspberry duckling. With a little luck, you'll snag a table on the rooftop deck.

ENTERTAINMENT
Bars & Live Music
Drinking is a Key West institution with a long and illustrious history of lushes, from rumrunners (the people, not the drink) to Hemingway. And the tradition is immortalized in Jimmy Buffet's song 'Margaritaville.' Spring break (mid-March) is a big deal here. Pub crawls are another institution, but bar owners freaked out when police enforced the open-container laws hindering customers from walking between bars carrying drinks. Enforcement isn't as gung-ho now, but it is illegal to walk with an open container holding an alcoholic drink – even if it's a plastic cup.

Most bars have live music most nights; happy hours and drink specials happen all the time. Bars stay open until people leave, at least until 2am and sometimes later.

The following watering holes are the most legendary.

Sloppy Joe's Bar (☎ *305-294-5717, 201 Duval St)* The Hemingway hangout of record, since 1937, has live entertainment nightly. Their Hemingway Hammer is made from 151-proof rum, banana and strawberry liqueur, blackberry brandy and a dash of white rum.

Margaritaville Café (☎ *305-292-1435, 500 Duval St)* Jimmy Buffet's very touristy place mixes its requisite namesake drink (there are better elsewhere), serves the requisite 'cheeseburgers in paradise' (there are better elsewhere) and puts on nightly bands. But, hey, Parrotheads will be Parrotheads.

Schooner Wharf Bar (☎ *305-292-9520, 202 William St)* With a fairly authentic 'sailor's bar' feeling, this real Conch hangout is great for waterside-sunset or post-cruise drinks. Local musicians – playing everything from banjos to reggae – perform nightly.

Rick's/Durty Harry's (☎ *305-296-4890, 202–8 Duval St)* This joint has nine bars and nightly live music that draws faithful tourists. People really like this meat market, and not just for their Wednesday and Thursday night specials: For $7 (low season) or $10 (high season) you get a wrist band allowing you to drink all you can from 9pm to 11:30pm (bring your ID). If you can maneuver the stairs, **Upstairs at Rick's** has dancing.

Captain Tony's Saloon (☎ *305-294-1838, 428 Greene St)* This old-fashioned saloon features live music almost daily and nightly.

Green Parrot (☎ *305-294-6133, 601 Whitehead St)* Open to the street, this locals' bar has been pickling its patron's livers with booze since 1890. Yup, this is what Key West is all about.

Gay & Lesbian Venues

The 'straight,' serious-drinking and partying section of town runs from Mallory Square to the 500 block of Duval St. From then on, it's a healthy mix of straight and gay. Gay and lesbian bars change as quickly as they do in Miami's South Beach, so ask around when you arrive. Check the Key West Business Guild's map and *Key West Columbia*

Fun Map, available at local gay-friendly businesses.

Atlantic Shores Resort (☎ *305-296-2491, 510 South St)* This popular local spot for men and women and au naturel sunning has a small snack bar, grill, pool, beach and Key West's largest tea dance on Sunday (7pm to 11pm). It's so popular that they added one on Wednesday, too (6pm to 10pm). And don't forget their Thursday night outdoor movies.

Bourbon St Pub (*no* ☎, *724 Duval St)* With three bars, this place dishes hot dancing, nightly videos and good 2nd-floor people-watching down onto Duval St.

801 Bourbon Bar (*no* ☎, *801 Duval St)* This great hangout has three bars, the island's longest happy hour (from noon to 8pm daily) and nightly drag and cabaret shows (11pm).

La Te Da (☎ *305-296-6706, 1125 Duval St)* Locals head over for the happy hour, live entertainment Thursday to Sunday and a few different bars.

Pearl's Rainbow (☎ *305-292-1450, 525 United St)* This outdoor patio bar, within a guest house, is Key West's only women-only bar.

SHOPPING

There is so much tourist stuff that you won't be able to avoid it. But hidden among the crud and T-shirt shops are some much cooler galleries and shops, including **Helio Gallery** (☎ *305-294-7901, 814 Fleming St)*, **Haitian Art Co** (☎ *305-296-8932, 600 Frances St)*, **Key West Lime Shoppe** (☎ *800-376-0806, cnr Greene & Elizabeth Sts)*, **Pandemonium** (☎ *305-294-0351, 825 Duval St)*, **Key West Cigar Factory** (☎ *305-294-3470, 306 Front St)* and **Key West Aloe** (☎ *305-294-5592, 524 Front St)*. You might want to procure a pair of Kino sandals, the classic Key West footwear. These Naugahyde sandals are slippery when wet, but they're cheap. If they ever break, bring them in and they'll be repaired.

GETTING THERE & AWAY
Air

Key West International Airport (EYW) is off S Roosevelt Blvd on the west side of the island. Expect to spend $150 to $180 for a roundtrip flight between Miami and Key West. With a little luck and good timing, you can get a direct, roundtrip flight between New York City and Key West for as low as $300. Flights from LA ($350 in summer, $575 in winter) and San Francisco ($400 year-round) usually have to stop in Tampa, Orlando or Miami first.

American Airlines (☎ 800-433-7300) and US Airways (☎ 800-428-4322) all have several flights a day. Cape Air (☎ 305-352-0714, 800-352-0714, w www.flycapeair.com) flies between Key West and Naples ($109/160-200 one-way/roundtrip), Fort Myers ($118/180-230) and Fort Lauderdale ($129/170-230).

Bus

Based at the Key West Airport, Greyhound (☎ 305-296-9072, w www.greyhound.com), 3535 S Roosevelt Blvd, has four buses daily between Key West and downtown Miami. Buses leave Key West at 6am (arriving at 10:55am), 8:45am (arriving 1:40pm), 11:30am (arriving 4:25pm) and 5:45pm (arriving 10:40pm). Fares are $32.25 weekdays, a tad more on weekends.

Car & Motorcycle

The 160 miles (3½ hours) from Miami to Key West along US Hwy 1 is as much the journey as the destination. Seriously. Take Florida's Turnpike Extension (toll) south and then pick up US Hwy 1 south at Florida City. Don't be in a hurry; enjoy the views. Besides, there are keenly enforced speed limits, high speeding fines, and you might hit a Key deer while speeding (see National Key Deer Refuge in the Lower Keys section of the Keys chapter).

GETTING AROUND

A city bus (75¢) runs between the airport and Duval and Caroline Sts every 40 minutes or so; take the blue route into Old Town. A taxi from the airport to the city will cost about $7.

The City Transit System (☎ 305-292-8160. w www.keywestcity.com) has six color-coded bus routes. Depending on the route,

buses run every 15 minutes or so, from about 6:30am to 10pm. Printed schedules are available on the bus and from the Web site, under transportation. The fare is 75¢ for adults, 35¢ for seniors.

The best thing to do with a car in Key West is to sell it: Parking is tough, the city is quick to ticket and tow, and traffic is restricted. Look for the main public parking garage at Caroline and Grinnell Sts ($1.25 hourly/$8 daily).

You don't need a license to rent a moped or scooter; prices average $18 a day (9am to 5pm or 6pm) or $25 for 24 hours. Try Keys Mopeds & Scooters (☎ 305-294-0399), 523 Truman Ave, or Moped Hospital (☎ 305-296-3344), 601 Truman Ave.

Bicycle rentals are also available many places, where prices average $10 daily, but the Key West Youth Hostel rents them for a bit less ($6 daily, $8 for 24 hours).

Dry Tortugas National Park

The Dry Tortugas (tor-**too**-guzz), a tiny archipelago of seven islands about 69 miles southwest of Key West, was first 'developed' 300 years after its discovery by Juan Ponce de León. He named Las Tortugas – 'The Turtles' – for the hawksbill, green, leatherback and loggerhead sea turtles that roam the islands. Sailors later changed it to Dry Tortugas since there was no freshwater here. Today it's a national park under the control of the Everglades National Park office (☎ 305-242-7700, w www.nps.gov/drto). You can only reach it by boat or plane.

Since the island was surrounded by rocky shoals, the first item of business was to build a lighthouse at **Garden Key**. When the US saw a need to protect and control the traffic flowing into the Gulf of Mexico, they began constructing **Fort Jefferson** in 1846. A federal garrison during the Civil War, Fort Jefferson was also a prison for Union deserters and for at least four people, among them Dr Samuel Mudd, arrested for complicity in the assassination of Abraham

Green sea turtle

Lincoln. In 1867, a yellow fever outbreak killed 38 people, and after a hurricane in 1873, the fort was abandoned. It reopened in 1886 as a quarantine station for smallpox and cholera victims. It was declared a national monument in 1935 by President Roosevelt, then in 1992, President George Bush Sr upped its status to a national park.

The park is open for day trips and overnight camping, which provides a rare perspective, so close to the hubbub of Key West and yet so blissfully removed and peaceful. The sparkling waters offer excellent **snorkeling and diving** opportunities. A visitor's center is located within the fascinating Fort Jefferson.

PLACES TO STAY & EAT
Garden Key has 13 *campsites* ($3 per person, per night) given out on a first-come, first-served basis. Reserve early by calling the Everglades National Park office (☎ 305-242-7700, Ⓦ www.nps.gov/drto). There are toilets, but no freshwater showers or drinking water; bring everything you'll need.

Since there is no freshwater, mosquitoes will not mar your trip. Even no-see-ums, tiny biting flies, are kept at bay most of the time; they only come out for about 15 minutes prior to sunset.

As for *food*, most of the time you'll find Cuban-American fishing boats trolling the waters. They'll happily trade for lobster, crab and shrimp; you'll have the most leverage trading beverages. Just paddle up to them and start bargaining for your supper. In March and April, there is stupendous bird-watching, including aerial fighting. Star-gazing is mind-blowing any time of the year.

GETTING THERE & AWAY
If you have your own boat, the Dry Tortugas are covered under National Ocean Survey chart No 11438.

Otherwise, the experienced and knowledgeable crew of the *Yankee Freedom II* (☎ 305-294-7009, 800-634-0939, Ⓦ www.yankeefleet.com) operates a fast ferry between Garden Key and the Key West Seaport (at the northern end of Margaret St). Roundtrip fare costs $109/99/69 adult/senior/child under 16 yrs. For an overnight drop-off (including gear), the cost is $130/99 adult/child. Board at the marina at 7:30am (the ferry leaves at 8am), and return at 5:30pm. Reservations are recommended. Continental breakfast, a picnic lunch, snorkeling gear and a 45-minute tour of the fort are all included.

If you don't have gear, the extraordinarily excellent folks at Dry Tortugas Kayak Outfitters (☎ 305-296-3009) will rent you first-rate kayaks and sometimes tents, coolers, grills and the like. Prices depend on how much gear you need.

Seaplanes of Key West (☎ 305-294-0709, Ⓦ www.seaplanesofkeywest.com) can take up to 10 passengers (flight time 40 minutes each way). A four-hour trip costs $179/129 adult/child under 12 yrs, an eight-hour trip $305/225. They'll also fly you out to camp for $329/235 per person, including snorkeling equipment; reserve at least a week in advance.

The Keys

The string of islands south of Miami have fascinated visitors beginning with the Spanish explorers of the early 16th century. But while divers and fisherfolk will have a great time here, the Florida Keys aren't exactly a romantic, untouched and steamy paradise (unless you have some cash to spare). If, however, you gear your expectations realistically, and take the time to unearth its treasures, there is an alluring, quirky and, yes, even sultry side to the Keys. Just bring the bug repellent and some cash.

Outside Key West you'll drive many miles between places of interest, but mostly you'll see innumerable islands and unbroken blue sky and ocean. And don't forget Key lime pie and conch chowder; when they're good, they *are* delightful.

Orientation

Hundreds of tiny islands, about 45 of which are populated, are strung from northeast to southwest and connected by US Hwy 1. Also called the Overseas Highway, US Hwy 1 is a combination of highways and causeways built on the foundations of the FEC Railway, which was destroyed in 1935. It's the main road through the Keys. In many areas it's the only road.

Diving & Snorkeling

Diving and snorkeling opportunities are outstanding – from natural coral reefs with fantastically colorful fish, to artificial reefs created by sunken boats and planes that attract sea life, to actual wrecked ships on the ocean floor. The reefs, which are fragile living entities that can be severely damaged by the slightest touch, are all about 5 miles offshore.

There are dive shops on every corner; we include ones recommended in Lonely Planet's Pisces Book *Diving & Snorkeling Florida Keys.*

Getting There & Around

Air Marathon Airport (☎ 305-743-2155) is the Keys' only commercial airport outside of Key West, but it's expensive to fly here, so most people make the two-hour drive from Miami.

Bus In essence, Greyhound (☎ 305-296-9072, w www.greyhound.com) serves all Key destinations along US Hwy 1. Buses depart downtown Miami for the Keys and Key West at 6:30am, 12:30pm, 4pm and 7pm. There are official stops with signs, but just tell the driver where you want to get off and they'll stop. Once you're on the Keys, just stand anywhere on the Overseas Highway (US Hwy 1) and when you see the bus in the distance, signal firmly and visibly, using all methods at your disposal – and the bus will stop to pick you up...if the driver sees you. To be really safe, ask Greyhound about the official stops.

Car & Motorcycle By car, there are two options: From Miami take I-95 south to US Hwy 1 and follow that until you can't go any farther – that'd be Key West. A shorter route is Florida's Turnpike Extension (toll) south to US Hwy 1 south from Florida City. Most of the route is just two lanes, often with a center turning lane, so traffic can crawl and dart in and out. Be patient.

Unless you're staying in one place the entire time, you'll need wheels to get around. There's no public transportation, and distances are too far to make bicycling a real option for anyone except experienced riders. You can rent bicycles in most larger Keys. Most major car rental companies have offices in Marathon and Key Largo.

Upper Keys

The Upper Keys stretch from Key Largo south to Long Key. Most visitors head down US Hwy 1 from Florida City, but you could also take the less trafficked FL 997 to FL 905 (toll $1), which passes the very colorful

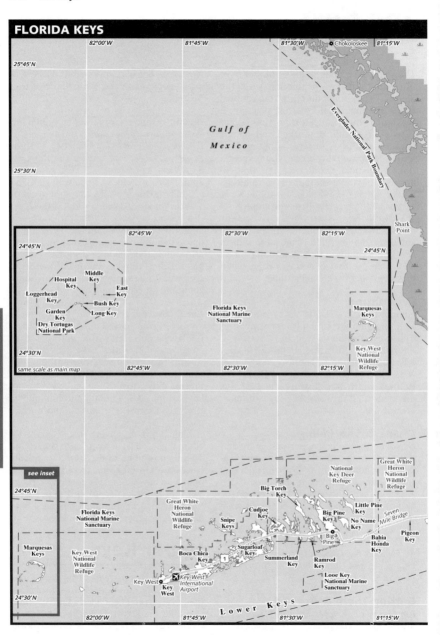

FLORIDA KEYS

82°00'W 81°45'W 81°30'W ◦ Chokoloskee 81°15'W

25°45'N

Everglades National Park Boundary

Gulf of

Mexico

25°30'N

Shark
Point

24°45'N 82°45'W 82°30'W 82°15'W 24°45'N

Middle
Key
Hospital East
Key Key
Loggerhead Bush Key
Key Florida Keys Marquesas
Garden Long Key National Marine Keys
Key Sanctuary
Dry Tortugas
National Park Key West
National
Wildlife
24°30'N Refuge
same scale as main map 82°45'W 82°30'W 82°15'W

THE KEYS

see inset

24°45'N
National Great White
Key Deer Heron
Refuge National
Wildlife
Big Torch Refuge
Key
Florida Keys Great White Cudjoe Little Pine
National Marine Heron Key Big Pine Key Seven
Sanctuary National Snipe Key No Name Mile Bridge
Wildlife Keys Key
Refuge Big Pigeon
Pine Key
Marquesas Bahia
Keys Key West Sugarloaf Honda
National Boca Chica Key Key
Wildlife Key 1 Summerland Ramrod
Refuge Key Key Looe Key
National Marine
24°30'N Key West ◦ Key West Sanctuary
Key International
West Airport

L o w e r   K e y s

82°00'W 81°45'W 81°30'W 81°15'W

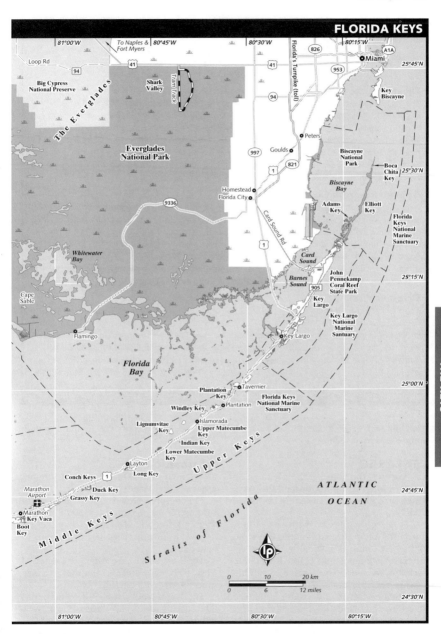

FLORIDA KEYS

Swimming with Dolphins

Experts say 'structured' programs – in which staff accompany swimmers in controlled areas for swims with dolphins that are accustomed to human contact – are safer and more humane than 'unstructured' ones. There are three swim-with-dolphins programs on the Keys.

Theater of the Sea

This Islamorada attraction (☎ 305-664-2431, ⓦ www.theaterofthesea.com, MM 84.5 bayside; admission $18/11 adult/child 3-12 yrs; open 9:30am-4pm daily) might look cheesy, but it's been here since 1946. Structured dolphin swims and sea lion programs include 30 minutes of instruction and 30 minutes of supervised swim. The swims ($135/95 for the dolphin/sea lion program) are by reservation only at 9:30am, noon and 2pm. They also run some other nice programs including continuous dolphin and sea lion shows; a marine exhibit with sharks, stingrays and tropical fish; a living shell exhibit; and a five-minute boat ride in their dolphin lagoon.

Dolphin Research Center

Near Marathon on Grassy Key, this open lagoon, nonprofit educational center (☎ 305-289-1121, ⓦ www.dolphins.org, MM 59 bayside; admission $15/12.50/10 adult/senior/child 4-12 yrs; open 9am-4pm daily) is dedicated to spreading understanding about dolphins. You can join a Dolphin Encounter program, in which you'll learn about and then swim with their dolphins for $135. Dolphin Splash programs, during which you'll stand on a submerged platform while a dolphin comes up to meet you, include 10 minutes in the water and 20 minutes spent preparing for it. General admission gets you into the center, where narrated demos are given every 30 minutes.

Dolphins Plus

This Key Largo center (☎ 305-451-1993, 866-860-7946; ⓦ www.dolphinsplus.com, off MM 99.5 bayside; admission $10/7 adult/child 7-17 yrs) specializes in recreational and educational unstructured swims. They expect you to already know a good deal before embarking upon the swim, even though a classroom session is included. Daily 30-minute natural swims ($100) are held at 9am and 1:45pm. Structured swims ($150), with a classroom session and hands-on interaction, are offered at 8:30am, 10:45am, 1pm and 3:15pm daily. It's tricky to find; call for specific directions.

Alabama Jack's (see Places to Eat & Drink in the Key Largo section).

KEY LARGO

Key Largo is the name of the island, at 33 miles the longest in the Keys, and the town, which stretches from about MM 106 to MM 97.

Key Largo is blessed with the largest concentration of dive sites in the Keys and its biggest allure is justifiably the underwater John Pennekamp Coral Reef State Park, the most accessible place to see the Florida reef. Divers will also love Jules' Undersea Lodge, an underwater hotel (see Places to Stay, later in this section). But then again, don't forget about Dolphins Plus (see the boxed text 'Swimming with Dolphins').

Information

Greyhound stops at the Key Largo Shopper grocery store, MM 99.6 oceanside.

The helpful Key Largo Chamber of Commerce (☎ 305-451-1414, 800-822-1088, ⓦ www.keylargo.org), MM 106 bayside, has area-wide information. It's open 9am to 6pm daily.

The Key Largo post office is located at MM 100 bayside. In Tavernier there's a post office at MM 91.5 bayside.

The Book Nook (☎ 305-451-1468), MM 99.6 oceanside, in Waldorf Plaza, sells nature, travel and Florida books.

Head to Mariner Hospital (☎ 305-852-4418), MM 91.5 bayside, in Tavernier, for health problems.

There are dozens of dive shops in Key Largo, most of which are located within Pennekamp Park (see below). Two others come recommended: **Silent World Dive Center** *(☎ 305-451-3252, 800-966-3483, MM 103.2 bayside)* and **Amoray Dive Resort** *(☎ 305-451-3595, 800-426-6729, MM 104.2 bayside)*.

John Pennekamp Coral Reef State Park

The first underwater park in the USA, Pennekamp *(☎ 305-451-1202, [W] www.pennekamppark.com, MM 102.5 oceanside; admission $4 per vehicle plus 50¢ per person or $2.50 for one person, $1.50 per pedestrian or cyclist; open 8am-sunset daily)* covers 75 sq miles of ocean containing living coral reef. It also has 170 acres of land with walking trails, including the Wild Tamarind Nature Trail, home to air plants, gumbo-limbo, wild bamboo, Jamaica dogwood, crabwood and, of course, wild tamarind.

Most importantly, the park's ranger-led programs and concession offer very convenient ways to experience the Florida reef. You can rent snorkeling or diving gear; take a glass-bottom boat, snorkeling or diving trip; or rent canoes and kayaks and explore a 3-mile network of canoe trails. And if you don't have the inclination to jump into the water, the **visitor's center** is billed as 'the reef you can walk out to.' You can't miss the 30,000-gallon aquarium showcasing living coral and tropical fish and plant life. But don't overlook the theater showing continuous nature videos. The park offers great ranger-led programs, including nature walks through mangrove and hardwood hammocks, a campfire program, and a lecture series discussing a range of environmental subjects, from crocodiles and raising bananas to native versus non-native vegetation.

Diving & Snorkeling Rangers and folks at the **scuba concession** *(☎ 305-451-6322)* are very helpful, and will assist you in planning specific trips. You can rent a full scuba outfit – mask, two tanks, regulator, BC and weight belt – for $38 a day. Four-hour, two-dive trips leave at 9:30am and 1:30pm and cost $41. They also offer certification in resort ($160), advanced ($325) and open water ($450) diving.

The **snorkel concession** *(☎ 305-451-1621)* rents equipment for $7 a day. They also operate 2½-hour snorkeling tours at 9am, noon and 3pm; adults/children pay $26/21, $3 extra for equipment. Four-hour sailboat snorkeling trips leave at 9am and 1:30pm for $32/27, plus $3 for equipment rental.

Canoeing & Kayaking Well-marked, easy **canoe trails** through mangroves begin at the marina. Canoes and kayaks (singles $10 hourly, doubles $15) are available from the park concession (☎ 305-451-1621).

Glass-bottom–boat Tours This 2½-hour tour *(☎ 305-451-1621; cost $18/10 adult/child under 12 yrs; departures at 9:15am, 12:15pm & 3pm daily)* goes out to Molasses Reef (named for a wrecked Jamaican ship carrying sugarcane molasses), which extends from Fort Lauderdale through the Dry Tortugas. If this is your only chance to see the reef, you'll be amazed by brilliant colors, the abundance of soft and hard coral and the sheer variety of tropical fish, from stingrays and turtles to barracuda and angelfish.

Key Largo Undersea Park

This place is a trip. Within a sheltered natural mangrove lagoon, the park *(☎ 305-451-2353, [W] www.jul.com, MM 103.2 oceanside; office open 8am-4pm daily)* is home to Jules' Undersea Lodge, an underwater hotel (see Places to Stay, later) reached only by diving. The 50-by-20-foot steel and acrylic structure, permanently anchored 30 feet beneath the surface of the lagoon, originally served as an underwater research lab off the coast of Puerto Rico. The lab was home to aquanauts exploring the continental shelf.

You can stay at the hotel or visit it during the day (by reservation only). Divers can use their own tanks or rent equipment here (a one-tank dive is $34 to $45). If you want to enter the hotel, sign up for a three-hour mini-adventure ($60), which also gives access to its facilities and three breathing hookahs – 120-foot-long air hoses for tankless diving. The lodge also offers many specialty diving courses, like diver propulsion vehicles, underwater archaeology and photography.

Snorkelers can use the area for $15 including gear. It's not in a coral reef, but you will see some reef fish. You may get lucky and see some of their local snorkeling Elvises.

Places to Stay

Camping You'll have choices ranging from inexpensive undeveloped sites to pricey, highly developed places.

John Pennekamp Coral Reef State Park (☎ 305-451-1202, 800-326-3521 reservations, **W** www.reserveamerica.com, MM 102.5 bayside) Sites without/with electricity $19/21. These 47 non-waterfront sites, most of which have water, are always in demand. If you come by boat, overnight moorings on buoys cost $17.50, which includes use of the dump station and showers (call ☎ 305-451-6322).

Hotels & Resorts *Sunset Cove Resort* (☎ 305-451-0705, fax 305-451-5609, MM 99.5 bayside) Rooms & cottages $85-100, waterfront suites $130-140. You'll know you've arrived when you spot the kitschy oversized dino guarding this family-friendly place. This good value offers 20 tidy rooms (some with full kitchen), lots of barbecue grills, a beach area and free use of their canoes and paddleboats. Inquire about their more unusual accommodations, like the Airstream trailer and motor home.

Largo Lodge (☎ 305-451-0424, 800-468-4378, MM 102 bayside) Apartments $95 off-season, $115 Dec-Apr. These six hidden cottages, tucked into a lush setting, feature efficiency kitchens, a living-dining room combination and a bedroom with two queen-size beds. A private swimming cove has enough tables and chairs for relaxing.

Westin Beach Resort (☎ 305-852-5553, 800-826-1006, fax 305-852-5198, **W** www.westin.com, MM 97 bayside) Rooms $109-309 off-season, $169-379 late Dec–Apr. This

first-rate resort has 200 airy rooms with balconies, two main restaurants, nature trails, two pools, a bar with happy hour specials, a myriad of water sports, a white-sand beach and a kids' program. The least expensive rooms face the parking lot, but at least they're mini-suites.

Kona Kai Resort & Gallery (☎ 305-852-7200, 800-365-7829, fax 305-852-4629, **W** www.konakairesort.com, MM 97.8 bayside) Rooms $109-168 off-season, $212-268 mid-Dec–mid-Apr, suites $146-319 off-season, $257-421 mid-Dec–mid-Apr. This intimate and magical hideaway features 11 airy rooms and suites (with full kitchens), all warmly contemporary and newly renovated. There's plenty to do – from nothing on your private patio, to tennis, kayaking and paddleboating. A white-sand beach, dotted with palms and hammocks, is more tempting than the curvaceous pool. The gallery, where you check in, is first rate, too.

Jules' Undersea Lodge (☎ 305-451-2353, fax 305-451-4789, **W** www.jul.com, MM 103.2 oceanside, 51 Shoreland Dr) Permanently anchored 30 feet beneath the water's surface, Jules' Undersea Lodge can accommodate six guests. The first question on everyone's mind is: Is it safe? Well, it was designed for scientists who lived onboard it for long periods of time. Even if all the backup generators and systems failed, there would still be about 12 hours of breathing time inside the hotel. Staff members are on duty 24 hours a day. In addition to two fairly luxurious private guest rooms, there are two common rooms, including a fully stocked kitchen/dining room and a wet room with hot showers and gear storage. Telephones and an intercom connect guests with the surface.

Noncertified divers can also stay here, but you'll have to get a quick limited certificate ($75). There are several accommodation packages, all of which require a reservation. The cheapest costs $250 per person; check-in at 5pm, out at 9am. The 'luxury aquanaut' package costs $350 per person and includes dinner and breakfast; check-in at 1pm, out at 11am. The 'ultimate romantic getaway' package costs $1050 for two people – for that, you get the place all to yourselves, with flowers and caviar and other little extras. Guests must be at least 10 years old; smoking and alcohol are not permitted.

Places to Eat & Drink

Mrs Mac's Kitchen (☎ 305-451-3722, MM 99.4 bayside) Breakfast & lunch $4-5, dinner $6-12. Open 7:30am-9:30pm Mon-Sat. Serving home-style cooking by and for locals, this packed diner (plastered with license plates and beer cans) leans toward meat and potatoes, stuffed pita pockets, steak sandwiches, Cajun shrimp baskets and burgers. Each night's menu is also supplemented by themed specials like Mexican or Italian.

Crack'd Conch (☎ 305-451-0732, MM 105 bayside) Lunch $9-15, dinner mains $11-25. Open noon-10pm daily. This fun seafood restaurant, with over 100 types of beer, has lunchtime sandwiches like crab cakes with bacon and cheddar, or steamed shrimp in a basket. The dinnertime mixed seafood platter is an appetite buster and a wallet killer, but well worth it.

Alabama Jack's (no ☎, 58000 Card Sound Rd) Dishes $10-16. This funky joint, on the banks of a mangrove swamp on the back road between Florida City and Key Largo, is a trip. More bar than eatery, it attracts everyone from Harley Davidson and pickup drivers to boaters and rich folks in stretch limos. Seafood and conch fritters take center stage under the open-air awnings.

The Fish House (☎ 305-451-4665, MM 102.4 oceanside) Lunch dishes $8-13, dinner mains $15-22. Open 11:30am-10pm daily. An easy favorite and a good value, this friendly and fun place has a nice tiled bar, fish nets hanging from the ceiling and hundreds of little holiday lights enlivening the scene. All the restaurants down here boast that they sell fresh fish, but this place *really* delivers. The smoked fish is a worthy specialty! Then again, oysters and clams from the raw bar are primo, too. Then again, so is the seviche. Hmmmm.

ISLAMORADA

Islamorada (eye-luh-murr-**ah**-da) is located on Upper Matecumbe Key, but the whole area spans about 20 miles from Plantation Key south to Long Key. Home to some significant state historic sites and the fun Theater of the Sea (see the boxed text 'Swimming with Dolphins'), Islamorada is worth a stop simply for its good restaurants. It's also the self-proclaimed sportfishing capital of the world. The promoters just might be right about that.

Information

Greyhound stops at the Burger King at MM 82.5 oceanside.

Look for the Islamorada Chamber of Commerce (☎ 305-664-4503, 800-322-5397, **w** www.fla-keys.com), MM 82.5 bayside, in an old caboose. It's open 9am to 5pm Monday to Friday, 10am to 3pm Saturday and Sunday.

The post office is at MM 82.9 oceanside.

Area dive shops include **Holiday Isle Dive Shop** *(☎ 305-664-3483, 800-327-7070, MM 84.5 oceanside)* and **Lady Cyana Divers** *(☎ 305-664-8717, 800-221-8717, MM 85.9 bayside)*.

Lignumvitae Key State Botanical Site

Only accessible by boat, this site *(lignum-vite-ee; ☎ 305-664-2540)* encompasses a 280-acre island of virgin tropical forest. Bring mosquito repellent! The simple attraction is the Matheson House (1919), with its windmill and cistern. The forest features strangler fig, mastic, gumbo-limbo and poisonwood trees, as well as native lignum-vitae trees, known for their extremely hard wood.

On the island, 1¼-hour guided walking tours are given at 10am and 2pm Thursday to Monday, but you can only visit by boat. From Robbie's Marina (see later in this section), boats depart for the 15-minute trip ($15/10 adult/child) about 30 minutes prior to each tour; reservations are highly recommended.

Indian Key State Historic Site

Also accessible only by boat, this 23-acre historic island *(☎ 305-664-2540)* has an interesting history. In 1831, renegade wrecker Jacob Housman bought the island and opened his own wrecker station after falling out with Key West wreckers. Housman developed it into a thriving little city, complete with a warehouse, docks, streets, a hotel and about 40 to 50 permanent residents. By 1836 Indian Key was the seat of Dade County. But Housman eventually lost his wrecker's license and in 1840 he lost the entire island after an attack during the Second Seminole War.

There's not much here today – just foundation remains, some cisterns, Housman's grave and lots of plant life. But there are trails and an observation tower. Free 1½-hour ranger-led tours (Thursday to Monday at 9am and 1pm) detail the fascinating history, not just of the wrecking operation, but also of the island's geological and natural history. There's a catch, though: You need to have a boat or take a 10-minute shuttle ($15/10 adult/child) from Robbie's Marina (see below). Shuttles depart about 30 minutes before the tours begin. Show up early since the boat can hold only six people.

Robbie's Marina

Robbie's (☎ 305-664-9814, W www.robbies .com, MM 77.5 bayside; open 8am to 6pm) rents all sorts of boats. Rates for a 15-foot boat start at $70 for half a day and, depending on the boat size and number of people, rise briskly from there. You can also feed tarpon right from the dock here ($1 to $2 per bucket of fish food); the best time is midmorning.

Organized Tours

The ever-opportunistic **Robbie's** also operates tours to Lignumvitae Key State Botanical Site (see earlier in this section), and two-hour scenic sunset cruises on Florida Bay ($25/15 adult/child under 12 yrs).

Places to Stay

Camping *Long Key State Recreation Area* (☎ 305-664-4815, 800-326-3521 reservations, W www.reserveamerica.com, MM 67.5 oceanside) Sites without/with electricity $24/26. Make reservations right this minute: It's tough to get one of these 60

sites, but once you do, you'll never want to leave. Most of the waterfront sites offer decent wooded privacy between one another.

Fiesta Key Resort KOA (☎ 305-664-4922, W www.koa.com, MM 70 bayside) Sites without/with hookups $40-50/58-78 off-season, $43-53/68-88 mid-Nov–mid-Apr; motel rooms & efficiencies $105-125 off-season, $143-163 mid-Nov–mid-Apr. For resort-style camping complete with organized social activities, nothing beats this highly developed campground, which has 350 sites, 20 motel rooms and seven efficiencies with kitchens. They also have an Olympic-sized pool, beach and full service marina.

Motels & Hotels *Ragged Edge Resort* (☎ 305-852-5389, W www.ragged-edge.com, 243 Treasure Harbor Rd) Rooms $48-83 off-season, $69-119 mid-Dec–mid-Aug. This low key and popular efficiency and apartment complex, far from the maddening traffic jams, has 10 quiet units and friendly hosts. The larger studios, which have screened-in porches, are the most desirable. There's no beach, but you can swim off the dock and at the pool.

White Gate Court (☎ 305-664-4136, 800-645-4283, fax 305-664-9746, W www.white gatecourt.com, MM 76 bayside) Units $110-195 off-season, $120-210 mid-Dec–Apr. With only seven studios and villas, these family-friendly places go fast – with good reason. Each well-equipped unit has a full kitchen, laundry, free local calls, barbecue grill and nice garden area with torch lights. Guests have free use of paddleboats, snorkeling gear and bicycles. You can swim off the dock.

Casa Morada (☎ *305-664-0044, 888-881-3030, fax 305-664-0674,* Ⓦ *www.casa morada.com, 136 Madeira Rd, off MM 82.2)* Suites $155-190 off-season, $200-230 mid-Dec–mid-May. This hidden enclave of 16 contemporary suites, decorated in an upscale, urbane, beachy sort of way, with iron beds and lots of periwinkle accents, is a romantic fave. A pool with lots of beach chairs and palm trees occupies some prime real estate on a point. Weekend Continental breakfasts are included.

Cheeca Lodge & Spa (☎ *305-664-4651, 800-327-2888,* Ⓦ *www.cheeca.com, MM 82 oceanside)* Rooms $149-450 off-season, $199-650 late Dec–mid-Apr. If you like angling, par-3 golf, tennis, spa amenities and kids' programs, this conference-style Rock-resort will fully satisfy you. The 203 upscale rooms are located in the main hotel or outlying villas; some are oceanfront, most have balconies. Their dive shop arranges all sorts of trips, or you can just wander the nature trails, rent a bike or kayak, laze by the seductive pool, kick around some white sand or retreat to the spa.

Places to Eat & Drink

Village Gourmet (☎ *305-664-4030, MM 82.7 oceanside)* Sandwiches $5-8. Open 5:30am-9pm Mon-Thur, 5:30am-10pm Fri & Sat, 6am-2pm Sun. With only about a dozen seats, this takeout place has good baked goods at breakfast, plus cold pastas, pizzas, sandwiches and perhaps a special like chicken parmigiana. The espresso is watery, though.

Manny & Isa's Kitchen (☎ *305-664-5019, MM 81.6 oceanside)* Lunch $5-8, dinner mains $11-18. Open 11am-9pm Wed-Mon. This Spanish/American, value-packed, no-frills joint has good daily specials, lobster enchiladas, *ropa vieja* (shredded beef) and chili con carne. Their Key lime pie rules.

Time Out Barbecue (☎ *305-664-8911, MM 81.5 oceanside)* Lunch $5-6, dinner $10-14. Open 11am-10pm daily. This low-brow eatery with linoleum floors dishes up killer barbecue. The smoky aroma wafts

---

Key Lime Pie

Many places claim to serve *the* original Key lime pie, but no one really knows who discovered the tart treat. Types of crust vary, and whether or not the pie should be topped with meringue is often debated. However, the color of Key lime pie is not open to question. Beware of establishments serving green Key lime pie: Key limes are yellow, not green. Restaurants that add green food coloring say that tourists expect it to be green. Steer clear. Always on the shortlist of 'Best Key Lime Pie' is Manny & Isa's Kitchen in Islamorada. Manny has picked Key limes from his backyard trees since the 1970s to make a pie with a short-crust pastry, luscious sweet-tart filling and thick meringue.

---

into your car the moment you pull up to the front door.

Papa Joe's (☎ *305-664-8109, MM 79.7 bayside)* Lunch dishes $8-13, dinner mains $13-23. Open 10am-10pm daily. Since the mid-1930s, this rustic, nautical landmark with sloping floors has offered value-conscious lunches ($6) and dinner specials ($11). But it's perhaps more popular for its rockin' outdoor tiki-style raw bar and sunset happy hours.

Mile Marker 88 (☎ *305-852-9315, MM 88 bayside)* Mains $15-24. Open 5pm-9pm Tues-Sun. This longtime, chef-owned institution serves creative seafood preparations – it's hard to go wrong when ordering. In season, delectable stone crabs will set you back about $38.

Morada Bay (☎ *305-664-0604, MM 81.6 bayside)* Lunch $9-16, dinner mains $21-27. Open 11:30am-10pm daily. If you can ignore the overwhelmed service, there's no more atmospheric and romantic beachfront place on the Keys. A whitewashed preppy boathouse ethos merges with a laid-back Caribbean setting, complete with powdery white sand, palm trees and nighttime torches. What, you want to know about the food? Patrons come for the drinks (served in jelly

Keys Beaches

The Keys are not well known for their beaches. Some are plagued by sandflies, but all are lapped by calm waters. Most are really narrow ribbons of white sand that tend to be even narrower in winter because of tides. For better or worse, the water is usually very shallow close to shore. The following are good public beaches, most with picnic tables, some with grills and all with toilets.

beach	mile marker
Harry Harris County Park	MM 92.5
Lower Matecumbe Beach	MM 73.5
Anne's Beach	MM 73
Long Key	MM 67.5
Sombrero Beach	MM 50
Little Duck Key Beach	MM 38
Bahia Honda State Park	MM 37

jars) and sunsets, but the 'Floribbean' seafood (Caribbean and Floridian influenced) is a-okay, too.

Pierre's (☎ *305-664-3225, MM 81.6 bayside)* Mains $25-30. Open 5:30pm-10pm daily. If you're only going to splurge once, let it be here. This two-story waterfront plantation house, owned by the wildly successful and adjacent Morada Bay, specializes in creative seafood preparations. At the very least, clean yourself up a bit and hang out in the handsome lounge with oversized rattan chairs or on the verandah.

LONG KEY STATE RECREATION AREA
Opened in 1969, this 965-acre recreation area *(☎ 305-664-4815, MM 67.5 oceanside; admission $3.25 per car plus 50¢ per person)*, about 30 minutes south of Islamorada's midsection, is filled with gumbolimbo trees, crabwood, poisonwood and lots of wading birds in the mangroves. Two short nature trails head through distinct plant communities. In addition to ranger-led programs a couple of times a week, Friday evening campfire programs and a two-hour

guided nature walk on Wednesday morning (10am), the park also has a 1½-mile canoe trail through a saltwater tidal lagoon and rents canoes ($4 hourly, $10 daily). While the park has both gulf and oceanside sections, its beach is small at low tide and gone at high tide.

Middle Keys

The Keys midsection runs from the tiny Conch Keys and Duck Key (MM 63 to MM 61), through Grassy Key (MM 60 to MM 57) and Key Vaca (MM 54 to MM 47), on which Marathon is located. The region ends with Pigeon Key (a National Historic District), which explores the building of the Overseas Highway (the lifeline of the Florida Keys), and the famed Old Seven Mile Bridge (MM 46.5 to MM 40).

MARATHON
People come to Marathon to fish, which is not to say that non-fishers will be bored. It's just that the area is really geared to fishing. The second largest town in the Keys (after Key West) also boasts the Dolphin Research Center (actually on Grassy Key), where you can swim with dolphins in supervised programs (see the boxed text 'Swimming with Dolphins').

Information
Greyhound stops at the Marathon Airport, MM 50.5 bayside.

The Marathon Visitors Center Chamber of Commerce (☎ 305-743-5417, 800-262-7284, Ⓦ www.floridakeysmarathon.com), MM 53.5 bayside, has a mother lode of information and sells Greyhound tickets. It's open 9am to 5pm daily.

Fisherman's Hospital (☎ 305-743-5533), MM 48.7 oceanside, has a major emergency room.

Food for Thought (☎ 305-743-3297), MM 51 bayside, in Gulfside Village Shopping Center, is a combination bookstore/health food shop.

Good dive shops include **Sombrero Reef Explorers** *(☎ 305-743-0536, 19 Sombrero Rd,* *off MM 50 oceanside)* and **Aquatic Adventures Dive Center** *(☎ 305-743-2421, 800-978-3483, MM 54 oceanside).*

Museums of Crane Point Hammock

This fun 63-acre complex *(☎ 305-743-9100, W www.cranepoint.org, MM 50 bayside; admission $7.50/6/4 adult/senior/student or child over 6 yrs; open 9am-5pm Mon-Sat, noon-5pm Sun)* encompasses both the Museum of Natural History of the Florida Keys and Children's Museum of the Florida Keys. It provides a geological and geographical history of the Keys, a rare early-20th-century Bahamian-style house, exhibits on pirates and wrecking, a treasure chest filled with dress-up clothes, and a walk-through coral reef tunnel featuring underwater sounds. There are short (1½-mile) but nice walking trails through the hammock, and the staff is very helpful and friendly.

Kayaking

Kayaking Adventures *(☎ 305-743-0561, 19 Sombrero Blvd, off MM 50 oceanside)* provides three-hour guided mangrove ecotours ($40 per person), three-hour sunset tours ($40 per person), instruction (included) and rentals (single/double $30/40 half-day, $45/60 full day).

Places to Stay

Camping ***Jolly Rogers Trailer Park*** *(☎ 305-289-0404, 800-995-1525, MM 59.5 bayside)* Sites $25 off-season, $40-50 mid-Nov–mid-Apr. There are 225 sites, all with hookups, here. Many tent sites are waterfront.

Knights Key Campground *(☎ 305-743-4343, 800-348-2267, MM 47 oceanside)* Tent sites without/with hookups $23/28, oceanfront/marina sites with hookups $55/65-70; sites cost less mid-Apr–Nov. On the northern end of the Seven Mile Bridge, this 200-site campground has only 17 sites specifically for tenters. It provides friendly service and 10% off for weekly summertime stays.

Motels & Hotels ***Siesta Motel*** *(☎ 305-743-5671, W www.siestamotel.net, MM 51 oceanside)* Rooms average $65 year-round. For the best, cheapest, cleanest place in the Keys, head here. The seven-room motel also provides great service.

Royal Hawaiian Motel Botel *(☎ 305-743-7500, MM 53 bayside)* Rooms $69-79 off-season, $105-115 mid-Jan–Mar. This family-run canalside place, with a boat dock and pool, has eight rooms that have waterfront balconies and sleep four. It's a very good inexpensive choice.

Coral Lagoon Resort *(☎ 305-289-0121, W www.corallagoonresort.com, MM 53.5 oceanside)* Efficiencies $75-100 off-season, $125 late Dec–late Apr. This lush, canalside complex, with 18 spacious units, boasts semi-private outdoor decks with hammocks and grills for each unit. Tennis racquets, rods and reels and plenty of personalized services are included. They also have slightly smaller units for $15 less and slightly bigger two-bedroom units for $25 more.

Conch Key Cottages *(☎ 305-289-1377, 800-330-1577, W www.conchkeycottages.com, MM 62.3 oceanside)* Units $74-147 off-season, $110-235 mid-Dec–early Sept, more for two-bedroom units; inquire about weekly rates. Nicely hidden from US Hwy 1 by a short pebbly causeway, this popular and nicely landscaped complex comprises 12 freestanding pastel cottages furnished with rattan, wicker and local pine. Each has its own hammock and kayak; all enjoy the small but lushly private pool.

Seascape Ocean Resort *(☎ 305-743-6455, fax 305-743-8469, 1075 75th St, off MM 50.5 oceanside)* Rooms $150-225. These nine rooms, several of which have a kitchen, hark back to the 1950s, but with updated amenities and a B&B ambience. Seascape, with a lovely waterfront pool and little sitting areas, was originally a private estate and the current residential neighborhood lends it a rare quietness. Rates include Continental breakfast and afternoon wine and snacks.

Hawk's Cay Resort *(☎ 305-743-9000, 800-432-2242, W www.hawkscay.com, 61 Hawk's Cay Blvd, off MM 61 oceanside, Duck Key)* Rooms $200-325 off-season, $240-295 Jan–mid-Apr, suites & villas much more. This five-story 400-room hotel, with tightly packed townhouse villas, is deco-rated in an upscale Caribbean style. The most developed self-contained resort in the Keys offers a sailing school, snorkeling, tennis, boat and kayak rentals, fishing pro-grams, dolphin encounters and scuba diving lessons.

Places to Eat & Drink

Leigh Ann's Coffee House *(☎ 305-743-2001, MM 50.5 oceanside)* Dishes $4-7. Open 7am-4pm daily. From breakfast frittatas to lunchtime bruschettas to smoothies and salads, the pleasant and friendly Leigh Ann's is a delightful oasis from the omnipresent conch fritters and seafood platters. The espresso is downright decent, unless you're a bean addict from Seattle.

7 Mile Grill *(☎ 305-743-4481, MM 45 bayside)* Breakfast $3-9, dinner $8-11. Open 7am-9pm Fri-Tues. This popular short-order place has bar service and some covered tables overlooking the parking lot. Go for a hearty morning serving of two eggs and a Delmonico steak, or lunchtime grilled-fish sandwiches or dinnertime shrimp steamed in beer.

Barracuda Grill *(☎ 305-743-3314, MM 49.5 bayside)* Mains $15-20. Open 5:55pm-10pm-ish Mon-Sat. This stylishly casual and chef-owned New American grill is making waves with its creative dishes and friendly service. If the timing is right, make it a point to eat here.

PIGEON KEY & OLD SEVEN MILE BRIDGE

This 5-acre island, about 2 miles west of Marathon and basically below the Old Seven Mile Bridge, is a National Historic District. As Henry Flagler's FEC Railway progressed southward, the construction of the Seven Mile Bridge between Marathon and Bahia Honda Key (actually Little Duck Key) became an immense project. From 1908 to 1912, Pigeon Key housed about 400 workers. Later it housed the rail-road maintenance workers. And after the hurricane that wiped out Flagler's railroad in 1935, the Key housed workers who con-verted the railroad to automobile bridges.

After a brief stint in the 1970s as a re-search facility leased by the University of Miami, the Pigeon Key Foundation pre-served the island's buildings and began telling the story of the railroad and its workers. Today the Key *(☎ 305-289-0025, w www.pigeonkey.org; admission $8.50/5 adult/child; tours 10am-3pm daily)* is open for touring and you can visit the old town, including the 'honeymoon cottage,' assistant bridge tender and bridge tender's houses, the section gang's quarters and the 'negro quarters.'

You can park at the southwestern end of Marathon (MM 47), and take the hourly shuttle out to the island; it runs from 10am to 3pm, with the last shuttle returning at 4:45pm. You can also ride or walk across the bridge.

The **Old Seven Mile Bridge** *(admission free)* serves as 'the World's Longest Fishing Bridge'; park at the northeastern foot of the bridge.

Lower Keys

The Lower Keys extend from Bahia Honda Key (MM 40) to Boca Chica Key (MM 7). Accommodation and dining choices in this stretch suffer in their proximity to Key West. Nonetheless, most are located on Big Pine Key. As for things to do, the National Key Deer Refuge is the main attraction, but you'll also find skydiving and great diving and snorkeling, especially at Looe Key Na-tional Marine Sanctuary and Bahia Honda State Park. You can also arrange wonderful kayak trips among the mangroves within the Great White Heron National Wildlife Refuge.

Information

The helpful Lower Keys Chamber of Commerce *(☎ 305-872-3580, 800-872-3722, w www.lowerkeyschamber.com)*, MM 31 oceanside, is on Big Pine Key. It's open 9am to 5pm Monday to Friday, 9am to 3pm Saturday.

The post office is at MM 30 bayside, on Big Pine Key.

Big Pine Shopping Center, at MM 30.5 bayside (turn northwest on Key Deer Blvd), has a Winn-Dixie, the biggest food market in the area, and the Big Pine Key public library (☎ 305-289-6303).

For emergencies, the closest facility is Lower Keys Medical Center (☎ 305-294-5531, 800-233-3119), 5900 College Rd, near MM 5, on Stock Island; it has a 24-hour emergency room.

Dive shops include **Looe Key Reef Resort & Dive Center** *(☎ 305-872-2215, 800-942-5397, MM 27.5 oceanside),* on Ramrod Key, and **Paradise Divers** *(☎ 305-872-1114, MM 38.5 bayside),* on Big Pine Key.

BAHIA HONDA STATE PARK

With one of the Keys' best sparkling-white-sand beaches, this 524-acre park *(☎ 305-872-2353, w www.bahiahondapark.com, MM 36.8 oceanside; admission $4 per car plus 50¢ per person; open 8am-sunset daily)* sits at the foot of the Seven Mile Bridge. (In summer sandflies are rife!) Even though it's very popular, the 2½-mile expanse and the shape of the beach allow for privacy. Don't get too private though: Topless and nude bathing are prohibited. Rangers will tell you once to put on clothes, after which you could be fined and ejected from the park. Bahia Honda is the southernmost Key with exposed limestone, and along its nature trails you'll find silver palms, yellow satinwood and endangered lily thorns.

Snorkeling & Kayaking

The **park concession** *(☎ 305-872-3210)* rents equipment ($10 for a mask, fins and snorkel) and offers daily excursions at 9:30am and 1:30pm ($26/21 adult/child under 18 yrs). Reservations are a good idea in high season. The concession also rents kayaks (singles/doubles cost $10/18 an hour and $30/54 per half day), and has a grocery store.

LOOE KEY NATIONAL MARINE SANCTUARY

Pronounced 'Loo,' this isn't a key but rather a grove reef off Ramrod Key and you can only visit with an organized trip. The Key Largo (see the John Pennekamp Coral Reef State Park section, earlier in this chapter) and Looe Key National Marine Sanctuaries were established in 1971 and 1981, respectively, to protect sensitive areas within the Keys. In reality, they are a compromise between commercial activities and environmental protection. Named for an English frigate that sank here in 1744, the Looe Key reef contains the 210-foot *Adolphus Busch* – used in the film *Fire Down Below* – which was sunk 60 to 120 feet in 1998. Activities permissible here include limited lobster-catching, crabbing and hook-and-line sport and commercial fishing. The sanctuary designation protects against damaging the natural features (which includes standing on, anchoring on or touching coral).

Diving & Snorkeling

Thousands of varieties of hugely colorful tropical fish, coral and sea life abound in the sanctuary. **Strike Zone Charters** *(☎ 305-872-9863, 800-654-9560, MM 29.5 bayside)* has four-hour snorkeling and diving trips aboard glass-bottom boats that depart at 9:30am and 1:30pm. Snorkeling trips cost $25 per person, plus $5 for equipment; diving trips are $40, plus $25 for equipment.

NATIONAL KEY DEER REFUGE

Key deer, an endangered subspecies of white-tailed deer, live primarily on Big Pine and No Name Keys. Once mainland-dwelling animals, the formation of the Keys stranded them on the islands, and evolution has wrought changes on their stature. Since it's warmer here than on the mainland, the deer don't need as much body mass. And to compensate for reduced grazing lands and scarce freshwater, the deer now have single births rather than multiple litters.

The National Key Deer Refuge *(headquarters: ☎ 305-872-2239/0774, MM 30.5 bayside, Big Pine Shopping Center; admission free; open 8am-5pm Mon-Fri)* sprawls over several Keys, but the sections that are open to the public – Blue Hole, Watson's Hammock and Watson's Nature Trail – are on Big Pine and No Name Keys. Besides these areas, all areas marked with signs that read 'US Fish & Wildlife Service – Unauthorized Entry Prohibited' are open to the public from a half-hour before sunrise to a half-hour after sunset. Key deer are best spotted in early morning and late afternoon.

From MM 30.5, take Key Deer Blvd north for 3½ miles. You'll first come to Blue Hole; Watson's Nature Trail and Watson's Hammock are a quarter mile farther on the same road. Less than a mile long, **Watson's Nature Trail** winds through the Key deer's natural habitat.

No Name Key gets fewer visitors than the Blue Hole or Watson's Nature Trail. Take Key Deer Blvd to Watson Blvd, turn right, go about 1½ miles to Wilder Blvd, turn left, follow it for 2 miles to Bogie Bridge, cross that and you'll be on No Name.

Blue Hole, an old quarry that's now the largest freshwater body in the Keys, has lots of alligators, turtles, fish and wading birds. Please don't feed the wildlife; many visitors do and it's illegal and irresponsible.

PLACES TO STAY
Camping
Bahia Honda State Park (☎ 305-872-2353, 800-326-3521 reservations, Ⓦ www.reserve america.com, MM 37) Sites without/with electricity $24/26, cabins $97 mid-Sept–mid-Dec, $125 other times; waterfront sites (reserve far in advance or forget it) are an additional $2. One of the Key's best camping places, this excellent park has 200 almost bayside and oceanside sites and six cabins, each sleeping six.

Big Pine Key Fishing Lodge (☎ 305-872-2351, MM 33 oceanside) Sites without/with hookups $30/37, motel efficiencies $89-115. This well-maintained canalside place has 60 tent sites, 97 RV sites and 16 efficiencies. Even with an artificial beach, ocean swimming isn't great, but there is a pool. The lodge, geared to fishing and diving, also has boat rentals.

Sugarloaf Key Resort KOA (☎ 305-745-3549, 800-562-7731, 251 County Rd, off MM 20 oceanside) Tent sites $40-43 off-season, $44-47 mid-Jan–mid-Mar, RV sites $60-80 off-season, $69-87 mid-Jan–mid-Mar. This

highly developed KOA has about 200 tent sites and 200 RV sites.

Motels & Hotels
Parmer's Place Guesthouse (☎ 305-872-2157, Ⓦ www.parmersresort.com, 565 Barry Ave, off MM 28.5 bayside) Units $55-130 off-season, $75-140 Jan-Aug. On 5 acres of Little Torch Key (call for directions), this lush and well-maintained 45-room waterfront resort has motel rooms, efficiencies, one- and two-bedroom units and lots of aviaries with chattering birds. Rates include Continental breakfast, a large pool and gas grills. You can swim from the docks.

Looe Key Reef Resort (☎ 305-872-2215, 800-942-5397, Ⓦ www.diveflakeys.com, MM 27.5 oceanside) Rooms $70-75 off-season, $95 Feb-Apr & July-Aug. Since the focus of this motel is diving, their 20 rooms are quite basic.

Little Palm Island Resort & Spa (☎ 305-872-2524, 800-343-8567, fax 305-872-4843, Ⓦ www.littlepalmisland.com) Suites $795. Accessible only by plane or boat, this 30-bungalow luxe retreat rewards guests with pampering service, romantic surroundings, white-sand beaches, a lagoon-like pool and Zen-style gardens. And for that price, it should! Spa services and the dining room are phenomenal. There's no better 6-acre place to stay if you can pay.

PLACES TO EAT & DRINK
Baby's Coffee (☎ 800-523-2326, MM 15 oceanside) Open 7am-6pm Mon-Fri, 7am-5pm Sat & Sun. It's the only coffee place in the area; they roast their own and luckily it's OK.

Good Food Conspiracy (☎ 305-872-3945, MM 30 oceanside) Open 9:30am-7pm Mon-Sat, 9:30am-5pm Sun. This health-food place has a limited amount of prepared foods, a juice bar, smoothies, vitamins and the like. If you are camping, they have healthful food supplies.

No Name Pub (☎ 305-872-9115, N Watson Blvd, off MM 30.5 bayside) Dishes $5-15. Open 11am-11pm. Perhaps the most colorful eatery in these parts, this smoky and hidden locals' roadhouse is wallpapered with dollar bills. The bar-cum-rustic restaurant serves great pizzas to families and drinkers.

Mangrove Mama's *(☎ 305-745-3030, MM 20 oceanside)* Lunch $10-15, dinner mains $19-25. Open 11:30am-3:30pm & 5:30pm-10pm daily. This hippish roadside eatery and rustic bar occasionally has live reggae. Check it out. As for the food, think good Caribbean-inspired seafood, like coconut shrimp, spicy conch stew and surf-and-turf. Even the locals hang out here, especially at happy hour.

The Everglades

Flying over South Florida makes it obvious: Vast tracts of the Everglades are completely inaccessible to the public. But the remainder, within Everglades National Park, contains some of the most accessible wilderness areas in the state. You'll find developed canoeing and kayaking routes, hiking and biking trails, and a very good information infrastructure.

Don't overlook Big Cypress National Preserve, a protected area at the northern end of the Everglades that is also open to hikers and drivers, or the colorful underwater Biscayne National Park, on the eastern shore.

The Tamiami Trail (US Hwy 41), the main artery linking Miami and the southwest Florida coast, is the easiest place to dip into the park. If you only have time to do one thing in the Everglades, it should be Shark Valley on the Tamiami Trail. At some point you will end up in Flamingo or Everglades City, which is near the 10,000 Islands; both make good bases for richer exploration.

Getting There & Around

The only sensible way to explore the area is by car. From Miami, take Florida's Turnpike Extension (toll) or US Hwy 1 to reach Florida City and Homestead; it's about 45 minutes with light traffic. From there to the entrance of Everglades National Park, it's another 15 minutes. And from there to Flamingo along Hwy 9336, add another hour without stopping.

From downtown Miami (assuming moderate traffic), it takes about 45 minutes to an hour to reach Shark Valley. There's no public transportation along the Tamiami Trail.

To reach Everglades City from the Tamiami Trail, head south on Hwy 29 until you're forced to turn right. At the traffic circle, turn left and the road leads you to the Gulf Coast Visitor Center. The whole trip from Miami takes a little less than two hours, 3½ to four if you add a side trip on Loop Rd.

Greyhound (☎ 800-231-2222) services Homestead, but not Florida City, Everglades City or Flamingo. There are four daily buses ($9.25/18.25 one-way/roundtrip) there from Miami. The only other way to reach Florida City by public transportation is idiotic: You can take Metrorail to Dadeland North, then bus No 1 to the Cutler Ridge Mall and then No 35 or No 70 to Florida City.

EVERGLADES NATIONAL PARK

The largest subtropical wilderness in the continental USA, and containing the second-largest US national park (after Yellowstone), the Everglades are a unique and delicate ecosystem made up of swamps and marshes at the southern tip of the Florida peninsula. It's also one of the most well-known and poorly understood areas of the USA. Visitors to South Florida hear about airboat tours and the Shark Valley Tram Tour, and of ecological threats to the area, but many don't have time to find out more. Or they're scared off by tales of renegade alligators and poisonous snakes lurking in the muck.

Whether you visit the Ernest Coe Visitor Center for an afternoon, take the Shark Valley Tram Tour, or embrace canoeing and camping in the 10,000 Islands and on the Wilderness Waterway, we can't urge you enough to visit.

Though the threat to the Everglades is very real, it is a spectacular place to get into the real nature of South Florida. From the brackish waters of the mangrove and cypress swamps, to hardwood hammocks, sawgrass flats, Dade County pinelands and marshes, to creatures like crocodiles, alligators, bottle-nosed dolphins, manatees, snowy egrets, bald eagles and ospreys, there is simply no other place like the Everglades.

History & Ecology

The Calusa Indians called the area Pa-hay-okee, or grassy water. The late and much-beloved Marjory Stoneman Douglas called it the River of Grass. In her book *The*

Alligator, Everglades National Park

An anhinga, or snake bird, Everglades

Boardwalk heading out to the Pa-hay-okee Overlook, Everglades National Park

JON DAVISON

Purple gallinule, Everglades National Park

TOM BOYDEN

Mature white ibis, Anhinga Trail, Everglades

LEE FOSTER

It's all about getting close to nature in the Everglades, and tours abound.

Everglades: River of Grass, she says Gerard de Brahm (a surveyor) named them River Glades, which on later English maps became Ever Glades.

The Everglades are part of a sheet-flow ecosystem, beginning at the Kissimmee River, which empties into Lake Okeechobee at the south center of the state. Before humankind's meddling, Okeechobee overflowed and sent sheets of water through the Everglades and finally into the Gulf of Mexico. The resulting ecosystem was home to thousands of species of flora and wildlife. Wading birds, amphibians, reptiles and mammals flourished.

Enter business, stage right. Sugar growers, attracted by mucky waters, swarmed in and pressured the government to make land available to them. In 1905, Florida governor Napoleon Bonaparte Broward personally dug the first shovelful of dirt for what was to become one of the largest and most destructive diversions of water in the world. The Caloosahatchee River was diverted and connected to Lake Okeechobee. Hundreds of canals were dug, slicing through the Everglades to the coastline to 'reclaim' the land. The flow of lake water was then restricted by a series of dikes. Farmland began to sprout up in areas previously uninhabited by humans.

Unfortunately, farming diverted the freshwater desperately needed by nature in the Everglades, and it produced fertilizer-rich wastewater, which promotes foliage growth, which in turn clogs waterways and further complicates matters. More recently, as chemicals spill into the Glades and local waters, the Florida Aquifer (the source of Florida's freshwater supply) is in great danger of being contaminated. Autopsies of local animals, including Florida panthers, have shown that mercury levels are extremely high. Pollution from industry and farming is killing foliage, and because of the freshwater diversion, saltwater from the Gulf of Mexico is flowing deeper into the park than ever before. There are 16 endangered and five threatened species of animals within the park.

Restoration Efforts to save the Everglades began as early as the late 1920s, but they were sidelined by the Great Depression. In 1926 and 1928, two major hurricanes caused Okeechobee to bust its banks; the resulting floods killed hundreds. So the Army Corps of Engineers came in and did a *really* good job of damming the lake. They constructed the Hoover Dike. Through the efforts of conservationists and prominent citizens like Douglas, the Everglades was declared a national park in 1947. But the threat is far from over.

Everglades restoration is one of the hottest potatoes in the USA's environmental community. In the mid-1990s, Congress voted to cut subsidies to Florida sugar growers by a penny a pound, and to use the savings to buy 126,000 acres of land to restore a natural flow of water through South Florida. About one-fifth of Florida's sugar-producing land was purchased and allowed to revert to marshland. Additionally, the federal and state governments would then spend $100 million to reroute and reconstruct South Florida's dikes, dams and levees, from northern Lake Okeechobee through the Glades.

The basic idea is to increase the quantity of freshwater within the Everglades, remove upstream phosphorus, employ mitigation projects to enhance the Everglades with restoration objectives, and maintain a diverse habitat to meet the needs of wildlife. It sounds great, but it's easier said than done. And the politics are highly divisive.

Thousands of scientists, environmentalists and business groups are still arguing about the best way to meet the goals of restoration. The Everglades Coalition, with 42 subgroups including the Conservancy, is the primary environmental group. They want to restore the remaining Everglades lands to conditions prior to developmental impacts while maintaining flood protection and providing freshwater needs for the growing South Florida populous. The Coalition also wants to continue restoring the Kissimmee River Basin, return Lake Okeechobee to a more natural state, proceed with land acquisition to preserve as much of the system as possible, and control urban sprawl.

THE EVERGLADES

THE EVERGLADES

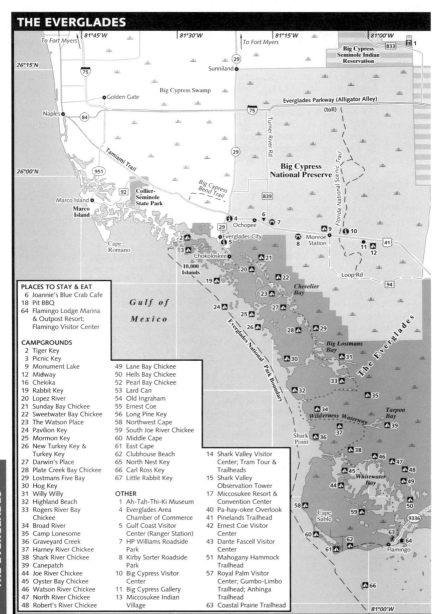

PLACES TO STAY & EAT
6   Joannie's Blue Crab Cafe
18 Pit BBQ
64 Flamingo Lodge Marina
    & Outpost Resort;
    Flamingo Visitor Center

CAMPGROUNDS
2   Tiger Key
3   Picnic Key
9   Monument Lake
12 Midway
16 Chekika
19 Rabbit Key
20 Lopez River
21 Sunday Bay Chickee
22 Sweetwater Bay Chickee
23 The Watson Place
24 Pavilion Key
25 Mormon Key
26 New Turkey Key &
    Turkey Key
27 Darwin's Place
28 Plate Creek Bay Chickee
29 Lostmans Five Bay
30 Hog Key
31 Willy Willy
32 Highland Beach
33 Rogers River Bay
    Chickee
34 Broad River
35 Camp Lonesome
36 Graveyard Creek
37 Harney River Chickee
38 Shark River Chickee
43 Canepatch
44 Joe River Chickee
45 Oyster Bay Chickee
46 Watson River Chickee
47 North River Chickee
48 Robert's River Chickee

49 Lane Bay Chickee
50 Hells Bay Chickee
52 Pearl Bay Chickee
53 Lard Can
54 Old Ingraham
55 Ernest Coe
56 Long Pine Key
58 Northwest Cape
59 South Joe River Chickee
60 Middle Cape
61 East Cape
62 Clubhouse Beach
65 North Nest Key
66 Carl Ross Key
67 Little Rabbit Key

OTHER
1   Ah-Tah-Thi-Ki Museum
4   Everglades Area
    Chamber of Commerce
5   Gulf Coast Visitor
    Center (Ranger Station)
7   HP Williams Roadside
    Park
8   Kirby Sorter Roadside
    Park
10 Big Cypress Visitor
    Center
11 Big Cypress Gallery
13 Miccosukee Indian
    Village

14 Shark Valley Visitor
    Center; Tram Tour &
    Trailheads
15 Shark Valley
    Observation Tower
17 Miccosukee Resort &
    Convention Center
40 Pa-hay-okee Overlook
41 Pinelands Trailhead
42 Ernest Coe Visitor
    Center
43 Dante Fascell Visitor
    Center
51 Mahogany Hammock
    Trailhead
57 Royal Palm Visitor
    Center; Gumbo-Limbo
    Trailhead; Anhinga
    Trailhead
63 Coastal Prairie Trailhead

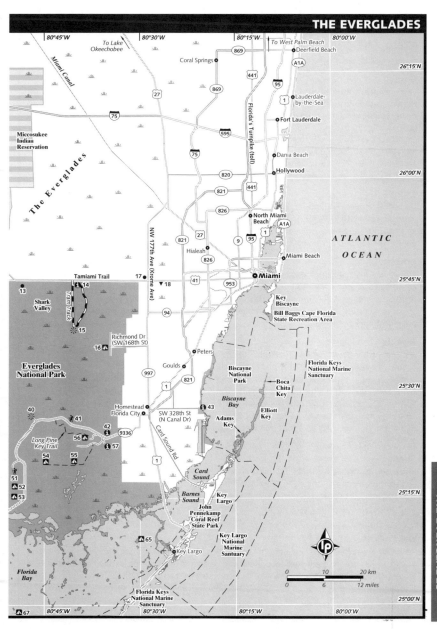

THE EVERGLADES

Panthers & Gators & Crocs, Oh My!

While panthers and gators and crocs lurk in the Everglades, the most exotic dangers you'll encounter will be weather, insects, bad tides, blistered hands and a sunburned face.

Gators

While alligators are common in the park, they are not very common in the area of the 10,000 Islands, as they tend to avoid saltwater. If you do see an alligator, it probably won't bother you, unless you do something overtly threatening or angle your boat between it and its young. If you hear an alligator making a loud hissing sound, you should get the hell out of Dodge. That hissing sound is a call to other alligators when a young gator is in danger. Finally, never, ever, *ever* feed an alligator – it's stupid and illegal. Alligators have a broad snout and black skin; only the upper teeth are visible when her jaw is clamped tight. Females build nests on mounds of vegetation in freshwater and will guard the nest long after the eggs have hatched.

Crocs

Crocodiles are less common in the park, as they prefer coastal and saltwater habitats. They are more aggressive than alligators, however, so the same rules apply. Crocs have a narrow snout and an envious olive-brown complexion; its teeth are visible even when its jaw is closed. With perhaps only a few hundred remaining in the US, they are also an endangered species.

Weather

Thunderstorms and lightning are more common in summer than winter. But in summer the insects are so bad you won't want to be out here anyway. In emergency weather, rangers will search for registered campers, but under ordinary conditions, they won't unless they receive information that someone's missing. If camping, have a friend or family member ready to contact rangers if you do not report back by a certain day.

Insects

In summer the Everglades surely double as the world's central mosquito-manufacturing plant. Insidious and almost invisible no-see-ums, ferocious at dawn and dusk, are god-awful biting machines. Avon Skin-So-Soft or REI Jungle Juice are key equipment. The insect problem in the dry season, though, isn't so bad. Information on mosquito levels during summer is available at ☎ 305-242-7700.

It's called DEET.

Snakes

There are four types of poisonous snake in the Everglades: diamondback rattlesnake (*Crotalus adamanteus*), pigmy rattlesnake *(Sistrurus miliarius)*, cottonmouth or water moccasin (*Agkistrodon piscivorus conanti*), which swim along the surface of water, and the colorful coral snake *(Micrurus fulvius)*. Wear long, thick socks and lace-up boots – and keep the hell away from them.

Other Critters

Raccoons and rats are less dangerous but very annoying. They will tear through anything less than a solid, sealed cooler to get your food. Keep your food and refuse inside a sealed cooler, and your water bottles sealed and inside your tent. (Open water can be smelled through your tent, and the last thing you want at 4am is a raccoon slashing through your tent for a sip of water.)

THE EVERGLADES

The Coalition has been working closely with local, state and federal officials on the best way to proceed, and the federal government has earmarked funds for Everglades restoration.

Planning

The Everglades' seasons consist of the dry season (roughly November to May) and the mosquitoes and no-see-ums season (June to October). While the park is open year-round, it's best to visit in the dry season. The summer season is brutal.

Rangers can help you develop specific itineraries with the assistance of the *Wilderness Trip Planner,* a very good National Park Service (NPS) guide to the park. Molloy's *A Paddler's Guide to Everglades National Park* is an excellent guide to the park's waterway trails. For nature information and identification, look for *Florida's Fabulous Birds* by Winston Williams, *Florida's Fabulous Reptiles & Amphibians* by Peter Carmichael and Winston Williams, the National Geographic's *Field Guide to Birds of North America* and *Peterson Field Guide to the Birds* by Roger Tory Peterson.

Tourist Offices

The main park entry points have visitor's centers where you can get maps, camping permits and ranger information. The principal one, the Ernest Coe Visitor Center (☎ 305-242-7700, W www.nps.gov/ever), on Hwy 9336, is packed with excellent information. It's open 8am to 5pm daily; the gate is open 24 hours daily. Admission is $10 per carload, $5 for pedestrians and cyclists. A quick stop here is the fastest and easiest way to see some of the Everglades. The center is about 15 miles south of Florida City and 38 miles north of Flamingo. The adjacent Royal Palm Visitor Center (☎ 305-242-7700), on Hwy 9336, is open from 8am to 4:15pm daily.

The Shark Valley Visitor Center (☎ 305-221-8776), on the Tamiami Trail, is open from 8:30am to 5pm daily. The Flamingo Visitor Center (☎ 941-695-3094), at the park's southern coast, is open from 7:30am to 5pm daily. The Gulf Coast Visitor Center (☎ 941-695-3311), on Hwy 29 in Everglades City, is the northwesternmost ranger station. It's open from 8:30am to 5pm daily and provides the best access to the 10,000 Islands area (see the boxed text 'Canoe Camping on 10,000 Islands').

Hiking

The Royal Palm Visitor Center is the starting point for two good trails: the three-quarter-mile **Gumbo-Limbo Trail**, with gumbo-limbo and royal palm trees, orchids and lush vegetation; and the **Anhinga Trail**, named for the odd anhinga birds (also called the snake bird, for the way it swims with its long neck and head above water). You'll probably run into alligators, turtles, waterfowl, lizards and snakes on this half-mile trail.

All along Hwy 9336 between the visitor's center and Flamingo, the 38-mile main road offers lots of opportunities for hiking, including: the **Pinelands**, a half-mile trail through Dade County pine forest – look for exposed limestone bedrock; **Pa-hay-okee Overlook**, a quarter-mile boardwalk trail with an observation tower; and **Mahogany Hammock**, a half-mile boardwalk leading into lush and overgrown vegetation. **Long Pine Key** is the starting point of a 15-mile series of walking trails where you may see many species indigenous to the Everglades, including, if you're very quiet and patient, Florida panthers.

Camping

In addition to camping in Flamingo and Big Cypress (see those sections, later), car campers shouldn't overlook *Long Pine Key* (☎ 800-365-2267; free off-season, $14 Nov-Apr), just west of the Royal Palm Visitor Center.

Attention canoe campers: See the boxed text 'Canoe Camping on 10,000 Islands.'

FLORIDA CITY & HOMESTEAD

Hurricane Andrew ripped through Homestead in 1992 at speeds of 200mph, leveling everything in its path. Even though it's been rebuilt, Homestead's economy never completely recovered. But this is still the 'gateway to the Everglades,' and the surrounding countryside still supports lots of farms, nurseries and 'u-pick' farm stands.

Krome Ave (Hwy 997) cuts through both towns; you'll find a few motels and fast-food restaurants like **Long John Silver's** here. The Chamber of Commerce (☎ 305-247-2332), 43 N Krome Ave, is open 9am to noon and 1pm to 5pm weekdays.

Places to Stay & Eat
Everglades International Hostel (☎ 305-248-1122, 800-372-3874, w www.everglades hostel.com, 20 SW 2nd Ave, Florida City) Dorm beds $13-16, doubles $33-39; add $1 per person for air-con in summer. This friendly hostel, in a 1930s boarding house and operated by the super-friendly Owhnn, has six-bedded dorm rooms and private doubles with shared bath. You'll find lots of information about Glades canoeing, kayaking and bicycling. (They also rent canoes and kayaks and give tours.) The hostel has a full kitchen, garden, Internet connections and laundry facilities.

Best Western Florida City/Homestead Gateway to the Keys (☎ 305-246-5100, 800-937-8376, fax 305-242-0056, w www.best western.com, 411 S Krome Ave, Florida City) Rooms $74-89 off-season, $94-109 Dec-May. This two-story motel has a pool and 114 standard-issue rooms with either two queens or one king bed. Some rooms have a microwave and refrigerator.

Robert is Here (☎ 305-246-1592, 19200 SW 344th St, Homestead) Open 8am-7pm daily Nov-Aug. For a slice of Old Florida, not to mention some exotic fruits and slices of heady mango (in summer), stop at Robert's. The mango shakes are otherworldly, but if you're here in the winter, try a Key lime milkshake. This is surely one of the best-known farmer's markets in the country.

El Toro Taco (☎ 305-245-8182, 1 S Krome Ave, Homestead) Dishes $2-9. Open 11am-9pm Tues-Thur & Sun, 11am-10pm Fri & Sat. The mythical aura surrounding El Toro Taco has a basis in reality, and it's reason enough for some to drive to Homestead from Miami. The fajitas, burritos, other

Mexican specialties and fresh salsa are exceptional at this family-run restaurant. Bring your own beer.

Farmer's Market Restaurant (☎ 305-242-0008, 300 N Krome Ave, Florida City) Lunch dishes $8-10, dinner dishes $12-14. Open 5:30am-9pm daily. This simple restaurant prepares homemade everything, from hot cakes and hearty breakfasts, to fried-fish baskets at lunch, to seafood combos and snapper at dinner.

FLAMINGO
From the Coe and Royal Palm visitor's centers, follow Hwy 9336 to the bitter end. Welcome to Flamingo, the most developed and least authentic Everglades experience you can get. With sightseeing and bay cruises, it's really geared toward holiday-makers. You'll find camping, houseboat rentals and a lodge, in addition to nature and bike paths, picnic tables, and short canoe trails.

If you 're overnighting in Flamingo, pick up the NPS brochure, which details nearby canoe and hiking trails. The 7.5-mile (one-way) **Coastal Prairie Trail** follows an old road once used by cotton pickers; it's only partially shaded by buttonwood trees, so bring plenty of sunscreen. Also see the boxed text 'Canoe Camping on 10,000 Islands' and Canoeing & Kayaking in the Everglades City section, later in this chapter, for more opportunities to canoe and kayak in the Everglades.

Flamingo Lodge Marina & Outpost Resort (☎ 941-695-3101, 800-600-3813, w www.flamingolodge.com, Hwy 9336; open daily) does it all. They rent kayaks for $27 for four hours, $43 for a full day and $50 overnight. A tandem costs $38/54/60. They also rent bicycles for $8/14 for four/eight hours, and lead sightseeing tours for two hours ($16/8 adult/child; departures at 10am, 1pm and 3:30pm) and four hours ($39 per person; departures at 8:30am and 1:30pm). The longer trips aren't really worth the extra time and money. In fact, the scenery is better out of Everglades City anyway, so if you have time, head west. The lodge also has laundry facilities, a post office, coolers, binoculars and fishing gear.

Places to Stay & Eat

National Park Service (☎ *800-365-2267,* Ⓦ *reservations.nps.gov)* Sites free off-season, $14 Nov-Apr. The campgrounds here are run by the NPS. None of these primitive, barely shaded sites have hookups. Depending on the time of year, cold-water showers arc either bracing or a welcome relief.

Flamingo Lodge Marina & Outpost Resort (see above) Rooms $65/95 off-

season/mid-Dec-Mar, suites & cottages $89-110/135-145. All 102 perfunctory units have two double beds, TV and air-con. It's better than camping in a rainstorm or with the mosquitoes. Suite and cottage rates are for four people (so they're a bargain, really) and cottages have full kitchen.

BISCAYNE NATIONAL PARK

Call it a living, breathing work of art, or a dazzling and garish spectacle of life. Either way, it's the world's third-largest reef (second to Australia's Great Barrier Reef and offshore Belize), and it contains the continental USA's only living coral. Fortunately, this unique 300-sq-mile park, 95% of which is under water, is very easy to explore independently with a canoe or via a glass-bottom–boat tour. Its offshore keys, accessible only by boat, also offer pristine opportunities for camping.

First things first though: Head straight to Convoy Point and the **Dante Fascell Visitor Center** (☎ *305-230-7275,* Ⓦ *www.nps.gov/ bisc, 9700 SW 328th St; open 8:30am-5pm daily)* to watch a great introductory film for a good overview of the park. Generally, summer and fall are the best times to visit the park; you'll want to snorkel when the water is calm.

Long **Elliott Key** has picnicking, camping and hiking among mangrove forests; tiny **Adams Key** has only picnicking; and equally tiny **Boca Chita Key** has an ornamental lighthouse, picnicking and camping. No-see-ums (tiny biting flies) are invasive, and their bites are devastating. Make sure your tent is devoid of miniscule entry points. Primitive *camping* costs $10 per night; self-pay with exact change on the harbor (rangers cruise the Keys to check your receipt). Bring in all supplies, including water, and carry everything out. There is no water on Boca Chita (only saltwater toilettes), and since it has a deeper port, it tends to attract bigger (and louder) boaters. There are cold-water showers and potable water on Elliott, but it's always good to bring your own since the generator might go out.

Biscayne National Underwater Park (☎ *305-230-1100)* offers glass-bottom–boat

---

Houseboating

One of the laziest, easiest and most fun ways to explore parts of the Everglades is on a houseboat. They're surprisingly simple to navigate and only reach cruising speeds of 6mph, so you needn't worry if your skills don't match a NASCAR driver's. Contact the *Flamingo Lodge Marina & Outpost Resort* (☎ *941-695-3101, 800-600-3813,* Ⓦ *www .flamingolodge.com, Hwy 9336)*. These folks rent two types of houseboat, which, if you're with five other people, is cheaper than you might think. Even with the top luxury model (the Gibsons), it only ends up being $41 per person per night. And the longer you keep it out, the cheaper it gets. All boats have a refrigerator/freezer unit, stove and oven, bathrooms with showers, propane, linen, kitchen utensils, pots, life vests and charts. The luxury boats have air-con and generators, while the pontoon boats do not.

Boxier pontoon boats, which can sleep six comfortably, cost $275 nightly or $340 for two nights off-season. From November to April the two-night minimum is $475. The Gibsons have a two-night minimum year-round, and cost $525 off-season, $575 November to April. Expect to pay an extra $40 a day for fuel. You don't need a special license; if you've never driven a boat before, they'll give you an hour-long orientation course and set you free with a seafaring RV.

THE EVERGLADES

viewing of the exceptional reefs, canoe rentals, transportation to the keys, and snorkeling and scuba diving trips. Here's the lowdown on the myriad of services offered: All tours require a minimum of six people, so call to make reservations. Three-hour glass-bottom–boat trips depart at 10am daily ($20/18/13 adult/senior/child under 12 yrs). Canoe rentals cost $8 hourly and kayaks $16; they're rented from 9am to 3pm. Transportation to Elliott Key for hiking or camping costs $25 per person roundtrip (make reservations at least a day in advance). A three-hour snorkeling trip ($30 per person) departs at 10am Monday to Thursday and at 1:30pm daily; you'll have about 1½ hours in the water. Scuba trips depart at 8:30am Friday to Sunday ($45). Two words of caution: Coral rock is very sharp (be careful wading in the water) and bring lots of mosquito repellent.

ALONG THE TAMIAMI TRAIL

Although the main attraction on the Tamiami Trail – which blazes between Miami and Tampa – is Shark Valley, a few other stops are worthy of your time. For the most part, it's straight as an arrow through monotonous swampland.

Miccosukee Resort & Convention Center

About 15 minutes west of the Miami airport, this resort (☎ 305-925-2555, 877-242-6464, Ⓦ www.miccosukee.com, 500 SW 177th Ave) has 302 contemporary guest rooms and suites ($99 Nov-Apr, inquire about off-season packages); wall-to-wall gaming tables that are open around the clock; second-tier nationally known entertainers; and five restaurants, including a deli and an all-you-can-eat buffet. Hotel guests have access to a nice fitness center. Inquire about special packages.

Shark Valley

This Everglades National Park entrance (☎ 305-221-8776; admission $8 per car; open 8:30am-5pm daily) offers a very popular and painless way to immerse yourself in the Everglades prairie. You can bike ($4.75 per

hour), walk or take a tram tour along the 17-mile **trail** between the entrance and the 50-foot-high **Shark Valley Observation Tower**, which offers a dramatic vantage point overlooking the park. The place is teeming with flora and fauna, including plenty of gators sunning themselves on the asphalt roadway. Give them wide berth.

The naturalist-led **Shark Valley Tram Tour** (☎ 305-221-8455 for reservations; tours $11/10/6.50 adult/senior/child under 12 yrs) takes two hours and is extremely worthwhile. If you only have time for one Everglades activity, this should be it. Trams leave hourly between 9am and 4pm in winter, and at 9am and 11am and 1pm and 3pm in summer. Reservations are recommended in high season. Shark Valley is 25 miles west of Florida's Turnpike.

Miccosukee Indian Village

For a more friendly and accessible introduction to Native American traditions and customs, see the Ah-Tah-Thi-Ki Museum section, later in this chapter. The Miccosukee Cultural Center is merely a collection of tourist shops and inhumane alligator wrestling displays. The filling station has expensive gasoline, and the restaurant is redolent with the scent of ancient frying oil. Move on.

Big Cypress Gallery

Clyde Butcher's photography gallery (☎ 941-695-2428, Ⓦ www.clydebutcher.com, Tamiami Trail; open 10am-5pm Wed-Mon) is a sanctified highlight of any trip to the Everglades. By all means stop here. In the great tradition of Ansel Adams, Clyde's large-format black and white images elevate the swamps to a higher level. He has found a quiet spirituality in the brackish waters and you just might, too, with the help of his eyes.

Big Cypress National Preserve

This 1139-sq-mile, federally protected preserve is the result of a compromise between environmentalists, cattle ranchers and oil-and-gas explorers. While allowing preexisting development to proceed to a certain

Air Boats & Swamp Buggies

Air boats are flat-bottomed skiffs that use powerful fans to propel themselves in the water. While capable of traveling in shallow water, they are very loud, and their environmental impact has not been determined. One thing is clear: Air boats in the hands of responsible operators have little impact, but irresponsible operators cause lots of direct and collateral damage to the ecosystem.

Swamp buggies are enormous balloon-tired vehicles that can go through swamps, causing ruts and damaging wildlife.

Air boat and swamp buggy rides are offered all along US Hwy 41 (Tamiami Trail). Please assess the motives behind the operator's existence before just getting on a 'nature' tour. You may be helping to disturb the Everglades' delicate balance.

extent, the preserve generally protects the land. The area is integral to the Everglades' ecosystem: Rains that flood the prairies and wetlands here slowly filter down through the Glades.

About 45% of the cypress swamp (which is not a swamp at all but a group of mangrove islands, hardwood hammocks, islands of slash pine, prairie and marshes) is protected preserve. Great bald cypress trees are nearly gone from the area, as lumbering and other industry took its toll before the preserve was established. These days, dwarf pond cypress trees fill the area.

Why is it called Big Cypress then? Because of the size of the preserve, not the cypress trees within it. Resident fauna include alligators, snakes, wading birds (white ibis', wood storks, tri-color herons and egrets), Florida panthers (rarely seen), wild turkeys and red cockaded woodpeckers.

Information The Big Cypress Visitor Center (☎ 941-695-4111), about 20 miles west of Shark Valley, sells off-road vehicle permits (4WDs are permitted; $50 annual permit required). It's open from 8:30am to 4:30pm daily. The National Preserve Headquarters (☎ 941-695-2000) is just east of Ochopee. It's open from 8am to 4:30pm weekdays.

Hiking You'll find 31 miles of the Florida National Scenic Trail (FNST), maintained by the Florida Trail Association, within Big Cypress National Preserve. From the southern terminus, which can be accessed by car via Loop Rd, the trail runs 8.3 miles north to the Tamiami Trail, passing the Big Cypress Visitor Center. There are two primitive campsites with water wells along the trail. Off-road vehicles are permitted to cross, but not operate on, the FNST. For the less adventurous, there's the short Tree Snail Hammock Nature Trail, off Loop Rd.

Driving On-road vehicles can drive on Loop Rd, a potholed dirt road, and Turner River Rd, which shoots straight as an arrow north off the Tamiami Trail. There are excellent wildlife-viewing opportunities along the entire stretch of Turner River Rd, especially in the Turner River Canal, which runs along the east side of it. The road leads to the northern area of the preserve where off-road vehicles are permitted.

Camping In addition to the two sites on the FNST, there are six primitive campgrounds on the preserve. You can pick up a map at the visitor's center. Be sure to bring your own water and food. Most campsites – **Bear Island**, **Midway**, **Loop Rd**, **Mitchell Landing** and **Pinecrest** – are free, and you needn't register. Mitchell Landing, Loop Rd and Pinecrest do not accommodate RVs. **Monument Lake** *(free off-season, $14 Nov-Apr)* has water and toilets.

Ochopee

Driving through the tiny hamlet of Ochopee (population about four)...no...wait...turn around, you missed it. That's right, folks, break out the cameras: Ochopee's claim to fame is that it has the USA's smallest official post office! In a former toolshed, a friendly postal worker patiently poses for snapshots.

Canoe Camping on 10,000 Islands

The finest way to experience the serenity and beauty of the Everglades – which is somehow desolate yet lush, tropical yet foreboding – is by canoeing or kayaking through the excellent network of waterways that skirt the northwest portion of the park. The **10,000 Islands** consist of many (but not really 10,000) tiny islands and a mangrove swamp that hugs the southwesternmost border of Florida.

The **Wilderness Waterway**, a 99-mile path between Everglades City and Flamingo, is the longest canoe trail in the area, but there are shorter canoe trails near Flamingo.

Most islands are fringed by narrow beaches with sugar-white sand, but note that the water is brackish, not clear, and very shallow most of the time. It's not Tahiti, but it's fascinating. The best part is that you can camp on your own island for up to a week.

Getting around the 10,000 Islands is pretty straightforward if you religiously adhere to NOAA tide and nautical charts. Going against the tides is the fastest way to make it a miserable trip. The Gulf Coast Visitor Center sells **nautical charts** and gives out free **tidal charts**. You can also purchase charts prior to your visit – call ☎ 305-247-1216 and ask for chart Nos 11430, 11432 and 11433.

Canoe & Kayak Itineraries

Near Everglades City, you can take a downstream trip on the Turner River alone or with a group. Take a drift-with-the-current trip to Chokoloskee Island, or add a bit of a challenge at the end and paddle upstream in the boating canal to the Gulf Coast Visitor Center (ranger station).

For an easy day of paddling, just cross the bay from the Gulf Coast Visitor Center and paddle out and around the mangroves to Sandfly Island or on the Chokoloskee Bay Loop.

For an easy one- or two-night trip, head to islands closest to the ranger station: Tiger, Picnic, Rabbit, New Turkey, Turkey and Hog Keys, all with beach campsites.

For a nice few days of canoeing, head south from the Gulf Coast Visitor Center, past Chokoloskee and up the Lopez River, north near Sunday Bay, and then southeast to Sweetwater Bay, where there's a chickee at which you can spend the night. The next morning head toward Watson Place and southwest to Pavilion Key for an overnight at the beach campsite. Then head north to Rabbit Key for a final night on the beach. In the morning, head back north to the ranger station.

There are hundreds of other combinations; check with a ranger at the Gulf Coast Visitor Center for more recommendations.

For the cost of a stamp, you can send a postcard or letter from here.

Places to Eat

Pit BBQ (☎ 305-226-2272, 16400 SW 8th St, between Miami & Shark Valley) Dishes $4-9. Open 11am-11:30pm daily. It doesn't get more real than this: authentic barbecue served on picnic tables in a dumpy joint with country & western music on the jukebox. You gotta love it (otherwise, don't stop).

Joannie's Blue Crab Cafe (☎ 941-695-2682, Tamiami Trail, east of Ochopee) Dishes $10-13. Open 9am-5pm daily. This quintes-

sential shack, with open rafters, shellacked picnic tables, wooden floors and alligator kitsch, couldn't be more atmospheric – in a *Deliverance* sort of way. Although the food served on paper plates is just so-so, the down-home charm of the place makes up for it. While stone crabs are a decided specialty, you can also get swamp dinners (with gator nuggets, gator fritters, frogs legs and Indian fry bread) and peel-and-eat shrimp.

EVERGLADES CITY

Everglades City survives rather than thrives from the trade of fisherfolk who pull into the marina and live in RVs, and tourists

Canoe Camping on 10,000 Islands

If you're going to make the eight- to 10-day Wilderness Waterway trek between Everglades City and Flamingo, you'll probably need help portaging (shuttling your car from one point to the other). Contact the very nice folks at the Everglades International Hostel (☎ 305-248-1122, 800-372-3874, **w** www.evergladeshostel.com), 20 SW 2nd Ave, Florida City. They're the only ones in the area who provide this service ($200 if you rent with them, $300 if you don't.) However you cut it, count on sacrificing one day for logistics: One person ferries the car around while another pulls permits for the backcountry trip.

Wilderness Camping

Three types of backcountry campsites are available from the Flamingo and Gulf Coast Visitor Centers: beach sites, on coastal shell beaches and in the 10,000 Islands; ground sites, which are basically mounds of dirt built up above the mangroves along the interior bays and rivers; and 'chickees,' wooden platforms built above the water line on which you can pitch a free-standing (no spikes) tent. Chickees, which have toilets, are the most civilized; they're certainly unique. There's a serenity in sleeping on what feels like a raft levitating above the water in the middle of nature. Beach sites are the most comfortable, though biting insects are rife, even in winter. Ground sites tend to be the most bug-infested.

Warning: If you're just paddling around and you see an island that looks perfectly pleasant for camping but it's not a designated campsite, beware – you may end up submerged when the tides change.

Rules & Permits

From November to April, camping permits cost $10; in the off-season sites are free, but you must still self-register at the Flamingo and Gulf Coast Visitor Centers.

All the park's resources are protected, including the plants, shells, artifacts and buildings. You can fish, but only with a state fishing license; check at any ranger station for information. Free permits, available at ranger stations, are required for overnight stays. In areas without toilets, you'll need to dig a hole at least 6 inches deep for waste. Campfires are prohibited except at certain beach sites: Use dead and down wood only, and build your fire below the high-tide line. Remove all your garbage from the park when you leave.

passing through to visit the Everglades. It's perfectly pleasant, in a fisherfolk's paradise kind of way – it's a sensible place to spend the night to get an early start on canoe trips in the 10,000 Islands.

Orientation & Information

Hwy 29 runs south through town.

At the corner of US Hwy 41 and Hwy 29, the Everglades Area Chamber of Commerce (☎ 941-695-3941), open 9am to 5pm daily, dispenses basic information. The Gulf Coast Visitor Center (☎ 941-695-3311), at the southern end of town, has loads of information on the 10,000 Islands

and the Everglades. It's open 8:30am to 5pm daily.

You can wash clothes at the coin laundry next to the Right Choice Market (it's the only choice, actually).

Bike rentals are available at the Ivey House Hotel (see Places to Stay & Eat, later) for $3/15 per hour/day.

Canoeing & Kayaking

Rangers with the **National Park Service** (☎ *941-695-3311, Gulf Coast Visitor Center; tours are free, canoes cost $24 per day; open mid-Nov–mid-Apr*) lead two different canoe trips through overhanging mangrove tunnels along the Turner River. Tours for more experienced paddlers depart at 9am on Saturday and last seven hours; the Sunday morning trips at 9:30am are four hours and geared to paddlers with average abilities.

The NPS also rents canoes by the day and for overnights ($24), and provides shuttle service ($150) if you'll be paddling from Everglades City to Flamingo and need to get back to pick up your car.

Everglades National Park Boat Tours (☎ *941-695-2591, 800-445-7724, Gulf Coast Visitor Center; tours $16/8 adult/child 6-12 yrs*) offer the simplest tours. Large pleasure boats depart every 30 minutes (9am to 4:30pm) from mid-December to mid-April and every hour or so in the off-season. Tours last 1¾ hours.

North American Canoe Tours (*NACT;* ☎ *941-695-3299/4666,* **W** *www.everglades adventures.com, Ivey House Hotel, 107 Camellia St; open Nov–mid-Apr*) rents camping equipment and first-rate canoes ($25/35/25 half/first/each additional day), recreational kayaks ($35/55/45 half/full/ each additional day) and touring kayaks ($45/65/55 half/full/each additional day), which have rudders and upgraded paddles that make going against the current a whole lot easier. You get 20% off most of these services and rentals if you're staying at the Ivey House Hotel, which NACT owns.

NACT is the best outfit for regular guided tours. For $75 to $95 per person (depending on whether you want to go out in a canoe or kayak), you get a guided six-hour canoe trip, with lunch, of the Turner River; daily tours depart at 9am. NACT also offers interesting day tours within the 10,000 Islands for approximately the same price. NACT will also customize multi-night excursions.

For those making the eight- to 10-day trip between the Gulf Coast and Flamingo Visitor Centers with an NACT rental boat, they will pick up boats in Flamingo for $100, but you'll still have to get yourself back to Everglades City. Call the Everglades International Hostel (☎ 305-248-1122, 800-372-3874) to make arrangements for that.

See the boxed text 'Canoe Camping on 10,000 Islands' for opportunities to canoe and kayak in the Everglades.

Places to Stay & Eat

Glades Haven (☎ *941-695-2746, Hwy 29*) Tent/RV sites $20/30. Across from the Gulf Coast Visitor Center, this 30-site commercial campground is geared more to RVs than tents, but tenters are welcome.

The ***Ivey House Hotel*** (☎ *941-695-3299, fax 941-695-4155,* **W** *www.iveyhouse.com, 107 Camellia St*) Rooms $50-90 Nov–mid-Dec, $70-125 mid-Dec–Apr; closed May-Oct. Deli open 7am-2pm. The town's premier lodging feels a tad institutional because of its newness, but this fine choice should be your first choice. In its former life, the low-slung hotel served as a recreation hall for Tamiami Trail laborers, but now the family-run hostelry has good meals (breakfast is included and there's not a deep fryer in sight), comfortable rooms and free use of bicycles (on a first-come, first-served basis). The newer inn rooms are more expensive, but they're much nicer. The older B&B rooms are smaller, with shared bath. Guests staying in these rooms do not have access to the pool at the inn. These folks also run NACT, which operates some of the best nature trips around; see Canoeing & Kayaking, earlier.

Rod & Gun Club Lodge (☎ *941-695-2101, 200 Riverside Dr*) Rooms $75 off-season, $105 mid-Oct–June. Built in the 1920s as a hunting lodge by Barron Collier (who needed a place to chill after watching workers dig his Tamiami Trail), this lodge is handsome and masculine, but the 17 guest house rooms aren't as much so. It sure harkens back to Olde Florida.

Captain's Table (☎ *941-695-4211, 800-741-6430, Hwy 29*) Rooms $45-75 off-season, $70-95 late Dec–Apr. At the jig in Hwy 29 east of the downtown traffic circle, Captain's Table has a nice staff and 48 barely tidy rooms and suites (with kitchen facilities).

Cheryl's Deli/Glades Haven (☎ *941-695-2746, Hwy 29*) Dishes $4-5. Open 6am-9pm daily. Across from the Gulf Coast Visitor

Center, Cheryl's/Glades has decent cold-cut sandwiches with lots o' toppings.

Susie's Station *(no ☎, Hwy 29)* Dishes $6-9. The atmosphere at Susie's is pleasant enough, but she only serves fried stuff: chicken strips, fried shrimp, french fries and the like. It's on the west side of the traffic circle.

Stock up on groceries before you come, since the **Right Choice Market**, just east of the traffic circle, is about 25% more expensive than any Publix.

AH-TAH-THI-KI MUSEUM

The best Everglades tourism news in years is the advent of this Seminole museum *(☎ 863-902-1113,* W *www.seminoletribe.com/ museum, Big Cypress Seminole Indian Reservation; admission $6/4 adult/senior & child; open 9am-5pm Tues-Sun),* 17 miles north of I-75. With educational exhibits on Seminole life, history and the tribe today, the museum was founded with Seminole gaming proceeds. Gambling receipts, an economic powerhouse, provide most of the Seminole tribe's multimillion-dollar operating budget.

Never before have the Seminoles opened so much up to the public. Sure, it's good for business, but they really are dedicated to giving visitors a closer understanding of the Seminole and Miccosukee people, and to enabling them to experience Seminole life. It's not the wild wild Glades, and there are aspects, like alligator wrestling, that leave something to be desired, but it's a breakthrough for the tribe. Until recently, they had kept to themselves where tourism was concerned.

Seminole Safari *(☎ 941-949-6101, 800-617-7516,* W *www.seminoletours.com)* offers day ($45) and overnight ($110) packages. Overnights include sleeping in a screened-in chickee hut, listening to campfire storytelling, taking an airboat or swamp buggy ride and having Indian meals (catfish, fry bread, gator nuggets). It's touristy, certainly, but the package is a rather unique opportunity.

Fort Lauderdale

As recently as the mid-1980s Fort Lauderdale was the unofficial spring break capital of the country. More American university students partook of this rite of passage in Fort Lauderdale than anywhere else in the country. The sand was sticky from beer and the streets were full of students drinking cheap drafts until they passed out. But since the late '80s, the town has divested itself completely of this scene. In essence, it's been outlawed. And the powers-that-be have done an exceedingly good job at renovating and grooming the whole place.

That's not to say this is not a partying town. There are dozens of clubs, pubs and beach nightspots, where you should dress respectably and behave yourself. These days, though, Fort Lauderdale is known more as an international yachting center than a party spot. Ships owned around the world are built and repaired here; huge yachts winter here; and some of the wealthiest European, Asian and American sailors can be seen fussing over details with the city's countless support staff.

Fort Lauderdale has some worthy cultural and historical sites (especially the Museum of Art), and lovely areas for walking – notably the district along E Las Olas Blvd and Riverwalk. There's also the Hugh Taylor Birch State Recreation Area and a river cruise to provide natural distractions.

History

Small bands of Indians lived in this region for about 4000 years before the arrival of the Spanish in the 16th century. During the early period of Spanish control and the later occupation of Florida by the British, fighting between the Europeans and Indian groups on the west coast of Florida kept settlers at bay. But during the second era of Spanish rule, white settlers slowly began to gain a regional foothold. In 1821 the USA took control of Florida, and by 1825, families had settled on the north banks of the New River.

In 1836, in the midst of the Second Seminole War, Seminoles attacked the Cooley family residence, killing all but Mr Cooley, who was away. The Cooley Massacre, a milestone in the city's history, led Major William Lauderdale (for whom the city is named) and troops from the Tennessee Volunteers to establish a fort and stockade here in 1838.

White settlement remained stagnant until the 1870s, but by the 1890s Fort Lauderdale was large enough to support a post office, and ferry and stagecoach services. Frank Stranahan established the city's first lodge.

The real boom came with the introduction of the Florida East Coast Railroad, connecting Miami, Fort Lauderdale and St Augustine with the rest of the eastern seaboard. Immigrant groups, including large numbers of Danes, Swedes and Japanese, moved in. In 1925, Port Everglades was established…just in time for the mid-1920s bust, and the 1926 hurricane, which killed dozens of people and wiped out thousands of acres.

As with Miami, WWII provided just the boost Fort Lauderdale needed. The public display of the captured German ship *Arauca* in Port Everglades served as a rallying point, and area German submarine maneuvers led to the establishment of military bases, which brought new settlers and money after the war. Prosperity grew during the 1970s construction boom, which also attracted hundreds of thousands of college students for spring break. The ritual of getting plastered as cheaply as possible was outlawed locally in the mid-1980s. Friendly police presence keeps things in order.

Orientation

Fort Lauderdale is set in a grid wherever physically possible (it's hard with all the water), and it's divided into three distinct sections: the beach, east of the Intracoastal Waterway; downtown, on the mainland; and Port Everglades, the cruise port south of the city.

US Hwy 1 (also called Federal Hwy) cuts through downtown, swooping under E Las Olas Blvd. Hwy A1A runs along the ocean, where it's also called Atlantic Blvd (south of Sunrise Blvd) or Ocean Blvd (north of Sunrise Blvd). At its southern end, Atlantic Blvd merges into Seabreeze Blvd and Seabreeze continues south until the curve where it becomes 17th St. The whole stretch is also known as, simply, Hwy A1A.

Streets and addresses are prefixed N, S, E or W according to their relation to Broward Blvd and Andrews Ave; Broward Blvd is the line dividing north from south, and Andrews Ave, just west of Federal Hwy, divides east from west.

The main arteries between downtown and the beach are Sunrise Blvd to the north, E Las Olas Blvd in the center and 17th St/ Seabreeze Blvd to the south (Seabreeze connects the beach to Port Everglades).

Between the beach and the mainland are almost two dozen small finger islands. This is yacht country, perhaps the yacht capital of North America, and you'll notice a mooring at every house. Along with yachts, of course, come the millionaires who putter around on them. If you're waterborne, cruise by Millionaire's Row on the New River, just west of the Intracoastal Waterway – that's south of E Las Olas Blvd, west of Las Olas Isles and east of downtown.

FORT LAUDERDALE AREA

1 Main Post Office
2 Gay & Lesbian Community Center
3 Baja Beach Club
4 Beach Hostel
5 Deauville Inn

You can walk 'downtown' Lauderdale-by-the-Sea easily. E Commercial Blvd is the town's main east-west artery, and Ocean Dr (Hwy A1A) is the main north-south route. The pier is at the end of Commercial Blvd at El Mar Dr, one block east of Ocean Dr.

Information

The excellent Greater Fort Lauderdale Convention & Visitor's Bureau (☎ 954-765-4466, 800-227-8669, w www.sunny.org), 1850 Eller Dr, is in Port Everglades. It's open 8:30am to 5pm weekdays. The CVB deliberately blurs Lauderdale neighborhood boundaries, marketing the region as a package to entice more visitors. For this reason, many pamphlets list hotels, attractions and events in the entire region within a Fort Lauderdale context.

The Lauderdale-by-the-Sea Chamber of Commerce (☎ 954-776-1000, 800-699-6764), 4201 Ocean Dr, is located in the middle of the triangle formed by the intersection of Ocean and Bougainvillea Drs. It's open 8:30am to 5pm weekdays, 9am to 3pm weekends.

The Gay & Lesbian Community Center (☎ 954-463-9005, w www.glccftl.org), 1717 N Andrews Ave, north of downtown, is quite helpful and friendly.

The main post office (☎ 800-275-8777) is at 1900 W Oakland Park Blvd, west of I-95.

Clark's Out of Town News (☎ 954-467-1543), 303 S Andrews Ave, in downtown, and the City News Stand (☎ 954-776-0940), 4400 Bougainvillea Dr, in Lauderdale-by-the-Sea, carry out-of-town and foreign newspapers. Clark's even has some travel books.

The *Sun Sentinel* and the *Miami Herald* are the major dailies for the area. *City Link* (w www.clo-sfl.com) is a good local weekly covering music, clubs, restaurants, art and other entertainment. *Hot Spots* covers the gay and lesbian club scene; pick it up at gay bars, clubs and guest houses.

Hobby House (☎ 954-463-1522), 1201 E Las Olas Blvd, downtown, offers one-hour developing and passport photos.

The Broward County main public library (☎ 954-357-7444, w www.broward .org/library) is at 100 S Andrews Ave in downtown.

The largest public hospital in the area is Broward General Medical Center (☎ 954-355-4400), 1600 S Andrews Ave, in Port Everglades.

THINGS TO SEE & DO
Downtown Fort Lauderdale

Museum of Art This museum (☎ 954-525-5500, w www.museumofart.org, 1 E Las Olas Blvd; admission $10/8/5 adult/senior/ student & child over 12 yrs; open 10am-5pm Tues-Sat, noon-5pm Sun) is simply one of Florida's best. The impressive permanent collection includes works by Pablo Picasso, Henri Matisse, Henry Moore, Salvador Dalí and Andy Warhol. Since the enormity of the collection far outpaces the available space, you never really know what will be showing. Don't overlook the growing and impressive collections of Cuban, ethnographic, African and South American collections.

Museum of Discovery & Science Fronted by the 52-foot Great Gravity Clock, Florida's largest kinetic energy sculpture, this environmentally oriented museum (MODS; ☎ 954-467-6637, w www.mods.org, 401 SW 2nd St; admission $14/13/12 adult/senior & student/ child; open 10am-5pm Mon-Sat, noon-6pm Sun) is one of Florida's best (of its genre). The admission price also includes one **IMAX** 3D show in the impressive five-story theater, which boasts wraparound sound. Before leaving, check out the **parabolic display** across the street: Two dishes face each other about 60 feet apart. Turn toward one dish and have a friend turn toward the other. Whisper into the dish and you'll hear each other perfectly.

Fort Lauderdale Historical Society This organization (219 SW 2nd Ave, w www.old fortlauderdale.org) maintains the 1905 **New River Inn** (☎ 954-463-4431, 231 SW 2nd Ave; admission $5/2 adult/child 6-16 yrs; open noon-5pm Tues-Fri), the **Philemon Bryan House** (1905; not open to the public) and the nearby **King-Cromartie House** (1907), which is only open for tours at 1pm, 2pm and 3pm on Saturday. The museum mounts exhibits on Fort Lauderdale and Broward County history and Seminole folk art.

Riverwalk This meandering pathway (☎ 954-468-1541, W www.goriverwalk.com), along the New River, runs from the Stranahan House to the Broward Center for the Performing Arts. It's very pleasant and lovely, and connects a number of sights.

Las Olas Riverfront (☎ 954-522-6556, SW 1st Ave at Las Olas Blvd), a giant shopping mall with stores, restaurants, a movie theater and live entertainment nightly, is also the place to catch many river cruises (see the Organized Tours section, later in this chapter).

Stranahan House One of Florida's oldest residences, this registered historic landmark (☎ 954-524-4736, W www.stranahanhouse .com, 335 SE 6th St; admission $5/2 adult/ child; open 10am-4pm Wed-Sun), behind the Hyde Park supermarket, is a fine example of Florida frontier design. Constructed from Dade County pine, the house has wide porches, exceptionally tall windows, a Victorian parlor, the original furnishings and fine tropical gardens. It was built as the home and store for Ohio transplant Frank Stranahan, who built a small empire trading with the Seminole. After real estate and stock market losses in the late 1920s, and the collapse of his Fort Lauderdale Bank, Stranahan committed suicide by jumping into the New River.

Fort Lauderdale Beach

Bonnet House This beautiful estate (☎ 954-563-5393, W www.bonnethouse.org, 900 N Birch Rd; admission $9/8/7 adult/ senior/student & child 6-18 yrs; open 10am-3pm Wed-Fri, noon-4pm Sat & Sun) features 35 subtropical acres filled with native and imported tropical plants, including a vast orchid collection. Although you must take a guided tour of the house (1¼ hours), you are free to walk the grounds and nature trails on your own.

International Swimming Hall of Fame If you know that a competition pool holds 573,000 gallons, you're enough of a swimming wonk to *really* enjoy this place (☎ 954-462-6536, W www.ishof.org, 1 Hall of Fame

Dr/SE 5th St; admission $3/1/5 adult/senior & student/family; open 9am-7pm daily). Exhibits include thousands of photographs, Olympic memorabilia from over 100 nations, medals, uniforms, paintings and sculptures.

Hugh Taylor Birch State Recreation Area This state park (☎ 954-564-4521, 3109 E Sunrise Blvd; admission $4 per vehicle of two to eight people, $1 per pedestrian or bicyclist; open 8am-sunset daily) contains one of the last significant maritime hammocks left in Broward County, as well as mangroves, a freshwater lagoon system and several endangered plant and animal species (including the gopher tortoise and golden leather fern). You can fish, picnic, hike, canoe or bike. Canoe rentals cost about $5.50 an hour and the canoe trail is half a mile long.

WATER SPORTS

Greater Fort Lauderdale has a three-tiered natural reef system with depths ranging from 20 to 55 feet. The region also has over 75 artificial reefs, which have been attracting fish and other reef life for about the last 20 years. Consequently, Fort Lauderdale has tons of dive operators. Your best bet is to pick up the 'Greater Fort Lauderdale Attractions Map and Events' brochure, which lists over 20 of them.

Water-skiing is possible on the ocean, but it's usually very expensive; check on the piers around Las Olas Blvd bridge and look for flyers in town. Jet-skis are popular here, but we really wish you wouldn't use them – see the Activities section in the Things to See & Do chapter for the rant.

Bill's Sunrise Watersports/Neptune Parasail (☎ 954-462-8962 main rental, ☎ 954-761-1672 parasailing, W www.sunrisewatersports .com, 2025 E Sunrise Blvd) These folks offer 10- to 12-minute parasailing flights for $65 per person, and they also rent six-person motorboats (by reservation only) for $50/ 85/150 an hour/two hours/four hours.

ORGANIZED TOURS

For sightseeing excursions down the New River and the Intracoastal Waterway to

FORT LAUDERDALE

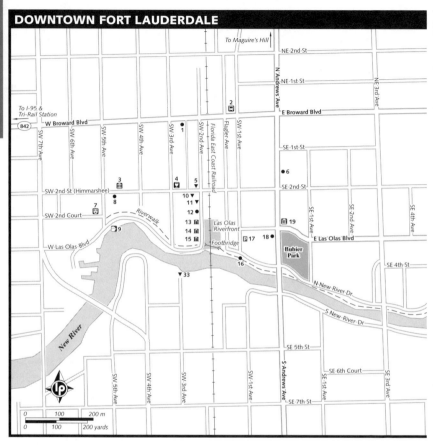

DOWNTOWN FORT LAUDERDALE

Port Everglades and back, hop aboard the 19th-century riverboat replica, the ***Carrie B*** (☎ *954-768-9920, SE 5th Ave on the River-walk; tours $11/6 adult/child 12 yrs & under*). Tours last about 1½ hours and depart at 11am, 1pm and 3pm daily.

Riverfront Cruises (☎ *954-463-3372, 800-499-2248,* W *www.riverfrontcruises.com, Las Olas Riverfront at SW 1st Ave; tours $14/8 adult/child*) offers 1½-hour yacht cruises along inland canals, past Million-aire's Row and down to Port Everglades. Tours leave every two hours from 10:30am to 8:30pm.

Pro Diver II (☎ *954-467-6030,* W *www. prodiveusa.com, 515 Hwy A1A/Seabreeze Blvd; tours $20/12 adult/child under 12 yrs*) is a glass-bottom boat revealing underwater ocean wonders that you could otherwise see only by snorkeling or diving. Speaking of which, if you do want to get closer, you can don snorkeling gear for an extra $9/6 adult/child. Some people in your party can view the fish the dry way, others can splash around with the fishes. Excursions leave at 9:30am Tuesday to Saturday and 2pm Sunday. Call at 8:30am the day of departure to check weather conditions.

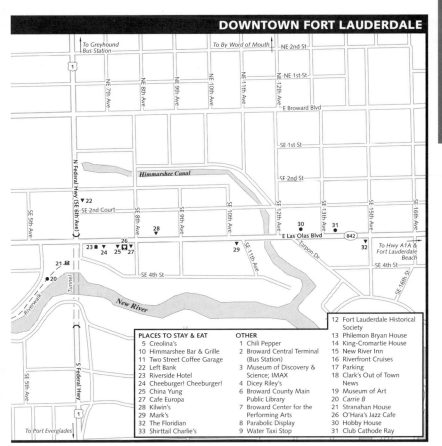

DOWNTOWN FORT LAUDERDALE

PLACES TO STAY & EAT	OTHER	
5 Creolina's	1 Chili Pepper	12 Fort Lauderdale Historical Society
10 Himmarshee Bar & Grille	2 Broward Central Terminal (Bus Station)	13 Philemon Bryan House
11 Two Street Coffee Garage	3 Museum of Discovery & Science; IMAX	14 King-Cromartie House
22 Left Bank	4 Dicey Riley's	15 New River Inn
23 Riverside Hotel	5 Broward County Main Public Library	16 Riverfront Cruises
24 Cheeburger! Cheeburger!	6 Broward County Main Public Library	17 Parking
25 China Yung	7 Broward Center for the Performing Arts	18 Clark's Out of Town News
27 Cafe Europa	8 Parabolic Display	19 Museum of Art
28 Kilwin's	9 Water Taxi Stop	20 Carrie B
29 Mark's		21 Stranahan House
32 The Floridian		26 O'Hara's Jazz Cafe
33 Shirttail Charlie's		30 Hobby House
		31 Club Cathode Ray

You'll have to decide for yourself about the **Jungle Queen** (☎ 954-462-5596, Ⓦ www.junglequeen.com, Radisson Bahia Mar Yacht Center, 801 Seabreeze Blvd; dinner cruises $27, sightseeing $12.50/8.25 adult/child under 10 yrs). This is either a wondrous journey to a tropical island, a great meal and a funny vaudeville show, or the kitschiest, cheesiest romp into Borscht-belt glitz around. Whatever else, this is a Fort Lauderdale tradition. The four-hour dinner tour (departing at 7pm nightly) goes like this: On the way to the 'tropical' island, where you dine on barbecue and shrimp,

the narrator dishes dirt on the rich folks who live on Millionaire's Row, leads group waves to the drawbridge attendants and offers trivia and local lore. If that sounds like a bit much, there are also three-hour afternoon tours, sans meal and show.

PLACES TO STAY

There are a few youth hostels and, if you're searching for work on a foreign-flag vessel, several inexpensive crew houses, too. You'll find the most hotels, motels and B&Bs on the beach, in the '-mars' area. Lauderdale-by-the-Sea lodging tends to be a bit pricier because rooms are right on the beach, but they're definitely the nicest.

Crew houses are not for the average backpacker, but rather for those seeking employment aboard yachts and ships moored nearby (see the Boat section in the Getting There & Away chapter). Generally these are the best places to pick up information on boat jobs; all have listings of the agencies in town. In most cases, backpackers just looking for lodging will not be admitted, so call first and make sure before showing up. The exception to the no-backpackers rule is Floyd's Youth Hostel & Crew House (see Port Everglades, in this section).

Wherever you go in town, be careful about advertised rates – many are for singles, with huge jumps for additional people. If you have complaints about a hotel, contact the Fort Lauderdale Division of Hotels and Restaurants (☎ 954-958-5520).

Downtown Fort Lauderdale

Riverside Hotel (☎ 954-467-0671, 800-325-3280, fax 954-462-2148, **w** www.riverside hotel.com, 620 E Las Olas Blvd). Rooms $95-149 off-season, $189 mid-Dec–mid-Apr (inquire about discounts). The best option downtown, Fort Lauderdale's oldest hotel has 105 large rooms with fluffy carpets and Jacobean oak furnishings. At press time an additional 116 rooms were under construction next door.

Fort Lauderdale Beach

Beach Hostel (☎ 954-567-7275, fax 954-567-9697, **w** www.fortlauderdalehostel.com, 2115 N Ocean Blvd; see the Fort Lauderdale Area map). Dorm beds $16. Affiliated with Floyd's and new in 2000, this hot-pink, 61-bed hostel is just one block from the beach and about a mile north of the main beach area. The mostly four-bed dorms are both single-sex and mixed. Canned goods are set out for the taking and breakfast foods, including eggs, are set out for the making. Free local calls, one Internet station and free snorkeling gear are also included. The hostel will pick you up anywhere in Fort Lauderdale during the day. Otherwise, bus No 11 runs by the hostel from the airport,

Greyhound bus station, downtown and the beaches. Most beds are filled with international visitors, since a passport is required to stay here.

The Winterset (☎ 954-564-5614, 800-888-2639, fax 954-565-5790, **w** www.thewinterset .com, 2801 Terramar St) Rooms & efficiencies $50-65/315-410 daily/weekly low season, $60-105/380-690 mid-Dec–Mar. This old-fashioned motel has 29 units, two pools surrounded by 40 varieties of palms, and friendly management. The furnishings date back to the 1970s (and not in a hip way, either).

La Casa Del Mar (☎ 954-467-2037, fax 954-467-7439, **w** www.lacasadelmar.com, 3003 Granada St) Rooms $80-100 off-season, $110-145 Dec-Apr. This family-owned, homey B&B has 11 rooms, studios and one-bedroom units. They're not ultra spiffy, but they're comfortable and surrounded by a tropical garden and a little pool. A full breakfast is included.

Nina Lee & Imperial House Motel (☎ 954-524-1568, 800-646-2533, fax 954-763-2931, 3048 Harbor Dr) Rooms/efficiencies/two-bedrooms $49/69/89 off-season, $79/99/119 late Dec–mid-Apr. Just a block from the beach, in a quiet neighborhood, this very friendly and clean motel has 26 units surrounding a pool, lawn and patio. This is a good choice for families, since some rooms connect and have sleeper sofas. Guests have use of the nearby Sheraton's facilities (including the pools, gym, business center and lounge).

Caribbean Quarters (☎ 954-523-3226, 888-414-3226, fax 954-523-7541, **w** www .caribbeanquarters.com, 3012 Granada St) Rooms $135-200 off-season, $150-250 Dec–mid-May. This three-story B&B features a lush private patio and 12 units with wicker and rattan furnishings and gauzy netting draped over the beds. Perfect for longer stays, some suites have a balcony, living room and even a dishwasher.

Radisson Bahia Mar Resort (☎ 954-764-2233, 800-327-8154, fax 954-523-5424, **w** www.bahiamar.net, 801 Seabreeze Blvd) Rooms $119-134 off-season, $199-239 Dec-May. A standard top-end place with 300

FORT LAUDERDALE BEACH

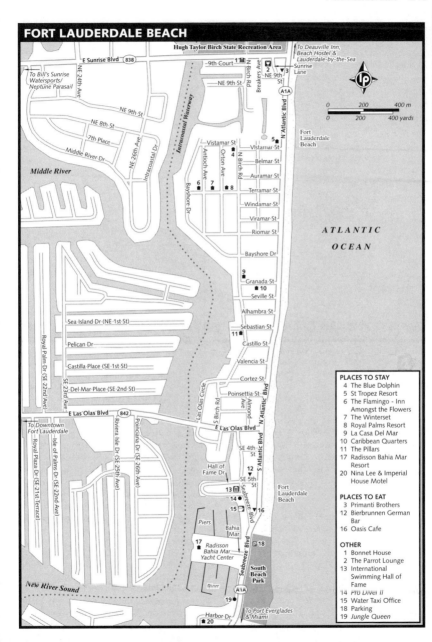

Hugh Taylor Birch State Recreation Area

To Deauville Inn,
Beach Hostel &
Lauderdale-by-the-Sea

E Sunrise Blvd (838)

To Bill's Sunrise
Watersports/
Neptune Parasail

9th Court
NE 9th St
NE 9th St
NE 8th St
7th Place
Middle River Dr

Sunrise
Lane

Middle River

ATLANTIC

OCEAN

Vistamar St
Belmar St
Auramar St
Terramar St
Windamar St
Viramar St
Riomar St

Bayshore Dr

Granada St
Seville St
Alhambra St
Sebastian St
Castillo St
Valencia St
Cortez St
Poinsettia St

Sea Island Dr (NE 1st St)
Pelican Dr
Castilla Place (SE 1st St)
Del Mar Place (SE 2nd St)
E Las Olas Blvd (842)

To Downtown
Fort Lauderdale

E Las Olas Blvd

SE 4th St
SE 5th St

Fort
Lauderdale
Beach

Hall of
Fame Dr

Piers
Bahia
Mar

Radisson
Bahia Mar
Yacht Center

**South
Beach
Park**

New River Sound

To Port Everglades
& Miami

Harbor Dr

PLACES TO STAY
4 The Blue Dolphin
5 St Tropez Resort
6 The Flamingo - Inn
  Amongst the Flowers
7 The Winterset
8 Royal Palms Resort
9 La Casa Del Mar
10 Caribbean Quarters
11 The Pillars
17 Radisson Bahia Mar
  Resort
20 Nina Lee & Imperial
  House Motel

PLACES TO EAT
3 Primanti Brothers
12 Bierbrunnen German
  Bar
16 Oasis Cafe

OTHER
1 Bonnet House
2 The Parrot Lounge
13 International
  Swimming Hall of
  Fame
14 Pro Diver II
15 Water Taxi Office
18 Parking
19 Jungle Queen

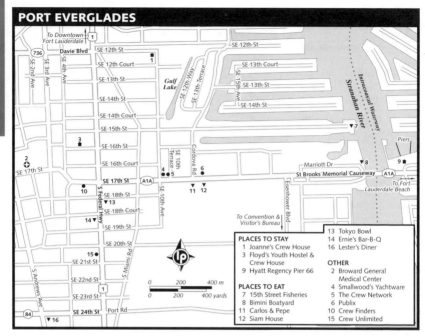

PORT EVERGLADES

PLACES TO STAY
1 Joanne's Crew House
3 Floyd's Youth Hostel &
   Crew House
9 Hyatt Regency Pier 66

PLACES TO EAT
7 15th Street Fisheries
8 Bimini Boatyard
11 Carlos & Pepe
12 Siam House
13 Tokyo Bowl
14 Ernie's Bar-B-Q
16 Lester's Diner

OTHER
2 Broward General
   Medical Center
4 Smallwood's Yachtware
5 The Crew Network
6 Publix
10 Crew Finders
15 Crew Unlimited

comfortable rooms, this resort also has the requisite amenities: pool, tennis courts and health club.

The Pillars (☎ 954-467-9639, 800-800-7666, fax 954-763-2845, W www.pillars hotel.com, 111 N Birch Rd) Rooms $119-159 June-Oct, $149-199 Nov, Dec & May, $189-259 Jan-Apr; suites $189-349 off-season, $279-389 Jan-Apr. Hands down the swankiest and loveliest lodging in town, this luxe retreat is *the* place to splurge for that special occasion. The Pillars boasts 23 suave plantation-style rooms surrounding a courtyard pool; waterfront tables lining its private dock (where you can have 'room' service) on the Intracoastal Waterway; and a host of amenities and pampering services.

Port Everglades

Floyd's Youth Hostel & Crew House (☎ 954-462-0631, fax 954-462-6881, W www .floydshostel.com, 445 SE 16th St) Dorm beds $15-16. Close to most crew placement

agencies (see Boat under Getting There & Away, later in this chapter), and a short bus ride to the beach, Floyd's is friendly and protective of their property and guests. Before you can stay you'll be vetted on the telephone. You must hold a valid passport; there's zero tolerance for illegal drug use. (Drinking is not monitored, but perhaps should be....) Floyd's provides many extras – free local calls, use of computers with DSL, incoming faxes, washer and dryer, basic food and cooking items, and barbecues every couple of weeks. They'll also pick you up from the airport, bus or train station.

Joanne's Crew House (☎ 954-527-1636, fax 954-527-1228, 916 SE 12th St) Rooms $135 per week. Fort Lauderdale's most established, best organized and cleanest crew house is in a residential area in a sprawling, ranch-style house. Fifteen people can await employment in five bedrooms (four bathrooms) in style: There's a big screened-in backyard, pool and a barbecue area on the 1-acre property. Joanne calls boat owners to tell them who's staying at the house.

Hyatt Regency Pier 66 *(☎ 954-525-6666, 800-327-3796, fax 954-728-3507,* W *www.hyatt.com, 2301 SE 17 St)* Rooms $179-259 off-season, $269-309 mid-Dec–Apr. The Hyatt has 380 very nice rooms, good service and great views from a rotating rooftop cocktail lounge.

Lauderdale-by-the-Sea

All three of these properties are right on the beach, not even a sandals' shuffle away.

A Little Inn by the Sea *(☎ 954-772-2450, 800-492-0311, fax 954-938-9354,* W *www.alittleinn.com, 4546 El Mar Dr)* Rooms & suites $79-149 off-season, $119-199 mid-Dec–Apr. All but one of these rooms and efficiencies face the ocean. Arranged around an interior and an exterior courtyard, many rooms have balconies and most have older bathrooms. Amenities include free bikes, free tennis, a pool and a breakfast buffet; children under age 12 stay free in their parents' room.

Tropic Seas *(☎ 954-772-2555, 800-952-9581, fax 954-771-5711,* W *www.tropicseasresort.com, 4616 El Mar Dr)* Rooms $85-160 off-season, $145-215 mid-Dec–Apr. This well-kept contemporary motel has 16 rooms. Only a few grains of sand stand between it, the pool and the ocean. Choose between simple rooms, ones that sleep three (with a kitchen), and one-bedroom suites. Children under 12 stay free in their parents' room.

Courtyard Villa *(☎ 954-776-1164, 800-291-3560, fax 954-491-0768,* W *www.courtyard villa.com, 4312 El Mar Dr)* Rooms $105-135 off-season, $159-175 mid-Dec–late Apr. With only four courtyard suites and four oceanfront efficiencies, these distinctive and classy European-style rooms go fast – with good reason. There are many added benefits: free bikes, barbecue grills, free access to over 450 movies, free tennis, a rooftop patio and free breakfast and drinks down the street at Mulligans restaurant. You may also wish to consider two-bedroom units ($150/250 off-season/winter) and off-season weekly rates ($588).

Gay Accommodations in Fort Lauderdale

Several charming men-only guest houses can be found in the '-mar' area, but the first entry is the only one that accommodates lesbians.

Deauville Inn *(☎ 954-568-5000, fax 954-565-7797,* W *www.ftlaud-deauville.com, 2916 N Ocean Blvd)* Rooms/efficiencies $60/90 off-season, $70/100 mid-Dec–Apr. Two blocks from the beach, this simple 10-room place welcomes anyone gay, straight, male or female.

The Blue Dolphin *(☎ 954-565-8437, 800-893-2583, fax 954-565-6015,* W *www.bluedolphinhotel.com, 725 N Birch Rd)* Rooms $99-119 off-season, $119-169 mid-Dec–Apr. This clean, renovated and comfortable place is just for men, who are quite comfortable around the clothing-optional pool. There are 16 rooms.

The Flamingo – Inn Amongst the Flowers *(☎ 954-561-4658, 800-283-4786, fax 954-568-2688,* W *www.theflamingoresort.com, 2727 Terramar St)* Rooms $100-195 off-season, $140-240 late Dec–Apr. With a tranquil garden, 13 tidy rooms, a completely renovated interior and a friendly staff, the Flamingo keeps its guests quite satisfied.

Royal Palms Resort *(☎ 954-564-6444, 800-237-7256, fax 954-564-6443,* W *www.royalpalms.com, 2901 Terramar St)* Rooms $149-229 off-season, $199-289 Dec-Apr. The premier gay guest house is a clothing-optional place that features 12 large, airy rooms (complete with CD/TV/VCR and library), a lush tropical garden, a pool with a waterfall and lots of perks, like free parking and breakfast. It's also isolated and serene.

FORT LAUDERDALE

PLACES TO EAT
Downtown Fort Lauderdale
Two Street Coffee Garage (☎ *954-523-7191, 209 SW 2nd Ave at 2nd St*) Open 7am-10pm Mon-Thur, 7am-midnight Fri, 8am-midnight Sat, 8am-10pm Sun. This independent coffeehouse pumps out excellent espresso and a comfortable vibe.

Shirttail Charlie's (☎ *954-463-3474, 400 SW 3rd Ave*) Dishes $9-11. Open 11:30am-10pm daily. Cantilevered over the banks of the New River, this casual outdoor eatery dishes up good fried seafood served in baskets. Service is friendly and the prices right. They provide ferry service from the Riverwalk that scoots you across the river to their place.

Creolina's (☎ *954-524-2003, 209 SW 2nd St*) Lunch mains $7-10, dinner mains $10-18. Open for lunch 11:30am-2:30pm Mon-Fri, dinner 5pm-9pm Sun & Mon, 5pm-10pm Tues-Thur, 5pm-11pm Fri & Sat. In the mood to be transported to the backwaters of Louisiana for some serious Cajun, Creole and jambalaya? This is *the* place.

Himmarshee Bar & Grille (☎ *954-524-1818, 210 SW 2nd St*) Lunch mains $10-13, dinner mains $16-25. Open 11am-2:30pm Mon-Fri, 6pm-10:30pm nightly. This upscale yuppie place has creative burgers and imaginative American dishes, but you can always keep it simple at lunchtime with a salad ($5). Outdoor tables are coveted; consider yourself lucky to get one. But then again, the indoor mezzanine provides a perfect perch to people-watch at the bar, where there's always a hip scene unfolding.

By Word of Mouth (☎ *954-564-3663, 3200 NE 12th Ave*) Lunch mains $10-16, dinner mains $19-35. Open 11am-3pm Mon-Fri, 5pm-10pm Wed-Sat. This successful catering operation also has a retail location that's truly known only 'by word of mouth.' Self-fulfilling marketing? Perhaps, but the New American daily specials (there is no set menu) live up to the reputation. The low-key atmosphere belies the high level of creative cooking. Check out the dishes in the glass case before ordering.

Along E Las Olas Blvd The following restaurants are all downtown along E Las Olas Blvd, which is dense with eateries.

Kilwin's (☎ *954-523-8338, 809 E Las Olas Blvd*) Open 11am-10pm Sun-Thur, 11am-midnight Fri & Sat. Since 1949, these folks have made tantalizing fudge, truffles, caramel, chocolate and ice cream.

Cafe Europa (☎ *954-763-6600, 726 E Las Olas Blvd*) Sandwiches $4-6. Open 9am-midnight Sun-Thur, 9am-1am Fri & Sat. You can't ask a good café for anything more than this: indoor and outdoor tables, great pastries, decent sandwiches and espresso. Can you?

Cheeburger! Cheeburger! (☎ *954-524-8824, 708 E Las Olas Blvd*) Dishes $5-10. Open 11am-9:30pm Mon-Thur, 11am-10pm Fri-Sun. Named after a *Saturday Night Live* sketch, this diner-like joint specializes in...you guessed it: cheeseburgers. Duh. It's kind on their part, letting you order a cheeseburger without the cheese 'for no extra charge.' They also make milkshakes, grilled cheese sandwiches, grilled-chicken sandwiches and Ham's 'burgersteak' dinners. It's a good family place.

The Floridian (☎ *954-463-4041, 1410 E Las Olas Blvd*) Dishes $5-15. Open 24 hrs daily. This institution has served very good diner food since the late 1930s. It's crowded on weekend mornings, with diners clamoring for huge omelets; but, you could break away from the pack and order the special 'Mess' for $7.

China Yung (☎ *954-761-3388, 720 E Las Olas Blvd*) Lunch $6-7, dinner $10-12. Open 11:30am-10pm Mon-Sat, 4pm-10pm Sun. A classic American Chinese restaurant, this joint has cheap lunch specials that include soup, egg roll and fried rice.

Mark's (☎ *954-463-1000, 1032 E Las Olas Blvd*) Lunch mains $7-18, dinner mains $16-38. Open for lunch 11:30am-2:30pm Mon-Fri, dinner 6pm-10pm Sun-Thur, 6pm-11pm Fri & Sat. Mark's has been one of the most exceptional South Florida restaurants since it opened in 1994. It's an upscale place with excellent service, a bustling open kitchen, cozy booths and rich mahogany tables. The chef uses classical cooking techniques on fresh local ingredients for his signature dishes. Look for cracked conch with black-bean mango salsa and vanilla rum butter sauce; crab-crusted grouper with wild mushroom ragout; and honey-balsamic–glazed wood-oven–roasted salmon.

Left Bank (☎ 954-462-5376, 214 SE 6th Ave) Mains $19-32, prix fixe menu $35. Open 5:30pm-9pm Sun-Thur, 5:30pm-10pm Fri & Sat. This elegant and romantic chef-owned restaurant has certainly evolved since it opened in the early 1980s, trending away from heavier classical French to lighter Provençal-style cooking. Gravitate toward the very good seafood dishes, either à la carte or with the value-laden fixed menu that includes an appetizer, main and dessert.

Fort Lauderdale Beach

There's not a whole lot worth jumping up and down about here, but you have to eat something.

Primanti Brothers (☎ 954-565-0605, 901 N Atlantic Blvd) Slices $2, pies $11-15. Open 24 hrs daily. The bros have great New York–style pizza in both Neapolitan and Sicilian versions.

Bierbrunnen German Bar (☎ 954-462-1008, 425 Fort Lauderdale Beach Rd) Dishes $7-15. Open 11am-2am Sun-Fri, 11am-3am Sat. Down a little alley, this bar-cum-restaurant serves authentic schnitzel (pork loin breaded and pan-fried), sauerbraten (sour roast beef with mashed potatoes and red cabbage), fresh bratwurst, and of course, excellent draft beer. You can always get something light like a mahimahi sandwich. It's a fun, partially open-air sort of place. Free appetizers lure patrons on weekdays, as do well-drink specials ($1.75).

Oasis Cafe (☎ 954-463-3130, 600 Seabreeze Blvd) Dishes $8-17. Open 11am-10pm Sun-Thur, 11am-11pm Fri & Sat, weather permitting. Almost within a traffic island across from the beach, this palm-studded café has only outdoor seating, with shaded gliding tables. Fare consists of sandwiches, wraps, good noshing appetizers, ribs and seafood.

Port Everglades

Crew-house dwellers will head to the *Publix* supermarket on 17th St.

Lester's Diner (☎ 954-525-5641, 250 Hwy 84) Dishes $6-8. Open 24 hrs daily. Universally hailed (in a most-affectionate way) as a greasy spoon, campy Lester's has been keeping folks happy since the late 1960s. Everyone makes their way here at some point: from business types on cell phones, to late-night clubbers, to blue-haired ladies with second husbands.

Carlos & Pepe (☎ 954-467-7192, 1302 SE 17th St) Dishes $7-15. Open 11:30am-11pm Mon-Thur, 11:30am-11pm Fri & Sat, noon-10:30pm Sun. Ignore the strip-mall location and overlook the casual interior. This authentic Mexican place has excellent salsa, fajitas and burritos, and strong margaritas. It's the best you'll find east of New Mexico.

Tokyo Bowl (☎ 954-524-8200, 1720 S Federal Hwy) Dishes $8-9; all-you-can-eat sushi $13.50. Open 11am-11pm Mon-Thur, 11am-midnight Fri & Sat, noon-11pm Sun. This Japanese fast-food place has good cheap eats, like beef and chicken teriyaki.

Ernie's Bar-B-Q (☎ 954-523-8636, 1843 S Federal Hwy) Dishes $7-13. Open 11am-1am Sun-Thur, 11am-2am Fri & Sat. This 'blues, booze and bbq' joint has been known for its good-time squalor and good, cheap food since 1957. Ernie's has everything from burgers to ribs to enormous portions of conch chowder, which itself can make a meal. Dishes are available for takeout, too, but the atmosphere is key. You could always just come for a drink.

Siam House (☎ 954-763-1701, 1392 SE 17th St) Lunch mains $6-7, dinner mains $10-14. Open 11:30am-3pm & 5pm-10pm daily. Siam House serves Asian cuisine, great Thai specialties and seafood dishes.

Bimini Boatyard (☎ 954-525-7400, 1555 SE 17th St) Lunch mains $10-12, dinner mains $14-22. Open 11:30am-10pm Sun-Thur, 11:30am-11pm Fri & Sat. If you suffer from boat envy, avoid this Intracoastal Waterway restaurant with great views of huge yachts. It also draws loud beautiful people to a lively bar or the dining room for a predictable California/American-style

FORT LAUDERDALE

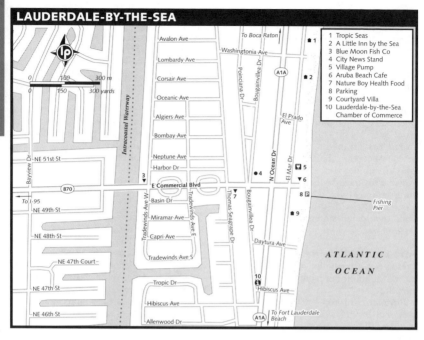

LAUDERDALE-BY-THE-SEA

0 — 150 — 300 m
0 — 150 — 300 yards

Intracoastal Waterway

Avalon Ave
Lombardy Ave
Corsair Ave
Oceanic Ave
Algiers Ave
Bombay Ave
Neptune Ave
Harbor Dr

NE 51st St
Bayview Dr

870

To I-95
NE 49th St
NE 48th St
NE 47th Court
NE 47th St
NE 46th St

E Commercial Blvd

Basin Dr
Miramar Ave
Capri Ave
Tradewinds Ave S
Tropic Dr
Hibiscus Ave
Allenwood Dr

Tradewinds Ave W
Tradewinds Ave E
Thomas Seagrape Dr

Washingtonia Ave
To Boca Raton
Poinciana Dr
Bougainvillea Dr

A1A

El Prado Ave

N Ocean Dr
El Mar Dr

Bougainvillea Dr
Daytura Ave

10

Hibiscus Ave

To Fort Lauderdale Beach
A1A

ATLANTIC OCEAN

Fishing Pier

1 Tropic Seas
2 A Little Inn by the Sea
3 Blue Moon Fish Co
4 City News Stand
5 Village Pump
6 Aruba Beach Cafe
7 Nature Boy Health Food
8 Parking
9 Courtyard Villa
10 Lauderdale-by-the-Sea Chamber of Commerce

---

menu. All in all, it's a lively place if you're in the mood for it.

15th Street Fisheries (☎ *954-763-2777, 1900 SE 15th St*) Lunch $3-16, dinner mains $16-40. Open 11:30am-10pm daily. A casual restaurant popular with families and tourists, this Intracoastal Waterway restaurant is big into seafood and lobster. A casual lunch menu (ie, a less-expensive one) is served throughout the day and evening in the lounge.

Lauderdale-by-the-Sea

Nature Boy Health Food (☎ *954-776-4696, 220 E Commercial Blvd*) Sandwiches $4-6. Open 10am-5pm Mon-Sat. Your body will appreciate the healthful salads, sandwiches, and fruit and veggie juice drinks on offer here.

Aruba Beach Cafe (☎ *954-776-0001, 1 E Commercial Blvd*) Dishes $12-22. Open 11am-11pm daily. An open-air party place overlooking the ocean, with sort of a

Caribbean-beach atmosphere, this place is pretty big and pretty loud. Weekday happy hour is popular, as are the Sunday breakfast buffet (9am to noon) and live music (Wednesday to Sunday). Stick to the simpler food items like sandwiches, pasta, burgers and salads. They're fine for a quick bite.

Blue Moon Fish Co (☎ *954-267-9888, 4405 Tradewinds Ave W*) Lunch mains $10-15, dinner mains $26-38. Open for lunch 11:30am-3pm daily, dinner 6pm-10pm Sun-Thur, 6pm-11pm Fri & Sat. Combine an excellent and eclectic seafood menu with good service and a spectacular waterside setting (indoor and outdoor) and you'll have this winning recipe. Come for Sunday brunch (11:30am to 3pm; $25 per person), when jazz often accompanies the spectacularly bountiful meal. Here's what you get: all-you-can-peel-and-eat shrimp and a seafood buffet, mains like seafood gumbo or salmon strudel (or both), dessert and either a Bloody Mary, mimosa or champagne. Sounds too good to be true, but it's not. The raw bar and sushi (not included in the buffet) are also very good.

ENTERTAINMENT
Bars
There's no cover for live music at these places.

Dicey Riley's (☎ 954-522-2202, 217 SW 2nd St) Open 11am-4am daily. If you can't make it to Dublin this season, head here. This downtown restaurant and lounge is as close to an Irish pub as you'll get, with traditional cuisine ($5 to $9) and draft Guinness, Bass and others. Dicey's is particularly packed on weekends, but traditional and contemporary live Irish tunes headline Tuesday to Saturday.

Maguire's Hill (☎ 954-764-4453, 535 N Andrews Ave) Open 11:30am-2:30am Sun-Thur, 11:30am-3am Fri & Sat (kitchen closed at 10pm Sun-Thur, midnight Fri & Sat). Another classic Irish pub, this one has classic Irish bands Thursday to Sunday. Dishes run $6 to $14.

O'Hara's Jazz Cafe (☎ 954-524-1764, 722 E Las Olas Blvd) Open 11:30am-2am Sun-Thur, 11:30am-3am Fri & Sat. For nightly jazz in a warm, comfortable atmosphere, head over here after 9pm. The menu ($4 to $9) features crab nachos, quesadillas, chicken wings, pizzas, salads and sandwiches.

The Parrot Lounge (☎ 954-563-1493, 911 Sunrise Lane) Open 11am-2am Sun-Thur, 11am-3am Fri & Sat. A mainstay since the 1970s, this popular dive bar draws a beer and peanuts kind of crowd.

Village Pump (☎ 954-776-5840, 4404 El Mar Dr) Open 8am-2am daily. This is a fun local dive bar, serving full meals throughout the day.

Nightclubs
'Fort Liquordale' is still a party town, and there are tons of clubs to suit a variety of tastes, persuasions, libidos and degrees of nuttiness. One thing is for sure, though: You can expect lots less attitude here than at South Beach clubs. Cover charges vary constantly, but coupons abound. For the latest in clubland, pick up the Fort Lauderdale version of the *New Times* (W www.newtimesbpb.com), a free weekly published on Thursday, or *City Link* (W www.clo-sfl.com). The following are simply the most enduring of the available options.

Baja Beach Club (☎ 954-563-7889, 3339 N Federal Hwy) Open 9pm-2am Sun-Fri, 9pm-3am Sat. At the northwest corner of Oakland Park Blvd and US Hwy 1, Baja Beach Club looks like an orgy at King Neptune's place. The enormous multilevel club features dance music, spring break parties (or what's left of them) and ladies' nights. Party hardy, dude.

Chili Pepper (☎ 954-525-0094, 200 W Broward Blvd) Open 10pm-3am Wed-Sat. This staggeringly huge and pretty minimalistic dance warehouse has lots of bars, an outside patio and balcony areas. They book excellent local and national rock bands. It's a hot club, spinning Euro, house, hip-hop and funk when the live music is on hiatus.

Gay & Lesbian Venues
Right up there with Provincetown, San Francisco and South Beach, Fort Lauderdale boasts dozens of gay bars and clubs scattered around town. It's best to check *Hot Spots* for the latest offerings. Again, these are simply the ones with staying power.

The Saint (☎ 954-525-7883, 1000 State Rd 84, W www.thesaintnightclub.net) Cover $4-5 Tues, Fri & Sun. Open 2pm-2am daily. This large, industrial music complex is a buzzy dance club – expect 500 people, minimum. Their cool Fetish Parties take place on the first Saturday of the month. Look for less buzzy and more down-home country & western bands on Tuesday and Sunday; 'ladies night' draws a crowd on Friday.

Club Cathode Ray (☎ 954-462-8611, 1307 E Las Olas Blvd) Open 2pm-2am Sun-Thur, 2pm-3am Fri & Sat. Pop over to this friendly, Guppie kind of hangout for two-for-one happy 'hour' (2pm to 8pm daily). A six-hour happy hour – you gotta love it.

Performing Arts
One of the state's largest and most important performing arts complexes is the

Broward Center for the Performing Arts
(☎ 954-462-0222, W www.browardcenter.org, 201 SW 5th Ave) Tickets $25-65/10-25 adult/child. Two venues, the 2688-seat Au-Rene Theater and the 588-seat Amaturro, host a wide variety of first-rate concerts, theatrical productions and kid-oriented theater. Call to see what's on.

SHOPPING

Swap Shop (☎ 954-791-7927, W www.florida swapshop.com, 3291 W Sunrise Blvd) Open 6am-5pm Mon-Fri, 5am-6pm Sat & Sun. This enormous circus-like flea market, the largest indoor/outdoor flea market in the country, boasts a real circus every day. They also have a drive-in movie, a little amusement park and lots of stuff to buy.

Sawgrass Mills (☎ 954-846-2350, 800-356-4557, W www.sawgrassmillsmall.com, 12801 W Sawgrass Blvd) Open 10am-9:30pm Mon-Sat, 11am-8pm Sun. With more than 2 miles of shops (that's 400 retail shops, 30 restaurants and an entertainment area), this place overwhelms even the most intrepid shopaholics. Grab a shopping cart and make a battle plan before waging war on your credit card; otherwise, you will be very quickly defeated by the enormity of it all. Bargain-hunters may wish to purchase, at the mall information desks, a $10 booklet with over $1500 worth of store coupons. (Some hotel concierges have them as giveaways.)

GETTING THERE & AWAY
Air

Fort Lauderdale-Hollywood International Airport (FLL; ☎ 954-359-1200, W www.fll .net) is served by more than 35 airlines, including some with nonstop flights from Europe.

Bus

The Greyhound station (☎ 954-764-6551, W www.greyhound.com), 515 NE 3rd St at Federal Hwy, is about four blocks from Broward Central Terminal (see the Getting Around section, later), the central transfer point for buses in the Fort Lauderdale area. Buses to Miami leave throughout the day

($5 one-way, 30 to 60 minutes) but, depending on when you arrive, you might have to wait as much as 2½ hours for the next one.

Train

Tri-Rail (☎ 800-874-7245, W www.tri-rail .com) runs between Miami and Fort Lauderdale ($6.75 roundtrip, 45 minutes). A feeder system of buses has connections for no extra charge. Free parking is provided at most stations. It's best to call Tri-Rail for route and scheduling information.

The Amtrak (☎ 800-872-7245, W www .amtrak.com) passenger trains run on Tri-Rail tracks. The Fort Lauderdale station, at 200 SW 21st Terrace, is just south of Broward Blvd and just west of I-95.

Car & Motorcycle

I-95 and Florida's Turnpike, the state's main toll road, run north-south. I-595, the major east-west artery, intersects I-95, Florida's Turnpike and the Sawgrass Expressway. It also feeds into I-75, which runs to Florida's west coast.

Boat

Port Everglades Authority (☎ 954-523-3404) runs the enormous Port Everglades cruise port (second busiest in the world after Miami). From the port, walk to SE 17th St and take bus No 40 to the beach or to Broward Central Terminal. If you're coming here in your own boat (not unlikely here), head for the Radisson Bahia Mar Yacht Center (☎ 954-764-2233).

Fort Lauderdale's premier unofficial crew agency is the three-ring binder at Smallwood's Yachtware (☎ 954-523-2282), 1001 SE 17th St. Owners come here, list their requirements in the book and wait for crew to get in touch. 'Official' agencies include Crew Unlimited (☎ 954-462-4624), 2065 S Federal Hwy; Crew Finders (☎ 954-522-2739), 408 SE 17th St; and The Crew Network (☎ 954-467-9777), 1053 SE 17th St.

GETTING AROUND
To/From the Airport

Fort Lauderdale-Hollywood International Airport (FLL), south of town off Federal

Hwy or I-95, is about a 20-minute drive from E Las Olas Blvd. Broward County Transit's bus No 1 goes from the airport to Broward Central Terminal. Tri-Rail shuttles connect the airport terminal with the Fort Lauderdale Airport train station (you can also take BCt bus No 3 or 6); trains head from there to the Fort Lauderdale station ($3) about once an hour at rush hours (there is no train service from about noon to 3pm). The trains run from about 5:30am to 9:15pm on weekdays, with less-frequent weekend service.

The official airport taxi is Yellow Cab Co (☎ 954-565-5400); it costs about $14 to go from the airport to a beach hotel. Tri-County Transportation Airport Express (☎ 954-561-8886) runs shuttles to hotels; a shared shuttle to most beach locations is $8 to $12. Pick up the shuttles as they circle the terminals. You must call 24 hours in advance to go *from* Fort Lauderdale *to* the airport. For information on getting from the airport to Miami, see the Getting Around chapter.

Bus
TMAX (☎ 954-761-3543), a free shuttle with service every 15 minutes or so, runs between downtown sights (7:30am to 6pm weekdays); between the beach and E Las Olas Blvd and the Riverfront (6pm to 1am Friday to Saturday); and between Tri-Rail and E Las Olas Blvd and the beaches (7:30am to 11pm Saturday, 7:30am to 9:30pm Sunday).

Broward County Transit (BCt; ☎ 954-357-8400), 200 W Broward Blvd, runs between downtown, the beach and Port Everglades. The fare is $1 for adults, 50¢ for seniors and children. You'll probably be better off, though, with an all-day pass ($2.50 adults, $1.25 seniors and children). Fare boxes onboard accept dollar bills. From Broward Central Terminal (its main

terminal), take bus No 11 to upper Fort Lauderdale Beach and Lauderdale-by-the-Sea; bus No 1 to Port Everglades; and bus No 40 to 17th St and Federal Hwy.

Car & Motorcycle
Having motorized wheels is the easiest way to go, though parking is tight in high season. Remember to remove all valuables from your car when parked. Pay parking lots are located north and south of E Las Olas Blvd ($1 per hour), and all-day parking at the beach costs $8 at the municipal parking lot on Hwy A1A just south of SE 5th St. Speed limits are strictly enforced. All major car rental companies have offices at Fort Lauderdale-Hollywood International Airport – see the Car & Motorcycle section in the Getting Around chapter for listings.

Bicycle
Fort Lauderdale's flatness makes it easy to get around by bike. Check with your hotel – many have bikes to loan or rent. The St Tropez Resort (☎ 954-564-8468), 725 N Atlantic Blvd, rents bicycles for $10 a day (8am to 7pm) or $40 per week.

Water Taxi
The Water Taxi (☎ 954-467-6677, w www .watertaxi.com), 651 Seabreeze Blvd, plies the canals and waterways between 17th St to the south, Atlantic Blvd/Pompano Beach to the north, the New River to the west and the Atlantic Ocean to the east. A $5 daily pass entitles you to unlimited rides. It's a great deal because it's cheap and because it's good to get out on the water in Fort Lauderdale. Call from any commercial location downtown on the New River or along the Intracoastal Waterway (any place with a dock) and they'll swing by and pick you up. Look for maps all along the route.

Language

SPANISH
Although visitors to Miami can get away with using only English, to do so is to essentially write off experiencing a huge chunk of the city's culture and life. Spanish may be more widely spoken in the metropolitan area than English, and you will certainly run into people who do not speak any English at all. See the Language section of the Facts about Miami chapter for phrasebook recommendations and other information.

Pronunciation
Spanish has five vowels: **a**, **e**, **i**, **o** and **u**. They are pronounced something like the highlighted letters of the following English words: f**a**ther, **e**nd, mar**i**ne, **o**r and p**u**ll. The stress is placed on the syllable with an accent over it (México=**meh**-hiko) or the second to last syllable (hasta luego=**ah**-sta loo-**eh**-go).

Greetings & Civilities
Hello/Hi.	*Hola.*
Good morning/day.	*Buenos días.*
Good evening/night.	*Buenas noches.*
See you later.	*Hasta luego.*
Goodbye.	*Adiós.*
Pleased to meet you.	*Mucho gusto.*
Please.	*Por favor.*
Thank you.	*Gracias.*
You're welcome.	*De nada.*
Excuse me.	*Perdóneme.*

Useful Words & Phrases
yes	*sí*
no	*no*
good/OK	*bueno*
bad	*malo*
best	*mejor*
more	*más*
less	*menos*
very little	*poco* or *poquito*

Shopping
How much does it cost?	*¿Cuanto cuesta?*
Can I look at it?	*¿Puedo mirarlo?*
I want...	*Quiero...*
What do you want?	*¿Qué quiere?*
Do you have...?	*¿Tiene...?*
Is/are there...?	*¿Hay...?*
I understand.	*Entiendo.*
I do not understand.	*No entiendo.*
Do you understand?	*¿Entiende usted?*
Please speak slowly.	*Por favor hable despacio.*

Getting Around
street	*calle*
avenue	*avenida*
corner (of)	*esquina (de)*
block	*cuadra*
to the left	*a la izquierda*
to the right	*a la derecha*
straight ahead	*adelante*
bus	*gua gua* or *autobús*
train	*tren*
taxi	*taxi*
toilet	*sanitario*
Where is...?	*Donde está...?*
the bus station	*el terminal de gua gua/ autobús*
the train station	*la estación del tren*

Numbers
0	*cero*	14	*catorce*
1	*uno*	15	*quince*
2	*dos*	16	*dieciséis*
3	*tres*	17	*diecisiete*
4	*cuatro*	18	*dieciocho*
5	*cinco*	19	*diecinueve*
6	*seis*	20	*veinte*
7	*siete*	30	*treinta*
8	*ocho*	40	*cuarenta*
9	*nueve*	50	*cincuenta*
10	*diez*	100	*cien*
11	*once*	500	*quinientos*
12	*doce*	1000	*mil*
13	*trece*		

CREOLE

Though French is Haiti's official language, most Haitians – especially those who emigrate to Miami – speak Creole. The language's origins are debated, but most scholars believe it arose from a pidgin that developed between French colonists and African slaves.

Haitians make up the third-largest group of immigrants in the area, after Cubans and Canadians. This brief glossary will help you as you navigate the small but very interesting pockets of Haitian Miami. See the Little Haiti section of the Things to See & Do chapter for more information.

Pronunciation

In terms of pronunciation, Creole is written phonetically. There are no silent consonants; a hard *c* is represented by a *k* (the letter *c* is never used in Creole, which itself is often spelled with a 'K'), and *g* is a hard *g*. There are no silent *'e'*s; all are pronounced as acute *e* unless they have the grave *(è)* accent. For example, *pale* (which means 'to speak') is pronounced 'palé.' The word for 'me' is *m* and is pronounced 'um.'

People

I	*m/mwen*
you	*ou*
he/she	*li*
you (plural)/we	*nou*
they	*yo*

Greetings & Civilities

How are you?	*Ki jan ou ye?*
Not bad.	*M pal pi mal.*
I'm getting along.	*M'ap kenbe.*
Good day. (used before noon)	*Bonjou.*
Good evening. (used after noon)	*Bonswa.*
See you later.	*Na wè pita.*

Useful Words & Phrases

My name is...	*M rele...*
May I take your photograph?	*Eske m ka fè foto ou?*
Where is the...?	*Ki kote...?*
What time is it?	*Ki lè li ye?*
What is your name?	*Ki jan ou rele?*
Do you speak English?	*Eske ou ka pale angle?*
I don't understand.	*M pa konpran.*
Where is/are...?	*Kote...?*
the toilets	*twalèt yo*
the hospital	*lopital la*
I am looking for...	*M'ap chache...*
What time is it?	*Kilè li ye?*
Stop.	*Rete.*
Wait.	*Yann.*
Help!	*Ede mwen!*

How much?	*Konbyen?*
Let's go.	*Ann ale.*
I would like to go (visit, speak with)...	*M ta vle ale (vizite, pale ak)...*
I am lost; where is...?	*M pèdi; kote...ye?*
Where does the bus leave?	*Kote taptap pati?*

Food

plat konplèt (or *plat complet*)	complete meal consisting of rice and beans, salad, plantains and meat of your choice
diri ak pwa	rice and beans
diri blan	white rice
griyo (often written as *griot*)	deep-fried pork
taso	deep-fried beef
poule	chicken
pwason	fish
lambi	conch
bannann peze	fried plantain
tomat	tomatoes
zonyon	onions
fig	banana
ju zoranj	orange juice
ju chadek	grapefruit juice
ju sitron	lime juice
koka	Coca-Cola
kiè	beer
dlo	water
dlo culligan	bottled water

Numbers

0	*zero*	9	*nèf*
1	*en*	10	*dis*
2	*de*	20	*ven*
3	*twa*	30	*trant*
4	*kat*	40	*karant*
5	*senk*	50	*senkant*
6	*sis*	100	*san*
7	*sèt*	1000	*mil*
8	*uit*		

Creole Proverbs

Creole has a small vocabulary, but, rather than limiting expression, it has sired a wealth of poetic and allegorical proverbs. The proverbs are a testament to the attitudes, struggles and lives of the majority of the Haitian people.

Dèyè mòn gen mòn.
Behind the mountains there are more mountains.

Apre dans tanbou lou.
After the dance the drum is heavy.

Men anpil chay pa lou.
Many hands make the load lighter.

Bèl antèman pa di paradi.
A beautiful burial does not guarantee heaven.

Kreyon pèp la pa gen gonm.
The people's pencil has no eraser.

Lè yo vle touye chen yo di'l fou.
When they want to kill a dog they say it's crazy.

Kay koule twompe solèy men li pa twompe lapli.
The leaky house can fool the sun but it can't fool the rain.

Milat pov se nég, nég rich se milat.
A poor mulatto is a black man, a rich black man is a mulatto.

Bay kou, bliye. Pote mak, sonje.
The one who gives the blow forgets. The one who gets hurt remembers.

Thanks

Many thanks to the travelers who used the last edition and wrote to us with helpful hints and interesting anecdotes:

Ian Barclay, Judith Berson, Jonathan Cameron, Andrea Carr, Miss de Vries, D Harriss, Richard Hastings, Sandra Hunter, Amanda Joun-Rosen, Eva Knoche, Alfio Levy, Bruce Maxwell, Ian Montrose, Matthew J Moore, Kristen Olson, Dr Peter Roper, Elisa Sohn, Sarah Tilley and Remco van Schellen.

LONELY PLANET

You already know that Lonely Planet produces more than this one guidebook, but you might not be aware of the other products we have on this region. Here is a selection of titles which you may want to check out as well:

Florida
ISBN 1 74059 136 4
US$19.99 • UK£12.99

Diving & Snorkeling Florida Keys
ISBN 0 86442 774 3
US$16.99 • UK£10.99

Latin American Spanish phrasebook
ISBN 0 86442 558 9
US$6.95 • UK£4.50

Miami City Map
ISBN 1 86450 177 4
US$5.99 • UK£3.99

USA
ISBN 1 86450 308 4
US$24.99 • UK£14.99

Cuba
ISBN 0 86442 750 6
US$19.99 • UK£11.99

Available wherever books are sold.

Index

Bold indicates maps.

Places to Stay in Miami

Places to Eat in Miami

Boxed Text

Miami Map Section

MAP 1 GREATER MIAMI

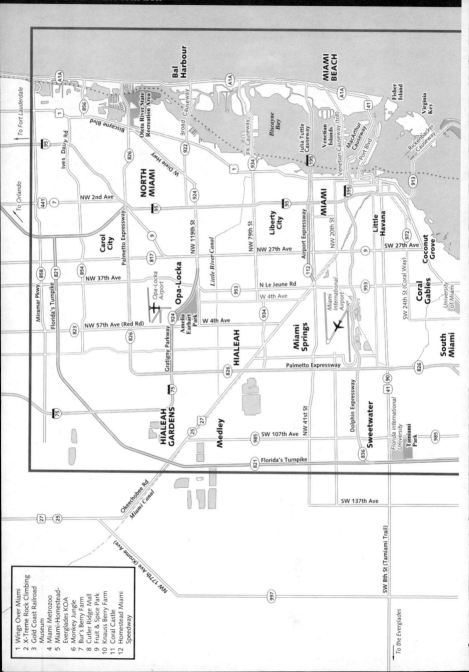

To Fort Lauderdale

To Orlando

Bal Harbour

MIAMI BEACH

Fisher Island

Virginia Key

Oleta River State Recreation Area

Biscayne Bay

Broad Causeway

JFK Causeway

Julia Tuttle Causeway

Venetian Islands

MacArthur Causeway (toll)

Port Blvd

Rickenbacker Causeway

Venetian Causeway (toll)

Biscayne Blvd

Ives Dairy Rd

NORTH MIAMI

W Dixie Hwy

NW 2nd Ave

NW 119th St

NW 79th St

Liberty City

MIAMI

Little Havana

Coconut Grove

SW 27th Ave

Carol City

Palmetto Expressway

NW 37th Ave

NW 27th Ave

Airport Expressway

NW 20th St

Coral Gables

University of Miami

SW 24th St (Coral Way)

Miramar Pkwy

Florida's Turnpike

Opa-Locka Airport

Opa-Locka

N Le Jeune Rd

W 4th Ave

South Miami

NW 57th Ave (Red Rd)

Gratigny Parkway

Amelia Earhart Park

W 4th Ave

Miami Springs

Miami International Airport

HIALEAH

Palmetto Expressway

HIALEAH GARDENS

Medley

Dolphin Expressway

Sweetwater

Florida International University

Tamiami Park

SW 107th Ave

NW 41st St

Florida's Turnpike

SW 137th Ave

Okeechobee Rd

Miami Canal

NW 177th Ave (Krome Ave)

SW 8th St (Tamiami Trail)

To the Everglades

Little River Canal

1 Wings Over Miami
2 X-Treme Rock Climbing
3 Gold Coast Railroad Museum
4 Miami Metrozoo
5 Miami-Homestead-Everglades KOA
6 Monkey Jungle
7 Bur's Berry Farm
8 Cutler Ridge Mall
9 Fruit & Spice Park
10 Knauss Berry Farm
11 Coral Castle
12 Homestead Miami Speedway

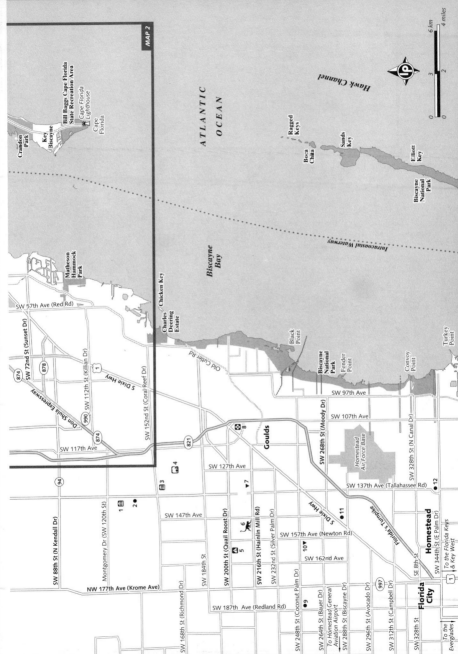

MAP 2

Bill Baggs Cape Florida
State Recreation Area

Crandon Park

Key
Biscayne

Cape Florida
Lighthouse

Cape Florida

ATLANTIC
OCEAN

Ragged
Keys

Boca
Chita

Sands
Key

Elliott
Key

Biscayne
National
Park

Hawk Channel

Intracoastal Waterway

6 km
4 miles

Matheson
Hammock
Park

Charles
Deering
Estate

Chicken Key

Biscayne
Bay

Black
Point

Biscayne
National
Park

Fender
Point

Convoy
Point

Turkey
Point

SW 57th Ave (Red Rd)

SW 72nd St (Sunset Dr)

SW 112th St (Killian Dr)

S Dixie Hwy

SW 152nd St (Coral Reef Dr)

Old Cutler Rd

Don Shula Expressway

SW 97th Ave

SW 107th Ave

SW 117th Ave

SW 268th St (Moody Dr)

SW 328th St (N Canal Dr)

SW 127th Ave

Goulds

Homestead
Air Force Base

SW 147th Ave

SW 137th Ave (Tallahassee Rd)

SW 200th St (Quail Roost Dr)

SW 216th St (Hainlin Mill Rd)

SW 232nd St (Silver Palm Rd)

SW 157th Ave (Newton Rd)

SW 162nd Ave

S Dixie Hwy

Florida's Turnpike

Montgomery Dr (SW 120th St)

SW 88th St (N Kendall Dr)

NW 177th Ave (Krome Ave)

SW 184th St

SW 166th Ave (Richmond Dr)

SW 187th Ave (Redland Rd)

SW 248th St (Coconut Palm Dr)

SW 264th St (Bauer Dr)

To Homestead General
Aviation Airport

SW 288th St (Biscayne Dr)

SW 296th St (Avocado Dr)

SW 312th St (Campbell Dr)

SW 328th St

Homestead

Florida
City

SW 344th St (E Palm Dr)

SE 8th St

To the Florida Keys
& Key West

To the
Everglades

1 🏛

2 ●

3 🏛

4 📷

5

6 🚶

7 ▼

8 ☒

9 ●

10 ▼

11 ●

9 ●

12 ●

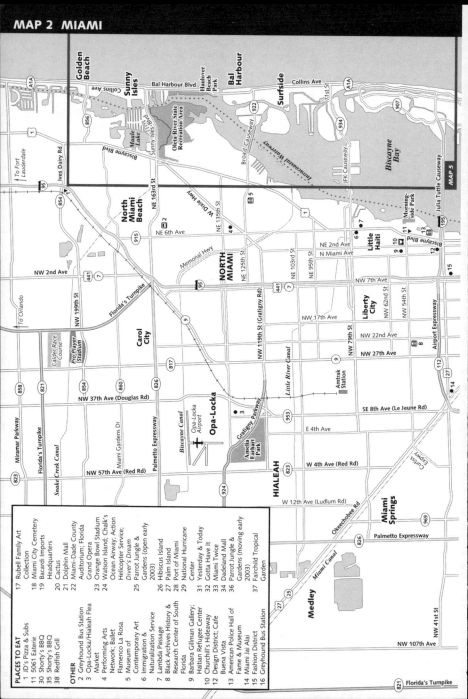

MAP 2 MIAMI

PLACES TO EAT
1 JD's Pizza & Subs
11 5061 Eaterie
30 Shorty's BBQ
35 Shorty's BBQ
38 Redfish Grill

OTHER
2 Greyhound Bus Station
3 Opa-Locka/Hialeah Flea Market
4 Performing Arts Network; Ballet Flamenco La Rosa
5 Museum of Contemporary Art
6 Immigration & Naturalization Service
7 Lambda Passage
8 Black Archives History & Research Center of South Florida
9 Barbara Gillman Gallery; Haitian Refugee Center
10 Churchill's Hideaway
12 Design District; Cafe Buena Vista
13 American Police Hall of Fame & Museum
14 Miami Jai Alai
15 Fashion District
16 Greyhound Bus Station

17 Rubell Family Art Collection
18 Miami City Cemetery
19 Bacardi Imports Headquarters
20 Cactus
21 Dolphin Mall
22 Miami-Dade County Auditorium; Florida Grand Opera
23 Orange Bowl Stadium
24 Watson Island; Chalk's Ocean Airway; Action Helicopter Service; Diver's Dream
25 Parrot Jungle & Gardens (open early 2003)
26 Hibiscus Island
27 Palm Island
28 Port of Miami
29 National Hurricane Center
31 Yesterday & Today
32 Gotta Have It
33 Miami Twice
34 Dadeland Mall
36 Parrot Jungle & Gardens (moving early 2003)
37 Fairchild Tropical Garden

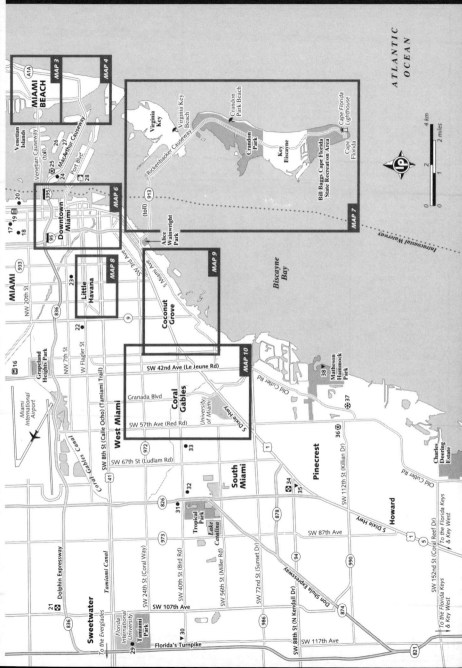

ATLANTIC OCEAN

Venetian Islands

MIAMI BEACH

MAP 3

MAP 4

Venetian Causeway (toll)

MacArthur Causeway

Port Blvd

Virginia Key

Virginia Key Beach

Rickenbacker Causeway

Crandon Park Beach

Crandon Park

Key Biscayne

Cape Florida

Cape Florida Lighthouse

Bill Baggs Cape Florida State Recreation Area

MAP 7

Intracoastal Waterway

Downtown Miami

MAP 6

(toll) 913

Alice Wainwright Park

MIAMI

MAP 8

Little Havana

23

22

MAP 9

Coconut Grove

S Miami Ave

SW 3rd Ave

Biscayne Bay

16

Grapeland Heights Park

Miami International Airport

NW 7th St

W Flagler St

SW 8th St (Calle Ocho) (Tamiami Trail)

West Miami

MAP 10

SW 42nd Ave (Le Jeune Rd)

Granada Blvd

Coral Gables

SW 57th Ave (Red Rd)

University of Miami

S Dixie Hwy

Old Cutler Rd

38

Matheson Hammock Park

37

SW 67th St (Ludlam Rd)

33

South Miami

972

32

34

35

Pinecrest

36

Charles Deering Estate

Old Cutler Rd

Coral Gables Canal

41

826

31

Tropical Park

Lake Carolina

SW 112th St (Killian Dr)

Howard

S Dixie Hwy

1

5

To the Florida Keys & Key West

To the Florida Keys & Key West

Dolphin Expressway

836

Tamiami Canal

SW 24th St (Coral Way)

973

SW 40th St (Bird Rd)

SW 56th St (Miller Rd)

SW 72nd St (Sunset Dr)

878

SW 87th Ave

94

Don Shula Expressway

990

874

SW 152nd St (Coral Reef Dr)

Sweetwater

21

836

Florida International University

Tamiami Park

29

30

Florida's Turnpike

To the Everglades

SW 107th Ave

SW 88th St (N Kendall Dr)

SW 117th Ave

986

821

4 km

2 miles

2

1

0

MAP 3 SOUTH BEACH (11TH TO 23RD ST)

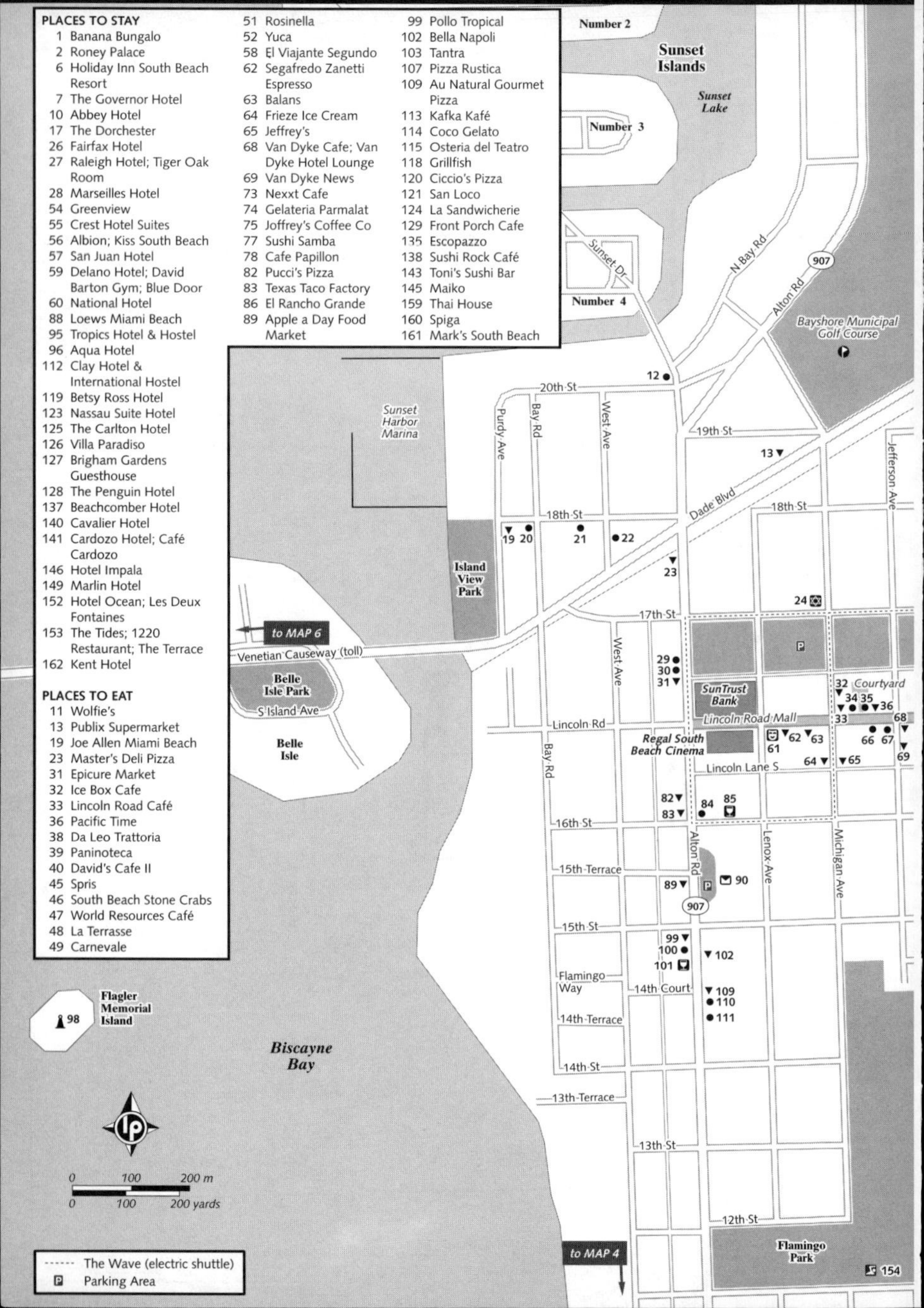

Number 2

Sunset Islands

Sunset Lake

Number 3

Number 4

Sunset Dr

N Bay Rd

Alton Rd

907

Bayshore Municipal Golf Course

20th St
19th St
Purdy Ave
Bay Rd
West Ave
Dade Blvd
18th St
Jefferson Ave

12 ●
13 ▼

Sunset Harbor Marina

18th St
19 ▼ 20 ▼ 21 ● ● 22
23 ▼
24 ⊞

Island View Park

17th St

to MAP 6
Venetian Causeway (toll)

Belle Isle Park
S Island Ave

Belle Isle

West Ave
Bay Rd

29 ●
30 ●
31 ▼

SunTrust Bank

32 Courtyard
34 35 ▼
33 ● ● 36
68

Lincoln Rd
Lincoln Road Mall

Regal South Beach Cinema

⊞ 62 ▼ 63
61
64 ▼ ▼ 65

Lincoln Lane S

66 67 ●
69

82 ▼
83 ▼

84 85
⊟

16th St

15th Terrace

89 ▼ ⊞ ✉ 90
907

Lenox Ave
Michigan Ave
Alton Rd

15th St

99 ▼
100 ●
101 ✉

Flamingo Way
14th Court

▼ 102

▼ 109
● 110
● 111

14th Terrace

14th St

13th Terrace

Biscayne Bay

Flagler Memorial Island

98

13th St

0   100   200 m
0   100   200 yards

to MAP 4

12th St

Flamingo Park

📠 154

----- The Wave (electric shuttle)
P Parking Area

to MAP 5

A1A

Miami Beach
High School

23rd St

Collins Ave

Miami Beach Boardwalk

Dade Blvd

22nd St

Collins Canal

Collins
Park

N Meridian Ave

Prairie Ave

Convention Center Dr

Washington Ave

Jackie Gleason Dr

Park Ave

Liberty Ave

21st St

20th St

19th St

Miami Beach
Convention
Center

Meridian Court

City
Park

18th St

City
Hall

Jackie
Gleason
Theater

James Ave

17th St

Burdines
Department
Store

Lincoln Lane N

Lincoln Rd

Meridian Ave

Euclid Ave

Pennsylvania Ave

Drexel Ave

16th St

15th St

Collins Canal

ATLANTIC

OCEAN

Española Way

14th Lane

(ped mall)

14th Place

14th St

13th St

Lummus
Park

12th St

Old
City Hall

A1A

The Promenade

Ocean Ln

Ocean Court

Collins Court

11th St

101	Irish House Bar & Grill
108	Blue
116	Crobar
117	Lost Weekend
132	Jazid
134	Mac's Club Deuce Bar
144	The Playwright
148	Level

OTHER

8	Bass Museum of Art
9	Miami Beach Public Library
12	Mark's Quality Cleaners
14	Miami Beach Chamber of Commerce
15	Holocaust Memorial
16	Miami Beach Botanical Garden
20	American Road Collections
21	Apeture Pro Supply
24	Cuban-Jewish Congregation
25	Temple Emanu El Synagogue
29	Ironworks
30	Pleasure Emporium
34	Books & Books
35	SEE
37	Brownes & Co Apothecary
42	New Concept Video
43	Senzatempo; Idol's Gym
53	Miami Surf Style
66	Carel Gallery
70	Britto Central
71	ArtCenter/South Florida
72	Fritz's Skate Shop
76	Lincoln Road Farmer's Market
79	Antiques & Collectibles Market
81	Eckerd
84	SoBe Liquor
87	Absolutely Suitable
90	Mail Boxes Etc
91	Cybr Caffe
94	Recycled Blues
98	Flagler Memorial Monument
100	Tropicolor Photo
104	South Beach Make-up
105	Española Way Art Center
106	Española Way Farmer's Market
110	Wash Time
111	Eckerd
122	Tattoos by Lou
130	Beach Dental Center
131	Art Attack
133	Post Office
136	Whittall & Shon
139	Public Toilets
142	Two Wheel Drive
147	Crunch
150	Carlyle Hotel
151	Leslie Hotel
154	Flamingo Park Swimming Pool
155	Flamingo Tennis Center
156	Miami Beach Police Station
157	Pop
158	Beatnix
163	Casa Casaurina

ENTERTAINMENT

3	Rain
4	Lola
5	Miami City Ballet
18	Mynt
22	Club 1771
41	Laundry Bar
44	Condal & Peñamil
50	Lincoln Theatre; New World Symphony
61	Colony Theatre
67	Touch
80	Rumi
85	Abbey Brewery
92	Liquid
93	Club Madonna
97	Billboard Live

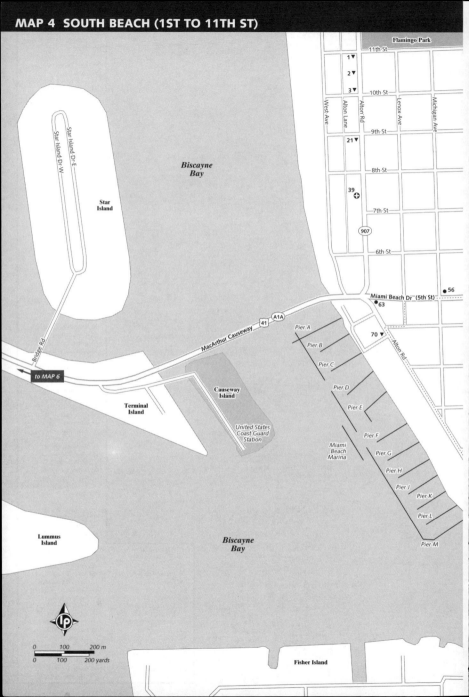

MAP 4 SOUTH BEACH (1ST TO 11TH ST)

Flamingo Park

11th St

1 ▼

2 ▼

3 ▼

10th St

West Ave

Alton Lane

Alton Rd

Lenox Ave

Michigan Ave

9th St

21 ▼

Biscayne Bay

8th St

39 ✚

7th St

907

6th St

Miami Beach Dr (5th St)

● 56

● 63

A1A

41

Pier A

70 ▼

Alton Rd

MacArthur Causeway

Pier B

Pier C

Bridge Rd

to MAP 6

Causeway Island

Pier D

Pier E

Terminal Island

United States Coast Guard Station

Pier F

Star Island

Star Island Dr W

Star Island Dr E

Star Island

Miami Beach Marina

Pier G

Pier H

Pier J

Pier K

Pier L

Lummus Island

Biscayne Bay

Pier M

Fisher Island

0   100   200 m

0   100   200 yards

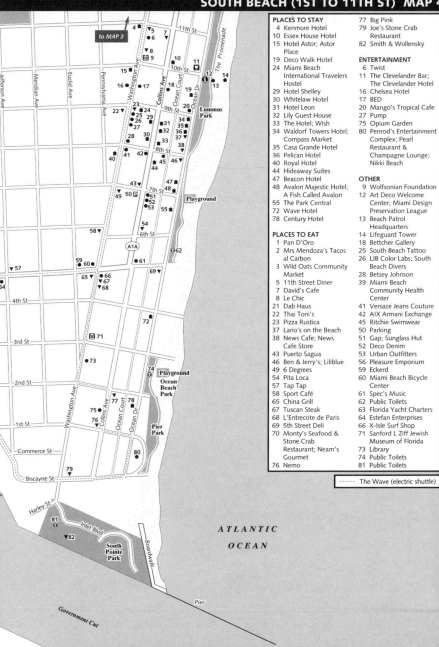

PLACES TO STAY
4 Kenmore Hotel
10 Essex House Hotel
15 Hotel Astor; Astor Place
19 Deco Walk Hotel
24 Miami Beach International Travelers Hostel
29 Hotel Shelley
30 Whitelaw Hotel
31 Hotel Leon
32 Lily Guest House
33 The Hotel; Wish
34 Waldorf Towers Hotel; Compass Market
35 Casa Grande Hotel
36 Pelican Hotel
40 Royal Hotel
44 Hideaway Suites
47 Beacon Hotel
48 Avalon Majestic Hotel; A Fish Called Avalon
55 The Park Central
72 Wave Hotel
78 Century Hotel

PLACES TO EAT
1 Pan D'Oro
2 Mrs Mendoza's Tacos al Carbon
3 Wild Oats Community Market
5 11th Street Diner
7 David's Cafe
8 Le Chic
21 Dab Haus
22 Thai Toni's
23 Pizza Rustica
37 Lario's on the Beach
38 News Cafe; News Cafe Store
43 Puerto Sagua
46 Ben & Jerry's; Liliblue
49 6 Degrees
54 Pita Loca
57 Tap Tap
58 Sport Café
65 China Grill
67 Tuscan Steak
68 L'Entrecote de Paris
69 5th Street Deli
70 Monty's Seafood & Stone Crab Restaurant; Neam's Gourmet
76 Nemo

77 Big Pink
79 Joe's Stone Crab Restaurant
82 Smith & Wollensky

ENTERTAINMENT
6 Twist
11 The Clevelander Bar; The Clevelander Hotel
16 Chelsea Hotel
17 BED
20 Mango's Tropical Cafe
27 Pump
75 Opium Garden
80 Penrod's Entertainment Complex; Pearl Restaurant & Champagne Lounge; Nikki Beach

OTHER
9 Wolfsonian Foundation
12 Art Deco Welcome Center; Miami Design Preservation League
13 Beach Patrol Headquarters
14 Lifeguard Tower
18 Bettcher Gallery
25 South Beach Tattoo
26 LIB Color Labs; South Beach Divers
28 Betsey Johnson
39 Miami Beach Community Health Center
41 Versace Jeans Couture
42 A!X Armani Exchange
45 Ritchie Swimwear
50 Parking
51 Gap; Sunglass Hut
52 Deco Denim
53 Urban Outfitters
56 Pleasure Emporium
59 Eckerd
60 Miami Beach Bicycle Center
61 Spec's Music
62 Public Toilets
63 Florida Yacht Charters
64 Estefan Enterprises
66 X-Isle Surf Shop
71 Sanford L Ziff Jewish Museum of Florida
73 Library
74 Public Toilets
81 Public Toilets

------ The Wave (electric shuttle)

MAP 5 NORTHERN MIAMI BEACH

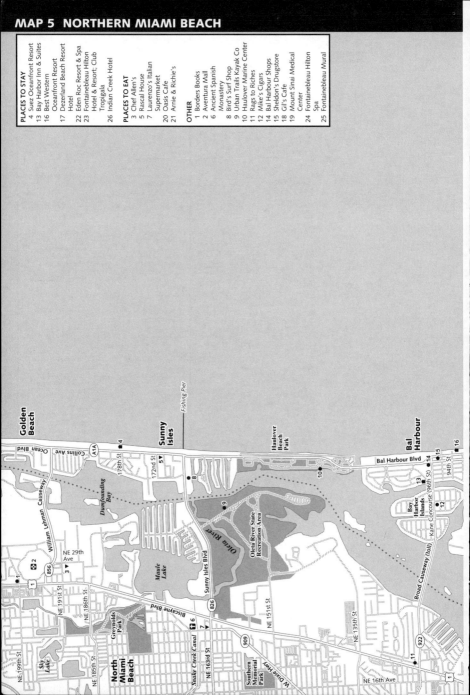

PLACES TO STAY
4   Suez Oceanfront Resort
13 Bay Harbor Inn & Suites
16 Best Western
    Oceanfront Resort
17 Dezerland Beach Resort
    Hotel
22 Eden Roc Resort & Spa
23 Fontainebleau Hilton
    Hotel & Resort; Club
    Tropigala
26 Indian Creek Hotel

PLACES TO EAT
3   Chef Allen's
5   Rascal House
7   Laurenzo's Italian
    Supermarket
20 Oasis Cafe
21 Arnie & Richie's

OTHER
1   Borders Books
2   Aventura Mall
6   Ancient Spanish
    Monastery
8   Bird's Surf Shop
9   Urban Trails Kayak Co
10 Haulover Marine Center
11 Rags to Riches
12 Mike's Cigars
14 Bal Harbour Shops
15 Sheldon's Drugstore
18 Gil's Cafe
19 Mount Sinai Medical
    Center
24 Fontainebleau Hilton
    Spa
25 Fontainebleau Mural

MAP 10 CORAL GABLES

PLACES TO STAY
5 Hampton Inn
7 Doubletree Hotel
11 Mayfair House
20 Sonesta Hotel & Suites
   Coconut Grove
21 The Mutiny Hotel

PLACES TO EAT
4 Daily Bread Marketplace
8 The Oak Feed
9 Paulo Luigi's
16 Anokha
17 Le Bouchon du Grove
18 Bacio
19 Johnny Rockets
22 Green Street Cafe

OTHER
1 Miami Museum of
   Science; Space Transit
   Planetarium
2 Vizcaya Museum &
   Gardens
3 Architectural Antiques
6 Ermita de la Caridad
10 CocoWalk; Cafe Tu Tu
   Tango; Cheesecake
   Factory
12 Improv Comedy Club
13 Streets of Mayfair
14 Coconut Grove
   Exhibition Center
15 Miami City Hall
23 Coconut Grove
   Playhouse
24 Coconut Grove
   Chamber of Commerce
25 Barnacle State Historic
   Site
26 Plymouth
   Congregational Church

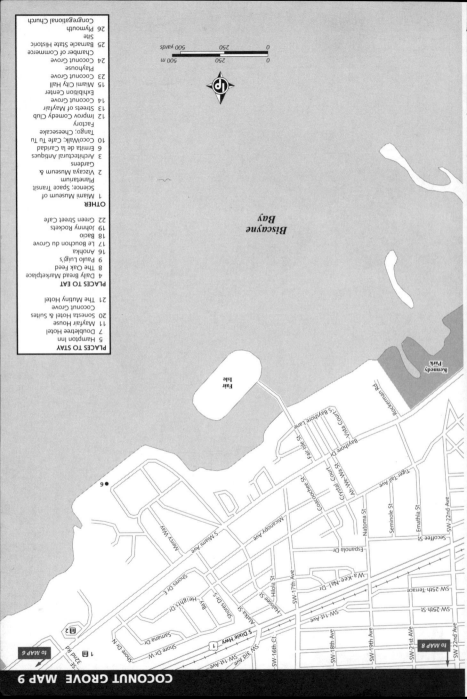

Biscayne Bay

Fair Isle

Kennedy Park

to MAP 6

to MAP 8

500 m
0   250   500
0   250   500 yards

MAP 9 COCONUT GROVE

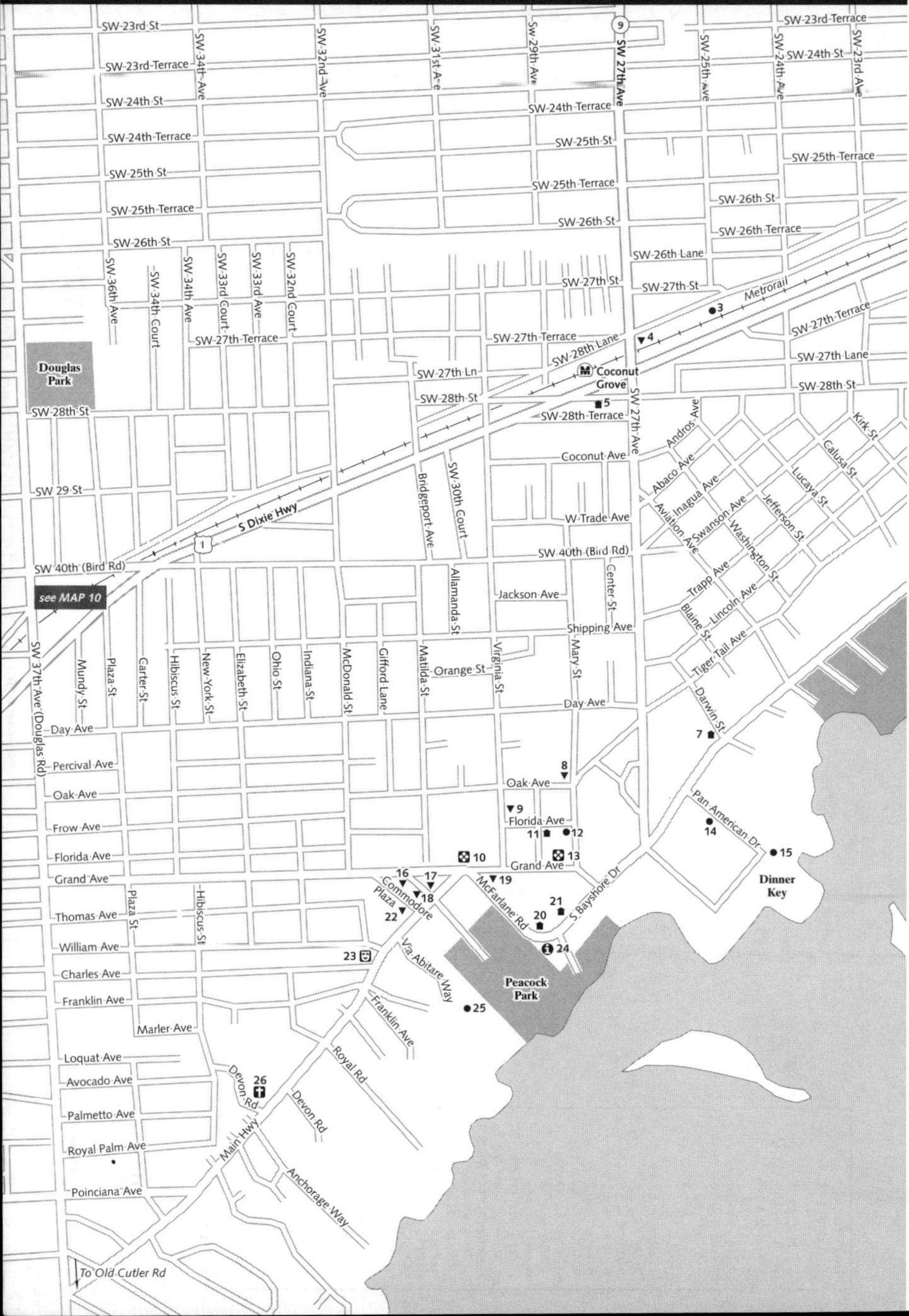

To Old Cutler Rd

Poinciana Ave
Royal Palm Ave
Palmetto Ave
Avocado Ave
Loquat Ave
Matter Ave
Franklin Ave
Charles Ave
William Ave
Thomas Ave
Grand Ave
Florida Ave
Frow Ave
Oak Ave
Percival Ave
Day Ave

Main Hwy
Anchorage Way
Devon Rd
Royal Rd
Franklin Ave
Kay Ave

Peacock Park

Dinner Key

Pan American Dr
Bayshore Dr
McFarlane Rd
Commodore Plaza
Via Abitare

Grand Ave
Florida Ave

Darwin St
Tigertail Ave
Blaine Ave
Lincoln Ave
Trapp Ave
Aviation Ave
Washington Ave
Inagua Ave
Jefferson Ave
Abaco Ave
Andros Ave
Coconut Ave

Mary St
Virginia St
Orange St
Matilda St
Gifford Lane
McDonald St
Indiana St
Ohio St
Elizabeth St
New York St
Hibiscus St
Carter St
Plaza St
Mundy St

Hibiscus St
Plaza St

Shipping Ave
Jackson Ave
Allamanda St
Bridgeport Ave

SW 37th Ave (Douglas Rd)
SW 40th (Bird Rd)
W Trade Ave
W 40th (Bird Rd)
SW 30th Court

See MAP 10

S Dixie Hwy
SW 29 St

Coconut Grove
Metrorail

Douglas Park

SW 28th St
SW 27th Ln
SW 28th Terrace
SW 28th Lane
SW 27th Terrace
SW 27th St
SW 26th St
SW 26th Lane
SW 26th Terrace
SW 25th St
SW 25th Terrace
SW 24th St
SW 24th Terrace
SW 23rd St

SW 27th Terrace
SW 27th St

SW 32nd Court
SW 33rd Ave
SW 33rd Court
SW 34th Ave
SW 34th Court
SW 36th Ave

SW 23rd Ave
SW 24th Ave
SW 25th Ave
SW 27th Ave
SW 28th Terrace
SW 29th Ave
SW 31st Ave
SW 32nd Ave
SW 34th Ave

Kirk St
Calusa St
Lucaya St

MAP 8 LITTLE HAVANA

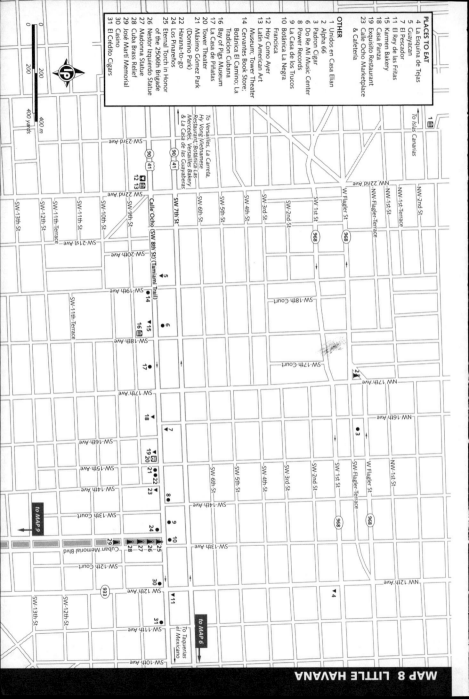

PLACES TO EAT
4 La Esquina de Tejas
5 Guayacan
7 El Pescador
11 El Rey de las Fritas
15 Karmen Bakery
18 Casa Panza
19 Exquisito Restaurant
23 Calle Ocho Marketplace
   & Cafeteria

OTHER
1 Unidos en Casa Elian
2 Alpha 66
3 Padron Cigar
6 Do Re Mi Music Center
8 Power Records
9 La Casa de los Trucos
10 Botánica La Negra
   Francisca
12 Hoy Como Ayer
13 Latin American Art
   Museum; Tower Theater
14 Cervantes Book Store;
   Botánica El Camino; La
   Tradicion Cubana
16 Bay of Pigs Museum
17 La Casa de Piñatas
20 Tower Theater
21 Máximo Gómez Park
   (Domino Park)
22 Havana-to-go
24 Los Pinareños
25 Eternal Torch in Honor
   of the 2506th Brigade
26 Nestor Izquierdo Statue
27 Madonna Statue
28 Cuba Brass Relief
29 José Martí Memorial
30 Casino
31 El Crédito Cigars

MAP 7 KEY BISCAYNE

ATLANTIC OCEAN

Cape Florida

Cape Florida
Lighthouse

Crandon Dr

Cape Florida
Channel

Bill Baggs
Cape Florida
State Recreation
Area

S. Martha Dr

Southwest
Point

Ocean Dr

E Wood Dr

Crandon Blvd

W Wood Dr

W Martha Dr

Harbor Point

Hurricane
Harbor

Galen Dr

W Heather Dr

E Heather Dr

Fernwood Dr

Harbor Dr

Ocean Lane Dr

East Dr

Crandon Blvd

Ocean Dr

13

12

11

10

6

8

Key
Biscayne

West
Point

Crandon
Park
Beach

7

Crandon
Park

Crandon Blvd

Biscayne
Bay

9

5

Northwest
Point

Bear Cut

Virginia
Key Beach

Rickenbacker Causeway

Duck
Lake

Virginia
Key

Intracoastal Waterway

Rickenbacker Causeway (toll)

3

Hobie
Island

Rickenbacker
Park

1

4

to MAP 6

0   5   1 km

0   .25   .5 mile

N

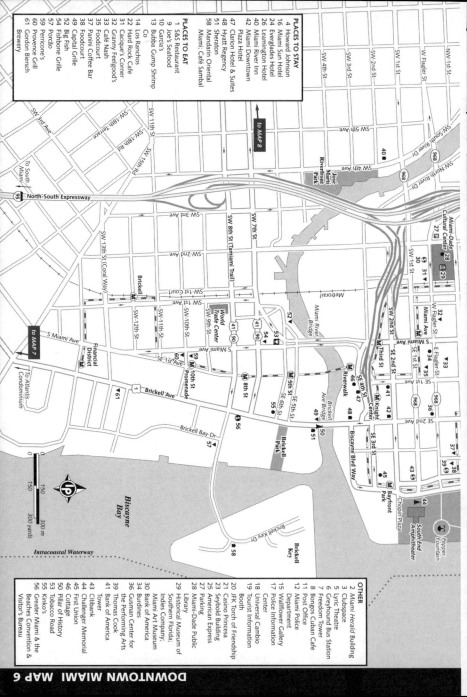

PLACES TO STAY

4 Howard Johnson
16 Miami Sun Hotel
24 Everglades Hotel
26 Leamington Hotel
40 Miami River Inn
42 Miami Downtown Plaza Hotel
47 Clarion Hotel & Suites
48 Hyatt Regency
51 Sheraton
58 Mandarin Oriental Miami; Café Sambal

PLACES TO EAT

1 S&S Restaurant
9 Joe's Seafood
10 Garcia's
13 Bubba Gump Shrimp Co
14 Los Ranchos
22 Hard Rock Cafe
31 Cacique's Corner
32 Granny Feelgood's
33 Café Nash
35 Foodcourt
37 Panini Coffee Bar
38 Foodcourt
49 Capital Grille
52 Big Fish
54 Fishbone Grille
57 Porcão
59 Perricone's
60 Provence Grill
61 Gordon Biersch Brewery

OTHER

2 Miami Herald Building
3 Clubspace
5 Lyric Theatre
6 Greyhound Bus Station
7 Freedom Tower
8 Bongos Cuban Cafe
11 Post Office
12 Miami Police Department
15 Wallflower Gallery
17 Police Information Center
18 Universal Cambio
19 Tourist Information Booth
20 JFK Torch of Friendship
21 Casino Princesa
23 Seybold Building
25 American Express
27 Parking
28 Miami-Dade Public Library
29 Historical Museum of Southern Florida; Miami Art Museum
30 Bank of America
34 Burdines
36 Gusman Center for the Performing Arts
39 Thomas Cook
41 Bank of America Tower
43 Citibank
44 Challenger Memorial
45 First Union
46 Cottage
50 Pillar of History
53 Tobacco Road
55 Kinko's
56 Greater Miami & the Beaches Convention & Visitor's Bureau

to MAP 8
to MAP 7

North-South Expressway
95

SW 8th St (Tamiami Trail)

World Trade Center

Financial District

Brickell Ave

Brickell Bay Dr

Brickell Park

Biscayne Bay

Brickell Key

Intracoastal Waterway

Miami-Dade Cultural Center

Metrorail

Miami River Bridge

Knight Center

Bayfront Park

Chopin Plaza

South End Amphitheater

Pepper Fountain

José Martí Riverfront Park

To South Miami
To Atlantis Condominium

0   150   300 yards
0   150   300 m

MAP 6 DOWNTOWN MIAMI

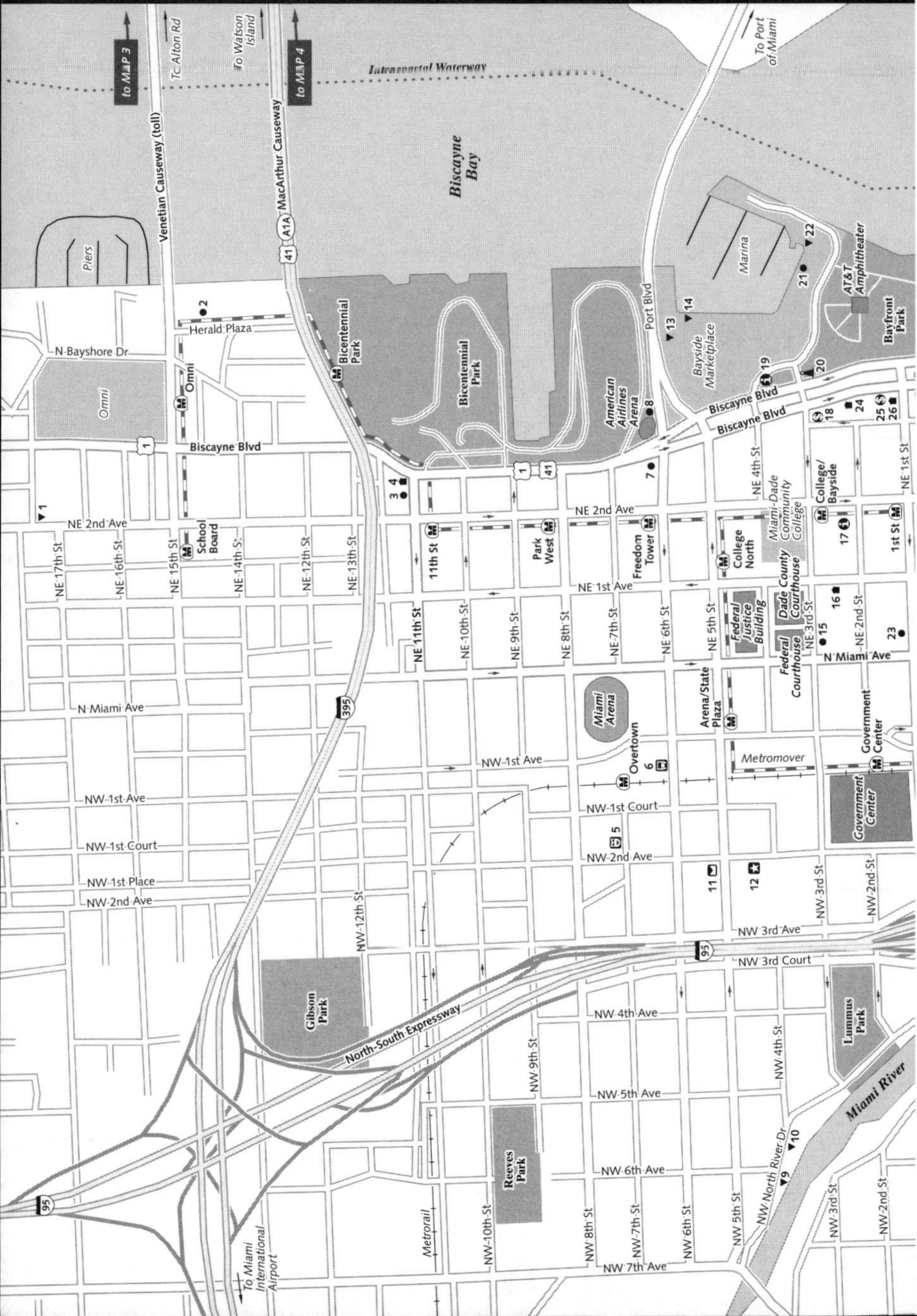

NW 2nd St
NW 3rd St
NW North River Dr
NW 5th St
NW 6th St
NW 7th Ave
NW 7th St
NW 8th St
NW 9th Ave
NW 10th St
Metrorail

To Miami International Airport

Miami River

Reeves Park

NW 6th Ave
NW 5th Ave
NW 4th Ave
NW 4th St

Lummus Park

NW 3rd Court
NW 3rd Ave
NW 2nd St
NW 3rd St
NW 2nd Ave

North-South Expressway

Gibson Park

NW 12th St

95

NW 2nd Ave
NW 1st Place
NW 1st Court
NW 1st Ave
NW 1st Court

Government Center

Metromover
Government Center

Overtown

Miami Arena

Arena/State Plaza

Metromover

N Miami Ave

95

395

NE 5th St
NE 6th St
NE 7th St
NE 8th St
NE 9th St
NE 10th St
NE 11th St
NE 13th St
NE 12th St
NE 14th St
NE 15th St
NE 16th St
NE 17th St

N Miami Ave

School Board

NE 2nd Ave

Federal Justice Building
Federal Courthouse
Dade County Courthouse

Freedom Tower

College North

Park West

11th St

41
1

NE 1st St

NE 2nd Ave

Miami-Dade Community College
College/Bayside

Biscayne Blvd

1st St

NE 1st St

Biscayne Blvd

Bayside Marketplace

Bayfront Park

AT&T Amphitheater

Marina

Port Blvd

American Airlines Arena

Bicentennial Park

Bicentennial Park

Herald Plaza

Omni

N Bayshore Dr

Omni

Biscayne Bay

Intracoastal Waterway

41 A1A/MacArthur Causeway

Venetian Causeway (toll)

To Watson Island

To Alton Rd

Piers

To Port of Miami

to MAP 4

to MAP 3

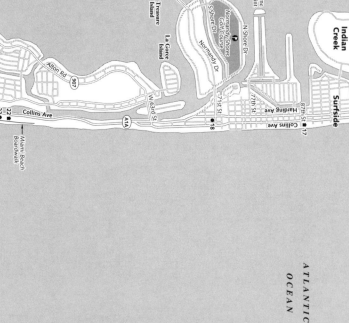

PLACES TO STAY
3 Hotel Place St Michel;
   Restaurant St Michel
7 Hyatt Regency Coral
   Gables
23 The Biltmore Hotel
32 Terrace Inn
33 Holiday Inn

PLACES TO EAT
4 Café Demetrio
5 Meza Fine Art Gallery &
   Cafe
6 La Dorada
9 Caffe Abbracci
11 Miss Saigon Bistro
13 Miracle Mile Cafeteria
16 Ortanique on the Mile
18 Taisho
19 Norman's
25 Allen's Drug Store

OTHER
1 Alhambra Watertower
2 Absinthe House
8 Merrick House
10 Books & Books
12 Coral Gables Chamber of
   Commerce;
   Omni-Colonnade Hotel
14 Coral Gables City Hall
15 Miracle Theater; Actors'
   Playhouse
17 Barnes & Noble
20 Venetian Pool
21 DeSoto Fountain
22 Coral Gables
   Congregational Church
24 Gable Stage
26 New Theatre
27 Bill Cosford Cinema
28 Jerry Herman Ring
   Theatre
29 Gusman Concert Hall;
   Miami Chamber
   Symphony
30 Lowe Art Museum
31 Mark Light Stadium
34 Titanic Brewery &
   Restaurant
35 The Shops at Sunset
   Place (IMAX,
   Gameworks, Virgin
   Megastore)

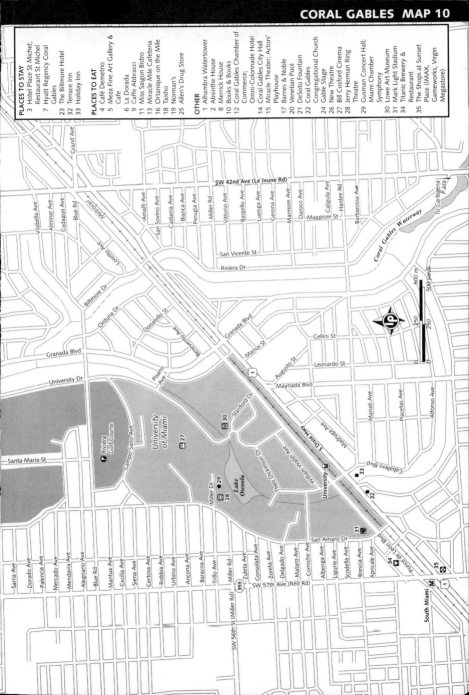

MAP LEGEND

ROUTES

City Regional
.... Freeway
.... Tollway
.... Primary Road
.... Secondary Road
.... Tertiary Road
.... Dirt Road
.... Pedestrian Mall
.... Steps
.... Tunnel
.... Trail
.... Walking Tour
.... Path

ROUTE SHIELDS

80 Interstate Freeway
101 US Highway
95 State Highway
G4 County Road

HYDROGRAPHY

.... River; Creek
.... Canal
.... Lake
.... Spring; Rapids
.... Waterfalls
.... Dry; Salt Lake

TRANSPORTATION

.... Train
M .... Miami Metromover
.... Bus Route
.... Ferry; Water Taxi

BOUNDARIES

.... International
.... State
.... Marine Park
.... County
.... Disputed
.... Cliff

AREAS

.... Beach
.... Building
.... Campus
.... Cemetery
.... Forest
.... Garden; Zoo
.... Golf Course
.... Park
.... Plaza
.... Reservation
.... Sports Field
.... Swamp; Mangrove

POPULATION SYMBOLS

○ NATIONAL CAPITAL ... National Capital
◉ STATE CAPITAL .... State Capital
● Large City .... Large City
● Medium City .... Medium City
● Small City .... Small City
○ Town; Village .... Town; Village

MAP SYMBOLS

■ .... Place to Stay
▼ .... Place to Eat
● .... Point of Interest

.... Airfield
.... Airport
.... Archeological Site; Ruin
.... Bank
.... Baseball Diamond
.... Battlefield
.... Bike Trail
.... Border Crossing
.... Buddhist Temple
.... Bus Station; Terminal
.... Cable Car; Chairlift
.... Campground
.... Castle
.... Cathedral
.... Cave

.... Church
.... Cinema
.... Dive Site
.... Embassy; Consulate
.... Footbridge
.... Fountain
.... Gas Station
.... Hospital
.... Information
.... Internet Access
.... Lighthouse
.... Lookout
.... Mine
.... Monument
.... Mountain

.... Museum
.... Observatory
.... Park
.... Parking Area
.... Pass
.... Picnic Area
.... Police Station
.... Pool
.... Post Office
.... Pub; Bar
.... RV Park
.... Shelter
.... Shipwreck
.... Shopping Mall
.... Skiing - Cross Country

.... Skiing - Downhill
.... Stately Home
.... Surfing
.... Synagogue
.... Tao Temple
.... Taxi
.... Telephone
.... Theater
.... Toilet - Public
.... Tomb
.... Trailhead
.... Tram Stop
.... Transportation
.... Volcano
.... Winery

Note: Not all symbols displayed above appear in this book.

LONELY PLANET OFFICES

Australia
Locked Bag 1, Footscray, Victoria 3011
☎ 03 8379 8000 fax 03 8379 8111
email talk2us@lonelyplanet.com.au

USA
150 Linden Street, Oakland, California 94607
☎ 510 893 8555, TOLL FREE 800 275 8555
fax 510 893 8572
email info@lonelyplanet.com

UK
10a Spring Place, London NW5 3BH
☎ 020 7428 4800 fax 020 7428 4828
email go@lonelyplanet.co.uk

France
1 rue du Dahomey, 75011 Paris
☎ 01 55 25 33 00 fax 01 55 25 33 01
email bip@lonelyplanet.fr
www.lonelyplanet.fr

World Wide Web: www.lonelyplanet.com *or* AOL keyword: lp
Lonely Planet Images: lpi@lonelyplanet.com.au